D0560129

Leading Edge Logistics
Competitive Positioning for the 1990's

Comprehensive Research on Logistics Organization
Strategy and Behavior in North America

by

Donald J. Bowersox, Ph.D
Patricia J. Daugherty, Ph.D
Cornelia L. Dröge, Ph.D
Dale S. Rogers
Daniel L. Wardlow

HD
38.5
·L4
1989

of

Michigan State University
Materials and Logistics Management Program
Department of Marketing and Transportation Administration

for the

COUNCIL OF LOGISTICS MANAGEMENT

Copyright© 1989 the Council of Logistics Management
2803 Butterfield Road, Oak Brook, Illinois 60521

Printed in the United States of America.
All rights reserved. No parts of this book
may be reproduced in any form or by any means,
without the permission in writing from the Publisher.

DEDICATION

In 1962, the American Management Association conducted one of the earliest Physical Distribution Seminars in Saranac Lake, New York. A group of speakers and attendees met to investigate the potential establishment of a professional society to serve as a regular forum for the exchange of physical distribution ideas. In St. Louis in January of 1963, the National Council of Physical Distribution Management was officially founded. That group, now the Council of Logistics Management, celebrated its 25th anniversary in 1988. Individual membership now exceeds 5,000. During those 25 years, the practice of logistics advanced to the point where it became integral to modern management. This research, which delineates leading edge logistical practice in 1988, is dedicated to my ten fellow founders and to a dozen others who gave their time and energy unselfishly during the very early years of NCPDM.

Founders

William T. Beckman
Warren Blanding
William H. Gribble
James J. Hardcastle
Burr W. Hupp
Eugene Landis
Bruce J. Riggs
Edward W. Smykay
John F. Varley
David R. Wood

Major Early Contributors

F. Harry Bergtholdt
Harry J. Bruce
Mark Egan
Kenneth U. Flood
Robert J. Franco
George A. Gecowets
James L. Heskett
Bernard J. LaLonde
H. George Miller
Andy C. Price
Harold T. Reed
Wendell M. Steward

Donald J. Bowersox
Principal Researcher
East Lansing, Michigan
January 1, 1989

6/12/90

ACKNOWLEDGEMENT

A research effort of this magnitude requires many different kinds of support. The research team is extremely grateful to numerous individuals and organizations for their extensive assistance.

Survey research supported with comprehensive interviewing is expensive. The research team is extremely grateful for the generous support of the Digital Equipment Corporation. DEC provided equipment as well as substantial financial and professional support during all phases of the research. All of this support was offered without proprietary restraint. As such, all logistics professionals who benefit from the research owe DEC a debt of gratitude for supporting public research.

Special appreciation and acknowledgement is due A. T. Kearney, Inc. A. T. Kearney provided generous financial support in the establishment of a post-doctoral faculty position at Michigan State University. The availability of this position has been invaluable to the completion of this research. A. T. Kearney's support included professional assistance, mailing lists and access to data concerning prior organization research.

Throughout the research, several individuals made a substantial contribution by serving on the Research Advisory Board. Advisory service necessitated several days of time and numerous trips to East Lansing. The Board was instrumental in the development of the Common Attributes Index that serves as the basis for comparative analysis. The Board members were also integral in helping to arrange interviews. Our thanks to the following individuals and their supporting organizations.

Judith Bielenberg Anderson	Union Pacific Corporation
William J. Best	A. T. Kearney, Inc.
Robert C. Camp	Xerox Corporation
Jack W. Farrell	Traffic Management Magazine
John E. Griggs	Gateway Systems Corporation
Bernard J. Hale	Bergen Brunswig Corporation
Charles P. Johansen	Digital Equipment Corporation
Clifford F. Lynch	Trammell Crow Distribution Corp.
Robert E. Sabath	A. T. Kearney, Inc.
Ronald E. Seger	A. T. Kearney, Inc.
Jeffrey R. Sims	The Kroger Company
James R. Stock	Michigan State University
Rodger D. Wasserman	American Delivery System Inc.

The Council of Logistics Management has made a major contribution by publishing this book. We appreciate the financial support and guidance provided by the Executive Committee, and thank George Gecowets and Elaine Winter who guided manuscript development and preparation. The Council provided editorial review through a team consisting of Robert C. Camp of Xerox Corporation, Robert E. Bowles of PPG Industries, Inc. and Kenneth E. Novak of W. W. Grainger, Inc. In addition, E. E. Wardlow, Retired Vice Chairman of Kmart Corporation, Robert E. Sabath of A. T. Kearney, Inc. and Bernard J. Hale of Bergen Brunswig Corporation provided valuable support by reviewing the manuscript in detail. A significant amount of overall support was provided by Charles P. Johansen who served as our coordinator with DEC. The Canadian Association of Physical Distribution Management was extremely helpful in providing a mailing list and handling receipt of Canadian questionnaires.

The support of Michigan State University was essential to completing the assignment. Dean Richard Lewis and Chairperson Robert Nason created an environment that permitted extensive research to be completed as scheduled. The manuscript is the result of substantial effort and tender care by Tricia Walters. Without Tricia and her desk top publishing, this book would not be a reality. Tricia was supported by Sharon Baker, Tarnie Nyquist and Pam Kingsbury to whom we extend our sincere appreciation. The following student assistants played a substantial role in the research: David Frayer, Richard Germain, Karen Griggs, David Hensel, Bill Meade, Matt Medick, Doug Sage and Kevin Steinke. In particular, Dave Hensel played a key role in final manuscript preparation.

With so much able assistance, it is difficult to offer any excuse to justify what what ever shortcomings the research may have. To the extent that there are faults, they are the sole responsibility of the research team.

RESPONDENT ACKNOWLEDGEMENT

The research team sincerely appreciates the support and unselfish participation of logistics executives who completed survey questionnaires and those who consented to interviews. A total of 909 questionnaires and 100 interviews formed the research data base. Following is an alphabetical list of interview firms.

Ace Hardware Corporation
Alco Health Services Corporation
American Delivery
   System Incorporated
American President
   Companies, Limited
Ancon, Incorporated
Arrow Electronics, Incorporated
Bank of Boston, Freight
   Management Services Division
Bearings, Incorporated
Beaver Lumber Company, Limited
Bender Warehouse Company
Bergen Brunswig Corporation
Bristol-Myers USPNG
Builders Transport Incorporated
Burlington-Northern Railroad
Campbell Soup Company
Canadian Tire Corporation, Limited
Carretta Trucking Incorporated
Caterpillar Logistics
   Services, Incorporated
Christian Salvesen (F.S.) Limited
Ciba-Geigy Corporation
Cincinnati Bell Telephone Company
Citgo Petroleum Corporation
Clairol Incorporated
Coast-to-Coast Stores, Incorporated
Columbian Storage and
   Transfer Company
Consumers Distributing
   Company Limited
Continental Freezers of
   Illinois, Incorporated
Crete Carrier Corporation

CSX/Sea-Land Logistics
CVN Companies Incorporated
Dauphin Distribution
   Services Company
Digital Equipment Corporation
Distribution Centers, Incorporated
Distribution Sciences, Incorporated
Domino's Pizza
   Distribution Corporation
Dow Chemical Canada Limited
Drug Transport, Incorporated
Dry Storage Corporation
Eastman Kodak Company
Eckerd Drug Company
Federal Express
Firestone Tire & Rubber Company
Fisher Scientific Group Incorporated
Fleming Companies
General Mills Canada
General Mills, Incorporated
General Motors Corporation
The Gillette Company
Gordon Food Service Incorporated
Grocery Products Distribution
   Services, Incorporated
Hardware Wholesalers, Incorporated
Helene Curtis Incorporated
Hershey Foods Corporation
The Hub Group, Incorporated
Itel Distribution Services
Jewel Companies, Incorporated
Johnson & Johnson
   Hospital Services
KLS Logistics Services
   Incorporated

Kellogg Company
Kimberly-Clark Corporation
Kinney Canada Incorporated
Kmart Corporation
The Kroger Company
Land O'Lakes, Incorporated
Lawson Products, Incorporated
Leaseway Transportation Corporation
Limited Distribution Services
Marshall Field & Company
McCrory Stores
McKesson Corporation
3M
Nabisco Brands Incorporated
National Freight Consortium p.l.c.
Owens-Corning Fiberglas Corporation
J.C. Penney Company, Incorporated
Pepperidge Farms, Incorporated
The Pillsbury Company
Professional Book
  Distributors, Incorporated
The Quaker Oats Company
Red Owl Stores, Incorporated

Rite Aid Corporation
Robin Transport, Incorporated
C.H. Robinson Company
St. Johnsbury Trucking
  Company Incorporated
Scott Paper Company
Sears, Roebuck and Company
Southern Bonded Warehouse
Spartan Stores, Incorporated
Steelcase Incorporated
Target Stores
Terminal Freight Handling Company
Trammell Crow
  Distribution Corporation
Union Pacific Corporation
United Parcel Service
USCO Distribution
  Services, Incorporated
Volume Shoe Corporation
Walgreen Company
Whirlpool Corporation
Xerox Corporation
Yellow Freight System, Incorporated

TABLE OF CONTENTS

LIST OF TABLES

Chapter 6

Chapter 7

Chapter 10

LIST OF FIGURES

Executive Overview

EXECUTIVE OVERVIEW

Leading edge logistics -- what is it and why can it have such a positive effect on corporate profitability? All too often, the answers to these questions are elusive and highly subjective. This ground breaking research into logistics organization structure, strategy and behavior pinpoints exactly what constitutes high-performance logistics. At the same time, it identifies the potential contribution logistics can make toward realizing strategic business goals and meeting bottom-line objectives.

The research provides overwhelming evidence that a small number of leading edge North American firms enjoy a superior level of logistical competency. These companies use logistics as a competitive weapon to secure and maintain customer loyalty. They are more responsive and flexible, are more committed to their customers, are more aware of their results, work more closely with their suppliers, are more likely to embrace technology and are more involved with their firm's strategic direction.

This book documents how 117 North American firms exploit their logistical competency. The leading edge firms -- manufacturers, retailers and wholesalers -- were selected from a field of 695 companies for microscopic examination. Analysis of these organizations revealed significant differences between the leading edge firms' approach to logistics organization structure, strategy and behavior and that of more typical firms. This book defines these comparative differences, explains results and offers benchmarking guidelines for companies seeking to improve their overall logistical performance.

LOGISTICS IN THE 1980'S: EVOLUTION TO REVOLUTION

During the 1980's, business throughout North America refocused attention on back-to-basic fundamentals such as product quality and value, customer service, and productivity. As management dealt with resources and efforts needed to achieve these goals, attention was drawn to logistics. Management began to recognize that this traditionally low-profile area of business operations is especially able to provide a needed edge in achieving back-to-basic objectives.

Logistics has always supported marketing and manufacturing by providing the correct assortment of inventory when and where needed, in a cost-effective manner. While the mission remained unchanged in the 1980's, the methods, approach and technology available to achieve these ends have changed significantly and rapidly.

i

This accelerated rate of change is new to the logistics discipline. Historically, developments in logistical practice occurred gradually and were evolutionary in nature. Primarily, they were motivated by the need to conquer the challenges of geography. At first, geographically-related logistical problems were formidable. As the industrial revolution provided technology to overcome transportation barriers, the significance of geographical obstacles declined. The costs of logistics, however, remained high.

Starting around 1950, fundamental logistical practices began to change, prompted by extreme profit pressures from domestic and foreign competition. Industries besieged by such pressures were the first to revamp logistical practices. Within these threatened industries, a small group of progressive firms began to rise to the top by reaping the benefits of improved logistical performance.

Senior executives at these firms recognized the benefits attainable through state-of-the-art logistics competency. They encouraged logistics staffs to innovate and gave them the necessary resources to do so. The majority of companies, however, maintained the status quo in their logistics practice, changing only what was absolutely necessary to survive. These companies adhered to the motto, "If it ain't broke, don't fix it."

Through the 1960's and 70's, the evolution continued. There was greater recognition of the importance of logistics. However, there were no major breakthroughs until the 1980's. At that time, the previously quiet logistics evolution became a revolution. At least four events acted as catalysts to create unprecedented opportunity to exploit the benefits of logistics excellence. These events -- political/legal change, exploding technology, North American business and economy structural change, and globalization of business -- are further discussed in Chapter One. Taken together, these events stimulated progressive North American enterprises to implement far-reaching changes in the culture and basic philosophy of logistics.

LEADING EDGE QUALITIES

As noted earlier, this book highlights the management practice of a relatively few leading edge organizations. In examining the 117 firms designated as logistics leaders, the researchers used a behavioral index to isolate the practices of high-performance organizations. Their findings show that leading edge firms come from all industries and levels in the distribution chain and include manufacturers, retailers and wholesalers of all sizes.

The research identified certain attributes that these leaders share. They are sensitive to customers needs and view logistical competency as a competitive resource. They have a clear understanding of what services create value for customers and of the costs associated with providing such services. They have developed day-to-day practices that produce the kind of performance needed to consistently satisfy customers.

To get a clearer picture of what differentiates leading edge firms from typical ones, a comparison is made of the specific practices of the leaders to those of a 458 member norm group. The norm group exhibit average or more typical logistical practice among North American manufacturers, retailers and wholesalers. Significant differences between leading edge and norm firms occur in three basic areas: organization structure, strategic posture and managerial behavior. These comparative differences are summarized.

Concerning organization structure, leading edge firms...

* Have had formal logistics organizations longer.

* Are more apt to have logistics headed by an officer level executive.

* Adopt a more fluid approach to logistics organization and encourage frequent reorganization to take advantage of opportunities.

* Tend to favor centralized control.

* Are becoming more centralized as they adapt organization structure to mission.

* Are responsible for more traditional staff and line functions.

* Are more apt to execute boundary-spanning or externally-oriented logistics functions.

* Tend to manage more beyond or extended functional responsibilities not traditionally considered part of logistics.

Concerning strategic posture, leading edge firms...

* Have a greater tendency to manage logistics as a value-added process.

* Reflect a stronger commitment to achieving and maintaining customer satisfaction.

iii

* Place a premium on flexibility, particularly in regard to accommodating special or non-routine requests.

* Are better positioned to handle unexpected events.

* Are more willing to use outside service providers.

* Place a greater premium on how well a service company performs in managing itself and its service to clients.

* Are more apt to view service-provider relationships as strategic alliances.

* Anticipate greater use of outside services in the future.

Concerning managerial behavior, leading edge firms...

* Expend more effort on logistics planning.

* Are more apt to publish their performance commitments and standards by issuing specific mission statements.

* Have chief logistics officers who are more apt to be involved in business-unit strategic planning.

* Respond effectively to non-planned events.

* Regularly use a wider range of performance measures, including asset management, cost, customer service, productivity and quality.

* Are more significant users of data processing technology and enjoy a higher quality of information system (IS) support.

* Typically have more state-of-the-art computer applications and are planning more updates and expansions.

* Are more involved in new technology such as electronic data interchange (EDI) and artificial intelligence (AI).

The above differences are indicative of how leading edge firms compare to their norm counterparts. Within the field of leaders, however, these differences disappear. The study uncovered a remarkable similarity in logistics practices among leading edge manufacturers, retailers and wholesalers.

Although these firms operate at different levels in the marketing channel and have distinctly different logistical missions, their structure, strategy and behavior are virtually identical.

In fact, similarities among leading edge performers can be categorized into ten propositions. Leading edge logistics organizations:

* Exhibit an overriding commitment to customers.

* Place a high premium on basic performance.

* Develop sophisticated logistical solutions.

* Emphasize planning.

* Encompass a significant span of functional control.

* Have a highly formalized logistical process.

* Place a premium on flexibility.

* Commit to external alliances.

* Invest in state-of-the-art information technology.

* Employ comprehensive performance measurement.

The research also examined logistics service providers. A profile emerged of today's aggressive new breed of logistics service firms. These firms represent leading edge competitors. The key characteristics of the new breed service leaders can be summarized in three words: relational, responsive and reliable.

Leading edge firms concentrate on building and maintaining long-term interactive relations. They actively seek to form strategic alliances with customers. Close working relationships with customers facilitate the development of tailored services. Services are modified and customized in response to specific demands. They place a premium on consistent, high quality service. By providing reliable service, the bonds between buyer and seller are strengthened and joint commitment to the relationship is intensified. The research identified that leading edge users and leading edge service providers are likely to find one another. In other words, the leading edge manufacturers, wholesalers and retailers choose to do business with leading edge service providers.

EXPLOITING OPPORTUNITIES

The leading edge firms do many things differently. These differences converge to form a common profile. First, leading edge organizations seek to use logistical competency to gain and maintain competitive superiority. Secondly, excellent companies seek to add value to the products and services they market, supporting this goal by operating a cost-effective logistics system. And lastly, leading edge firms leverage their assets by forming strategic alliances with service suppliers. These alliances help the firms achieve preferred-supplier status with key customers.

As the 1990's approach, the pressures for logistical excellence will be fueled by the continuing need to improve productivity and remain competitive in a shrinking global environment. In addition, senior management's growing awareness of the strategic importance of logistical superiority will place added performance demands upon logistics organizations.

Senior top management's understanding of and appreciation for logistics' profitability potential is increasing. With this situation in mind, this research had one overriding objective -- to further define the role that outstanding logistical performance can play in achieving strategic business goals.

To that end, the chapter contents are organized as follows. The main body of the document -- divided into four parts -- presents the findings within a format of discussion and interpretation. Part One identifies and establishes the concept of a leading edge logistical performer and highlights comparative findings among business types by channel position. In combination with the Executive Overview, Part One is designed to provide the casual reader with an overview of the research.

Part Two discusses the research findings in detail. Data are presented in the form of benchmarking guidelines to assist managers seeking to improve logistical performance. Three chapters compare leading edge structure, strategy and behavior to the more typical respondent. Chapter six reports findings regarding career progression of chief logistics officers.

Part Three closely examines the changing nature of service companies and how they assist leading edge firms in their pursuit of excellence. A total of three chapters are devoted to basic logistics services, strategic alliances and tailored services.

Lastly, Part Four outlines challenges and opportunities expected to confront logistical managers in the future. The chapters present logistical challenges as viewed by respondents and detail the research team's interpretation of areas most likely to offer future opportunities for improving logistical performance. The final chapter summarizes research findings. Supporting appendices present detailed technical matters and data, including a description of methodology, data tabulation and supporting analysis.

PART I

When It Comes To Logistics
There Are Excellent Companies

STATEMENT ON EXCELLENCE

For several years, a few business managers from different types and sizes of business organizations have been dealing proactively with the chaos of the 1980's. This select group has been innovatively applying information and transportation technology to dramatically revamp the way their firms exploit logistics. Operating in a permissive legal environment, these proactive managers have radically modified logistical organization structure, strategy and behavior to gain competitive superiority.

There are many testimonials:

* *The story of a small bakery previously buried as a low performer in the portfolio of a large conglomerate. This bakery is currently revolutionizing the fresh bake industry. In just a few short years, they introduced new technology and totally revamped logistics practice to dramatically increase order delivery performance. Today, this rapidly growing division is an industry leader.*

* *The story of a world class mass merchandiser who is using logistical competency to surpass traditional industry leaders. This retailer is pioneering value-added partnership alliances with key vendors who literally manage the mass merchandiser's warehouse inventory. Using a paperless environment for order and financial transactions and a quarterly open-to-buy, this alliance is resulting in reduced warehouse inventory and significantly improved customer service at retail stores.*

* *The story of a supplier of building materials that regularly meets and even exceeds the just-in-time delivery capability popularized by the Japanese. This firm has proactively installed communication technology to permit job site delivery within a plus or minus 30 minute window. This extraordinary accomplishment is being achieved across the entire geography of North America to a customer base that is continuously shifting delivery destinations as construction jobs begin and end.*

* *The story of a drug wholesaler who a few short years ago faced what appeared to be overwhelming competition from vertically integrated drug chains. This wholesaler took a quantum leap forward in technology application to offer inde-*

pendent drug retailers a unique and better way of doing business. The result is a cost effective logistics network for independent retailers that outstrips the value-added performance of the leading integrated drug chains.

These brief testimonials are but a few of the many leading edge success stories. Despite the fact that the United States expended 462 billion dollars on logistics in 1987, logistics *is not* sufficiently interesting to attract widespread attention. The fact that annual expenditure on logistics for over a decade has been ten times greater than all advertising expenditure *is not* sufficient to attract widespread attention. However, recognition that an increasing number of firms are gaining competitive leadership in industry after industry based on their logistical competency *is* sufficient to attract widespread attention.

Excellence in logistics is grounded in management practice. It is not the exclusive property of any nation or area of the world. This book will present conclusive evidence that excellent logistics operations exist throughout North America. Evidence suggests that excellent logistical performers exist throughout the free world. The key point should not be missed -- select North American firms are clearly world class and rank with the best of the best in terms of logistical proficiency.

Part I introduces the concept of leading edge logistical performance. In Chapter One, the substance and methodology of the research is established. In Chapter Two, logistical positioning is developed within the framework of the distribution channel. The universal characteristics of leading edge performance are shown to be independent of business type or distribution chain position.

6

Chapter One

SCOPING THE BEST OF THE BEST

During the decade of the 1980's, remarkable advancement has occurred in the practice of logistics. In a broad sense, logistics is that aspect of business operations concerned with the strategic positioning of inventory. Such inventories consist of raw materials, component parts, work-in-process and finished goods. The average inventory holdings of all United States businesses during 1987 approximated 683 billion dollars, which was equivalent to 15.17 percent of the gross national product. Every business, whether service or merchandise, requires inventory to exist. This research examined in-depth how the very best North American businesses manage the logistics of inventory. It is an examination of how leading companies deploy their resources and use their logistical capability to gain and maintain competitive advantage.

It is evident that some firms are easy to do business with while others, unintentionally, make doing business quite difficult. Being easy to do business with is not a cliché. It means that placing an order with such a firm is effortless, often handled electronically by computer to computer data interchange (EDI). Order entry and management systems are designed to readily accommodate customer-generated changes with minimal or delay. These firms plan their operations to have inventory available for shipment and to arrange delivery as promised. Easy to do business with firms avoid surprises. In the event that an operational snag occurs, adjustments or alternatives are implemented, frequently in a manner transparent to customers. If an inventory or capacity shortfall develops, easy to do business with firms offer alternatives and negotiate solutions before problems become critical.

Information is the key to ease of doing business. Nothing can be more frustrating than being unable to find order status or details about a shipment, an invoice, returns or other similar aspects of business. Easy to do business with firms specialize in providing one call accurate information response. All of the above attributes exemplify commitment to customers through quality logistics. They demonstrate a customer responsiveness, a caring. They illustrate how select firms use their logistical competency to help achieve their strategic objective of becoming and remaining preferred suppliers to selected customers.

During the course of carefully examining the logistical operations and involvements of North American companies, a profile of practices and behaviors emerged that shows the logistical capability of some firms is competitively superior. This select group of firms comes from all areas of North American industry and represents all levels of the distribution chain from manufacturers to wholesalers to retailers. These leaders have emerged as being ahead of the competitive pack in terms of exploiting strategic logistics. These are the firms designated in this research as *leading edge*. The practice and behavior of leading edge performers provide ideal benchmarking guidelines for others seeking to improve their overall logistical performance. Prior to looking more closely at the functional, structural and behavioral practices of leading edge companies, some background regarding the development of logistics offers a useful foundation.

ABOUT LOGISTICS

Senior management in North America is becoming increasingly aware that logistical competency can attract and retain key customers. Logistics suffers from a jargon complex. Logistics jargon is aggravated by the fact that even the word logistics is a mongrel term used to cover the integration of several basic business activities. An early logistician, the late and eminent Dr. E. Grosvenor Plowman, provided the first comprehensive definition of business logistics by building upon the logic of early Greek scholars and by a careful examination of military history. Logistics was defined by the Greeks as the "science of correct reasoning by means of mathematics." The first modern use of the term logistics was in the military, where it was employed to identify the process of coordinating the planning and implementation of personnel, supplies, facilities and weapon support strategies. Dr. Plowman viewed business logistics as a combination of the comprehensive military mission and the precise Greek logic adapted to commercial enterprise. He viewed business logistics as the integrated management of: (1) the pre-production or inbound factors of a business; and (2) the post-production or outbound factors. The objective of business logistics, as perceived by Dr. Plowman, was "to achieve the optimum coordination of inbound material movement, raw material storage, work-in-process handling and the outbound packaging, warehousing and movement of finished products."[1]

The unique feature of Dr. Plowman's pioneering contribution was his vision of logistics as a single manageable process that spanned the value-added chain from material origin to finished product customer delivery. This vision, while deceptively simple, did not become common management practice until the 1980's.

In 1963, the National Council of Physical Distribution Management, the predecessor organization to the Council of Logistics Management, was founded to foster the development of logistics. During the initial meetings of the Council, the potential use of the term logistics was rejected by business executives because of its "predominate military connotation." In 1984, the Council officially adopted the term logistics in its revised name. The Council then defined logistics as[2]:

"the process of planning, implementing, and controlling the efficient, cost effective flow and storage of raw materials, in-process inventory, finished goods and related information from point of origin to point of consumption for the purpose of conforming to customer requirements. This definition includes inbound, outbound, internal and external movements."

The potential contribution of logistics to achieving the goals of commercial enterprise is based upon two basic propositions: (1) the integrated management of all activities related to inventory so as to achieve operating objectives at lowest possible total cost; and (2) the proactive use of logistical competency to help achieve customer satisfaction.

The appropriate activities to be integrated through the logistical value-added process differ depending whether an organization is a manufacturer, retailer or wholesaler. In fact, to confuse the issue, the specific activities managed by two directly competitive firms' logistical organizations can be different based on a host of circumstances. The key word to understanding the potential of logistics is integration. Research findings clearly support the conclusion that how activities are managed is far more significant than how many functions are managed. Table

1-1 provides a list of business functions typically involved in logistics at the manufacturing, retail and wholesale levels of distribution.

TABLE 1 - 1
LOGISTICS FUNCTIONS CLASSIFIED
BY CATEGORY

Function	Manufacturer	Retail Wholesale
Outbound Transportation	X	X
Logistics Administration	X	X
Intra-Company Transportation	X	X
Finished Goods Field Warehousing	X	X
Logistic Systems Planning	X	X
Order Processing	X	X
Customer Service	X	X
Finished Goods Inventory Management	X	X
Inbound Transportation	X	X
Logistics/Facility Design	X	X
Materials Handling	-	X
Production Planning	X	-
Sourcing/Purchasing	X	X
Raw Materials/Work in Process Invty.	X	-
Sales Forecasting	X	X
International Logistics	X	X
Capital Equipment Procurement	-	X
Data Processing for Distribution Applications	-	X

No X means the function is not typically performed at the channel position or was not included in the applicable questionnaire.

WHY NOW?

As great as the rate of expansion of human knowledge and experience was during the 1980's, predictions call for even more rapid change through the year 2000. If it is true that knowledge quadrupled during the 1980's, how will logistics professionals cope with changes to come? Which areas of logistics management will be most affected?

Multiple external factors impact business practice. This section focuses on four factors that have had a significant effect on the practice of logistics. The political/legal infrastructure, exploding technology, changes in the North American business and economy structure and the globalization of business were among the most significant forces stimulating change in the way logistics is managed. The combined impact of these four factors creates a major opportunity to move logistical performance to new heights of excellence. They support the belief that today's professional managers can and should more proactively exploit logistics than their predecessors.

THE POLITICAL/LEGAL INFRASTRUCTURE

In the United States during the late 1970's and throughout the 1980's, the Carter and Reagan administrations have brought about landmark changes in regulatory philosophy. Competitive free market forces were restored to service industries such as transportation and communications. Similar deregulation has since occurred in Canada. This restoration of a major sector of the North American economy to a free market established the conditions necessary for managers to creatively shape formerly disparate logistics functions into an integrated force.

The gradual awakening of the North American business community to the realities of global competition set the stage for deregulation. To succeed, it was essential to remove infrastructural barriers to efficient competition. Transportation and communications were among the most highly regulated and protected industries during most of the 20th century.

The effects of deregulation have been felt throughout the world. In Canada, the more recent deregulation of trucking and the increased competition in rail and air freight services have opened new possibilities for creatively managing the long haul problems of that nation's geography. The relaxation of trade barriers between the United States and Canada is expected to stimulate economic activity on both sides of the border. The opportunities to improve competitive position through strategic logistics are unlimited.

The long moribund British economy has similarly responded to the liberalization of the business environment brought about by the Thatcher government. Renewed levels of investment in the private sector and the de-nationalization of many key industries have stimulated the competitive spirit in the United Kingdom.

The overall European Economic Community is attacking open market structures in a similar way. The targeted 1992 dropping of trade barriers and the standardization of regulation will create a true European economy. While the member nations of the EEC are nominally a customs union now, there are many protective and restrictive barriers in the areas of consumer and industrial trade practices, technical standards, currency rates, inspection laws and other commercial policies. Through careful and detailed intra-community negotiation, it will be possible in the future for an Italian telecommunications company to sell telephones at competitive prices in Britain -- a feat long impossible due to varying manufacturing standards.

After 1992, the combined European economy will surpass that of the United States by most financial and demographic measures. Foreign producers, especially those already operating in Europe, will be able to manufacture and sell in a more homogeneous market. No longer will suppliers have to manufacture to different technical standards, and to package and ship in unique ways to each nation.

Forms of deregulation are also occurring throughout the Pacific Rim nations and Australia. The net result of a more permissive political/legal environment around the globe is the creation of greater opportunity for logistics to take an active role in competitive practice. The recent anti-trust philosophy of the United States Government has supported the need for increased competition in world markets. The passage of the National Cooperative Research Act of 1984, which permits basic research alliances among competitors, is reflective of this rapidly changing regulatory attitude.

EXPLODING TECHNOLOGY

For less than $7,000, it is now possible to own a computer which is faster and more powerful than those used to control the Apollo moon missions of the early 1970's. Nowhere in day-to-day business existence is the force of change more apparent than in data processing. Astounding price breakthroughs in hardware have brought enormously powerful low cost computing support to the logistical integration process.

The impact of computer technology on logistical practice is far reaching. Formerly complex tasks such as truck routing and scheduling are now routinely managed using desk top computers. Simulations of entire logistical systems can be conducted to determine the least-cost approach to achieving desired customer service performance. Knowledge-based computer application software is expanding the boundaries of logistics information. It is possible to computerize the knowledge of logistics experts and combine it with current data to synthesize new strategic alternatives. For the first time, the potential exists to create a truly seamless transaction processing system. Such systems offer the potential to link status and control information from material procurement to finished product customer delivery. The creation and management of such a huge database would have been unthinkable a few years ago. Today, such systems are on the drawing boards. Firms are implementing flexible controls to enable seamless systems to function throughout a logistics organization. The computing capacity exists now -- it is only lack of human imagination and development time that limits availability.

The vast potential of low cost computing is being magnified by significant advances in communication technology. Combining magnetic and optical media with communication satellite technology enables the movement of vast quantities of information at high speed and very low cost. One firm interviewed during the research has installed satellite dishes on the roofs of all retail stores. Their communication network allows real time point of sale transmission of individual product sales.

Currently available systems such as bar-coding are being improved and combined with data communication transmission to achieve logistical control. With the advent of satellite tracking of trucks and trains, a shipper or carrier will be able to pinpoint the exact location and schedule of an individual package at any time throughout the entire logistical pipeline. Throughout the service infrastructure, carriers, warehouses and special service providers are implementing positive control systems. In many situations, transportation vehicles are being equipped with on-board computers and transmission devices. For the logistics of business, the information age has arrived.

BUSINESS AND ECONOMY
STRUCTURAL CHANGE

The eighties have been a period of significant change in both the structure of business and the concentration of markets. Business has experienced a series of far-reaching mergers. As a result, surviving business enterprises tend to be either very large or very small, with fewer medium-sized firms than before. The movement toward large businesses has stimulated two diametrically different logistical management strategies.

On one hand, combining businesses has created a potential for synergy by consolidating logistical operations across newly acquired business units. In direct contrast, many senior managers desire to retain divestment options by maintaining each business unit's logistical self sufficiency. Each of these polar strategies, in its unique way, has stimulated interest in logistical competency.

Business restructuring has forced logistics to prominence in another way. The overall desire to implement flatter organizations in an effort to increase flexibility and reduce cost has forced the delegation of authority down the organization closer to the customer. The off-shoot has been an increased concern for quality customer service.

The leaning or flattening of organization has also stimulated increased outsourcing. The streamlined firm of the late 1980's is flexible. It is able to direct limited assets to areas of maximum yield and leave areas beyond its expertise to specialty firms. The new, more hollow corporation is inclined toward the development of alliances with significant material vendors and service providers. The result is an extended corporate network of strategic alliances between buyers and providers of key services and materials.

At the same time that firms restructure and rethink their logistical strategy, markets continue to concentrate. In 1987, 49.2 percent of all retail sales and 65.1 percent of wholesale sales took place in the top 50 Metropolitan Statistical Areas (MSA). Less than ten percent of retail store locations account for more than one-half of all retail sales. The top 50 retailers in 1987 accounted for roughly 21 percent of all retail sales. About 9 percent of the wholesalers conducted 60 percent of the 1987 wholesale transactions. In the same year, approximately 10 percent of all factories turned out 75 percent of the total value-added by manufacturing. The 45.18 percent of the population that lives in the top 50 MSA's represented 52.13 percent of 1987 disposable income. Canada is experiencing similar concentration.

This concentration of retail, wholesale and manufacturer demand is stimulating extensive and elaborate product and service segmentation strategies. The response of logistics has been the development of tailored distribution capability to support segmented or niche marketing strategies. New demand for higher levels of customer service performance has stimulated the development of exacting logistical performance measurement.

The combined effect of structural change has been a dramatic alteration of the logistics playing field. New requirements exist demanding the movement of increasingly greater tonnage into and throughout increasingly more congested environments. While opportunities for freight consolidation are greater, impediments from potential gridlock in congested areas are also significant. In the long term, these revolutionary structural changes may cause a significant revision of what constitutes the ultimate logistical organizational structure.

GLOBALIZATION

The emergence of large multinational corporations as power players in international business has dominated recent news. As businesses enter new geographical markets, effective support of manufacturing and marketing operations across national boundaries becomes critical to success. Simple logistical competence is no longer adequate for off-shore firms competing with domestic companies. Only through excellent logistical management can complex, multinational arrangements become a reality.

Logistics cost as a percentage of revenue is greater for firms operating internationally than for domestic firms. Task complexity, increased lead times, market-unique product and service requirements and foreign business environmental factors combine to create a challenging and potentially costly climate for international logistics. Success in such a climate relies on the creation and management of an intricate logistical network of interactive relationships. The expansion of strategic logistics to the international arena is a dominant long-term trend.

In the manufacturing arena, North America has been attempting to reposition itself as a true global competitor. As manufacturing strategy has been redirected to capitalize on technology, the most significant advancements have increased logistical dependency.

Time based manufacturing strategies place emphasis on speed and flexibility in process or model/product changeovers. These strategies are typically called market-paced, demand driven or flexible manufacturing. This neo-jobshop strategy tends to sacrifice low per-unit manufacturing cost in favor of reducing total elapsed time from production to customer delivery. While such time based strategies have the potential to dramatically reduce finished goods inventory and enable quick competitive response, small shipment distribution and reliance on just-in-time procurement increases the importance of logistics.

Focused manufacturing strategies emphasize full utilization of the latest technology to realize maximum economies of scale. These strategies are intended to achieve the lowest cost per unit, but require a great deal of anticipatory manufacturing and long haul logistics to ensure that demand is satisfied.

To succeed, both flexible and focused manufacturing strategies require exacting logistics support. The logistical implications of these alternate manufacturing strategies are developed in greater detail in Chapter Two. Each typically employs just-in-time procurement techniques to realize maximum efficiency. While flexible strategies potentially reduce commit-ment to anticipatory inventory, they increase the need for highly responsive customer delivery capability. Focused strategies work just the opposite with respect to outbound logistics. Greater quantities of inventory need to be effectively positioned in anticipation of future demand. Excellence in manufacturing is not entirely in-plant. The movement of goods is the visible, make-or-break side of manufacturing as viewed by customers.

Wholesalers and retailers are not exempt from the impact of globalization. The degree to which wholesalers and retailers participate in off-shore sourcing fluctuates with the value of the dollar. However, many retail/wholesale organizations are firmly committed to off-shore sourcing arrangements that are not amenable to short-term modification.

Some firms now commit to production capacity without specifying exact products or styles to be manufactured until relatively late in the selling season. The advantages are tremendous. Such arrangements can postpone manufacturing until the fashion selling season begins, with the firm committing to exact color and style assortments only after consumer buying trends develop. One obvious benefit is the elimination of excessive markdowns. Such close international production scheduling requires exacting logistical support.

Compare such postponement to traditional international buying, transportation and warehouse practices. Working through brokers, typical overseas lead times can be 180 days or longer. For the typical retailer, the ordering of Christmas promotional merchandise is a one-shot effort committed more than six months in advance with little or no chance for modification. In a rapidly changing market, the risk is significant that goods procured under traditional international arrangements will be inadequately supplied, obsolete or incorrectly styled. As wholesale and retail firms increase international operations exacting logistics will become increasingly important.

In summary, the intensity of competition has forced corporate attention to focus on the development of logistical competency. Managers today are reaching to improve logistical performance out of necessity. The combined impact of deregulation, technology, concentration and globalism has been to increasingly draw logistical planning and performance to center stage.

CUSTOMER SATISFACTION
AND LOGISTICAL QUALITY

The dominant characteristic of successful firms in the competitive environment of the late 1980's and the foreseeable future is the degree to which they are customer driven. Such firms have made an uncompromising commitment to total quality control throughout their operations. Because logistics is event oriented, quality and customer satisfaction become one and the same. The only satisfactory logistical performance is one that delivers products and services to customers **when** they want it, **where** they want it and **how** they want it.

From the customer's viewpoint, each and every order is a unique event that must be delivered as specified by terms of sale. Logistics quality compliance is either black or white. If delivery is as anticipated, the result will be customer satisfaction. Conversely, if delivery is late, damaged or consists of less than ordered quantities, the result will be dissatisfaction. Quality in logistics is complex because it involves the orchestration of a wide variety of somewhat independent events across a vast geographical area. Quality logistics is not as simple as measuring the percentage of defects or reworks. In essence, quality logistics represents the culmination of all activities that occur during the logistics value-added process. In today's competitive world, customer expectations regarding error free, damage free and timely delivery have been raised to high levels. These expectations will increase in the 1990's as customers demand faster and more flexible service.

Leading edge firms have a clear vision of what services and performance levels create value for their customers. They also have a very good handle on the costs associated with creating such value. It is the capability to consistently meet customer needs that distinguishes a firm in the market place.

TRACK RECORD OF THE 1980'S

For several decades three statements regarding contemporary logistical practice have been widely publicized: (1) logistics is expensive; (2) inventory investment to support business practice is high; and (3) productivity of human resources in logistics is comparatively low. The 1980's have seen significant response to these traditional areas of concern. Comprehensive data concerning each area is presented in Appendix F.

CONCERNING COST ACCOMPLISHMENTS

The exact cost of logistics has always been a topic for interesting debate. The controversy centers around what costs should be included in the tabulation of total logistics expenditure and how they should be allocated. Using a conservative procedure, Robert V. Delaney estimated that the United States economy expended 14.3 percent of Gross National Product (GNP) or 377 billion dollars for logistical support in 1980[3]. From 1980 to 1987, this expenditure dropped to 10.3 percent of the United States GNP. Transportation expenditure alone dropped from nearly 8 percent to 6.3 percent of GNP.

To paint the picture in different terms, consider the following relationship. If the logistical efficiency of 1980 had remained status quo at 14.3 percent of GNP to 1987, total logistics cost would have been 182 billion dollars higher and transportation expenditures alone would have been almost 65 billion dollars greater than that actually experienced in 1987. It is clear that the relative efficiency of logistics has improved substantially during the decade of the 1980's.

CONCERNING INVENTORY INVESTMENTS

One valuable way to view asset productivity is to relate aggregate inventory holdings to industrial output. From the viewpoint of asset productivity and inventory velocity, the 1987 United States GNP of $4.5 trillion was supported by an average national inventory of $683 billion. Thus, average national inventory in 1987 was equal to 15.17 percent of United States GNP.

In 1980, the comparative measurement was 17.57 percent of GNP.

Inventory is the focal asset of business. For many retailers, inventory commitment far exceeds net worth, and soundness of inventory management is often the difference between success and total failure. Advanced economies are characterized by anticipatory manufacturing where production is to inventory or stock rather than to specific customer orders. The practice of building to stock means that all costs associated with the value-added process, including most of logistics, are expended in anticipation of future transactions. The composition of inventory, and the potential impact of forward imbalance are discussed in Chapter Eleven.

CONCERNING LABOR PRODUCTIVITY

A major part of the logistics success equation is the effective utilization of labor. Logistics is labor intensive. As an advanced economy reaches near full employment, the labor pool available and the number willing to perform logistics tasks dwindles.

The logistics problems related to labor productivity are double edged. First, while United States labor productivity has increased during the 1980's, this rate lags behind other industrialized nations such as Japan, Great Britain, France, and Italy. Second, the quality of logistics jobs, that typically must be performed manually, are not viewed by potential workers as attractive. Given their choice, most available labor will be attracted to less physical endeavors. The acceleration of labor productivity in the logistics process remains a critical challenge for the 1990's.

SELECTING LEADING EDGE FIRMS

The concept of leading edge benchmarking is to isolate select firms for microscopic examination. To operationalize the concept, it was necessary to develop a methodology that permitted the identification of leading edge firms from among research participants. To this end, a scale called the Common Attributes Index (CAI) was developed.

Based on exploratory interviews with fifteen senior executives who are generally recognized corporate logistical leaders, twenty desired behaviors were identified. As Phase I of the major study began, additional interviews were conducted to finalize the initial list of attributes. To formalize the index, an expert panel was used consisting of two senior logistics managers, two experienced consultants and two logistics educators. The panel ultimately selected fifteen attributes and their associated point allotments. The Common Attributes Index score reflects a logistical organization's behavior and practices in key areas. The index allocates a maximum of 100 points based on the presence of the fifteen attributes and on performance capability assessment. The attributes chosen include such practices as the formalization of a logistics plan, frequency of plan revision, organizational level of the senior logistics executive, involvement in business unit strategic planning, publication of a mission statement and extent of functional span of control. The CAI also assigns points related to the scope and quality of information systems, flexibility and ease of handling logistical operations and problems.

The CAI index was used to rate all study respondents, with only slight adjustments to reflect unique characteristics of manufacturers, wholesalers and retailers. Using basic statistical analysis, the CAI score distributions for each type of respondent were determined to be approximately normal. The mean and the standard deviation were used to separate respondent groups into three categories for comparative analysis. Those scores equal to or greater than the mean plus one standard deviation were labeled leading edge.   Likewise, scores equal to or less than the mean minus one standard deviation were labeled emerging.   The range of scores falling within one standard deviation of the mean, approximating 67 percent of the respondents, were labeled as the norm or typical group. The majority of analyses presented in this report examine how leading edge firms differ from the average or norm group. Table 1-2 provides the CAI distributions by business type.

A review of Table 1-2 identifies four categories of respondents.   Up to this point, no mention has been made of the respondent category identified as hybrids. The definition of a hybrid is a firm that is simultaneously engaged in business for profit at more than one level in the distribution channel. For example, a firm actively selling products at both the retail and wholesale levels of distribution would be classified as a hybrid. These respondents were considered sufficiently unique to justify their analysis as a separate category of respondent.

TABLE 1-2
RESPONDENTS CAI GROUPING
CLASSIFIED BY CATEGORY

CAI GROUPS

Business Type	Emerging	Norm	Leading Edge	Total
Manufacturer	62	254	64	380
Wholesaler	28	98	22	148
Retailer	17	57	16	90
Hybrid	13	49	15	77
Total	120	458	117	695

THE ANALYSIS BASE

Table 1-2 clearly illustrates that the concept of leading edge is not limited to manufacturing. In total, 117 firms were identified as leading edge out of a data set consisting of 695 respondents. Firms meeting the leading edge standard represent all sizes of enterprise, are found in all basic industries and exist at all levels in the distribution chain. They represent industrial and consumer goods businesses. Finally, they are found in near equal proportions within Canada and the United States.

Overall, the generalizations and interpretations of this research are based on a total of 1009 responses resulting from 909 questionnaires and 100 interviews. While this is a very comprehensive data base, the results are not statistically representative of all firms in North America. Rather, the results should be viewed as a comparative analysis of the practices and behavior among respondent firms. As a group, the research participants are, because of the method of selection, logistically sensitive firms. In all probability, the firms studied are above the overall average of North American firms with respect to logistical sophistication. Three separate data sets were constructed for analysis based on compatible questionnaires.

Data Set I - 695 North American respondents used to measure, compare and contrast leading edge to norm structural, strategic and behavioral practices.

Data Set II - 187 United States manufacturers that completed update questionnaires designed to examine adjustments in logistical practices across time.

Data Set III - A set of 27 Canadian manufacturers used for comparison to the United States manufacturers respondents (380).

To assist in the interpretation of questionnaire responses, a total of 100 interviews were completed. Of particular value were thirty-nine interviews conducted with firms who provide logistics services. Table 1-3 provides a detailed summary of interviews by business type.

In terms of research design, the questionnaire and the interviews were conducted in three phases. Phase I consisted of the initial manufacturer mail survey and 25 interviews completed during 1987. Phase II consisted of the retailer/wholesaler mail survey, a mail survey of Canadian manufacturers and a total of 37 additional interviews. Phase II was completed during 1988. Phase III consisted of interviews with 38 service providers during 1988. The results of all phases were grouped into the three data sets described earlier. Research results are drawn from the data sets and interviews.

TABLE 1-3
INTERVIEW FIRMS CLASSIFIED BY BUSINESS TYPE

Manufacturer		30
Retailer		17
Wholesaler		15
Service Providers		38
Transportation	(17)	
Warehousing	(10)	
Special Service	(11)	
		100

Appendices are critical to the presentation of the full range of research findings. As noted above, general conclusions are, with only rare exception, drawn from a comparison of leading edge to norm respondents. Appendices A, B and C provide detailed research methodology and data presentation. The results of all tabulations and cross tabulations for each of the four business types and the three CAI groupings are presented in these three appendices. These data, including degrees of statistical significance, are detailed for the benefit of other researchers. Appendix D provides a brief review of past organizational structure studies that are referenced in the functional discussion of Chapter Three. Appendix E provides a comprehensive description of CAI construction, statistical tabulation and testing. Results of internal bias and external anchor analyses are presented. The index was judged to be internally consistent and relatively free of bias with respect to respondent sales or industry. The external anchor of CAI to public financial performance was not conclusive. Appendix F presents cost and inventory data.

The major limitation of this research is its restriction to the United States and Canada. Significant differences exist in structure, culture and political settings throughout the world and care must be taken to limit generalization. Based upon presentations and discussions with logistics executives in England, France, Italy and Australia, there are reasonable grounds to hypothesize that the concept of leading edge as operationalized in North America is potentially useful for benchmarking throughout the industrialized free market world. Because of overall space limitations comparative analysis of structure, strategy and behavior by industry classification is not reported. This analysis was provided to firms who participated as research respondents.

28

FOOTNOTES

(1) E. Grosvenor Plowman, Elements of Business Logistics, (Stanford, CA: Stanford University, Graduate School of Business), 1964, pp. 3-4.

(2) Definition provided by the Council of Logistics Management, Oak Brook, IL, 1984.

(3) Robert V. Delaney, "Freight Transportation Deregulation," Seminar T9 on Road Transport Deregulation: Experience, Evaluation and Research, (Cambridge, MA: Arthur D. Little, Inc.), 1988.

30

Chapter Two

COMPARATIVE LOGISTICAL PRACTICE

To facilitate a comparison of leading edge logistical practice among different types of businesses, the overall research was designed around the distribution chain or marketing channel. The marketing channel is the arena for the performance of logistics services. A major conclusion of the research is that the best practice as typified by leading edge firms is remarkably similar regardless of a firm's channel position. In other words, manufacturers, wholesalers and retailers exhibit similar organization structure, strategic posture and management behavior when it comes to logistical practice, despite significantly different overall business missions and objectives. Firms that master integrated logistics exhibit high performance regardless of where they fit into the channel structure. This chapter presents conclusions concerning the similarities and differences in logistical practices of leading edge firms compared by channel position.

The initial section provides background discussion of channel structure to serve as an analysis framework. The section examines and compares the traditional logistical mission of primary channel members. The information used to develop this section was obtained from interviews and secondary data. The final section provides comparative analyses of leading edge performance among different types of channel participants based upon survey data.

CHANNEL STRUCTURE AND STRATEGY

In a technical sense, a marketing channel is a managerially determined system of relationships that exist between businesses to facilitate ownership and physical transfer of products and services. *Primary channel participants* are manufacturers, wholesalers and retailers who buy and sell products to each other and ultimately to consumers and industrial users. In some situations, a firm may participate simultaneously at more than one primary channel position. These firms are identified as hybrids. To support the primary channel participants, a vast assortment of facilitating firms provide services and perform key functions essential to overall channel operations. Such facilitating firms are typically referred to as *secondary channel participants*.

The main distinction between primary and secondary channel participants is the degree of risk they take in the value-added distribution process. A typical manufacturer, wholesaler or retailer has significant financial investment in facilities, inventory, systems and human resources. The risks associated with these commitments are typically concentrated and focused on specific products or a limited geographical area. In contrast, a facilitating firm traditionally restricts risk to the performance of specific services or activities. For example, the risk of a carrier has traditionally been limited to the transport of a given shipment to a specified destination. The overall business risk of the service provider is typically hedged by simultaneous involvement in a number of different channel arrangements. This traditional distinction between primary and secondary participants is being blurred by the rapid growth in strategic alliances between users and providers of services. The trend toward the development of extended risk sharing arrangements represents a significant dimension of leading edge logistics that is treated in greater detail in Part III.

From a logistics performance viewpoint, there are significant differences in firm mission based on distribution channel position. The specific logistical requirements confronted by a firm are directly related to channel position. In this section attention focuses on what makes each channel position unique, what is included in the typical logistical mission and what constitutes business type logistical excellence.

MANUFACTURERS

In the North American economy, manufacturers are highly visible. Because manufacturers create and promote the sale of branded products, they often have distinct corporate images. In the eyes of the consuming public and professional purchasing agents, manufacturing firms are responsible for product and service performance. The typical manufacturing operation spans the continent or globe to achieve low cost procurement of materials, component parts and labor. They require finished goods distribution systems that operate in a low total cost manner and which are capable of providing reliable high quality customer service. The complexity of manufacturing has encouraged the development of integrated logistics.

Manufacturers typically operate across broad geographical areas. The requirement for market logistics, as a result of channel position, means that manufacturers must assume a great deal of risk with respect to distribution of their product line. Although manufacturers have significant product and service development risk, their overall inventory exposure is relatively narrow in comparison to a wholesaler or retailer. Where a manufacturer may have a few hundred stock-keeping units, the typical wholesaler and retailer have thousands.

A final distinguishing characteristic of manufacturing logistics is the typical requirement to manage a broad array of inbound materials and component parts. The typical manufacturing process requires substantial material and parts inventory to support assembly and conversion. The sophistication of inbound logistics has greatly increased as a result of widespread adoption of the popular just-in-time (JIT) procedure of bringing materials and parts into the manufacturing process only as they are required.

Phase I of the research, completed in 1987, resulted in 380 qualified questionnaire responses. To track change in logistical practice while the research was under way, 187 of the same firms supplied additional data in 1988 during Phase II. These two sets of questionnaire responses were supplemented by 30 interviews with highly respected corporate logistics officers. Based on the data collected, manufacturers logistics missions were grouped into three strategic categories.

The first and most popular strategy is process based. It is concerned with managing a broad group of logistics activities as a value-added chain. The emphasis of a process strategy is to achieve efficiency from managing purchasing, manufacturing scheduling and physical distribution as an integrated system. Approximately 60 percent of the respondents indicated adoption of a process strategy.

The second strategy is market based. This strategy is concerned with managing a limited group of logistics activities across a multi-division business or across multiple business units. The logistics organization when following a market based strategy seeks to: (1) make joint product shipments to customers on behalf of different business units or product groups; and (2) facilitate sales and logistical coordination by a single order-invoice. Often the senior sales and logistics executives report to the same senior manager. Thirty percent of the manufacturing respondents utilize this strategy.

The third strategy is channel based. This strategy focuses on managing logistics activities performed jointly in combination with dealers and distributors. The channel orientation places a great deal of attention on external control. Firms that concentrate on a channel base strategy typically have significant amounts of finished inventories forward, or downstream, in the distribution channel. Just under ten percent of the firms reported this strategy.

While no single logistics strategy is dominant among all manufacturers, over seventy percent of the respondents have established formal logistics organizations within their firms. This fact alone demonstrates the commitment and progress among manufacturers toward implementing integrated logistics.

While manufacturing conversion strategies cover a wide spectrum, two are becoming popular in North America: (1) focused factories; and (2) flexible or market-paced manufacturing. The concept of a focused factory is to concentrate manufacturing or conversion at a single geographical location where it is possible to deploy the most advanced or state-of-the-art manufacturing technology. Focused factories often are scheduled to operate around the clock. The focused concept is logistically dependent. Materials must flow into the factory as needed and finished products must be effectively distributed in order to gain and maintain focused factory efficiency. One firm interviewed has a focused factory under development that will require several million dollars of increased logistical support to achieve manufacturing economies. However, the projected economies of the focused factory will far exceed the required logistical expenditures, with the overall result being increased profitability. The focused concept will not work without dependable and economical logistics.

The second popular concept of manufacturing is often described as flexible or market paced. This strategy strives to schedule manufacturing time as close to the development of market demand as possible in an effort to eliminate the risk of anticipatory manufacturing. The central concepts of flexible manufacturing are quick line change-over and short interval scheduling. In the ideal flexible manufacturing situation, production capacity is not committed until customer orders are in the system. Interviewed firms report dramatic reductions in order processing time, set up time and production scheduling intervals. One firm reported a reduction in average order lead-time to approximately one-fifth of the original time. In other situations, products that formally required 6 to 8 weeks from order receipt to delivery now required ten days or less. This ability to directly react to customer demands will work only with dependable and economical logistics.

It is clear that manufacturing in North America is and has been rapidly changing. Logistics is becoming more critical as new manufacturing strategies are developed and implemented.

WHOLESALERS

As the most opportunistic and perhaps most flexible members of the channel, wholesalers make a living out of working in the middle. Their purview is the ground between manufacturing and retailing. They provide functions that manufacturers and retailers find undesirable or uneconomical to perform. Wholesalers are specialists who link manufacturers and retailers. In total, 15 wholesalers were interviewed and 148 completed Phase II questionnaires.

In a sense, the total business of a wholesaler is logistics. Their sole function is the facilitation and delivery of goods and services through the channel to final destination. Wholesalers buy and sell, collect assortments, allocate and disperse the products and services of others through time and across geography. For industrial products, wholesale activities are frequently performed by a channel member called a distributor.

The prominence of wholesalers in specific industry channels has varied over time. During the 1960's, it appeared that drug wholesalers might vanish as a result of the growth of the integrated drug retail chains. As selected drug wholesalers redefined their product lines and target customers, they emerged in the 1980's as very strong organizations. Food wholesalers have declined to an all time low during the 1980's. It remains to be seen whether they will revitalize their channel position. In general, however, the role and number of specialty wholesalers has increased over the past twenty years.

Contemporary wholesalers perform a broad line of services. Their organizations are no longer simply movers and holders of merchandise. Wholesalers now provide value-added services such light manufacturing, finishing of goods, assembly, pricing and the customized development of promotional displays.

While their primary value-added function remains the provision of a customized assortment of products, wholesalers are beginning to offer customers a wide range of such new services such as information management, order processing, inventory management and logistics system design. Wholesalers expansion into such non-traditional services continues to blur the traditional definition of what constitutes a wholesaler's responsibilities. Traditional categories of merchant middlemen are not relevant to wholesaling in the 1980's. Traditional titles such as agent, broker, distributor, importer, exporter and merchandiser, have become obsolete. Furthermore, as manufacturers and retailers diversify, they essentially become wholesalers by providing wholesaling functions for their own products and often for other firms.

Regardless of the precise definition of a wholesaler, they do a tremendous amount of business. In 1987, the 321,000 United States wholesalers did just under $2 trillion in sales. Wholesalers have persevered and prospered despite the long standing criticism that they are parasites in the distribution chain. The simple truth remains that while wholesalers can be eliminated, the functions they provide cannot be omitted.

The typical scope of wholesale logistical operations tends to be local to regional. The typical operation serves a wide variety of small accounts. Some wholesalers have a few very large customers. There is a select number of large scale distributors that operate on a truly national level. Because of the relative size of these firms, they are potent forces within their distribution channel.

One type of wholesaler deserves special mention -- the merchant cooperative. An old idea, cooperatives are again on the rise. During the research, executives at several such member-owned wholesalers were interviewed. Their singular dedication of purpose -- satisfying their membership -- has created an innovative customer service environment. At one billion dollar co-op, the entire management team has been restructured around the logistics mission. Duplicate efforts within the firm were disbanded or reassigned under the executive vice president for logistics who has become the most powerful operating executive in the organization. Six vice-president level departments were eliminated as management drove decision-making down the organization and consolidated under the logistics banner. The result was improved profitability and employee morale, a dramatic reduction in member complaints, greater inventory turnover, higher warehouse utilization and innovative new service programs for the membership. This firm realized the value of integrating all aspects into a unified customer-oriented logistics system.

It is clear that wholesalers are a distinctive and important part of distribution practice in North America. The relative importance of wholesaling varies by type of distribution channel and appears to change over time. Logistics is the essence of wholesaling and the foundation from which many significant value-added services are launched.

RETAILERS

Retailers constitute the most forward point in the distribution channel. The store and its customer image represent the product offering of a retailer. From an operations viewpoint, retailing is a business of detail. The typical retailer stocks a very broad product assortment. For example, typical food chain store stocks well over 11,000 individual products. Large mass merchandisers or department stores stock even more. In total, 17 retailers were interviewed and 90 completed Phase II questionnaires.

Specialty retailers have experienced explosive growth during the 1980's. One need only visit a large regional shopping mall to observe specialty retail proliferation.

Retailing is highly dispersed in the United States. There are over 1.5 million retail store locations and they had 1987 sales of over $1 trillion. That works out to be approximately one retail establishment for each 170 people in the United States. However, the sales volume of retailers is highly concentrated. The top ten retail firms enjoy 12.4 percent of the total national retail sales.

The logistical operations of retailers are geographically focused and highly detailed. Retail distribution warehouses are generally located within one or two day's travel distance from a cluster of store locations. The delivery destinations of retailers' distribution systems are well known, making transportation planning relatively straightforward. Retailers generally ship large numbers of stock-keeping units from their distribution warehouses, creating the need for intricate control systems. The notion of an *inventory pipeline* is critical in retailing due to the high cost of retail space. Proper timing of store deliveries is essential to the maintenance and velocity of store inventory.

During the interview process it became clear that selected retailers have made substantial organizational changes to better coordinate merchandising and operations. In some cases, the traditional split between the buyers and logistics is rapidly disappearing in favor of an integrated approach. The traditional split in organizational responsibility continues to prevail in the food and department stores interviewed. In contrast, many mass merchandisers and specialty retailers have integrated organizations in an effort to improve coordination.

Historically, large retailers have utilized a central warehouse approach as the nucleus of their distribution system. A high level of vertical integration aimed at absorbing or eliminating traditional wholesale activities was popular among retailers during the 1950's and 1960's. The prime motivation for vertical integration was cost reduction. During this period, retailers felt that the key to cost efficiency was owning and operating warehouses and trucks. This trend has begun to reverse in the 1980's as a result of the general acceptance of outsourcing and the development of strategic alliances. Warehousing and trucking do not generate cash flow, and thus are losing appeal for retailers who operate in increasingly competitive situations. With today's scarcity of economic resources, one popular strategy is to invest assets only if revenue is generated. By purchasing their logistics support, retailers are able to focus on store operation -- the business they know best.

Retailers today have a broad range of purchase options ranging from every day low prices to the practice of forward buy and possible diversion. In the strategy of every day low price, retailers seek to reduce the complexity of manufacturer promotional allowances and concentrate on rapid turnover.

The motivation for forward buy is to take advantage of deep discounts offered by manufacturers during promotional periods. In the simplest form, a forward buy may only represent deal hopping wherein the retailer buys regular stock inventory from one deal to the next. However, many forward buys are for immediate resale. Merchandise is often resold through a diversion network for a few percent profit. Such profits are highly attractive to retailers who typically enjoy slim profit as a percent of sales. One firm interviewed discussed the example of forward buy and diversion wherein they actually picked up at the manufacturer's factory and delivered as a for-hire carrier to the final buyer's destination. The combination of product margin, pickup allowance and transportation fee made this a very profitable transaction.

A related development is the increased use by retailers of direct-to-store deliveries from manufacturers. Through greater cooperation and electronic data interchange, central retail buying offices are able to create combination truckload shipments for stop-off distribution to retail stores. One retail food chain and a large consumer paper company interviewed during the research have joined together to bypass the retailer's distribution system entirely, thus lowering the overall total cost of logistics from manufacturer to the retail store. The trend is for further expansion of direct-to-store deliveries from manufacturers because significant cost economies can be achieved.

It is clear that logistics is one key to unlocking the productivity door in retailing. Leading edge retailers are developing unique and innovative ways to offer consumers broad product assortments without increasing inventory risk. Most of these new solutions involve changes in traditional logistics practice.

HYBRIDS

Hybrid organizations are firms that simultaneously engage in business for profit at more than one level in the distribution channel. This concept is distinct from vertical integration in that these firms operate, for example, both wholesale and retail operations as profit centers. This combination of wholesale and retail is the most common, though manufacturer/wholesaler and manufacturer/retailer were also encountered during the research. In total, 77 hybrids completed questionnaires during Phase II of the research. Eleven of the sixty-one manufacturer, wholesaler and retailer interviews were with hybrid organizations.

An example of a typical hybrid organization is a large food-service company that was interviewed. This company operates a number of regional distribution centers, each serving approximately 5,000 restaurants or other food-service establishments. Products are sold at wholesale prices to these traditional customers. Over the past ten years, this firm has begun to open retail stores which sell wholesale products at discount retail prices directly to consumers. Typically, the firm operates a single retail location in a given city. The image maintained at retail is one of a large, institutional package size store with few conveniences. The appeal is price, unusual products or large sizes, coupled with the feel of shopping at wholesale.

Consumers love bargains, and the feel of shopping in a warehouse/wholesale environment has brought forth the warehouse club shopping concept. Firms such as Price Club pioneered this wholesale type of retail environment. Explosive growth is resulting from the market entry of such firms as Wal-Mart's Sam's Wholesale Club. Consider the logistics of a typical warehouse club outlet. They are usually located in communities with a minimum of 150,000 people and at least 500,000 people within a 30 mile radius. The location is normally not a prime retailing site and is often in an industrial park. Customer membership fees typically cover overhead such as rent, maintenance and utilities of an outlet. The warehouse store sets prices below those of other retailers and normally sells in product multiple units. Logistically, a hybrid operation like the wholesale store is a low cost operation. Wholesale stores restrict their SKU assortment to rapidly turning items and operate essentially as a satellite distribution warehouse.

A common hybrid is a manufacturer who has retail stores to sell directly to consumers. Retail operations may be limited to selected geographical areas or specific branded products. The hybrid operation typically continues to sell through wholesalers or other retailers while operating its own stores. The logistical support of the hybrid operations will be distinctly different in that the firm performs the typical services provided by the wholesale/retail level of the distribution chain. A limited number of manufacturers and wholesalers are involved in non-store retailing wherein they sell products direct by catalog or mail order to consumers.

The hybrid takes many different forms. In almost every situation, the decision to do business at two different channel positions requires the development of logistical support capability. While difficult to generalize such innovations, the complex operations of the hybrid are highly dependent upon logistics.

SERVICE PROVIDERS

The logistical glue that holds channel arrangements together is provided by service companies who specialize in transportation, warehousing and special services. In Phase III of the research, 38 service providers were interviewed.

With the deregulation of transportation in the United States and Canada, carriers have begun to develop new levels of service through intermodalism. Combining transportation modes under one carrier responsibility has resulted in a significantly different transportation resource. New transportation options such as double stacked container trains are playing a major role in the revitalization of the rail pipeline between major markets. Innovative new equipment such as the Road-Railer has facilitated boundary spanning between the long and short haul traffic, resulting in minimum handling and reduced shipment times.

Transportation deregulation has also increased competition between carriers. To gain competitive advantage, carriers have joined in alliances with primary channel members to become an integral part of the value-added chain that leads to the final consumer. Just-in-time systems have drawn carriers into the strategic operation of many manufacturers, wholesalers and retailers. The bywords for carriers have become flexibility and customer service.

Public warehouses have also expanded their role in the distribution chain. With the growing popularity of focused retailing, outsourced warehouse services have attained new prominence. A public warehouse which offers contract arrangements can become an integral part of a firm's inventory deployment system. Warehouse firms are capable of providing sophisticated inventory tracking, customized light assembly manufacturing, order fulfillment and other services desired by manufacturers, wholesalers and retailers.

A growing number of service companies have developed the capability to manage all or part of the logistics operations for a firm. These carriers or warehouse companies offer logistics system design consultation and then are willing to operate all or part of the system on a turnkey basis. By specializing in logistics expertise, such service firms offer high levels of logistical management skill to help resolve unique requirements.

There is a clear trend among all types of service providers to seek more formal longer term business arrangements. The alliance concept is a key ingredient of strategic logistics. The resulting long-term relationships enable powerful economies of scale. In strategic logistics, cooperation enhances competitive strength.

One newer type of alliance involves a formal agreement between a primary channel participant and one or more logistical services providers. The growth of such relationships has been exceptional during the 1980's. The basic concept is for the channel member to focus on core business requirements, while the service provider performs specialized logistics and related business services. This trend has spawned a whole crop of new firms whose sole business is participation in such alliances. These new firms perform services that have traditionally been classified as both logistical and non-logistical. They do whatever is necessary to enhance the overall value-added process. No longer is it a simple matter of discussing manufacturer, wholesale and retail channels when it comes to channel structure and strategy.

COMPARATIVE ANALYSIS - LEADING EDGE FIRMS

The departure point for this analysis was to establish the comparative behavior of leading edge firms who function as primary participants at different levels or positions in the distribution channel. An initial premise was that manufacturers would be typically more committed to integrated logistics than either retailers or wholesalers.

Table 2-1 provides the comparative CAI scores and groupings of manufacturers, wholesalers, retailers and hybrid respondents. Statistical tests support the conclusion that no significant differences exist in overall mean CAI or score distribution by type of firm. In fact, the CAI statistical distributions for the types of firms were near identical with all four being acceptable normal distributions.

TABLE 2-1
CAI ANALYSIS AND GROUPING LEADING EDGE
ORGANIZATIONS BY BUSINESS TYPE

Business Type	CAI Mean	CAI Standard Deviation	Leading Edge Minimum Score	Firms	Percent Leading Edge
Manufacturer	52.89	14.39	68	64*	16.84
Wholesaler	48.44	14.51	63	22	14.86
Retailer	53.88	15.03	69	16	17.78
Hybrid	50.92	13.87	65	15	19.48
Overall or Mean	51.93	14.43	67	117	16.83

* For the comparative analysis of selected attributes, conclusions are drawn from a base of 93 leading edge firms. The group of 117 is reduced to 93 as a result of substituting 40 leading edge manufacturers from the 1988 Phase II update for the 64 leading edge manufacturers from the 1987 original Phase I. The update respondents are statistically compatible to the Phase I respondents (see Appendix A). The prime reason for substitution is to compare responses on identical question/responses.

All 117 leading edge firms are similar in that they have CAI scores which are one standard deviation or more above the mean of all respondents in their business type. Figure 2-1 illustrates comparative CAI score means of all respondents and the minimum score necessary to be classified as leading edge. These data are displayed for all business types. These scores were assigned based on the existence of specific CAI attributes that could have been significantly different depending on the type of firm. In other words, a given retailer and manufacturer could both qualify as leading edge in terms of CAI score, but under careful examination this could reflect substantially different practices and behaviors. In this section, comparative practices regarding organization structure and managerial behavior of leading edge firms are examined across business type.

FIGURE 2-1
CAI MEAN SCORE BY BUSINESS TYPE AND LEADING EDGE MINIMUM SCORE

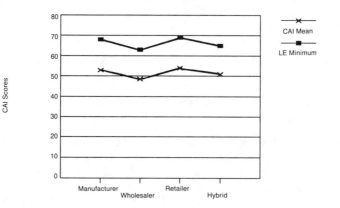

ORGANIZATION STRUCTURE

The comparative missions of manufacturers, wholesalers, retailers and hybrids necessitate some differences in organization structure. In fact, analysis of the data regarding specific organization titles and reporting relationships showed no single or dominate organization chart as ideal across all leading edge firms. Data were collected regarding several indicators of organization structure. Comparative analysis of leading edge organization attributes is based on: (1) length of time logistics has been formally organized; (2) rate of organization change; (3) degree and trend regarding centralization and decentralization; (4) traditional logistics functions; (5) beyond functions; and (6) senior logistics officer level, reporting relationship and longevity.

Leading edge firms are committed to formal logistics organization. As a group, leading edge respondents have been formally organized an average of about 16.5 years. In comparison by type, retailers and wholesalers have been formally organized significantly longer than manufacturers and hybrids. In fact, retailers reporting average formal logistics organization of 22.0 years and wholesalers at 22.2 years have both been formally organized on the average more than twice as long as manufacturers, 11.31 years, and three times as long as hybrids at 7.71 years. This analysis supports the conclusion that leading edge firms independent of business type have significant commitment to the concept of integrated logistics.

The longevity of any specific organization structure is short among leading edge organizations. The fluidness of organization reflects a willingness to modify structure to accomplish an ever changing mission. The average leading edge firm has reorganized 2.2 times within the last five years. Hybrids lead with an average of 2.43 times while wholesalers were low at 1.77 times. Leading edge retailers and manufacturers reported 2.40 and 2.33 reorganizations during the past five years. There are no statistically significant differences in the frequency of reorganization by business type among leading edge firms. The update questionnaire among 187 manufacturers (data set II) revealed that about half of the respondents had reorganized their logistics effort during the past year. This analysis supports the conclusion that leading edge logistical organizations are dynamic, independent of type of business or channel position.

The trend in leading edge logistical organization is toward more centralization. On a scale of 1 to 5, with 5 being fully centralized, leading edge firms reflect an average score of 3.7. No statistically significant difference exists between leading edge firms based on channel position. Table 2-2 provides data con-

48

cerning degree of centralization and trend over the past three years. Figure 2-2 illustrates the centralization trend by business type. This analysis supports the conclusion that leading edge firms prefer centralized logistics organization structure and the trend is toward more centralization.

TABLE 2-2
LEADING EDGE ORGANIZATIONS
CURRENT CENTRALIZATION AND TREND BY TYPE

Business Type	Centralization Score 1-5*	Percent - Three Year Trend		
		More Centralized	More Decentralized	No Change
Manufacturer	3.69	57.5	22.5	20.0
Wholesaler	3.41	31.8	22.7	45.5
Retailer	3.81	62.5	12.5	25.0
Hybrid	3.60	64.3	21.4	14.3

* Scale: 1 = completely decentralized
          5 = completely centralized

A significant aspect of organization structure is the number of traditional logistics functions that report to the senior logistics officer. The traditional logistics functions among manufacturers, wholesalers and retailers were detailed in Table 1-1. The responsibility for a specific function can be line or a combination of line and staff. Among leading edge firms, retailers and manufacturers are likely to have significantly greater functional responsibility than either wholesalers or hybrids. When it comes to line responsibility, manufacturers are likely to have significantly more total line functions than other leading edge organizations. Table 2-3 presents leading edge total functions and total line functions by business type. This analysis supports the general conclusions that manufacturers and retailers have broader overall logistical responsibility than wholesalers and hybrids and that manufacturers are likely to have more line responsibility.

FIGURE 2-2
LEADING EDGE ORGANIZATION
CENTRALIZATION TREND PAST THREE YEARS
BY BUSINESS TYPE

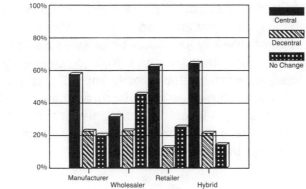

TABLE 2-3
FUNCTIONAL ANALYSIS
LEADING EDGE ORGANIZATIONS

Business Type	Average Functions	
	Total Overall Functions	Total Line Functions
Manufacturer	12.19	9.89*
Wholesaler	10.86	5.77
Retailer	13.25**	6.06
Hybrid	11.93	6.80

*   Statistically significantly higher than wholesalers, retailers and hybrids.
** Statistically significantly higher than wholesalers.

Significant differences exist between type of firm or channel position when it comes to the likelihood of having or not having responsibility for a specific traditional logistics function. Table 2-4 lists six functions wherein leading edge respondent's organizational structures differ between business types. For all other functions (Table 1-1) no difference exists among leading edge firms, independent of business type. Table 2-4 lists the percentage of leading edge respondents that reported responsibility for each of the six functions. The statistical likelihood of having any specific function varied across of business types. This analysis highlights the key functional differences between leading edge firms. Manufacturers are more likely to be directly involved in those logistical activities that directly impact customers. Over 85 percent of all leading edge manufacturers have responsibility for order processing, inventory management and customer service. This analysis illustrates the tendency among manufacturers to be more line oriented.

TABLE 2-4
LEADING EDGE ORGANIZATIONS COMPARATIVE
ANALYSIS OF SIX SIGNIFICANTLY DIFFERENT
FUNCTIONS BY ORGANIZATION TYPE

Traditional	Percent			
Logistics Function*	Manufacturer	Wholesaler	Retailer	Hybrid
Inventory Management	93.7^M	63.6^L	75.0	66.7
Intra-Company Transportation	92.2^M	68.2^L	93.8	60.0^L
Order Processing	85.9^M	40.9^{FL}	93.8	66.7
Customer Service	89.1^M	54.5^L	62.5	73.3
Facility Design	59.4^L	86.4	93.8	86.7
International	67.2^M	13.6^L	37.5	40.0

M = more likely to have; L = less likely to have; FL = far less likely to have

* All other functions listed in Table 1-1 had no significant difference indicating an equal likelihood that leading edge firms would or would not have functional responsibility.

Another aspect of functional organization is the degree to which leading edge organizations are responsible for beyond functions. Beyond functions are defined as functions that extend beyond the traditional logistics functions. Beyond functions are generally accepted as an indicator of the entrenchment of logistics in the overall formal structure of the enterprise. In other words, a logistics organization that has significant beyond functional responsibility is viewed as being more established than one that has fewer or no beyond functional responsibilities. Among leading edge organizations, 55.4 percent report responsibility for beyond functions. No significant difference exists between channel position and the likelihood or extent of beyond functional responsibility. As will be reported in Part II, leading edge firms as a group are significantly more involved in beyond responsibility than overall respondents. This analysis supports the conclusion that leading edge organizations are equally likely to have beyond responsibility, independent of business type.

A final aspect of comparative leading edge organizational analysis dealt with the reporting level and longevity of the senior logistics executives. Across leading edge organizations, the formal logistics effort is headed by a Vice President or higher title executive in 79.5 percent of the cases. This was true of 90 percent of all wholesalers, retailers and hybrids but only 70.3 percent of manufacturers. The likelihood that formal logistics in a leading edge manufacturer would be headed by an executive at a non-officer level was statistically greater than among other channel members. In terms of reportability of the chief logistics officer, the same pattern holds. Among wholesalers, retailers and hybrids, 94.3 percent of senior logistics executives reported to a senior vice president or higher. Among manufacturer leading edge organizations, the comparable percentage was 67.1 percent. In terms of longevity, manufacturer senior logistics officers have been in the job a significantly shorter period than other types of leading edge executives. Hybrid senior logistics officers have been in the job an average of 7.60 years which is almost as long as they report having had formal logistics organizations (7.71 years). In comparison, retail senior logistics officers have been in the job an average of 6.38 years, whole-salers 5.77 years and manufacturers 4.17 years. This analysis supports the conclusions that the senior logistics officers in manufacturing organizations are less elevated in the organization structure and have shorter tenure than their leading edge counterparts.

MANAGERIAL BEHAVIOR

A fundamental premise of the overall research was that practice of management is more basic to superior logistical performance than organization structure. In other words, while no single or ideal organization arrangement may exist within or between business types, it was expected that the best practices of logistics management could be identified. Data were col-lected regarding several different management practices. Comparative analysis of leading edge managerial behavior is based on: (1) logistics planning; (2) logistics mission state-ment; (3) participation in business unit strategic planning; (4) operational flexibility; (5) performance measurement; (6) competitive benchmarking; (7) computer sophistication; and (8) technology deployment.

The quality of leading edge logistics practice is highlighted by the careful attention that is given to formal planning. Across all leading edge respondents, no less than 95.7 percent reported commitment to a regular and comprehensive formal logistics planning procedure. The typical planning time horizon was 3.5 to 4 years with the average horizon being 3.81 years. The most common timeframe for plan update was on an annual basis. There was no significant difference between the incident of planning, the time duration of the plan nor the frequency of update among manufacturers, wholesalers, retailers and hybrids. This analysis supports the conclusion that formal logistics plan-ning is a common commitment among leading edge organiza-tions regardless of channel position.

The formal mission statement represents a firm's commitment to a specified level of logistics performance. The typical practice is to publish mission statements so that internal and external logistics customers are informed in advance of what performance to expect. About seventy percent of the leading edge firms report the practice of publishing formal mission statements. The likelihood of having a formal mission statement is independent of channel position. This analysis supports the conclusion that leading edge manufacturers, wholesalers, retailers and hybrids are equally committed to the practice of publishing formal logistics mission statements.

To effectively perform in concert with business unit strategic direction, it is imperative that logistics management be informed and ideally should participate in the strategic planning process. Only two leading edge firms indicated that their senior logistics officer was not in some way involved in business unit strategic planning. The vast majority of senior logistics officers, 92.5 percent, are formal participants in the strategic planning process. Another 5.4 percent provide input through other executives. Comparing by channel position, more manufacturing executives report participation by providing input through other executives (12.5%) than is true in wholesaling, retailing and hybrid organizations. In fact, 100 percent of the leading edge wholesale and retail senior logistics officers reported direct participation in business unit strategic planning. However, no statistically significant difference exists concerning the likelihood of strategic planning involvement by channel position. This analysis supports the conclusion that participation in business unit strategic planning is a universal practice among senior logistics executives in leading edge firms. It also reflects a general attitude among leading edge firms to treat logistical competency as a strategic resource.

To evaluate operational flexibility, respondents were asked to judge capability of their logistical organization to accommodate various events that reflect typical day-to-day operating situations. Leading edge firms demonstrated more operational flexibility than overall respondents. Table 2-5 lists the events

TABLE 2-5
FLEXIBILITY ANALYSIS OF
LEADING EDGE ORGANIZATIONS

Event	Manufacturer	Wholesaler	Retailer	Hybrid
Special Customer Service Request	3.22*	2.81	3.06	3.15
Sales and Marketing Incentive Programs	3.18	3.01	3.31	3.35
Product Introduction	3.27	3.22	3.30	3.25
Product Phase Out	3.06	2.84	3.00	3.20
Disruption in Supply	2.91**	2.53	2.80	2.50
Computer Breakdown	2.25	1.82	2.13	2.13
Product Recall	3.02	2.70	2.80	2.67
Customization of service levels to specific markets or customers	2.98	2.57	3.08	2.95
Product modification or customization while in the logistics system	2.76	2.32	2.71	2.85
Average across events	2.96	2.68	2.92	2.89

* Statistically different from the hybrid at $p = 0.08$.
** Statistically different from wholesalers and hybrids at $p = 0.07$.

Scale: 1 = cannot accommodate
        5 = accommodates very easily

and average response among leading edge firms by channel position. With two exceptions, the comparative ability of leading edge firms to handle special events is remarkably similar. The exceptions are that manufacturers report significantly more flexibility in handling: (1) special customer service requests; and (2) disruptions in supply. The ability to accommodate special customer service requests appears to reflect a trend among progressive manufacturers to capitalize upon flexible or tailored distribution practices. On an overall basis manufacturers exhibit the greatest flexibility across the nine events, 2.96, followed by retailers at 2.92, hybrids at 2.89, and wholesalers with a 2.68

score. The differences are not statistically significant by channel position.

All leading edge firms express limited flexibility to deal with computer breakdowns and supply disruptions. These scores reinforce the importance of information in the managerial practices of leading edge firms. The inability of dealing with supply disruptions reflects increased reliance on just-in-time inventory procurement strategies. In general, leading edge firms have mastered the logistics of product introduction, phase out and general support of marketing and sales incentive promotions. Areas of low flexibility include: (1) customization of service levels, characteristic of niche and tailored distribution strategies; and (2) the ability to customize products in the logistics system, reflective of postponement strategies. This analysis supports the conclusion that leading edge firms regardless of channel position place a great deal of emphasis on being flexible in the achievement of their logistical missions.

No area reflects the commonality of leading edge practice better than performance measurement. In total, 38 performance measures were examined. The measures covered five performance areas: (1) asset management; (2) cost; (3) customer service; (4) productivity; and (5) quality. Across channel position, leading edge firms reported regular use of 31 to 32 out of the 38 listed performance measures. Table 2-6 indicates the number of measures by performance category and type of firm. Leading edge firms follow almost identical performance measurement practices in the areas of cost, customer service and asset management. Performance measurement in quality and productivity is less uniform. However, no statistically significant differences exist between the practice of any category of performance measurement and channel position. This analysis confirms the almost compulsive commitment among leading edge firms to all forms of performance measurement independent of channel position.

TABLE 2-6
PERFORMANCE MEASUREMENT PRACTICES
LEADING EDGE ORGANIZATIONS

Performance Measurement Category	Listed Measures	Average			
		Manu-facturer	Whole-saler	Retailer	Hybrid
Asset Management	6	5.10	5.46	5.06	5.13
Cost	12	10.25	10.27	10.13	10.20
Customer Service	9	7.45	7.46	7.31	7.40
Productivity	6	3.93	4.77	4.13	4.67
Quality	5	4.35	3.96	4.50	4.27
TOTAL	38	31.08	31.91	31.13	31.66

An important part of leading edge performance is the practice of benchmarking. Leading edge firms are true believers that it is essential to continuously evaluate what other firms, both direct and indirect competitors, are doing in their pursuit of logistics excellence. Respondents were asked to report their benchmarking practices in ten different areas. Table 2-7 presents the percentage of firms reporting benchmarking practice by area.

In general, leading edge retailers are less involved in benchmarking than their manufacturing, wholesale and hybrid counterparts. In particular, retailers are less concerned than other channel members with comparative analysis of customer service, productivity and quality. On an overall basis, leading edge firms appear to be most interested in benchmarking cost, customer service and quality, and least interested in asset management and order processing operations. However it is important to stress that even in areas of limited interest, leading edge firms report near 50 percent participation in the bench-marking process. This analysis confirms that leading edge firms are avid benchmarkers. Retailers are less involved in bench-marking than other leading edge firms. The retailers' lower overall interest in customer service, productivity and quality benchmarking appears to be directly related to the restriction of typical retail logistics operation to the support of a unique store network.

TABLE 2-7
BENCHMARKING PRACTICES LEADING EDGE ORGANIZATIONS

	Percent			
Benchmark Area	Manufacturer	Wholesaler	Retailer	Hybrid
Cost	87.2	81.8	68.8	66.7
Asset Management	59.5	61.9	31.3	33.3
Customer Service	87.5	90.9	31.3*	66.7
Productivity	73.7	76.2	37.5*	60.0
Quality	85.0	80.9	50.0*	73.3
Logistics Strategy	74.4	60.0	50.0	60.0
Technology Deployment	63.2	76.2	50.0	53.3
Transportation Operations	65.8	76.2	62.5	46.7
Warehouse Operations	60.5	85.7	68.8	53.3
Order Processing Operations	61.5	60.0	43.8	33.3
Average Across Areas	71.8	74.9	49.6	55.6

* In each test of statistical significance, retailers were more likely to say no and less likely to say yes.

Computer sophistication appears to go hand-in-hand with the concept of leading edge logistics. When asked to compare their logistics information system to that of other areas of their business, leading edge firms felt logistics was treated well. On a scale of 1 to 5, where 5 equals much better, leading edge firms reported a composite score of about 3.6, with no significant difference by channel position. Naturally, specific computer applications that are of highest priority differ somewhat by channel position. Figure 2-3 illustrates the number of computer applications reported by channel position. Respondents were given an opportunity to indicate how many out of a list of 20 common computer applications they currently have installed. The list of 20 applications is included in Appendix C. As a group, leading edge firms have significantly more computer applications than the typical respondent.

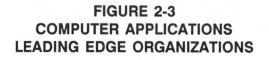

FIGURE 2-3
COMPUTER APPLICATIONS
LEADING EDGE ORGANIZATIONS

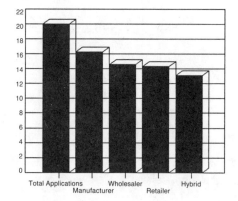

Of particular importance are the characteristics of information used to manage logistics. On an overall basis, leading edge firms have higher quality information. However, manufacturers reported that their information was less accurate than their channel counterparts. Table 2-8 ranks five information characteristics on a five point scale by channel position. On an overall basis, wholesalers, retailers and hybrids have better information to guide logistical operations than reported by their manufacturing counterparts. Several possible explanations exist for this minor information deficiency among manufacturers. The most likely is that the typical manufacturer logistics operation needs to compete with other functional areas such as production and sales for information services. In contrast, logistics in firms operating at other channel positions are automatically part of the mainstream transaction process. This analysis confirms that leading edge firms have extensive computer applications and high quality information. To the extent that one business type does not measure up to the overall leading edge competency, manufacturers rate lower with respect to accurate information to manage the logistics process.

TABLE 2-8
CHARACTERISTICS OF INFORMATION
LEADING EDGE ORGANIZATIONS

Characteristic	Manufacturer	Wholesaler	Retailer	Hybrid
Timely	4.00	4.27	4.25	4.33
Accurate	4.13*	4.55	4.44	4.47
Readily Available	4.00	3.95	4.19	4.26
Formatted On An Exception Basis	3.23	3.62	3.50	3.67
Appropriately Formatted Formatted To Facilitate Use	3.76	3.95	3.81	4.00
Average Across Characteristics	3.82	4.06	4.04	4.15

* Statistically significantly lower than other channel members ($p = 0.01$).

Scale: 1 = Never
        5 = Always

Leading edge firms are ahead of the pack when it comes to technology deployment. Two areas of deployment were of particular interest with respect to comparative leading edge behavior: (1) Electronic Data Interchange (EDI) and (2) Artificial Intelligence (AI). Tables 2-9 and 2-10 provide a summary of leading edge firms currently involved in EDI by type of applications and the degree to which AI is being used. In terms of EDI, it is clear that leading edge firms are beginning to deploy this technology irrespective of channel position. The level of deploying artificial intelligence in logistics has not reached expected penetration among leading edge firms. Leading edge manufacturers are the most involved in testing and evaluating AI logistics applications. Across the leading edge category, 57.5 percent of all respondents either do not have plans to install logistics AI applications or have not evaluated the potential. These data show that involvement in EDI and AI is not significantly different by channel position. EDI is a rapidly growing technology that appears to have appeal throughout a cross section of leading edge firms. AI is more prevalent in manufacturing and less common in retailing. Too few leading edge firms are currently using AI in logistics to permit conclusions regarding statistical significance of practice by channel position.

TABLE 2-9
INVOLVEMENT IN SELECTED TECHNOLOGY
LEADING EDGE ORGANIZATIONS

| | Percent | | | |
EDI Application	Manufacturer	Wholesaler	Retailer	Hybrid
Manufacturer	---	47.6	40.0	60.0
Wholesaler	35.9	---	26.7	33.3
Public Warehouse	33.3	0.0	14.3	15.4
Carrier	37.5	10.5	37.5	28.6
Financial Institution	31.2	52.4	50.0	53.9
Retailer	27.8	45.0	---	46.2
Customer	51.3	61.9	42.9	53.3
Co-Packer/Contractor	10.8	17.7	6.7	0.0

TABLE 2-10
ARTIFICIAL INTELLIGENCE IN LOGISTICS
LEADING EDGE ORGANIZATIONS

Percent

Activity	Manufacturer	Wholesaler	Retailer	Hybrid
Currently Used or Planned	48.6	33.3	12.5	38.50
Not Planned or not Evaluated	43.2	61.9	81.3	61.50

SUMMARY

The practices of leading edge firms are nearly identical independent of channel position. These findings make it clear that the leading edge firm can be expected to place a premium on specific managerial behavior regardless if they are manufacturing, wholesale, retail or hybrid organizations.

In terms of mission, firms that operate at different positions in the channel of distribution have distinctive logistical goals. To accomplish these goals, they have adopted unique and highly customized organization structures. What leading edge firms have in common across business types is a commitment to formal logistics organization, a willingness to modify organization as necessary to achieve their goals, a tendency to operate logistics on a centralized basis, responsibility for a broad array of traditional logistical functions, a tendency to have organizational responsibility for non-traditional logistics functions and senior logistics executives who are officers reporting to the inner circle of top management. In general, these senior logistics executives have held their positions in leading edge firms sufficiently long to have made a major impact. While selected differences exist on specific organizational features, a common profile emerges concerning how leading edge firms approach the organization of their logistical affairs.

When it comes to managerial behavior and practice, leading edge firms are remarkably similar independent of business type. Leading edge firms place a premium on formal planning, follow the practice of advanced commitment to a formal mission statement, are deeply involved in business unit strategic planning, demonstrate operational flexibility, are compulsive performance measurers, engage in competitive benchmarking, enjoy sophisticated computer support and are leaders in technology deployment.

Clearly there are basic and important differences between firms based on size, industry or class of trade as well as position in the distribution channel. These differences are evident in the establishment of their strategic posture. However, the practices they follow to achieve stated logistical objectives are nearly identical. Part II offers specifics regarding how leading edge firms measure up to the more typical firm within each business type.

PART II

Benchmarking Leading Edge Performers

STATEMENT ON BENCHMARKING

A pioneer in competitive benchmarking, the Xerox Corporation defines the activity as "the continuous process of measuring their products, services and practices against their toughest competitors or those companies renowned as leaders." Part II of this research book is devoted to the establishment of logistical benchmarks.

Using the Common Attributes Index (CAI) as the criterion for selection, leading edge organizations were isolated from among manufacturing, wholesale, retail and hybrid respondents. Assessing the logistical performance of the best competitors can identify standards of excellence. Benchmarking data can be useful for formal planning activities; strategies can be developed and implemented incorporating the knowledge gained from the benchmarking process. A thorough understanding of competitors' strengths and weaknesses helps to identify appropriate goals. It can help in the establishment of priorities and in the identification of new ways of doing business.

In Part I, the analysis concluded that few significant or meaningful differences exist in the practice of logistical management based on position in the distribution chain. In fact, regardless of business type, leading edge organizations are remarkably similar in terms of organizational structure, strategic posture and managerial behavior. In Part II, specific practices of leading edge organizations are isolated for microscopic examination.

Part II contains four chapters. The approach of each chapter is similar. Data are presented on specific attributes of organizational structure in Chapter Three, strategic posture in Chapter Four and managerial behavior in Chapter Five. The presentation first reports comparative performance of all respondents. Next, leading edge performance is directly isolated and contrasted to norm or typical respondent practice. Each chapter concludes with a summary statement regarding benchmarking conclusions.

The final chapter in Part II is devoted to Logistical Executive Career Pathing. While Chapter Six is not directly related to management practice, it provides significant insight into where today's logistical executives come from and where they are going.

The overall purpose of Part II is to establish a benchmarking start for firms who are interested in improving the quality of their logistical performance. For additional information on benchmarking, refer to the articles listed below[1]. A thorough understanding of what the best of the best do is an effective starting point. However, benchmarking is not a one-time tool. To be productive, benchmarking should be an on-going process. Continuous assessment of competitors and a willingness to integrate the knowledge gained from such benchmarking procedures are imperative to insure success in today's competitive environment.

66

FOOTNOTE

(1)   John E. Kelsch, "Benchmarking: Shrewd Way to Keep Your Company Ahead of Its Competition," _Boardroom Reports_, December 15, 1982 and Frances G. Tucker, Seymour M. Zivan, and Robert C. Camp, "How to Measure Yourself Against the Best," _Harvard Business Review_, Vol. 87, No. 1, Jan-Feb, 1987.

Chapter Three

ORGANIZATION STRUCTURE

The most visible dimension of logistics is the organizational structure adopted by a firm to conduct day to day operations. The study of logistics organizational structure, however, consists of a great deal more than span of control and reporting relationships.

An understanding of logistics organization starts with a careful review of functional span of control. Line and overall responsibilities for traditional logistics functions as well as the most common and least common functional responsibility are analyzed by business type. The analysis of span of control is rounded out by a review of functions likely to be added in the future and the most common beyond or extended functions that report to logistics organizations.

The second section of this chapter discusses structural preference. Manufacturers can select from a broad range of structural alternatives for organizing core logistics functions. The chapter identifies the most common structural alternatives among

North American manufacturers. Structural alternatives for wholesalers, retailers and hybrids are more varied. Therefore, it was not feasible to develop representations of typical organizational structures for these channel members.

Next, attention is directed to the degree and trend of centralization of organizational structure. Once again analysis results are presented by business type. The final chapter section views the dynamic nature of logistics organization. Patterns of formalization are reviewed in terms of longevity and frequency of reorganization.

Comparative benchmarking of leading edge firms to the norm or more typical respondent is used to present major conclusions. Each section contains a benchmarking sub-section relevant to the content being discussed. Benchmarking generalizations are presented in summary form at the end of the chapter.

FUNCTIONAL SPAN OF CONTROL

A traditional way to study logistical organization is to analyze the span of control or number of functions that the unit is directly responsible for on a line and staff basis. An analysis of span of control offers a convenient and necessary starting point for future generalizations concerning organization strategy and managerial behavior. The basic orientation of this research was to emphasize how functions are managed as contrasted to only examining how many functions report directly to the logistics executive.

Several questions were designed to address the issue of span of control. Comparative information is reported by business type concerning: (1) average line and overall functional responsibility; (2) most common functions; (3) least common functions; (4) functions most likely to be added in the future; and (5) beyond functions.

AVERAGE LINE AND OVERALL FUNCTIONS

Table 1-1 lists fifteen functions for manufacturers and sixteen functions for other business types that are generally accepted as the traditional responsibilities of logistics organizations. Survey respondents indicated which of these traditional functions were the formal responsibility of the logistics organization and classified their responsibility as line or staff.

The baseline for studying span of control is research that was completed over the past fifteen years by A. T. Kearney, Inc. and Traffic Management magazine. Separate studies completed in 1973, 1981 and 1985 all concluded that direct functional responsibility of the logistics organization was increasing. The 1988 data confirms the continuation of this trend. These studies are discussed in greater detail in Appendix D.

Table 3-1 reports the average number of functions for each year. The data in the years 1985 and 1987 distinguish between line and overall functions. Overall functions are a combination of line or staff accountability for the fifteen or sixteen traditional logistics functions. Both overall and line responsibility have increased during the 1980's. These data are plotted in Figure 3-1 to illustrate the rapid rate of functional expansion since 1981. Of particular interest is the increase in average line responsibility from 4.01 to 5.65 functions in the years 1985 to 1987. This expansion of line functional responsibility reflects a significant degree of formalization of logistics in the overall organizational structure of respondent firms.

Table 3-2 reports data from the 1987-88 research by business type. As shown, manufacturers had the highest average number of line functions with responsibility for 6.57 out of the fifteen traditional functions. The line functional responsibility for all other business types was lower. Out of sixteen traditional functions, hybrids averaged 5.66, retailers 4.55 and wholesalers 3.95.

TABLE 3-1
AVERAGE NUMBER OF TRADITIONAL FUNCTIONS

YEAR	OVERALL	LINE
1973	2.24	--
1981	3.62	--
1985	6.99	4.01
1987	8.68	5.65

FIGURE 3-1
AVERAGE NUMBER OF TRADITIONAL
LOGISTICS RESPONSIBILITIES
1973 - 1981 - 1985 - 1987

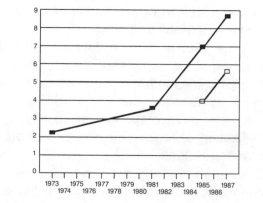

TABLE 3-2
AVERAGE NUMBER OF TRADITIONAL FUNCTIONS
BY BUSINESS TYPE

BUSINESS TYPE	OVERALL	LINE	RESPONDENTS
Manufacturer	8.82	6.57	380
Wholesaler	7.61	3.95	148
Retailer	8.48	4.55	90
Hybrid	8.94	5.66	77
Average Across Type	8.68	5.65	
Total Respondents			695

When staff or advisory functions were examined, the overall responsibility for all respondents jumped from 5.65 (line only) to 8.68 combined line and staff. Manufacturers averaged 8.82, wholesalers 7.61, retailers 8.48 and hybrids 8.94 overall functions. While the manufacturer list of traditional functions only contained fifteen choices as contrasted to sixteen for all other business types, the average overall responsibility between manufacturers, wholesalers, retailers and hybrids was nearly equal.

These data, in comparison to earlier A. T. Kearney and Traffic Management magazine results, make it clear that the average line and overall responsibility for traditional logistics functions is increasing. This suggests that the critical mass is in place to make integrated logistics a reality. Comparisons across business types support the conclusion that logistics at the manufacturing level is more line oriented than in the other business types. In particular, wholesalers and retailers have broad overall responsibilities, but relatively narrow line responsibilities. This variation in staff and advisory responsibility is viewed as a direct reflection of the logistical mission confronted by different business types.

MOST COMMON FUNCTIONS

Table 3-3 presents the five most common logistical line functions. Responses were rank ordered based upon the number of firms reporting direct line authority for each of the selected functions.

TABLE 3-3
THE FIVE MOST COMMON TRADITIONAL LOGISTICS LINE
LINE FUNCTIONS RANKED BY BUSINESS TYPE

Line Function	Manufacturer	Wholesaler	Retailer	Hybrid
Outbound Transportation	1	2	2	1
Intra-Company Transportation	2	3	5	4
Warehousing	3	1	1	1
Inbound Transportation	4	--	3	5
Logistics Administration	5	--	--	--
Materials Handling	--	3	4	3
Inventory Management	--	5	--	--

1 = most common

The greatest number of manufacturer respondents indicated they have line responsibility for outbound transportation. In fact, three of the five most common line functions among the manufacturing firms were transportation-related: outbound, intra-company and inbound transportation.

The line function most often cited by wholesalers was warehousing. This was followed by outbound transportation, intra-company transportation, materials handling and inventory management. These five functions reflect the traditional scope of a basic wholesaling operation. Wholesaling firms are in business to transport, store and manage inventories as they move through the channel.

The most common line responsibility among retail respondents was warehousing. This was followed by materials handling and the three transportation services. Once again, the basic services or those most integral to providing logistical needs were cited most frequently.

The same five functions are most common among hybrid firms. However, the rank ordering was slightly different. Responsibilities for outbound transportation and warehousing were most commonly reported by hybrids. These were followed by materials management, intra-company transportation and inbound transportation.

The most common logistics line responsibilities revealed no surprises. The line responsibilities detailed in Table 3-3 are the core logistics functions needed to perform business operations.

LEAST COMMON FUNCTIONS

Whereas the most common logistical line responsibilities were fairly consistent across business types, more diversity was shown in the range of least common line functions. Results are presented in Table 3-4. Once again, responses are ranked.

The fewest number of manufacturers reported line responsibility for sales forecasting. This was followed by logistics engineering, raw materials/work in process inventory, international logistics and production planning. There appears to be a sharp organizational distinction between production-related responsibilities for manufacturers.

Wholesaling firms were least likely to have line responsibility for international logistics. This was followed by data processing for distribution applications, sales forecasting, capital equipment procurement and facilities design.

Retailers were least likely to have line responsibility for sales forecasting followed by international logistics, facilities design, purchasing and customer services.

TABLE 3-4
THE FIVE LEAST COMMON TRADITIONAL LOGISTICS
LINE FUNCTIONS RANKED BY BUSINESS TYPE

Line Function	Manufacturer	Wholesaler	Retailer	Hybrid
Sales Forecasting	1	3	1	3
Logistics Engineering	2	--	--	--
Raw Materials WIP Inventory	3	--	--	--
International Logistics	4	1	2	2
Production Planning	5	--	--	--
Data Processing/ Distribution Applications	--	2	--	1
Capital Equipment Procurement	--	4	--	--
Facilities Design	--	5	3	4
Purchasing	--	--	3	5
Customer Service	--	--	5	--
Logistics Systems Planning	--	--	--	5

1 = least common

The fewest hybrid firms reported line responsibility for data processing for distribution applications. The other functions least reported by hybrids included international logistics, sales forecasting, facilities design, purchasing and logistics system planning.

Two of the least cited line functions -- sales forecasting and international logistics -- were common to all four of the business types. Based upon interviews and the general trend toward globalization of business operations, it can be expected that more logistical organizations will be assuming responsibility for international business. The fact that few logistics organizations have responsibility for sales forecasting is significant. Historically, low sales forecast accuracy has been identified as a critical contributor to logistics problems. This deficiency is further elaborated in Chapter Five. Across all respondents, only 14 percent reported direct responsibility for sales forecasting. More direct involvement and coordination between logistics personnel and those responsible for forecasting is essential to improving logistical performance.

FUTURE FUNCTIONS

A significant insight into future logistics responsibilities is gained from examining the functions respondents believe are most likely to be added in the future. The functions identified varied widely by channel position. Logistics system planning and inbound transportation were the only traditional functions that made the most likely to be added list of all business types. These data are reported in Table 3-5. The percentages presented are based upon the number of firms who did not have responsibility for the specific function, but indicated they were likely to add it in the future.

Manufacturers chose logistics systems planning as the function most likely to be added in the future. The next most likely functions to be added were inbound transportation, logistics administration, outbound transportation and finished goods inventory.

Among wholesalers, the most likely function to be added was logistics system planning. The next most likely to be added function was materials handling. Other functions most likely to be added to wholesalers' logistics organizations in order were outbound transportation, warehousing, inventory management and inbound transportation.

Among retailers, warehousing was the function viewed as most likely to be added in the future. It was followed by logistics systems planning, logistics administration, inbound transportation and capital equipment procurement.

Hybrid respondents listed intra-company transportation as the function most likely to be added in the future. The next most likely to be added were outbound transportation, data processing for distribution applications, logistics systems planning and inbound transportation.

These data reflect a somewhat uncertain future concerning where logistics functional responsibility will expand in the future. There is evidence to suggest a concern with more formalized logistics system planning and a desire to assume control over inbound transportation independent of distribution channel position.

TABLE 3-5
LOGISTICAL FUNCTIONAL RESPONSIBILITIES
MOST LIKELY TO BE ADDED BY BUSINESS TYPE

Traditional Function	Percent			
	Manufacturer	Wholesaler	Retailer	Hybrid
Logistics Systems Planning	68.2	55.6	54.5	35.7
Inbound Transportation	63.0	40.0	44.4	33.3
Logistics Administration	62.3	--	50.0	--
Outbound Transportation	58.3	46.2	--	42.9
Finished Goods Inventory	44.8	--	--	--
Materials Handling	--	46.7	--	--
Warehousing	--	41.7	100.0	--
Inventory Management	--	40.0	--	--
Capital Equipment Procurement	--	--	41.7	--
Intra-Company Transportation	--	--	--	45.5
Data Processing/ Distribution Applications	--	--	--	36.0

BEYOND FUNCTIONS

Respondents were asked if they have responsibilities not traditionally identified as logistics functions. Because the overall responsibility of logistics executives has increased, it follows that they could have also been assigned functional responsibility only tangentially related to logistics.

Respondents were asked to list such beyond functions managed by their logistics organization. The beyond functions were self-reported, in response to an open-ended question. As would be expected, the answers varied widely. However, certain beyond functions were frequently cited. The most common beyond function from the manufacturer survey was data processing for distribution applications, with 11.8 percent of the respondents specifying functional responsibility. The next most commonly named beyond functions by manufacturers were facilities management at 10.3 percent, selected sales activities at 9.2 percent, manufacturing operations at 7.4 percent, and real estate activities at 4.5 percent.

In the Phase II Wholesale/Retail survey, data processing for distribution applications was added to the list of traditional logistics functions. Over 26 percent of the wholesalers reported responsibility for data processing for distribution applications. The next most common beyond functions named by wholesalers were real estate at 16.2 percent, security/loss prevention at 6.1 percent, and selected sales activities, personnel and maintenance/repair all at 4.7 percent.

Similar to wholesalers, 18.9 percent of retailers listed facilities management, the most common beyond function. Real estate and security/loss prevention were tied for second at 7.8 percent. Fleet administration was fourth, with 4.4 percent of the retail respondents naming it as part of the logistics organization's direct responsibility. No other beyond function was named by more than 3 percent of the retail respondents.

Facilities management and real estate were both named by 15.6 percent of the hybrid firms. In third place was selected sales activities at 6.5 percent, followed by personnel at 3.9 percent.

Beyond functions represent a gradual expansion of formal logistics responsibility into tangentially related areas. The fact that a significant number of respondents reported beyond functions is interpreted as a measure of formalization of logistics within the enterprise. The assignment of beyond functions means that the logistics organization and its senior officer have gained sufficient organizational longevity to be viewed as part of the permanent management structure. The downsizing and overall flattening of organizational structure could increase the incident of beyond functions in the future.

LEADING EDGE BENCHMARKING - SPAN OF CONTROL

The basic benchmarking procedure is to compare leading edge firms to the norm or more typical respondent. When leading edge firms were compared to norm firms, they were typically responsible for more traditional line and overall logistics functions. As discussed previously, overall functions are comprised of those responsibilities for which the logistics organization has direct line control or a staff-advisory role. These data are presented in Table 3-6.

TABLE 3-6
AVERAGE LINE AND OVERALL FUNCTIONAL
RESPONSIBILITIES BY BUSINESS TYPE
AND CAI CATEGORY

CAI Group	Manufacturer Line/Overall	Wholesaler Line/Overall	Retailer Line/Overall	Hybrid Line/Overall
Leading Edge	9.89/12.19	5.77/10.86	6.06/13.25	6.80/11.93
Norm	6.64/ 9.10	4.32/ 8.11	4.95/ 8.77	6.37/ 9.51

Leading edge manufacturers averaged 12.19 overall functions while norm firms averaged 9.10. Leading edge manufacturers averaged 9.89 line functions as compared to 6.64 for norm firms. The mean number of line functions for all CAI categories of manufacturers was 6.57.

The pattern for wholesalers was similar to manufacturers. Leading edge wholesalers averaged 10.86 overall functions. Norm wholesalers averaged 8.11 overall functions. Looking specifically at line functional control, leading edge wholesalers averaged 5.77 line functions while norm wholesalers averaged 4.32. The mean number of line functions for all CAI categories of wholesalers was 3.95.

Similar to manufacturers and wholesalers, leading edge retailers reported responsibility for more overall and line functions than did norm retailers. Leading edge retailers on average had 13.25 overall functions while norm retailers had 8.77. Leading edge retailers had an average of 6.06 line functions compared to 4.95 for norm firms. The mean number of line functions for all CAI categories of retailers was 4.55.

Leading edge hybrids averaged 11.93 overall functions compared to an average of 9.51 for norm hybrids. Leading edge hybrids average 6.80 line functions and norm hybrids had a mean number of 6.37 line functions. The mean number of line functions for all CAI categories of hybrids was 5.66.

Of particular interest is the extensive involvement in boundary spanning functions by leading edge firms. Table 3-7 lists five traditional functions that involve interaction with groups either within or external to their enterprise. For example, order processing and customer service typically interface directly with customers. In contrast, purchasing typically interfaces with vendors. Sales forecasting requires internal coordination with such units as marketing and finance. The analysis supports the conclusion that leading edge organizations are more involved in boundary spanning functions than typical respondents. Table 3-7 reports involvement by business type. In this comparison, the percentage involvement of leading edge firms is benchmarked to the norm or more typical respondent. The phenomenon of greater involvement in boundary spanning is characteristic of leading edge firms independent of distribution chain position. Further boundary spanning information is included in materials covering external alliances reported in Chapter Seven.

TABLE 3-7
BOUNDARY SPANNING INVOLVEMENT
BY BUSINESS TYPE AND CAI GROUP

Percent

Boundary Spanning Function	Manufacturer LE/Norm	Wholesaler LE/Norm	Retailer LE/Norm	Hybrid LE/Norm
Sales Forecasting	56.3/30.7	45.5/31.6	33.3/19.7	50.0/46.0
Purchasing	59.4/49.6	54.6/41.8	58.3/39.3	57.1/58.0
Order Processing	85.9/55.9	40.9/47.9	91.7/44.3	64.3/52.0
Customer Service	89.1/57.9	54.6/44.9	58.3/29.5	71.4/46.0
International	67.2/47.6	13.6/16.3	33.3/37.7	42.9/24.0

Leading edge firms are also typically responsible for more beyond functions. Average beyond functions per respondent cross tabulated by CAI group and business type is illustrated in Figure 3-2. Core logistics functions are easier to define for manufacturing firms than for the other business types. This in part explains the lower incident of beyond functions among manufacturing firms.

The consistency of the responses has benchmarking significance. Without exception, leading edge firms have a greater critical mass of traditional and beyond functional span of control than the more typical firm. These results are consistent independent of position in the distribution channel. These data are further elaborated and statistically analyzed in Appendices A and B. As noted earlier, it is more important to develop an understanding of how leading edge firms manage logistics functions rather than to focus on the number of functions managed. Nevertheless, it is significant that leading edge firms independent of business type are typically responsible for more traditional and beyond functions than their norm counterparts. This analysis supports the conclusion that comprehensive functional span of control is a universal prerequisite to integrated logistics.

FIGURE 3-2
AVERAGE NUMBER OF BEYOND FUNCTIONS
PER FIRM BY BUSINESS TYPE AND CAI GROUP

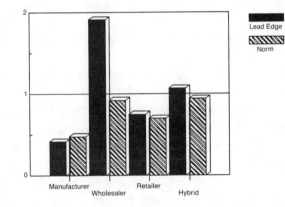

STRUCTURAL PREFERENCE

Previous research has concluded that no ideal or model organization exists that fits all firms. This is even true for firms at a specific position in the distribution chain. For example, careful examination of two large successful mass merchandisers revealed that one was irrevocably committed to distribution warehouses while the other looked upon such facilities as necessary evils to be minimized in favor of direct store vendor shipments.

To gain insight into formal organization structure, two techniques were utilized. In the Phase I study of manufacturers, firms were presented five organization charts and asked to indicate which most closely resembled their organization. This procedure could not be employed in the Phase II study of retail and wholesale organization because preliminary research was not successful in identifying typical organizations that could be graphically represented.

In the Phase II research, retail and wholesale firm representatives were asked to complete an organization profile indicating the title, level and function of each person who reported directly to the senior logistics executive. These responses were useful in the determination of span of control and level of responsibility.

The five organizational charts used in Phase I are illustrated in Figure 3-3. The charts depict the varying degree to which logistics activities are dispersed or consolidated.

Table 3-8 presents the breakdown of organizational structure responses for manufacturing firms. Over one-half of the manufacturing firms reported a functional organization structure versus a divisionalized organization structure. Responsibilities are organized based upon functional activities such as logistics, manufacturing and accounting for the enterprise rather than by division or business unit.

Viewing the responses from a different perspective, a very strong preference was reported for consolidated or formalized logistical responsibilities. Only 28.5 percent of the manufacturing respondents reported logistical functions dispersed throughout the organization. The vast majority indicated logistics functions were either partially or totally integrated, thus demonstrating more formalized commitment of logistical resources. This analysis reflects a strong preference for centralized control of logistical operations. Organization types B and D, which are centralized, were selected by 35.3 percent of respondents.

FIGURE 3-3
ALTERNATIVE ORGANIZATION STRUCTURES MANUFACTURING FIRMS

Type A - Functional Organization:
Dispersed Responsibilities for Logistics Activities

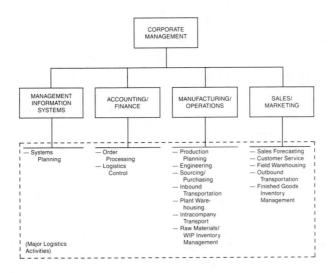

Type B - Functional Organization:
Consolidated Logistics Responsibilities

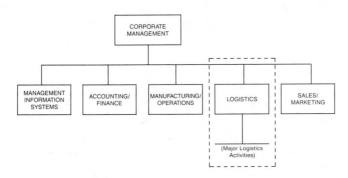

FIGURE 3-3 con't.

Type C - Divisional Organization:
Logistics Functions Consolidated within Business Units

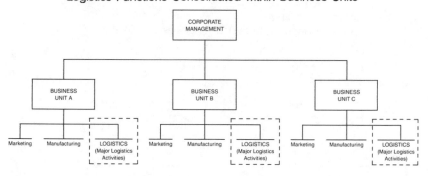

Type D - Divisional Organization:
Centrally Consolidated Logistics Responsibilities

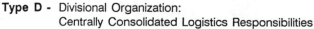

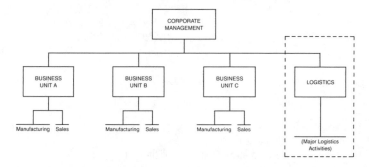

Type E - Divisionalized Organization:
Corporate Staff Logistics Function with Line Logistics Functions
in the Business Units (essentially a combination of Type C and D)

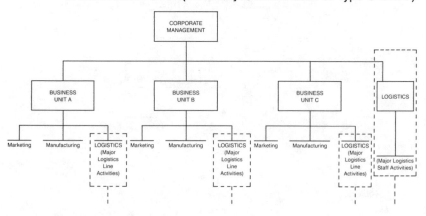

TABLE 3-8
ORGANIZATION PREFERENCE AMONG MANUFACTURING FIRMS

Organization Type	Number of Respondents	Percentage of Respondents
TYPE A: Functional Organization, Dispersed Logistics Responsibilities	108	28.5
TYPE B: Functional Organization, Consolidated Logistics Responsibilities	93	24.5
TYPE C: Division Organization, Logistics Functions Consol- idated within Business Units	59	15.6
TYPE D: Divisionalized Organization, Centrally Consolidated Logistics Responsibilities	41	10.8
TYPE E: Divisionalized Organization Corporate Staff Logistics Function with Line Logistics Functions in the Business Units	59	15.6
OTHER	19	5.0

Because of the wide variations in structural organization of wholesalers and retailers, it was not practical to provide respondents a selection of organization charts. In order to determine the organization structure of wholesale, retail and hybrid firms, respondents were asked to indicate the reporting relationships of logistics executives within their firms. The number and type of direct reports to the senior logistics executive mirrors the overall logistics organization structure. Reporting to top-level executives is indicative of greater visibility and recognition.

Table 3-9 presents a breakdown of personnel reporting to the senior logistics executive. Overall, wholesalers have more upper level executives reporting to the senior logistics executive than do retailers or hybrids. The nature of wholesaling as predominantly a logistics oriented business is reflected by the number of senior and executive vice presidents reporting to the chief logistics executive.

TABLE 3-9
PERSONNEL REPORTING DIRECTLY TO THE
SENIOR LOGISTICS EXECUTIVE BY BUSINESS TYPE

Title	Number by Type of Firm		
	Wholesalers	Retailers	Hybrids
Executive Vice President	18	1	4
Senior Vice President	14	2	0
Vice President	85	52	45
Director	74	116	66
Manager	222	170	99
Supervisor	56	3	47
Other	30	16	25

On an overall basis, the traditional belief that no single organization structure is ideal was confirmed. In the manufacturing study, 70 percent of all respondents reported the existence of a formal logistics organizational structure. The retail/wholesale survey results indicate that 80 percent of the respondents report a formal logistics organizational structure. These data support the belief that dispersed organizational responsibilities are rapidly being replaced by formalized structure. Evidence also clearly supports the common belief that logistical organization development is evolutionary.

LEADING EDGE BENCHMARKING - ORGANIZATION STRUCTURE

When benchmarking the manufacturing firms by CAI category, it is clear that leading edge manufacturers are far less likely than norm manufacturers to operate with a dispersed organization responsibility. Almost 90 percent of the leading edge firms have formal organizational structures. Leading edge manufacturers prefer centralized organizational structures. They are likely to pattern their organizational structure to consolidate logistical responsibilities (Type B or Type D; see Figure 3-3). Among leading edge respondents 65 percent favored either structure B or D. Because these structure types consolidate logistical responsibilities, they increase the likelihood of improved efficiencies and economies of scale. In comparison, norm manufacturers show no specific structural preference. While 72 percent of the norm respondents indicate formal organizations, only 35 percent favored Type B and Type D structures. Therefore, from a benchmarking perspective, the analysis supports the conclusion that leading edge manufacturers have far greater tendency to have formalized and centralized organizational structure than norm manufacturing respondents.

No significant differences were identified between the organizational structures of leading edge and norm firms for wholesaler, retailer or hybrid business types. However, leading edge firms do have more high level personnel reporting directly to the senior logistics executive.

CENTRALIZATION/DECENTRALIZATION OF LOGISTICS

As noted earlier, manufacturer respondents indicated a clear preference for centralized organization structures. Among manufacturers, 35.3 percent of respondents indicated existence of centralized organization structures. Among leading edge firms, centralized preference jumped to 65 percent. Nearly 60 percent of manufacturers responding to the update survey had centralized structures.

In the Phase II survey of retailers and wholesalers, respondents were asked to directly calibrate their degree of centralization as well as the trend over the past three years. Table 3-10 presents the degree of centralization by business type. Retailers reported greater incidence of centralized logistical organizations. On a scale of 1 to 5, with five being totally centralized, comparative scores were 3.84 for retailers, 3.62 for manufacturers from the update survey, 3.53 for wholesalers and 3.24 for hybrids.

Respondents were also asked to indicate any shift in centralization/decentralization policy over the previous three years. These data are presented by Figure 3-4. Responses indicated a strong movement toward centralization of logistical responsibility independent of business type. Across the board, almost 1 out of 2 respondents indicated that their logistical organization is becoming more centralized.

This overall analysis is very conclusive. Logistics organizations are typically centralized and are becoming more centralized. This conclusion is valid independent of business type.

TABLE 3-10
CENTRALIZATION DEGREE BY BUSINESS TYPE

Degree	Percent			
	Update Manufacturer	Wholesaler	Retailer	Hybrid
Completely Centralized	25.3	26.2	34.8	15.8
Somewhat Centralized	33.3	24.8	28.1	23.7
Combination	24.7	31.0	27.0	35.5
Somewhat Decentralized	11.8	11.7	6.7	18.4
Completely Decentralized	4.8	6.2	3.4	6.6
Mean*	3.62	3.53	3.84	3.24

* Scale: 1 = completely decentralized
         5 = completely centralized

FIGURE 3-4
STRUCTURAL PREFERENCE TRENDS
BY BUSINESS TYPE

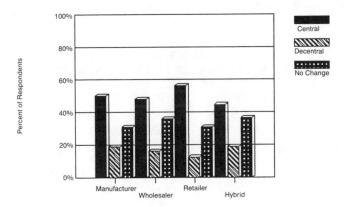

LEADING EDGE BENCHMARKING -
CENTRALIZATION/DECENTRALIZATION

Table 3-11 presents corporate degree of centralization for leading edge and norm respondents by distribution channel position. Retailers have the highest degree of centralization, and no statistically significant difference exists between leading edge and norm respondents. Data for each of the other business types, also reflects a preference for centralization. Table 3-12 presents centralization trends by business type for leading edge and norm respondents. Once again there is a remarkable similarity in respondent data. No statistically significant difference exists between leading edge and norm respondents. The trend toward centralization was stronger among manufacturers, retailers and hybrids than for wholesale firms. As shown in

Table 3-12, norm wholesalers reported greater movement to centralized operations than did leading edge wholesalers.

Benchmarking guidelines suggest that both leading edge and norm firms are committed to centralized organizations. The fact that no measurable difference exists between CAI categories serves to validate the commitment to centralized organization structure independent of business type.

TABLE 3-11
CENTRALIZATION DEGREE BY BUSINESS TYPE
AND CAI GROUP

| | Scale* | |
Business Type	Leading Edge	Norm
Manufacturer (Update)	3.69	3.70
Wholesaler	3.41	3.53
Retailer	3.81	3.81
Hybrid	3.60	3.18

* Scale: 1 = completely decentralized
          5 = completely centralized

TABLE 3-12
CENTRALIZATION TRENDS BY BUSINESS TYPE
AND CAI GROUP

| | | Percent | | |
Trend	Update Manufacturer LE/Norm	Wholesaler LE/Norm	Retailer LE/Norm	Hybrid LE/Norm
Centralization	57.5/52.1	31.8/50.0	62.5/55.4	64.3/43.8
Decentralization	22.5/17.7	22.7/17.0	12.5/14.3	21.4/20.8
No Change	20.0/30.3	45.5/33.0	25.0/30.4	14.3/35.4

DYNAMIC STRUCTURE

Several aspects of the research address the longevity of the logistics organization and the frequency of change. Both sets of data provide insight into the dynamics of logistics organization.

YEARS ORGANIZED

The four business types revealed similar patterns regarding the length of time logistics has been formally organized, although retailers on average have been formally organized slightly longer than other business types. The average length of formal organization of logistics by business type is: manufacturers 10.90 years, wholesalers 10.14 years, retailers 11.82 years and hybrids 10.39 years. This mirrors the increasing recognition of the importance of logistics within the business organization and the increasing acceptance of the integrated logistics concept during the late 1970's. For reasons reviewed in Chapter One, during the past decade logistics has gained greater recognition and significantly more responsibilities have been delegated to logistical organizations. The longevity data confirm these common beliefs regarding logistical evolution.

LEADING EDGE BENCHMARKING - YEARS ORGANIZED

From the perspective of benchmarking, leading edge wholesalers and retailers have been organized formally considerably longer than their norm counterparts. The difference in length of time of formalization between leading edge and norm wholesalers is especially dramatic. Wholesaling firms in the leading edge category have been formally organized for an average of 22.2 years versus only 8.8 years for the norm wholesalers. Leading edge retailers have been formally organized approximately twice as long as have norm retailers, 20 years versus 10.1. Leading edge manufacturers have been organized slightly longer at 11.31 years than norm manufacturers at 10.59 years. Hybrids are an anomaly. Leading edge hybrids have been organized 7.7 years, which is fewer than the overall average of 10.4 years. This suggests a faster evolutionary process, but no data exists to confirm this conclusion.

Leading edge hybrids formalize or establish rules and procedures to guide day-to-day operations at a faster pace than norm hybrids. They tend to reflect advanced characteristics after having been organized a relatively short period of time. A useful hypothesis is that the complex nature of hybrid business operations necessitates early development of formalized rules and procedures. Figure 3-5 illustrates the length of time leading edge and norm firms have been organized by business type. It is clear from the data that commitment to formal logistics structure is an essential ingredient of leading edge performance.

FREQUENCY OF REORGANIZATION

Longevity is not the only indicator of the logistics organization's dynamic nature. The typical respondent had undergone between one and two reorganizations during the past five years. This rate of organization adaptation is illustrative of a general philosophy of responsiveness by incorporating flexibility into even the most formal operations. Rules and procedures are developed to guide everyday operations. However, organizations also attempt to build flexibility into their operations so that they can respond to an ever-changing mission. Internal reorganization and adaptation enable firms to capitalize on developing opportunities. In fact, change or reorganization is typical among the leading edge firms.

FIGURE 3-5
NUMBER OF YEARS LOGISTICS HAS BEEN
FORMALLY ORGANIZED BY BUSINESS TYPE
AND CAI GROUP

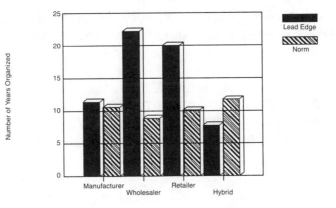

Overall, retailers and hybrids have reorganized more frequently than manufacturers and wholesalers. As the channel members closest to the consumers, retailers are most likely to sense changing customer service requirements. Reorganizations among retailers reflect their desire to modify business practices in line with customer demands. Retailer reorganizations could also be viewed as an indication of the increased formation rate of new types or forms of retailing. Average number of reorganizations over the past five years by business type are: manufacturers 1.9; wholesalers 1.6; retailers 2.3; and hybrids 2.1.

LEADING EDGE BENCHMARKING - REORGANIZATION

Leading edge firms reported significantly more reorganizations than their norm counterparts. Figure 3-6 illustrates the average number of reorganizations by business type and CAI group. The most significant difference is between leading edge manufacturers and norm manufacturers. Leading edge manufacturers were involved in an average of 2.3 reorganizations during the previous five years compared to an average of 1.9 for norm

FIGURE 3-6
NUMBER OF REORGANIZATIONS OF LOGISTICAL
ACTIVITIES WITHIN THE LAST FIVE YEARS
BY BUSINESS TYPE AND CAI GROUP

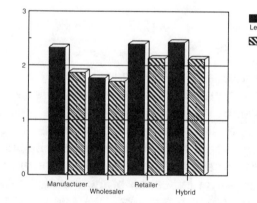

manufacturers. While the difference is not as dramatic, leading edge respondents in all other business types also reported more frequent reorganizations than norm respondents. The update of 187 manufacturers indicated that 50 percent had reorganized during the year between Phases I and II of this research. It is clear that logistical organizations are not rigid throughout North American industry. The analysis also supports the conclusion that leading edge firms continue to seek improved organization structures at a more frequent rate than the typical firm.

SUMMARY

The research clearly documents the fact that the typical logistics organization's average number of line and overall logistics functions is increasing. Logistical span of control at the manufacturing level of distribution tends to be more line oriented than typical of other business types. The distinction between line and staff responsibilities by business type reflects differences in logistics mission by position in the distribution chain.

Manufacturers appear to have a generally accepted core of logistics functions that are typically part of the formalized structure. For retailers and hybrids, the logistical core constitutes outbound transportation and warehousing, with a variety of other functions rounding out the typical respondent's logistical structure.

Few logistics organizations have responsibility for sales forecasting. This is true independent of business type. Increased attention to international concerns has not, with the exception of some manufacturers, filtered down to logistical structure. Based upon interviews and survey data, a look to the future suggests that the most likely functions to be added are logistics systems planning and inbound transportation. These future directions are independent of business type.

The current frequency of beyond functions is impressive. Delegated responsibility for a function only tangentially related to logistics is reflective of a general formalization of the unit in the enterprise's overall culture.

In terms of structural preference, logistics organizations are formalized and centralized. Analysis suggests that organization structures are becoming increasingly centralized at all levels in the distribution chain. The dynamic nature of logistics is high-lighted by the longevity of formal organizations and the fre-quency of reorganization. Formal logistics organizations have considerable longevity but the frequency of reorganization clearly suggests constant adjustment of structure to mission.

In terms of benchmarking leading edge firms to the norm, analysis supports the following generalizations concerning leading edge organizations. Leading edge firms:

* Have had formal organizations longer.

* Are more apt to have logistics headed by an officer level executive.

* Adopt a more fluid approach to logistics organization structure and encourage frequent reorganizations to take advantage of opportunities.

* Tend to favor centralized control.

* Are becoming more centralized as they adapt organization structure to mission.

* Are responsible for more traditional staff and line functions.

* Are more apt to execute boundary-spanning or externally-oriented logistics functions.

* Tend to manage more beyond or extended functional responsibilities not traditionally considered part of logistics.

Manufacturing Strategic Preference
    Leading Edge Benchmarking - Strategic Preference
Flexibility
    Ease of Accommodating Special Events
    Leading Edge Benchmarking - Special Events
External Alliances
Newborns
Summary

Chapter Four

STRATEGIC POSTURE

The strategic posture of a logistics operation is concerned with relationships. Such relationships involve everyday contact with customers. The relationships also extend to channel associates and service providers. Finally, the relational spectrum of logistics spans the internal interfaces and conflicting objectives that must be considered within the business enterprise. To accommodate the varied relations, it is essential for a logistics organization to be responsive and exhibit a high degree of flexibility. It is essential to realize that a logistics operation has many different customers, both external and internal.

The strategic posture of respondents was examined to better understand how leading edge logistical operations accommodate special events. In particular, attention focused on which events were viewed as routine and which events were difficult to accommodate. Likewise, attention was directed to anticipated future use of external alliances with service providers. The objective was to identify what, if any, difference exists between leading edge firms as contrasted to norm or more average respondents.

In the case of manufacturers, it was possible to isolate overall logistics strategic posturing. A comparative analysis of the strategic orientation by business type was presented in Chapter Two. Because of the nature of manufacturing enterprises, it was possible to identify three primary operational strategies during preliminary research. Manufacturing respondents were asked to identify which of these three strategies most closely approximated their firm's orientation.

For reasons discussed in Chapter Two, the strategic mission of wholesalers and retailers does not distill into a clear or easy to define strategic pattern. Therefore, the research design of Phase II dealing with wholesalers and retailers took a somewhat different approach from the Phase I manufacturing survey to examining strategic preference. The initial section reports data on manufacturing strategic preference.

The second section presents analysis and conclusions relating to flexibility and responsiveness. The final section examines a unique subset of respondents who have special strategic significance because of their recent entry into formal logistics. These *newborns* are "Johnny come lately's" in that they have only been committed to formal logistics three years or less.

As in Chapter Three, major conclusions regarding strategic posture are presented in a framework of comparative benchmarking between leading edge and the norm or more typical respondent data. With the exception of the discussion concerning newborns, each section contains one or more benchmarking sub-sections relevant to the content. Benchmarking generalizations are presented in summary form at the end of the chapter.

MANUFACTURING STRATEGIC PREFERENCE

Manufacturing firms were asked to choose from among three alternative strategies, the one strategy which most closely approximated their own. These strategic orientations had been identified during the pilot study that preceded Phase I of the overall research. The strategies are presented in Table 4-1.

Overall, the most frequently selected strategy was a process orientation. More than one-half of all manufacturer respondents indicated their primary strategy most closely approximated the process description. A process strategy reflects recent efforts to better integrate stages of the value-added logistics chain. The process strategic orientation seeks to integrate inbound and outbound logistical operations. Figure 4-1 provides a breakdown of strategic choice as reported by manufacturing respondents.

TABLE 4-1
PRIMARY LOGISTICS STRATEGY MANUFACTURING RESPONDENTS

Process Strategy -- A process-based strategy is concerned with managing a broad group of logistics activities as a value added chain. Emphasis is on achieving efficiency from managing purchasing, manufacturing, scheduling and physical distribution as an integrated system.

Market Strategy -- A market-based strategy is concerned with managing a limited group of logistics activities for a multi-division single business unit or across multiple business units. The logistics organization seeks to make joint product shipments to common customers for different product groups and seeks to facilitate sales and logistical coordination by a single order-invoice. Often the senior sales and logistics executives report to the same manager.

Channel Strategy -- A channel-based strategy is concerned with managing logistics activities performed jointly with dealers and distributors. The strategic orientation places a great deal of attention on external control. Significant amounts of finished inventory are typically maintained forward or downstream in the distribution channel.

LEADING EDGE BENCHMARKING -
STRATEGIC PREFERENCE

No statistically significant differences were noted between the strategic choice of leading edge and those of norm manufacturing firms. The dominant choice of both respondent groups was a process strategy. However, leading edge firms indicated a stronger tendency toward the process strategy than the norm respondents. Table 4-2 presents the strategic choice of the two respondent groups.

FIGURE 4-1
STRATEGIC SELECTION MANUFACTURING FIRMS

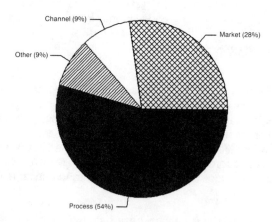

TABLE 4-2
STRATEGIC ORIENTATION BY CAI GROUP

Strategy	Leading Edge		Norm	
	Number	Percent	Number	Percent
Process	42	70.0	129	55.6
Market	14	23.3	78	33.6
Channel	4	6.7	25	10.8

FLEXIBILITY

Flexibility is a popular word in today's business community. Buyers expect suppliers, regardless of their position in the distribution chain, to be capable of rapid response to service requests. Much of the expected responsiveness relates to logistical operations. To achieve responsiveness, logistical organizations must develop operations sufficiently flexible to respond to customer needs without sacrificing organizational efficiency. This section examines how this balancing act is achieved. The presentation focuses on operational areas that logistical organizations have learned to handle with ease as well as on those areas that represent problems.

To evaluate flexibility, respondents were asked to indicate their logistical organization's ability to accommodate special customer requests or events. Responses were analyzed to identify events that were relatively easy for logistical systems to handle and those that were more difficult.

EASE OF ACCOMMODATING SPECIAL EVENTS

Table 4-3 presents comparative rankings of ten events. A rank of 10 indicates that the overall respondents by business type found that event the easiest to accommodate. A rank of

1 indicates that respondents found the event most difficult to accommodate. The data are presented by business type.

TABLE 4-3
EASE OF ACCOMMODATING SPECIAL REQUESTS
BY BUSINESS TYPE

Event	Manufacturer	Wholesaler	Retailer	Hybrid
Special Customer Service Requests	10	8	6	9
Sales and Marketing Incentive Programs	9	9	8	8
Product Introduction	8	10	10	10
Product Phase Out	7	6	9	7
Disruption in Supply	3	2	3	2
Computer Breakdown	1	1	1	1
Product Recall	6	4	4	3
Customization of Service Levels to Specific Markets or Customers	4-5 (tie)	5	5	4
Product Modification or Customization while in the Logistics System	4-5 (tie)	3	2	5
Returned Goods	2	7	7	6

Scale: 10 = easiest to accommodate
          1 = most difficult to accommodate

There was unanimous agreement among all business groups that computer breakdowns constitute a very difficult event to accommodate. Stated differently, computer breakdowns, because of the degree of dependency on data processing, create the greatest problems and are the most difficult to work around. Given the high degree of data processing dependency, the relative impact of breakdown is not surprising nor is it likely to change in the future.

The next most difficult overall event to accommodate was supply disruption. If inbound supply is disrupted, whether it be raw materials for manufacturing or finished products bound to retailers, operations must be curtailed and in extreme situations closed down. Supply disruption was reported as a serious event independent of distribution channel position.

Throughout the distribution chain, respondents indicated some degree of difficulty in performing value-added services involving unique capabilities. Retailers and wholesalers in particular indicated that modification or customization of manufacturer's products was difficult. All business types indicated that providing customized customer service to specific markets or customers was difficult. These results suggest that the majority of respondents have difficulty accommodating requests that are unique and outside of normal operations.

The events that respondents indicated were easiest to accommodate were product introduction, support of sales and marketing promotions and product phase out. While each of these events represents a special request, they occur frequently and in a somewhat repetitive pattern. Product introductions are operationally similar to phase outs. Support of sales and marketing promotions are also recurring events. The general response during interviews was that the logistics of these events can be accommodated providing advanced information is provided. The advanced warning associated with these easier to handle events contrasts sharply with events identified as most difficult to accommodate. In the difficult to handle events, formal notification does not arrive prior to the event. In the instance of a disruption in supply, the logistics organization typically finds out about the breakdown at a point when routine corrective action would be too late to resolve the disruption. At best, in such emergency situations the logistics organization is forced to operate in a reactive mode. In events they handle with relative ease, they typically have the opportunity to proactively plan operational adjustments.

While many similarities among the business types exist regarding ease and difficulty of handling events, a few dramatic differences were noted. For example, wholesalers, retailers and hybrids find returning goods to manufacturers only moderately difficult. Manufacturers report that the returns are operationally difficult to handle. Returned goods bound for manufacturers move backward through the entire distribution chain. In a traditional channel arrangement, they will be shipped from the retailer to a wholesaler and then on to the manufacturer. The efforts must be coordinated, documented and fully funded by manufacturers who are not in a position to control actual operations. Reverse logistics, as this process is called, is both costly and time consuming for manufacturers. The manufacturer bears the cost burden whereas retailers and wholesalers, while perhaps experiencing inconvenience, normally assume no risk. Perhaps the most uneconomical aspect of reverse logistics is the complete loss of economy of scale designed into the outbound flow of merchandise.

Manufacturers, wholesalers and hybrids characterize special customer service as requests moderately easy to accommodate. Such requests represent minor variations in standard service packages such as delivery to a secondary or non-typical destination. For retailers, similar service requests were reported as moderately difficult to accommodate. Manufacturers especially, and to a significant degree wholesalers, are organized to provide prompt response to special requests from their regular channel customers. The structure of retailing and the fact that they deal with so many different customers makes accommodation of special requests typically non-economical. It is important to note however, that the unique type of specialty retailing that offers customized services was not accessed by the data collection procedures of this research.

Product phase outs are more difficult for wholesalers to accommodate than for manufacturers, retailers and hybrids. The strategic positioning of wholesalers puts them in the middle when the channel must accommodate a phase out. It is often necessary for phased out products to be retrieved from retailers and then returned to manufacturers. Product recalls also present a moderate amount of difficulty for wholesalers. In each instance, wholesalers must react to market demands rather than being able to plan or schedule the events in advance.

LEADING EDGE BENCHMARKING - SPECIAL EVENTS

Table 4-4 presents the comparative analysis of the capability of leading edge versus norm respondents to accommodate special requests. In almost all situations, leading edge firms can accommodate such events more easily than norm respondents.

Leading edge manufacturers indicated significantly greater ease than norm firms in handling product introduction, product recall and customization of service levels to specific markets or customers. In all other instances, except for accommodating computer breakdowns, leading edge firms found the events somewhat, but not significantly easier to accommodate. Regarding computer breakdowns, both leading edge and norm manufacturers experience service difficulty when confronted with loss of data processing support.

A somewhat unexpected result was reported by wholesalers. Norm wholesalers reported significantly fewer difficulties in providing modification or customization of products while in the logistical system than the leading edge. A priori, it would have been hypothesized that leading edge firms would be more adept at dealing with such requests. Norm wholesalers also indicated slightly better ability to deal with special customer service requests, to customize service for specific markets or customers and computer breakdowns. Leading edge wholesalers reported greater ease in accommodating sales and marketing incentive programs, product introduction, product phase out, disruption in supply, product recall and returned goods. The research contains no data to explain the norm respondents' unexpected superior capability to handle special requests. One possible, but unvalidated, explanation may be the large overall size of the typical leading edge wholesaler respondent.

110

TABLE 4-4
EASE OF ACCOMMODATING SPECIAL EVENTS
BY BUSINESS TYPE AND CAI GROUP

Average

Event	Manufacturer L.E./Norm	Wholesaler L.E./Norm	Retailer L.E./Norm	Hybrid L.E./Norm
Special Customer Service Request	3.22/3.11	3.41/3.60	3.75/3.38[B]	3.87/3.40
Sales and Marketing Incentive Programs	3.18/3.03	3.68/3.54	4.08/3.50[B]	4.14/3.21[A]
Product Introduction	3.27/2.99[A]	3.95/3.70	4.06/3.80	4.00/3.57
Product Phase Out	3.06/2.92	3.45/3.20	3.67/3.57	3.93/3.34[B]
Disruption in Supply	2.91/2.77	3.05/2.92	3.40/3.10	3.00/2.78
Computer Breakdown	2.25/2.26	2.09/2.30	2.50/2.35	2.50/2.26
Product Recall	3.02/2.77[B]	3.27/3.04	3.40/3.15	3.21/2.84
Customization of Service Levels to Specific Markets or Customers	2.98/2.72[B]	3.09/3.30	3.77/3.15[B]	3.60/3.00[B]
Product Modification or Customization while in the Logistics System	2.76/2.59	2.76/3.19[C]	3.29/2.92	3.47/3.16
Returned Goods	---	3.59/3.51	3.63/3.28	3.67/3.37

A, B, C - Significantly different from the norm at 0.01, 0.05 and 0.10 respectively.

For Hybrids, Retailers and Wholesalers scale is:
1 = cannot accommodate; 5 = accommodates very easily.

For Manufacturers scale is:
1 = cannot accommodate; 4 = accommodates easily.

Leading edge retailers report significantly greater ease in handling special customer service requests, customization of service levels to specific markets or customers and sales and marketing incentive programs than do norm retailers. For all of the other special requests, leading edge retailers only accommodate events slightly more easily than norm retailers.

Leading edge hybrids indicate significantly greater ease of accommodation for customization of service levels to specific markets or customers, sales and marketing incentive programs and product phase out. For the remainder of the events, norm hybrids indicated slightly greater difficulty in dealing with the special requests than leading edge hybrids.

With few exceptions, leading edge firms report greater to far greater capability when it comes to handling service requests or events. In a number of situations requiring special treatment, leading edge firms are significantly ahead of their norm counterparts. Flexibility is viewed as a key strategic element in that customer expectations can be satisfied and problems resolved if a firm is positioned to do whatever is necessary to accommodate requests. This analysis supports the conclusion that leading edge firms have developed more flexible operations than the typical respondent. With the exception of selected non-routine events in the wholesale area, the leading edge superiority generalizes across business types.

EXTERNAL ALLIANCES

One strategic practice increasingly evident in logistics is the formation of external alliances or what are often called third party partnerships. Such alliances extend beyond the boundaries of a firm and include close working relationships with service providers and materials vendors. The justification for the formation of external alliances is reduced cost and/or improved customer service. Key to the concept of external alliance is the fact that the traditional adversarial buyer-seller interface is replaced by a win-win relationship.

Chapter Seven presents the detailed information on the use of external logistics services by respondent firms. Data analysis revealed a difference between the expected usage of outside physical services and information services. Physical services include transportation and warehousing. Information services, as the name implies, are communications-related. This includes such services as order entry/processing, inventory management and freight audit/payment services. All respondents indicated greater anticipated external purchase of physical services than information-related services. Interview responses suggest that the heavy capital commitment required to develop private capacity and the high quality of available for-hire services combine to encourage outsourcing. By purchasing these services externally, firms can focus available assets on basic business requirements. External purchase also offers flexibility. Firms can gain immediate entry into new markets and/or shorten their response time for specific customer requests by purchasing available services.

Explanations for the lower indicated usage of information services include a desire for maintaining control, security and the general availability of low cost/high capability computer systems. Some firms expressed a hesitance to relinquish control over vital data due to management philosophy and concern for the security. Reluctance to outsourcing information may also be based on the belief that service providers will not be sufficiently familiar with the specific business requirements and, therefore, would not be as efficient as the firm's own employees. Finally, information technology has resulted in affordable systems. Many firms prefer to invest in a system that can be customized to their operations.

As noted earlier, detailed analysis of strategic alliances has been reserved for Chapter Seven. Since such arrangements could be appropriately discussed either here or at that later point, materials were placed in Part III.

NEWBORNS

A select grouping of respondents warrant special consideration and discussion with respect to strategic posture. This subset is labelled newborns. Newborns are firms who initiated formal logistics operations within the past three years. Table 4-5 details the number of newborns by business type. Newborns are classified by length of time committed to formal logistics organization.

TABLE 4-5
NEWBORNS FORMAL LOGISTICS ORGANIZATION

Years Organized

Organized	Manufacturer	Wholesaler	Retailer	Hybrid	Total
1 year	28	6	5	6	45
2 years	27	12	7	3	49
3 years	23	11	8	3	45
Total	78	29	20	12	139

The newborn represents a relatively recent entry into formal logistics. As a new entry, for whatever reason, their senior management did not see fit to formalize logistical operations until after 1985. The number of newborn logistics organizations among the overall respondent base was surprisingly large. Of the 695 respondents, 139 or 20 percent qualified as newborns. The distribution of newborns is illustrated by age distribution in Figure 4-2.

The feature of newborns that is particularly interesting is their fast evolution. Table 4-6 provides a year by year tabulation of newborns by CAI group. Over the past three years, an average of 46 respondent firms have committed to formal organizational structure each year. As one might expect, no newborn reached leading edge status during their organizational year. What was unexpected was that the majority of newborns were classified as norm during their initial year of formal logistics operations. For firms that have been formally organized for two years, 88 percent were categorized as norm or leading edge. Analysis of those firms formally organized three years indicated

114

that 82 percent qualified as either norm or leading edge. It is clear that newborns pursue logistics with a mission to become among the very best as fast as possible.

FIGURE 4-2
NEWBORNS BY BUSINESS TYPE
AND AGE DISTRIBUTION

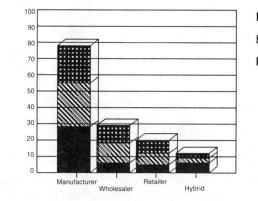

TABLE 4-6
NEWBORNS BY CAI GROUP AND YEARS ORGANIZED

CAI Group	One Year	Two Years	Three Years	Total
Emerging	16	5	5	26
Norm	29	38	32	99
Leading Edge	0	6	8	14
Totals	45	49	45	139

This rapid rate of evolution through CAI classification has widespread strategic implications. Keep in mind that newborns are not typically new businesses. They are businesses that only committed to formal organization relatively late in terms of overall general business acceptance of integrated logistics. Nevertheless within two years they are as advanced as the typical firm that has been committed to formal logistics considerably longer. By the end of three years, newborns have more than their fair share of leading edge representation. This rapid advancement suggests a very clear mission when these firms select to embrace formal logistics. It suggests specific operational objectives, adequate resources and overall senior management support. The strategic implication is that newborn firms pro-actively formalized logistics as a means of differentiating competitive positioning.

Newborn respondents were not concentrated within an industry. They are representative of a mix of different types and sizes of businesses. Manufacturing firms had a higher representation of newborns than the other types of businesses classified by distribution channel position. Table 4-7 provides the distribution by business type. The newborn group consisted of 78 manufacturers, 29 wholesalers, 20 retailers, and 12 hybrids. This distribution is close to the overall percentage frequency of each business type in the respondent base. Only hybrids appear to have less than their fair share of newborns. Retailers have slightly more than their fair share. These data are presented in Table 4-8.

TABLE 4-7
NEWBORNS BY BUSINESS TYPE AND CAI GROUP

CAI Group	Manufacturer Number/%	Wholesaler Number/%	Retailer Number/%	Hybrid Number/%
Emerging	15/10.8	6/ 4.3	3/ 2.1	2/ 1.4
Norm	54/38.8	22/15.8	14/10.0	9/ 6.5
Leading Edge	9/ 6.5	1/ 0.7	3/ 2.1	1/ 0.7
Totals	78/56.1	29/20.9	20/14.4	12/ 8.6

TABLE 4-8
NEWBORN REPRESENTATION IN TOTAL RESPONSE BASE
BY BUSINESS TYPE

Business Type	Total Respondents	Percent Total Respondents	Newborn Respondents	Percent Total Newborn
Manufacturer	380	54.7	78	56.1
Wholesaler	148	21.3	29	20.9
Retailer	90	14.4	20	14.4
Hybrid	77	8.6	12	8.6
Totals	695	100.0	139	100.0

The significant difference among newborns is the relatively short time it took for manufacturer organizations to reach advanced status. After three years, all manufacturer newborns were either classified as norm or leading edge. The manufacturing CAI profile across three years in comparison to all other newborns as a group is presented in Table 4-9. This analysis clearly supports the conclusion that newborn manufacturers have a clear vision of what they are trying to accomplish by formalizing logistics. In Chapter Three, it was pointed out that, among

TABLE 4-9
MANUFACTURER NEWBORNS COMPARED TO ALL
OTHER NEWBORNS BY CAI GROUP

Business Type CAI Group	Number of Years Organized		
	One	Two	Three
Manufacturer			
Emerging	12	3	0
Norm	16	22	16
Leading Edge	0	2	7
All Others			
Emerging	4	2	5
Norm	13	16	16
Leading Edge	0	4	1

all respondents, manufacturers' logistics organizations had been formalized fewer years on the average in comparison to other respondents (Figure 3-5). Analysis of newborns clearly reflects the intensity of the catch-up effort.

The newborn represents an interesting cross section of respondents. The firms are seeking to close the gap. All evidence suggests that they get up to speed well within a three year horizon. From a strategic perspective, firms that are late to commit to formal organization appear to be very proactive in their effort to rapidly exploit logistical competency.

SUMMARY

Strategic posture is difficult to calibrate because of its extreme customization to the strengths and weaknesses of specific firms. While the final story on logistics strategy has not been written, the respondents provided interesting insight into the capabilities they seek to perfect. It is clear leading edge firms placed a premium upon flexibility and communications independent of business type. Flexible operations result in a capability to respond to changing customer requests, market trends and internal objectives.

While the manufacturer's strategic orientation is somewhat easier to pin down than that of other business types, some common strategic practices across business type were observed. Leading edge respondents place a great deal of emphasis on both internal and external communications. They are aware of the direct impact of service vendors and customers upon their logistical performance. Leading edge firms are increasingly becoming involved in boundary spanning alliances and are committed to outsourcing selected service requirements. In the future, they expect to increase their outsourcing of transportation and will retain their use of external warehousing, but will decrease use of information based services. These trends are further substantiated in Chapter Seven.

While a portion of the advantage enjoyed by leading edge firms results strictly from their longevity as formal organizations, the research clearly illustrates that firms need not be organized for an extensive period of time to be leading edge. In the past, recognition and appreciation of logistical operations and their contribution to the total corporate success has sometimes been slow in coming. There is evidence that the speed of acceptance is changing. Newborns were defined as a group of firms who have had formal logistics organizations for three years or less. These newborns enjoy their fair share of sophisticated organizations. Based upon a clear vision of desired objectives, newborns appear to have benefitted from the knowledge of others. They have implemented state of the art logistical practices that often allow them to avoid traditional pitfalls or excessive trial and error.

The many dimensions of strategic posture provide significant insight into how the best of the best logistics organizations function. In terms of benchmarking leading edge firms to the norm respondent, survey data supplemented by interview responses support the following generalizations concerning leading edge strategic posture. Leading edge firms:

* Have a greater tendency to manage logistics
  as a value-added process.

* Reflect a stronger commitment to achieving and
  maintaining customer satisfaction.

* Place a premium on flexibility, particularly in
  regard to accommodating special or non-routine
  requests.

* Are better positioned to handle unexpected
  events.

*   Are more willing to use outside logistics service providers.

*   Place a greater premium on how well a service company performs in managing itself and its service to clients.

*   Are more apt to view service provider relationships as strategic alliances.

*   Anticipate greater use of outside logistics services in the future.

Planning
 Mission Statement
 Leading Edge Benchmarking - Formal Mission Statement
 Logistics Plan
 Leading Edge Benchmarking - Logistics Plan
 Planning Horizon
 Leading Edge Benchmarking - Planning Horizon
 Logistics Plan Update Interval
 Leading Edge Benchmarking - Plan Update Interval
 Senior Logistics Executive Participation in Business Unit Planning
 Leading Edge Benchmarking - Participation in Business Unit Planning
 Effect of Specific Planning Related Events
 Leading Edge Benchmarking - Effect of Specific Planning Related Events
 Conclusion - Planning
Performance Measurement
 Performance Measurement Data Collection Methodology
 Average Performance Measurements
 Respondent Use of Specific Measures
 Availability of Information
 Relative Importance of Performance Measurements
 Competitive Benchmarking
 Leading Edge Benchmarking - Performance Measurement and Benchmarking
 Conclusion - Performance Measurement
Computer Applications
 Most Commonly Installed Computer Applications
 Plans to Install Computer Applications
 Quality of Information
 Comparison to Other Information Systems
 Leading Edge Benchmarking - Computer Applications
 Conclusion - Computer Applications
Information Technology Adoption
 Electronic Data Interchange
 Planned EDI Applications
 Artificial Intelligence/Knowledge-Based Systems
 Hardware Technologies
 Leading Edge Benchmarking - Information Technology
 Conclusion - Information Technologies
Summary

Chapter Five

MANAGEMENT BEHAVIOR

The true measure of a firm's logistics organization success is its ability to get the job done in an efficient and effective manner. This chapter focuses on what organizations actually do in the practice of logistics management.

This chapter is divided into four sections. The first presents data concerning the commitment of logistics organizations to formal planning. Planning was found to be an activity in which leading edge firms excel. The second section reviews performance measurement practice. Leading edge firms are compulsive measurers of all aspects of their logistics operations. The third section details current and planned computer applications and the quality of information available to support logistics operations. The final section provides an in-depth look at the acceptance level of information technologies. The discussion focuses on hardware technologies being adopted by logistics organizations and on the rate of acceptance of Electronic Data Interchange (EDI) and Artificial Intelligence (AI). As in previous chapters, comparative benchmarking of leading edge firms to norm respondents is presented in each section. Benchmarking generalizations are summarized at chapter end.

PLANNING

A primary concern of the research was the planning practice of logistics organizations. Data were collected concerning: (1) the existence of a formal logistics mission statement; (2) the existence of a formal logistics plan; (3) the planning horizon of the logistics strategic plan; (4) the planning update intervals; (5) the input of the senior logistics executive in overall business unit strategic planning; and (6) the impact of the business unit's sales forecast and excessive end-of-month or end-of-quarter surges on logistical performance.

MISSION STATEMENT

A mission statement expresses the objectives of a logistics organization. It serves to communicate such objectives to customers as well as across internal organization units. Finally, the mission statement anchors formal logistics planning. As such, the existence and quality of a firm's mission statement are prime indicators of the formalization of logistics.

Respondents were asked whether they had a formal written logistics mission statement and the content of that statement. The response by business type was surprising. Only 29.3 percent of all respondents indicated that they had formal logistics mission statements. The percent of respondents by business type that reported having mission statements are illustrated in Figure 5-1. The data are reported in Table 5-1. In general, retailers were the most apt to have mission statements, followed by manufacturers and hybrids. Wholesalers indicated the lowest incident of logistics mission statements with 17.9

FIGURE 5-1
MISSION STATEMENT BY BUSINESS TYPE

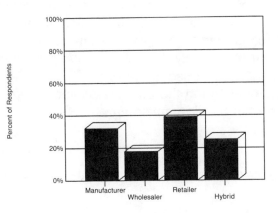

TABLE 5-1
MISSION STATEMENT BY BUSINESS TYPE

Business Type	Have Number/Percent	Do Not Have Number/Percent	Respondents
Manufacturer	120/32.2	253/67.8	373
Wholesaler	26/17.9	119/82.1	145
Retailer	34/39.1	53/60.9	87
Hybrid	19/25.3	56/74.7	75
Total	199/29.3	481/70.7	680

percent. To some degree, this low percentage can be attributed to the fact that the primary business of wholesaling is logistics. The nature of a wholesaler's overall business mission statement may negate the necessity for a separate logistics mission statement. The reported existence of formal mission statements across all respondents was very low.

LEADING EDGE BENCHMARKING - FORMAL MISSION STATEMENT

In sharp contrast to norm respondents, the existence of formal mission statements was dramatically higher for leading edge respondents. Figure 5-2 presents percentage frequency of formal logistics mission statements of leading edge in comparison to norm respondents. Across all business types, leading edge firms were far more likely than norm firms to have mission statements. All the comparisons were statistically significant. Little doubt exists concerning the practice of leading edge firms with respect to formal mission statements.

FIGURE 5-2
MISSION STATEMENTS BY BUSINESS TYPE AND CAI GROUP

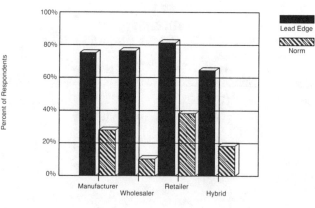

LOGISTICS PLAN

The logistics plan is a formal document that guides allocation of human and financial resources toward the attainment of selected logistics objectives. The plan defines how the logistics organization intends to accomplish its stated mission and, if properly positioned, helps achieve the goals and objectives of the overall business unit.

Among business types, retailers indicated the highest frequency of formal logistics plans with 57.5 percent. This was followed by manufacturers at 45.4 percent, hybrids with 37.8 percent and wholesalers at 31.3 percent reporting logistics plans. The overall incident of having a logistics plan across all business types was 43.1 percent. These percentages were lower than expected. These data are reported in Table 5-2.

TABLE 5-2
LOGISTICS PLANS BY BUSINESS TYPE

Business Type	Have Number/Percent	Do Not Have Number/Percent	Respondents
Manufacturer	171/45.4	206/54.6	377
Wholesaler	46/31.3	101/68.7	147
Retailer	50/57.5	37/42.5	87
Hybrid	28/37.8	46/62.2	74
Total	295/43.1	390/56.9	685

LEADING EDGE BENCHMARKING - LOGISTICS PLAN

As illustrated in Figure 5-3, leading edge firms are considerably more involved in logistics planning than norm respondents. More than 90 percent of all leading edge business types have written logistics strategic plans. In the norm group, retailers were highest with 60 percent and wholesalers were lowest with 25.8 percent. The responses of leading edge firms were remarkably consistent independent of position in the distribution channel. Among manufacturers, all 64 leading edge respondents had logistics plans. Across business types, the likelihood of leading edge firms having plans was statistically significantly higher than the likelihood of norm firms having plans.

FIGURE 5-3
LOGISTICS PLAN BY BUSINESS
TYPE AND CAI GROUP

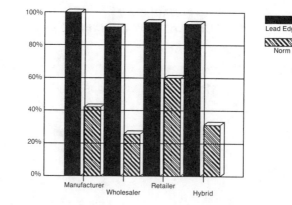

PLANNING HORIZON

The length of the formal planning horizon is a key indicator of how serious planning is in the logistical management process. The primary difference between a budget and a plan is the time horizon. The typical budget covers a single year while a plan projects operations further into the future. Comprehensive logistics plans were expected to cover at least a three year horizon and contain a detailed financial budget for the base or current year. As the plan extends into the future, it naturally becomes less specific or detailed.

Table 5-3 provides data regarding planning horizon by business type. Across all business types, the average planning horizon was 3.9 years. While retailers tend to have longer average planning horizons than other business types, no significant difference exists by distribution channel position.

TABLE 5-3
PLANNING HORIZON BY BUSINESS TYPE

Business Type	Number of Respondents	Average Year Horizon
Manufacturer	170	3.9
Wholesaler	44	3.8
Retailer	47	4.1
Hybrid	27	3.6
Total	288	3.9

LEADING EDGE BENCHMARKING - PLANNING HORIZON

Figure 5-4 compares planning horizon responses of leading edge to norm firms. In the case of manufacturers and wholesalers, planning horizons of leading edge firms were longer than those for norm respondents. The reverse was true for retailers and hybrids. Once planning becomes part of normal management practice, the average time horizon ranged between three and five years. There was no significant difference between leading edge and norm respondents.

FIGURE 5-4
LOGISTICS PLANNING
BY BUSINESS TYPE AND CAI GROUP

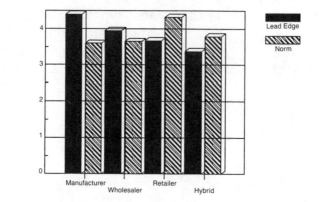

LOGISTICS PLAN UPDATE INTERVAL

The update frequency of logistics plans is a prime indicator of the management commitment to the overall planning process. The expectation was that plans would be updated at least annually. The overall average interval between updates across business types was 10.5 months. The mean update interval for hybrid firms was 12.1 months, for wholesalers 11.4 months, and for retailers 11.9 months. Manufacturers reported the most frequent updates at 9.7 months. These data are presented in Table 5-4.

TABLE 5-4
PLANNING UPDATE BY BUSINESS TYPE

Business Type	Number Respondents	Average Months Horizon
Manufacturer	170	9.7
Wholesaler	45	11.4
Retailer	47	11.9
Hybrid	26	12.1
Total	288	10.5

LEADING EDGE BENCHMARKING - PLAN UPDATE INTERVAL

No difference exists between leading edge and norm respondents with respect to frequency of logistics plan updates. The key, similar to conclusions with respect to planning horizon, is participation in logistics planning. If a firm has adopted the practice of logistics planning, a strong likelihood exists that they will update the plan at least on an annual basis.

SENIOR LOGISTICS EXECUTIVE PARTICIPATION IN BUSINESS UNIT PLANNING

The degree to which the logistics officer participates in business unit strategic planning is viewed as a direct indicator of a firm's senior management perception of the importance of logistics. Firms that include their senior logistics executive in the overall strategic planning should be better positioned to exploit logistics' strengths and capabilities.

Across business types, respondents reported a high degree of regular involvement in overall strategic planning. Among all respondents, 78.7 percent reported direct participation. While the incident of participation varied by business type, the differences were not significant. The data are reported in Table 5-5. Questions were redesigned in the Phase II research to determine the degree of strategic planning involvement ranging from indirect input to direct participation. In terms of direct involvement and input information, 97 percent of respondents reported involvement in business unit strategic planning.

TABLE 5-5
SENIOR LOGISTICS OFFICER PARTICIPATION IN
OVERALL PLANNING BY BUSINESS TYPE

Business Type	Participates Number/%	Provides Input Number/%	Does Not Participate Number/%	Total
Manufacturer Phase I	279/74.8	---	94/25.2	373
Manufacturer Phase II	125/67.6	54/29.2	6/3.2	185
Wholesaler	122/84.1	18/12.4	5/3.4	145
Retailer	76/86.4	9/10.2	3/3.4	88
Hybrid	58/78.4	15/20.3	1/1.3	74
Total/Average with Phase I Manufacturer	535/78.7	42/6.2	103/15.1	680
Total/Average with Phase II Manufacturer	381/77.5	96/19.5	15/3.0	492

This analysis supports the conclusion that one of the first indicators of formal acceptance of logistics is the participation of the senior logistics executive in the business units strategic planning process. Across the board, approximately eight out of every ten respondents indicated direct involvement.

LEADING EDGE BENCHMARKING - PARTICIPATION IN BUSINESS UNIT PLANNING

Norm and leading edge firms across business type indicated a high involvement of senior logistics executives in business unit strategic planning. All retail and wholesale leading edge firms reported that senior logistics executives were routinely involved. Norm wholesale and retail firms indicated a near 90 percent rate of involvement. Leading edge manufacturers had a 98 percent involvement rate, while leading edge hybrid companies were lowest at 93 percent. The lowest rate of involvement and a major exception was reported by norm manufacturers, who indicated that only 76.8 percent of senior logistics executives were included in business unit strategic planning. In both Phase I and II manufacturing surveys, there was a significant difference between the likelihood of leading edge and norm manufacturers' senior logistics officers being included in business unit strategic planning. In both situations, analysis indicated that leading edge manufacturing executives were more likely to be involved than the norm respondents. These data are illustrated in Figure 5-5.

EFFECT OF SPECIFIC PLANNING RELATED EVENTS

The research isolated the impact which different types of planning problems or breakdowns have upon logistical performance. Table 5-6 provides responses by business type concerning sales forecasting, excessive end-of-month or end-of-quarter business surges and timely information. With the exception of timely information, respondents across business type indicated that these events had medium to high impact. All business types are highly reliant on timely information.

FIGURE 5-5
SENIOR LOGISTICS EXECUTIVE'S
PARTICIPATION IN OVERALL PLANNING
BY BUSINESS TYPE AND CAI GROUP

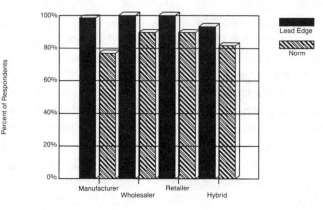

LEADING EDGE BENCHMARKING -
EFFECT OF SPECIFIC PLANNING
RELATED EVENTS

Some significant differences were found when comparing leading edge to norm respondents. The statistically significant differences between leading edge and norm firms by business type are shown in Table 5-6. Generally, respondents reported sales forecasting accuracy had a medium to high effect on planning. However, fifty-three percent of the leading edge hybrids reported that sales forecasts had low to medium impact. Few would argue about the importance of accurate sales forecasting. Therefore, the responses of the leading edge hybrids seems to indicate logistics planning among these firms is not directly tied to sales forecasting.

TABLE 5-6
**EFFECT OF SPECIFIC PLANNING RELATED
EVENTS ON PERFORMANCE BY BUSINESS TYPE**

Event	Manufacturer	Wholesaler	Retailer	Hybrid
Sales Forecast Accuracy	3.06^M	3.54^M	3.73	3.62
End-of-Period Surges	2.76	3.19^L	3.85	3.37^L
Timely Information	3.25^M	4.02^M	4.07	3.99

Manufacturer: 4-point scale with
1 = no impact and 5 = very high impact.

Wholesaler/Retailer/Hybrid: 5-point scale with
1 = no impact amd 4 = very high impact.

L = Leading edge firms indicated significantly less impact
M = Leading edge firms indicated significantly greater impact

Questions concerning the impact of end-of-period surges were designed to examine the logistics organization's capability to accommodate wide swings in shipment requirements that occur near the end of selling periods. A little over one-half of norm wholesale and hybrid firms said that end-of-period demand swings had no or low effect on logistics operations. More than 70 percent of leading edge wholesalers and hybrids indicated the impact of end-of-period surges was low. These responses demonstrate organizational flexibility. Firms that plan well anticipate the need to handle surges and develop contingencies for handling such situations.

Manufacturers and retailers responded differently concerning the impact of end-of-period surges. Only 31 percent of leading edge retailers and 38 percent of leading edge manufacturers reported a low to medium effect of such surges on their logistical operations. Unplanned surges affect the logistics operations of manufacturers and retailers to a greater degree than for either wholesalers or hybrids. Despite considerable attention to planning, the traditional end-of-period volume surge remains a serious logistical management concern.

Leading edge firms were especially concerned about obtaining timely information. Leading edge manufacturers and wholesalers indicated timely information has a significantly greater effect on operations than did their norm counterparts. The impact of timely information was not significantly different for leading edge versus norm groups for retailers and hybrids.

CONCLUSION - PLANNING

The following generalizations are noted concerning the six facets of planning examined. First, it appears that an initial step toward formalization of logistics planning is for logistics executives to get involved in overall business unit strategic planning. The incidence of such involvement among respondents is almost as high as the existence of formal logistics organization. Thus, formal organization and strategic planning involvement among respondents seem to go hand-in-hand regardless of business type.

Once firms choose to develop logistics plans, they select a three to five year horizon and typically update on an annual basis. The incidence of planning was lower than expected. Likewise, the number of firms that follow the practice of maintaining a formal mission statement was surprisingly low. With respect to mission statements and planning, leading edge firms are far ahead of norm respondents. This is independent of position in the distribution channel. To an impressive degree, firms that regularly plan appear to be able to better cope with breakdowns or unexpected events that impact their logistical operations.

PERFORMANCE MEASUREMENT

Increased competition for market share coupled with expanding product lines has made the job of the logistician increasing difficult. Greater demands are made on logistical systems to perform customer service faster and more accurately with less overall inventory to support operations than in the past. Logistics systems have become increasingly complex. As a result, sophisticated measurement systems are being developed to help control and direct day-to-day logistical operations. Performance measurement act as the logistics organization's guidance system.

The research was designed to collect very detailed information regarding how logistics managers measure and benchmark their systems. This section reports conclusions regarding overall and leading edge performance measurement.

PERFORMANCE MEASUREMENT
DATA COLLECTION METHODOLOGY

The Phase I manufacturers survey offered respondents an open-ended question and asked that they describe specific performance measures regularly used in the areas of cost, customer service, productivity and quality. The responses were impressive in that respondents indicated an almost compulsive commitment to performance measurement. Emerging firms generally concentrated on cost performance measurement. Norm respondents reported the practice of measuring both cost and customer service. Leading edge firms indicated a general concern with all four of the categories of the above listed performance measurements.

Based on the Phase I results, the Phase II wholesale/retail and manufacturer update questionnaires were structured to allow respondents to select from a list of specific measures in five performance areas. Measurement of asset management was added to cost, customer service, productivity and quality. The data from Phase II respondents are presented in this section.

Respondents were asked if they used a specific measurement, whether or not the necessary information was available and the importance of each measure in the day-to-day monitoring of their logistics organization. In addition, respondents were asked to report their competitive benchmarking practices in ten specific areas.

AVERAGE PERFORMANCE MEASUREMENTS

The frequency of performance measurement was remarkably consistent across business types. Table 5-7 provides a recap of the average number of measures used by business type within each of the five performance categories. Figure 5-6 illustrates the overall percent of respondents using each category of performance measurement.

TABLE 5-7
PERFORMANCE MEASUREMENTS
BY CATEGORY AND BUSINESS TYPE

Performance Measurement Category and Number	Average			
	Manufacturer	Wholesaler	Retailer	Hybrid
Asset Management (6)	4.32	4.26	3.69	4.38
Cost (12)	9.05	7.74	8.51	8.43
Customer Service (9)	6.52	5.53	5.23	5.18
Productivity (6)	3.11	2.90	3.30	3.34
Quality (5)	3.34	2.54	2.64	2.66
Overall (38)	26.34	22.97	23.37	23.99

Of the six asset management performance measurements, each business type averaged over three measures. Hybrid firms had the highest average using 4.38 asset management performance measures. Manufacturers were second with 4.32, wholesalers averaged 4.26 and retailers averaged 3.69 asset management performance measurements.

The average usage rate with respect to cost performance measures was high. A choice of twelve cost performance measurements was listed in the questionnaire. Manufacturers reported the highest average use with 9.05 cost performance measurements. The average number of cost performance measurements for other business types was 8.51 for retailers, 8.43 for hybrids and 7.74 for wholesalers.

FIGURE 5-6
PERFORMANCE MEASUREMENT BY CATEGORY AND BUSINESS TYPE

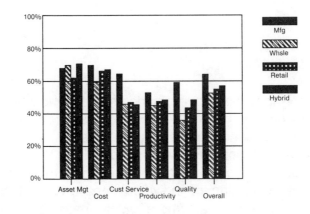

Manufacturers employed the highest number of customer service performance measurements averaging 6.52 out of a possible nine. Wholesalers were second with 5.53, retailers reported 5.23 and hybrids indicated the use of 5.18 measures on the average.

Respondents were asked to indicate the number of productivity performance measures used on a regular basis. Out of six choices, hybrids used an average of 3.34, retailers 3.30, manufacturers 3.11 and wholesalers 2.90.

Out of the five quality performance measurement options, the average use reported by manufacturers was substantially higher than the other three business types. Manufacturers reported average use of 3.34 of the listed quality measures. Hybrids averaged 2.66, retailers 2.64 and wholesalers 2.54 measures. A possible explanation for manufacturers reporting a higher frequency of quality performance measurement is the overall drive for total quality that characterizes current manufacturing operations. The intense effort to improve the quality level of North American products appears not to have extended to all levels of the distribution channel.

RESPONDENT USE OF
SPECIFIC MEASURES

The emphasis on performance measurement is observable from an analysis of the frequency of use of the thirty-eight specific performance measures by business type. Use of specific performance measures varied widely. Usage also varied across business type with no consistent pattern. It is clear from the percent utilization of individual measures that asset, cost and customer service are more widely measured than productivity or quality. The percentage utilization data is presented in Table 5-8. Commentary on usage pattern is presented for each performance measurement category.

TABLE 5-8
SPECIFIC PERFORMANCE MEASUREMENTS
BY BUSINESS TYPE

Performance Measure	Percent			
	Manufacturer	Wholesaler	Retailer	Hybrid
Asset Management				
Inventory turns	81.9	85.2	82.6	84.2
Inventory carrying costs	68.6	68.3	55.6	74.3
Inventory levels, # days supply	86.9	80.7	74.1	88.0
Obsolete inventory	85.7	79.7	73.1	84.9
Return on net assets	66.9	65.9	55.0	54.3
Return on investment	74.6	74.8	67.9	71.2
Cost				
Total cost analysis	87.6	74.8	82.1	82.9
Cost per unit	79.7	63.8	78.6	79.7
Cost as percentage of sales	83.3	81.2	79.5	83.6
Inbound Freight	86.0	80.0	87.5	73.6
Outbound Freight	94.4	88.3	90.6	90.3
Warehouse costs	89.0	85.7	89.9	89.0
Administrative costs	80.0	79.1	76.7	77.0
Order processing	52.0	45.8	45.7	33.8
Direct labor	78.6	71.4	86.2	85.7
Comparison-actual vs. budget	96.6	86.6	86.5	90.3
Cost trend analysis	76.9	59.1	61.4	62.3
Direct product profitability	59.2	46.8	27.8	58.6
Customer Service				
Fill rate	78.2	71.0	66.2	61.2
Stockouts	80.6	72.9	71.6	67.2
Shipping errors	83.0	78.9	81.9	73.5
On time delivery	82.7	70.5	76.9	67.2
Backorders	77.1	69.2	58.7	63.1
Cycle time	69.9	34.7	56.4	46.8
Customer feedback	90.3	85.6	84.1	88.7
Sales force feedback	87.9	85.0	51.5	80.3
Customer surveys	68.8	51.6	58.9	47.8
Productivity				
Units shipped per employee	54.8	53.1	61.4	60.0
Units per labor dollar	51.9	43.7	63.9	61.1
Orders per sales representative	38.7	51.7	15.5	42.2
Comparison to historical standards	76.3	74.6	86.4	83.1
Goal programs	76.2	69.2	82.1	76.1
Productivity index	55.8	44.9	56.3	44.9
Quality				
Frequency of damage	67.4	44.7	60.8	50.0
Dollar amount of damage	74.6	55.6	67.1	58.8
Number of credit claims	75.7	68.9	67.5	62.7
Number of customer returns	77.1	69.0	63.9	72.9
Cost of returned goods	68.0	57.7	54.2	55.1

ASSET MEASUREMENT

Over 80 percent of manufacturers reported regularly measuring inventory level, inventory turns, and obsolete inventory. Each of the six listed asset management performance measurements was used by over 65 percent of manufacturing respondents. The lowest individual measure used by manufacturers was return on net assets at 66.9 percent.

The most common asset management measurement used by wholesalers was inventory turns, with 85.2 percent reporting use of that particular measure. Inventory level, number of dayssupply, obsolete inventory and ROI were all used by more than 70 percent of wholesalers. The least used asset management performance measure by wholesalers was return on net assets.

Among retailers, the most common asset measure was inventory turns with 82.6 percent using that measure. Inventory level, number of days supply, obsolete inventory and ROI were used by more than two-thirds of the retailers. Interestingly, only 55 percent of the retailers reported using inventory carrying costs and return on net assets.

More than 80 percent of hybrids listed inventory turns, inventory levels, number of days supply, and obsolete inventory as regularly used asset management performance measurements. Only 54.3 percent of hybrid respondents reported using return on net assets.

COST MEASUREMENT

Generally, respondents reported heavy use of cost performance measures. The least used cost measure for a particular business type was direct product profitability (DPP) among retailers with only 27.8 percent reporting use. While direct product profitability analysis has recently become popular in the food industry, it does not appear to be widely employed across industries. Also, it may be identified by another name such as retail margin analysis. Manufacturers and hybrids report the most extensive use of DPP.

Among manufacturers, the most commonly used cost performance measures were comparison of actual to budgeted costs and outbound freight. The least used cost measure among manufacturers was order processing, with approximately one-half of the respondents indicating use.

Nearly 90 percent of wholesale respondents reported measuring outbound freight cost. Use of comparison of actual to budgeted and measurement of warehouse cost were both in the mid 80 percent range. The least used cost performance measurement among wholesalers was order processing at 45.8 percent.

The cost performance measurement having the highest usage among retailers was outbound freight at 90.6 percent. Warehouse costs, inbound freight, comparison of actual to budgeted cost, direct labor and total costs analysis were all used by more than 80 percent of the retail respondents.

Over 80 percent of the hybrid respondents reported regular measurement of outbound freight, actual to budgeted costs, warehouse costs, direct labor, cost as a percentage of sales and total cost analysis. The least used cost performance measurement was order processing at 33.8 percent.

CUSTOMER SERVICE MEASUREMENT

With the exception of manufacturers, reported customer service measures utilization was lower than either cost or asset measurements. Each of the customer service performance measurements included in the research was used by at least two-thirds of all manufacturer respondents. Over 80 percent of manufacturers use both customer feedback, feedback from the sales force, shipping errors, on time delivery and stockouts to monitor their customer service performance.

Wholesalers recorded relatively low customer service performance measurement. Customer feedback and sales force feedback were the most used measurement at about 85 percent. Measurement of cycle time was lowest at 34.7 percent.

The highest ranked customer service performance measure among retailers was customer feedback with 84.1 percent indicating regular usage. Shipping errors were a close second with 81.9 percent usage. The lowest usage was sales force feedback at 51.5 percent. Backorders, cycle times and customer survey usage rates were also used by fewer than 60 percent of the retail respondents. To a significant degree, the failure to use these conventional customer service measures is a direct reflection of the retailing logistics mission as discussed in Chapter Two.

Nearly 90 percent of hybrids use customer feedback to determine how well they are doing. About 80 percent of hybrids reported using feedback from sales force. As with wholesalers, measurement of cycle time was lowest at 46.8 percent.

PRODUCTIVITY MEASUREMENT

Productivity performance measurement was relatively low among all respondents. Regular measurement of productivity is typically found in more advanced organizations. The two most common productivity measures for all business types were comparison of operating results to historical standards and goal programs. Comparative analysis of one operating period to another and of actual to planned operations are the first levels of productivity measurement.

Following standards and goals, manufacturers reported frequent use of a productivity index at 55.8 percent and units shipped per employee at 54.8 percent. The third most common choice of wholesalers was units shipped per employee at 53.1 percent. The third choice of retailers and hybrids was units per labor dollar at 63.9 and 61.1 percent respectively.

QUALITY MEASUREMENT

Only manufacturers and hybrids recorded the use of any listed quality performance measurements above the 70 percent level. Number of customer returns was reported as a regular quality measure among 77.1 percent of manufacturers.

The most used quality measures among wholesalers were customer returns and number of credit claims, both at 69 percent. The least used measure among wholesalers was damage frequency at 44.7 percent.

Among retailers, no quality performance measurement was used by more than 68 percent of respondents. However, each of the quality measurements was used by more than 50 percent. Highest usage levels were number of credit claims at 67.5 percent and the dollar amount of damage at 67.1 percent. The least used quality performance measurement was cost of returned goods at 54.2 percent.

For hybrids, the most commonly used quality performance measurement was number of customer returns at 72.9 percent. The least used quality performance measurement among hybrid firms was for frequency of damage at 50 percent.

AVAILABILITY OF INFORMATION

In order to gain a better understanding of utilization patterns for specific performance measures, respondents were asked if adequate information was available. With a few minor exceptions, the percentages of respondents having information available corresponded closely to respondents reporting use of the performance measurements. Table 5-9 presents the percentage of respondents by business type who have the required information to measure each specific performance measurement.

Review of Table 5-9 indicates substantial variation in the availability of performance measurement information. The lowest percentages of available performance measurement information

TABLE 5-9
AVAILABILITY OF SPECIFIC PERFORMANCE MEASUREMENT INFORMATION BY BUSINESS TYPE

Performance Measure	Percent			
	Manufacturer	Wholesaler	Retailer	Hybrid
Asset Management				
Inventory turns	88.5	92.7	89.5	92.5
Inventory carrying costs	72.9	81.9	76.5	75.0
Inventory levels, # days supply	92.1	89.7	85.5	93.9
Obsolete inventory	87.5	87.8	81.5	91.7
Return on net assets	76.7	86.8	79.0	82.5
Return on investment	80.3	89.8	85.9	88.3
Cost				
Total cost analysis	87.9	78.8	85.1	86.9
Cost per unit	88.9	71.4	84.9	79.7
Cost as a percentage of sales	91.7	90.3	93.2	88.7
Inbound freight	87.4	87.6	86.5	81.0
Outbound freight	96.2	92.0	94.3	95.2
Warehouse costs	91.3	91.8	93.4	85.9
Administrative costs	92.1	91.0	90.7	89.4
Order processing	62.3	63.2	61.5	58.6
Direct labor costs	85.3	81.0	91.5	90.3
Comparison of actual vs. budget	95.5	88.7	91.9	91.9
Cost trend analysis	77.5	66.3	77.9	74.6
Direct product profitability	67.5	56.0	41.3	68.9
Customer Service				
Fill rate	81.9	77.2	77.6	62.3
Stockouts	82.7	76.0	80.6	69.8
Shipping errors	86.0	71.6	83.9	71.4
On time delivery	80.1	62.1	85.0	61.8
Backorders	83.3	73.5	66.7	70.6
Cycle time	76.3	39.8	67.2	44.2
Customer feedback	86.6	74.8	81.0	78.9
Sales force feedback	85.6	75.7	58.1	80.8
Customer surveys	68.9	52.1	68.8	47.3
Productivity				
Units shipped per employee	73.2	63.0	76.2	67.9
Units per labor dollar	69.5	59.6	77.8	70.7
Orders per sales representative	60.0	72.8	36.1	56.9
Comparison to historical standard	81.6	79.6	95.2	82.5
Goal programs	75.0	72.1	85.7	77.8
Productivity index	61.0	53.0	66.0	54.9
Quality				
Frequency of damage	66.0	41.5	71.7	60.7
Dollar amount of damage	73.0	54.1	75.0	63.2
Number of credit claims	79.5	74.0	70.2	73.2
Number of customer returns	80.4	78.1	72.5	75.0
Cost of returned goods	71.5	65.2	67.4	64.2

were in the productivity and quality areas. The highest percentages of information availability were in the asset and cost areas.

RELATIVE IMPORTANCE OF
PERFORMANCE MEASUREMENTS

Respondents were asked to indicate the relative importance of specific performance measurement areas to their specific logistics operation. These data reflect the prevailing attitude by business type regarding the use of specific measurements.

Respondents were asked to indicate the importance of each measure on a scale of 1 to 5, with five being most important. The responses were then averaged for each measure and performance category. No performance measurement in any category averaged lower than three. Most measurements averaged near 4.0. This illustrates that respondents believe that these performance measurements are fairly important even if they dp not use them or do not have the information to use them. These measures of importance are presented in Table 5-10.

IMPORTANCE OF ASSET MEASURES

Wholesalers at 4.48, retailers at 4.35, and hybrids at 4.27 rated the measurement of inventory turns as the most important asset to be measured. Manufacturers select number of days of supply at 4.13, with inventory turns a close second at 4.10. The lowest average asset management importance rating was given by retail and manufacturing firms to the measurement of obsolete inventory. However, those particular importance ratings still averaged around 3.7.

TABLE 5-10
PERFORMANCE MEASUREMENTS BY BUSINESS TYPE

Performance Measure	Ratings			
	Manufacturer	Wholesaler	Retailer	Hybrid
Asset Management				
Inventory turns	4.1	4.5	4.4	4.3
Inventory carrying costs	3.7	4.0	3.9	3.7
Inventory levels, # days supply	4.1	4.0	4.0	4.2
Obsolete inventory	3.7	4.0	3.7	3.9
Return on net assets	3.9	3.9	3.8	3.8
Return on investment	4.0	4.1	4.1	4.1
Cost				
Total cost analysis	4.5	4.2	4.3	4.3
Cost per unit	4.1	3.7	3.9	4.2
Cost as a percentage of sales	3.9	4.2	4.1	4.0
Inbound freight	3.8	3.8	4.1	3.6
Outbound freight	4.4	4.1	4.4	4.1
Warehouse costs	4.1	4.2	4.4	4.0
Administrative costs	3.6	3.8	3.6	3.5
Order processing	3.3	3.5	3.3	3.1
Direct labor costs	3.8	4.0	4.3	4.0
Comparison actual versus budget	4.2	4.2	4.5	4.2
Cost trend analysis	3.8	3.7	3.9	3.9
Direct product profitability	3.8	4.0	3.3	3.8
Customer Service				
Fill rate	4.3	4.6	4.2	4.4
Stockouts	4.2	4.4	4.3	4.2
Shipping errors	4.1	4.3	4.2	4.1
On time delivery	4.4	4.3	4.3	4.4
Backorders	3.9	4.1	3.8	4.0
Cycle time	3.8	3.4	3.5	3.7
Customer feedback	4.4	4.3	4.3	4.5
Sales force feedback	4.0	4.1	3.8	4.3
Customer surveys	3.8	3.8	3.9	3.7
Productivity				
Units shipped/employee	3.4	3.9	4.0	3.8
Units per labor dollar	3.4	3.7	4.1	3.8
Orders per sales representative	3.0	3.6	3.1	3.8
Comparison to historical standard	3.6	3.9	4.0	4.1
Goal programs	3.8	4.1	4.3	4.3
Productivity index	3.7	3.7	4.0	4.1
Quality				
Frequency of damage	3.8	3.7	3.9	3.8
Dollar amount of damage	3.7	3.9	4.0	3.7
Number of credit claims	3.7	3.9	3.8	3.7
Number of customer returns	3.8	4.0	3.6	4.0
Cost of returned goods	3.6	3.9	3.6	4.0

Scale - 1 = unimportant; 5 = important

IMPORTANCE OF COST MEASURES

In terms of relative importance, respondents indicated that total cost, outbound freight and comparison of actual to budgeted costs were the most important cost measurements. This was generally true independent of business type. Wholesale and retail firms placed great importance on warehouse cost measurements. The least important cost measurement was order processing.

IMPORTANCE OF CUSTOMER SERVICE MEASURES

Customer service performance measurements received high average ratings across business types. With the exception of cycle time and use of customer surveys, all other customer service performance measurement were rated above 4.0 by at least two of the four business types. The sensitivity to customers is illustrated in Figure 5-7. The area of customer service performance measurement was judged the most important by all business types.

IMPORTANCE OF PRODUCTIVITY MEASURES

Among productivity measurements, goal programs received the highest individual average importance rating across all business types. The lowest importance was given to orders per sales representative.

IMPORTANCE OF QUALITY MEASURES

Quality performance was generally rated lower in importance than other types of measures. However individual measures were ranked consistently across business types. No

148

FIGURE 5-7
IMPORTANCE OF PERFORMANCE MEASUREMENT
BY CATEGORY AND BUSINESS TYPE

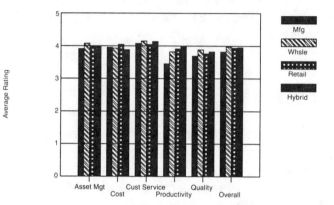

Scale: 1 = Unimportant; 5 = Important

single quality measure was rated above 4.0 in importance across business types.

COMPETITIVE BENCHMARKING

More and more firms have adapted benchmarking as a technique to compare their operations to their competition and to leading firms in closely related businesses. Manufacturers in particular are using benchmarking in key strategic areas as a tool to calibrate their logistics operations. Use of benchmarking was measured in ten specific areas of operation. Data are presented in Table 5-11.

TABLE 5-11
BENCHMARKING PRACTICES BY
AREA AND BUSINESS TYPE

Percent by Business Type

Benchmarking Area	Manufacturer	Wholesaler	Retailer	Hybrid
Asset Management	36.6	30.3	24.3	26.4
Cost	78.1	59.7	56.4	61.1
Customer Service	84.8	53.7	40.3	47.1
Productivity	57.5	41.5	46.8	38.9
Quality	79.1	46.2	38.2	52.8
Strategy	53.0	27.8	39.2	26.5
Technology	47.2	36.4	34.8	40.6
Transportation	56.3	44.4	60.5	40.0
Warehousing	51.1	51.5	57.9	37.7
Order Processing	51.9	39.5	28.8	27.5
Overall	59.6	43.1	43.4	40.5

Over 78 percent of the manufacturing respondents report using benchmarking to review and compare their costs, customer service and quality performance. Among manufacturers, greatest use of benchmarking was reported for customer service performance. Productivity, logistics strategy, transportation, warehousing and order processing were all reported as being benchmarked by more than 50 percent of manufacturing respondents. The overall average usage of the ten benchmark areas was 59.6 percent for manufacturers compared to 43.4 percent for retailers, 43.1 percent for wholesalers and 40.5 percent for hybrids. It is clear that manufacturers have adopted the concept of benchmarking to a greater extent than the other channel members.

Nearly 60 percent of wholesalers use benchmarking for cost comparisons. Over fifty-three percent of the wholesalers used benchmarking for customer service and 51.5 percent for warehouse operations. Only 27.8 percent use benchmarking for logistics strategy.

Among retailers over 60 percent benchmark in the transportation area. Cost and warehouse operations each are benchmarked by over 56 percent of retail firms. For retailers, the lowest benchmark areas are asset management and order processing. Even though these areas have relatively low benchmarking percentages, approximately one in four retail firms report activity.

The highest use of benchmarking among hybrids is in the cost area with 61.1 percent reporting measurement activity. Customer service at 47.1 percent and quality at 52.8 percent benchmarking were the next highest areas for hybrid respondents. The lowest areas of reported hybrid benchmarking are in asset management, comparative logistics strategy and order processing. This analysis illustrates that benchmarking is a common practice. Manufacturers are the most deeply involved in benchmarking.

LEADING EDGE BENCHMARKING - PERFORMANCE MEASUREMENT AND BENCHMARKING

Leading edge firms, no matter what their position in the channel, tend to measure all five areas of performance to a greater degree than norm respondents. In every category of performance measurement, leading edge firms use significantly more measures than norm respondents. These conclusions are independent and significant across all business types.

Figure 5-8 illustrates comparative benchmarking areas by business type and CAI group and Table 5-12 presents statistical significance. Perhaps the most distinguishing feature of leading edge firms is their commitment to performance measurement.

151

In the area of benchmarking, leading edge firms are more active than their norm counterparts. In terms of the extent of benchmarking within individual areas, leading edge firms are significantly ahead of their norm counterparts. Manufacturer leading edge firms are significantly more involved in asset management, productivity, logistics strategy and technology deployment benchmarking. Leading edge wholesalers are significantly more involved in every area of benchmarking than norm wholesalers with the exception of order processing. No significant difference exists between leading edge and norm retailers with respect to specific benchmark areas. Leading edge hybrids are significantly more involved in customer service, quality and logistics strategy benchmarking than their norm counterparts. In no area did norm respondents report more involvement in benchmarking than the leading edge firms within their business type.

TABLE 5-12
PERFORMANCE MEASURES USED
BY BUSINESS TYPE AND CAI GROUP

| | Average | | | |
Performance Measure	Manufacturer LE/Norm	Wholesaler LE/Norm	Retailer LE/Norm	Hybrid LE/Norm
Asset Management	5.10^A/4.25	5.45^A/4.29	5.06^A/3.67	5.13^B/4.20
Cost	10.25^A/8.96	10.27^A/7.94	10.13^A/8.68	10.20^A/8.51
Customer Service	7.45^B/6.54	7.45^A/5.89	7.31^A/5.35	7.40^A/4.73
Productivity	3.93^B/3.14	4.77^A/2.99	4.13^A/3.46	4.47^A/3.33
Quality	4.35^A/3.15	3.95^A/2.69	4.50^A/2.60	4.27^A/2.41

A, B - Significantly different from the norm at 0.01 and 0.05 respectively.

The analysis supports the conclusion that leading edge firms are fully commited to performance measurement and benchmarking. In these areas, excellence clearly stands out.

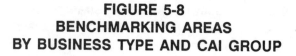

**FIGURE 5-8
BENCHMARKING AREAS
BY BUSINESS TYPE AND CAI GROUP**

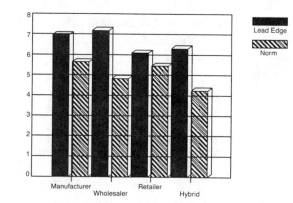

CONCLUSION - PERFORMANCE MEASUREMENT

In all five performance measurement categories, respondents indicated extensive activity. The intensity is indicated by the average number of performance measures regularly used. Desired activity is reflected by the importance that respondents assigned to measures not currently being used. For the most part, respondents are measuring performance activity in all areas where information is available. Consequently, the most active areas of performance measurement are financial.

Patterns with respect to benchmarking are somewhat surprising. Despite the fact that all business types rate customer service the most important performance measurement area, only manufacturers rank it as first in current benchmarking effort. The lack of information and structural definition may be primary reasons for this apparent inconsistency.

Leading edge firms are clearly the pacesetters in both performance measurement and benchmarking. They are significantly ahead of their norm counterparts. As a general conclusion, the analysis supports the generalization that the emerging firm is interested in cost measurement, norm firms add customer service to their measurement portfolio and leading edge firms are committed to the comprehensive measurement in all five of the performance areas.

COMPUTER APPLICATIONS

One inescapable conclusion from this research is that information is the key to successful logistics management. At the center of a logistics organization's information management capabilities are the installed computer applications that generate information. It is not enough to have a big computer that produces masses of paper. The information used by the logistics organization must be specific, timely and high quality. Without a strong information base, no logistics organization can be successful.

Research respondents were asked a series of questions dealing with information management requirements of their logistics organization. One set of questions examined logistics computer applications. Respondents were presented with the comprehensive list of common logistics computer applications presented in Table 5-13. Respondents were queried about whether data processing applications were: (1) currently installed with no plans for revision; (2) currently installed but planned for revision during the next three years; (3) not currently installed but planned to be installed in next three years; or (4) not currently installed with no plans to install. The data reported in this section summarizes current and planned applications.

TABLE 5-13
LOGISTICAL COMPUTER APPLICATIONS

Freight Audit and Payment
Purchasing
Sales Forecasting
Inventory Control (Raw, In Process, & Finished Goods)
Warehouse Order Selection
Warehouse On-Line Receiving
Warehouse Merchandise Locator
Warehouse Short Interval Scheduling
Order Processing
Order Entry
Vehicle Routing and Scheduling
Inbound Freight Consolidation
Outbound Freight Consolidation
Supporting Financials
Performance Measurement
Distribution Modeling
Direct Product Profitability
Direct Store Delivery
Shelf Management
MRP
DRP

Respondents were also requested to describe the information used to manage logistics. Issues of concern were, whether information is: (1) timely; (2) accurate; (3) readily available; (4) formatted on an exception basis; and (5) appropriately formatted to facilitate use. A final question asked respondents to compare their overall logistics information systems to systems used to support other operational areas of their enterprise such as marketing or manufacturing. The data presented deals with quality of information and overall comparison of logistics systems to other information management applications. In total, the objective was to develop a clear profile of the precise role that information plays in leading edge logistical management.

MOST COMMONLY INSTALLED
COMPUTER APPLICATIONS

In the Phase I manufacturing survey, the computer applications were somewhat different from those included in the Phase II retail/wholesale survey. The Phase II questionnaire was modified to take into consideration applications unique to wholesalers and retailers. For example, production scheduling was dropped and warehouse applications were expanded in numbers. In addition, retail applications such as direct product profitability and electronic shelf management were added. The results are presented in Table 5-14.

For manufacturers, the most commonly installed computer applications were order entry at 96.2 percent and order processing at 96.1 percent. This was true for both the Phase I and the Phase II manufacturing update. Close behind were finished goods inventory control at 92.8 percent, supporting financials at 82.9 percent, work in process inventory at 80.3 percent and raw materials inventory control at 79.4 percent. It is clear that manufacturers are greatly concerned about the management of inventory assets.

Over 90 percent of wholesalers reported that they have order entry, order processing and inventory control applications installed. The next most common wholesale applications were purchasing at 81.6 percent and supporting financials at 76.6 percent.

Similar to manufacturers, retailers listed order entry at 92 percent and order processing at 90.7 percent as two of the most commonly installed logistics computer applications. Other common applications were inventory control at 87.5 percent,

TABLE 5-14
LOGISTICAL COMPUTER APPLICATIONS
BY BUSINESS TYPE

		Percent		
Application	Manufacturer	Wholesaler	Retailer	Hybrid
Freight Audit/Payment	63.9	46.8	58.0	43.1
Purchasing	73.1	81.6	81.9	83.6
Sales Forecasting	77.8	64.9	71.9	64.8
Inventory Control	---	92.4	87.5	89.5
Warehouse Order Selection	70.6	71.2	81.5	68.5
Warehouse On-Line Receiving	60.7	61.2	69.0	52.1
Warehouse Merchandise Locator	59.9	56.8	76.5	59.7
Warehouse Workload Balancing	31.8	27.0	38.0	26.4
Warehouse Short Interval Schedule	31.7	23.1	29.5	21.4
Order Processing	96.1	91.6	90.7	89.3
Order Entry	96.2	92.0	92.0	89.2
Vehicle Routing & Scheduling	32.7	28.6	34.2	28.2
Inbound Freight Consolidation	39.8	25.2	35.4	24.0
Outbound Freight Consolidation	53.8	36.8	45.7	43.1
Supporting Financials	82.9	76.6	83.6	85.3
Performance Measurement	71.0	57.8	67.1	66.7
Distribution Modeling	46.3	21.8	42.5	30.0
Direct Product Profitability	48.3	49.6	24.4	40.0
Direct Store Delivery	31.7	30.5	45.1	34.9
Shelf Management	26.5	28.5	26.0	22.6
MRP	60.9	---	---	---
DRP	37.6	---	---	---
Raw Material Inventory Control	79.4	---	---	---
In Process Inventory Control	80.3	---	---	---
Finished Goods Inventory Control	92.8	---	---	---

Note: Those applications showing no response were not included in the Phase I or Phase II questionnaires.

purchasing at 81.9 percent, supporting financials at 83.6 percent and warehouse order selection at 81.5 percent.

The most commonly installed computer application for hybrid firms were inventory control at 89.5 percent followed by order processing at 89.3 percent, order entry at 89.2 percent, supporting financials at 85.3 percent and purchasing at 83.6 percent.

The data on most common computer applications are very consistent across business types. Applications dealing with order entry, order processing, inventory control, purchasing and supporting financials are popular independent of business type. Beyond these popular applications, the pattern is inconsistent.

PLANS TO INSTALL
COMPUTER APPLICATIONS

Table 5-15 provides a comparative analysis of plans to install computer applications. As one might expect, the most popular applications are those offering cost reduction potential.

The computer applications most likely to be installed within the next three years were consistent across business types. More than 20 percent of each business type plans to install vehicle routing and scheduling. A significant number of firms in each channel position plan to install inbound freight consolidation, warehouse workload balancing, direct product profitability and warehouse on-line receiving.

QUALITY OF INFORMATION

Respondents were asked to rate the quality of information available to manage logistics on a scale of one to five. The information attributes used were: (1) timeliness; (2) accuracy; (3) availability; (4) formatted on an exception basis; and (5) appropriately formatted to facilitate use. A response of one

TABLE 5-15
PLANS TO INSTALL
LOGISTICS COMPUTER APPLICATIONS BY BUSINESS TYPE

Application	Percent			
	Manufacturer	Wholesaler	Retailer	Hybrid
Freight Audit/Payment	16.9	19.2	17.3	20.8
Purchasing	20.3	8.5	13.3	8.2
Sales Forecasting	14.2	14.1	17.1	15.5
Inventory Control	---	2.8	10.2	5.3
Warehouse Order Selection	13.6	9.4	7.4	9.6
Warehouse On-Line Receiving	24.2	23.7	19.1	23.3
Warehouse Merchandise Locator	18.6	18.7	9.4	15.3
Warehouse Workload Balancing	23.3	22.6	29.1	26.4
Warehouse Short Interval Schedule	17.6	14.9	23.1	21.4
Order Processing	3.3	4.2	9.3	6.7
Order Entry	3.8	5.5	6.9	6.8
Vehicle Routing & Scheduling	23.9	27.9	22.8	28.2
Inbound Freight Consolidation	27.1	20.0	24.4	12.7
Outbound Freight Consolidation	17.6	19.1	14.8	18.1
Supporting Financials	10.3	9.9	7.6	6.7
Performance Measurement	17.5	23.2	18.3	16.7
Distribution Modeling	23.7	22.6	23.8	21.4
Direct Product Profitability	19.0	27.5	23.1	27.1
Direct Store Delivery	9.4	10.2	11.0	12.1
Shelf Management	11.1	13.1	15.6	12.9
MRP	15.9	---	---	---
DRP	26.1	---	---	---
Raw Material Inventory Control	14.3	---	---	---
In Process Inventory Control	11.3	---	---	---
Finished Goods Inventory Control	5.0	---	---	---

Note: Applications indicating no response were not included in the Phase I or Phase II questionnaire

means never true whereas a score of five indicates always true. Data concerning information quality is displayed in Figure 5-9.

FIGURE 5-9
QUALITY OF INFORMATION
BY BUSINESS TYPE

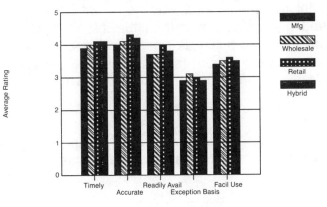

5 - point scale with
  1 = never and
  5 = always.

On average, all of the business types reported their support information as accurate. The average rating across channel position was over 4.0 on a five point scale. Retailers and hybrids averaged above 4.0 for timeliness of information while the mean score for manufacturers and wholesalers was just below or at 4.0. The lowest scores recorded for all business types was in the area of the frequency of information being formatted on an exception basis. Only wholesalers averaged above 3.0 for exception formatting. In general, the quality of

160

information available to manage logistics is good. The presentation of the information appears to leave something to be desired. Results were consistent across business types.

COMPARISON TO OTHER INFORMATION SYSTEMS

Respondents were asked to compare logistics information to that available for managers of other areas of the business. A five-point scaling method was used, with one being much worse and five much better than the information available in other areas. Across business types, respondents rated logistics information as being about the same as that available to other areas. These data are presented in Table 5-16.

TABLE 5-16
COMPARISON OF LOGISTICS INFORMATION SYSTEMS TO
OTHER INFORMATION SYSTEMS BY BUSINESS TYPE

	Phase II Manufacturer	Wholesaler	Retailer	Hybrid
Systems Comparison	3.08	2.96	3.08	2.88

5 - point scale with
    1 = much worse and
    5 = much better.

LEADING EDGE BENCHMARKING - COMPUTER APPLICATIONS

This research found that leading edge firms have more computer applications currently installed than norm firms. These data are illustrated by business type and CAI category in Figure 5-10. These differences are all statistically significant. Leading edge firms also plan to install more new computer applications and enjoy superior data processing support. Leading edge logistics management information systems compare favorably to information system support systems available to other areas of

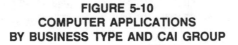

FIGURE 5-10
COMPUTER APPLICATIONS
BY BUSINESS TYPE AND CAI GROUP

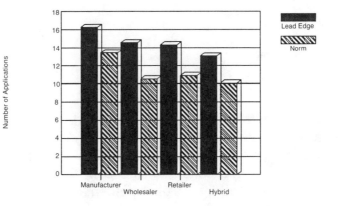

the business. Table 5-17 indicates comparative rating of logistics information systems between leading edge and their norm counterparts. For all business types except retailing, leading edge information systems were rated significantly better than norm respondents.

CONCLUSION -
COMPUTER APPLICATIONS

Across business types, logistics computer applications are extensive and projected to grow. In every area, leading edge firms enjoy superior computer support. In most cases, the difference between leading edge and norm respondents is statistically significant.

TABLE 5-17
COMPARISON OF LOGISTICS INFORMATION SYSTEMS TO OTHER INFORMATION SYSTEMS BY BUSINESS TYPE AND CAI GROUP

CAI Group	Phase II Manufacturer	Wholesaler	Retailer	Hybrid
Leading Edge	3.50	3.68	3.56	3.60
Norm	3.01	2.92	3.16	2.73

5 - point scale with
   1 = much worse and
   5 = much better.

Leading edge firms typically receive data in better and more usable format than do norm firms. They currently use and plan to use more decision support models. Most of the logistics oriented computer applications included in the research were listed as being installed by a higher percentage of leading edge than norm firms.

INFORMATION TECHNOLOGY ADOPTION

The future success or failure of many logistics organizations will likely depend on how effectively they use emerging technology. Over the last few years, there has been an explosion of advancements in both software and hardware. Today's logistics managers face the challenge of keeping pace with fast moving advancements. Managers of leading edge companies are keenly aware that they must exploit new technology. While such technology covers a broad spectrum of different application areas, questions in this research were aimed at the adoption of specific new information technology.

As the rate at which new hardware and software is introduced accelerates, logistics managers confront a staggering number of options. One of the results of the explosion in technology has been the development of an *information gap*. This information gap evolved as technology expanded exponentially. The manager's ability to implement technology has not kept pace with the rate of development. Only a small portion of the available software and hardware has been adopted by logistics organizations. In today's rapidly changing environment, software and hardware quickly become obsolete.

An example of how quickly technology changes is the personal computer (PC). The original PC was introduced in the early 1980's. PC's were widely adopted by logistics organizations. These machines are no longer being produced. The PC AT class was introduced in the mid 1980's and was also widely adopted by logistics organizations as an enhancement over the original PC. Today, the 80286-based PC is also out of production. The replacement PC's, 80386-based machines, have been commercially available for over two years and offer greatly increased computing power. Intel has recently announced that the successor to the 80386 chip is ready for initial distribution.

The Phase II questionnaire contained a set of questions aimed at determining what information technologies are currently being used by logistics organizations and at identifying future adoption plans. The questions were designed to gauge the nature and magnitude of the information gap.

One application of technology that is particularly relevant to logistics is electronic data interchange (EDI). Much has been written about EDI. Survey respondents were questioned as to whether they were currently use or plan to use EDI. Specified EDI applications included communication with manufacturers, wholesalers, public warehouses, carriers, financial institutions, retailers, customers and copackers/contractors.

Another area of emerging information technology application for logistics organizations is artificial intelligence/knowledge--based systems (AI). According to some proponents, AI is "bursting out of the laboratories and into corporate boardrooms."

Knowledge based systems offer the potential to capitalize on the experience of experts by computerizing a set of rules that replicate the expert's knowledge. One research objective was to measure the real and planned rates of AI technology adoption.

Other questions on information technologies focused primarily on hardware. The specific hardware technology applications examined in the research are listed in Table 5-18.

TABLE 5-18
HARDWARE TECHNOLOGIES

Bar Coding
Optical Scanning
Robotics
Automated Storage and Retrieval Systems
Automated Material Handling Equipment
Local Area Networks
Computer-Aided Warehouse Design
Handheld Data Entry Devices
Electronic Order Transmission
On Board Computers-Delivery Vehicles
On Board Computers-Lift Trucks
Voice Data Capture
PC or PC XT Compatible
80286 Microcomputers (AI or compatible)
80386 Microcomputers
CD-ROM (Read Only Memory)
WORM (Write Once, Read Many) Discs
68020-Based Microcomputers (Mac 2 or Sun)
Fiber Optics

ELECTRONIC DATA INTERCHANGE

Responses to the questions on installed EDI applications were fairly consistent. No individual EDI application is currently used by more than 40 percent of the respondents in any business type. At the same time, all EDI applications included in the research were reported as being installed by at least some respondents. These data are reported in Table 5-19.

Among manufacturers, the most common EDI application was linkage to financial institutions at 28.5 percent. The lowest installed EDI usage rate for manufacturers was with copackers/contractors at 6 percent.

Among wholesalers, the most popular linkage was with customers with 39.6 percent reporting on-line. One-third of wholesalers were electronically linked with manufacturers. The next most common wholesale EDI links were with financial institutions at 26 percent and retailers at 22.1 percent. Only 13.6

TABLE 5-19
CURRENTLY INSTALLED ELECTRONIC DATA INTERCHANGE
APPLICATIONS BY BUSINESS GROUP

EDI Application	Percent			
	Manufacturer	Wholesaler	Retailer	Hybrid
Manufacturers/Vendors	23.2	33.3	38.0	31.5
Wholesalers	24.6	16.4	17.6	17.7
Public Warehouses	21.0	1.6	10.8	10.5
Carriers	25.4	13.6	30.4	22.1
Financial Institutions	28.5	26.0	38.7	30.3
Retailers	17.2	22.1	23.2	26.5
Customers	27.5	39.6	21.9	37.0
Copackers/Contractors	6.0	4.0	4.1	6.2

percent of respondent wholesalers mentioned that they were on-line with carriers, 4 percent with co-packers and only 1.6 percent with public warehouses. However, it should be noted that very few wholesalers are active users of warehousing.

For retailers, the most common EDI connection was with financial institutions with 38.7 percent on line. Links with manufacturers at 38 percent and carriers at 30.4 percent were in second and third place. Links with other retailers were reported by 23.2 percent of retail respondents. This presumably refers to links with other stores in the same retail chain.

For hybrid firms, the most common EDI link at 37 percent was with customers. Over thirty percent of hybrid firms reported links with manufacturers. Close behind were links with financial institutions at 30.3 percent, retailers at 26.5 percent and carriers at 22.1 percent.

PLANNED EDI APPLICATIONS

Respondents were questioned concerning their future plans to install EDI. Some firms reported moving quickly to expand EDI applications. Table 5-20 provides a summary of applications planned for implementation during the next three years. These data cover all respondents that do not currently have a given application, but plan to implement one.

Manufacturers anticipate the greatest future EDI expansion. Among other business types, with some very notable exceptions, the general expansion strategy appears to be one of reacting to manufacturer proposals rather than taking EDI leadership.

ARTIFICIAL INTELLIGENCE/ KNOWLEDGE-BASED SYSTEMS

Based on respondent data, it is clear that AI/knowledge based systems are viewed as technology of the future. During the interviews, some logistics executives expressed hope that they would be able to move toward testing of AI techniques, but to date little specific progress was reported.

TABLE 5-20
PLANNED EDI APPLICATION BY BUSINESS TYPE

	Percent			
EDI Application	Manufacturer	Wholesaler	Retailer	Hybrid
Manufacturers/Vendors	30.5	29.0	32.9	26.0
Wholesalers	27.4	12.7	17.6	26.5
Public Warehouses	26.7	3.9	8.1	7.5
Carriers	41.4	16.7	34.2	16.2
Financial Institutions	21.8	13.0	17.3	10.6
Retailers	19.0	14.5	12.2	13.2
Customers	42.1	23.0	11.0	23.3
Copackers/Contractors	19.2	5.6	9.5	3.1

Only 6 percent of the Phase I manufacturing respondents reported currently installed AI systems. The Phase II results for wholesalers, retailers, hybrids and manufacturing update firms reported current use of AI/knowledge based systems at below 4 percent. The planned future use of AI was, of course, substantially higher. Among manufacturers, 21.5 percent of the Phase II respondents plan to install logistics AI applications. Across other business types, 5.9 percent of wholesalers, 15.1 percent of retailers and 11.4 percent of the hybrids are planning to test AI technologies. It appears safe to conclude that at least for logistics organizations, widespread use of AI technology is still in the future.

HARDWARE TECHNOLOGIES

The data concerning installed and planned hardware technologies were fairly consistent across business types. This implies that logistics organizations are installing the same kinds of hardware technologies independent of business type.

**MOST COMMONLY INSTALLED
HARDWARE TECHNOLOGIES**

The data regarding currently installed hardware technology are presented in Table 5-21. Among the technologies the most commonly installed were the PC, PC XT or compatibles. Manufacturers were the leaders with 82.8 percent installed and wholesalers were low with 70.1 percent. Approximately 20 percent of all business types are using 80386-based microcomputers, the currently most available PC technology. The analysis shows that PC's remain more popular among respondents than more advanced technology.

**TABLE 5-21
INSTALLED INFORMATION TECHNOLOGIES
BY BUSINESS TYPE**

	Percent			
Technology	Manufacturer	Wholesaler	Retailer	Hybrid
Bar Coding	26.9	22.5	47.2	28.0
Optical Scanning	16.2	18.3	41.4	20.6
Robotics	8.3	2.9	3.5	5.4
AI/Knowledge Systems	4.0	3.0	3.5	4.3
ASRS	18.0	11.0	18.4	8.2
Automated Material Handling	24.6	25.7	42.5	18.9
Local Area Networks	25.1	14.1	23.5	15.5
CAD Warehouse Design	17.3	15.3	26.7	16.4
Handheld Data Entry Devices	19.4	28.8	31.8	31.5
Electronic Order Transmission	54.9	56.1	54.5	53.4
On Board Computers - Delivery Vehicles	16.3	14.8	4.8	9.5
On Board Computers - Lift Trucks	12.4	4.3	2.4	5.4
Voice Data Capture	6.4	8.1	2.4	5.5
PC or PC XT Compatible	82.8	70.1	77.8	71.2
80286 Micros (AT or compatible)	47.7	45.1	53.7	44.9
80386 Microcomputers	26.0	26.8	24.1	33.3
CD-ROM (Read only memory)	7.4	8.9	6.7	8.9
WORM (Write once, read many)	9.0	4.0	4.0	6.4
68020 - Based Micros	8.4	10.4	6.5	7.8
Fiber Optics	6.7	4.2	5.3	4.6

The next most commonly installed hardware technology for all business types was electronic order transmission. Over 50 percent of all respondents are currently using electronic order transmission. This type of transmission includes the majority of EDI applications. In actual practice, applications range from document FAX to computer-to-computer linkage.

After microcomputers and electronic order transmission, the next most commonly used hardware technologies among manufacturers and retailers were bar coding, followed by automated material handling systems and local area networks. For wholesalers, the next most commonly used hardware technologies after microcomputers and electronic order transmission were handheld data entry devices and automated material handling systems. Similar to wholesalers, many hybrid firms reported that they are currently using handheld data entry devices.

**MOST COMMONLY PLANNED
HARDWARE TECHNOLOGIES**

The most commonly planned hardware technologies were also consistent across business types. These data are presented in Table 5-22. Over 40 percent of manufacturers, 38.7 percent of wholesalers, 34.7 percent of hybrids and 27 percent of retailers plan to install bar coding within the next three years. Handheld data entry devices were the second most popular new technology on the drawing boards. Other frequently noted hardware technologies included optical scanning and local area networks.

LEADING EDGE BENCHMARKING - INFORMATION TECHNOLOGY

Leading edge firms are exploiters of information technology. They report having many more hardware technologies installed than their norm counterparts. These data are illustrated by Figure 5-11. Leading edge firms are generally more involved in electronic data interchange than norm companies and typically focus on marketing related applications. Leading edge firms report an average of two to three EDI applications, which is significantly greater than norm firms.

TABLE 5-22
PLANNED TECHNOLOGIES BY BUSINESS TYPE

	Percent			
Technology	Manufacturer	Wholesaler	Retailer	Hybrid
Bar Coding	41.4	38.7	27.0	34.7
Optical Scanning	25.1	30.7	16.1	34.3
Robotics	6.1	4.4	5.8	9.5
AI/Knowledge Systems	21.5	5.9	15.1	11.4
ASRS	7.9	13.1	12.6	11.0
Automated Material Handling	17.9	15.0	19.5	17.6
Local Area Networks	21.1	18.5	24.7	12.7
CAD Warehouse Design	12.8	15.3	17.4	13.7
Handheld Data Entry Devices	33.3	35.3	30.7	23.3
Electronic Order Transmission	23.1	19.4	19.3	23.3
On Board Computers - Delivery Vehicles	15.7	14.1	20.2	16.2
On Board Computers - Lift Trucks	16.9	14.4	22.6	17.6
Voice Data Capture	9.2	5.2	7.3	5.5
PC or PC XT Compatible	7.5	9.7	3.3	13.7
80286 Micros (AT or compatible)	9.1	5.3	6.1	7.3
80386 Microcomputers	6.5	9.8	11.4	10.6
CD-ROM (Read only memory)	5.6	6.5	2.7	7.1
WORM (Write once, read many)	3.0	4.0	1.3	4.8
68020 - Based Micros	3.0	3.2	1.3	0.0
Fiber Optics	2.4	3.4	4.0	1.5

Leading edge firms currently use and plan to use more artificial intelligence than norm respondents. A few of them see AI capabilities as a supplement to or improvement of current transaction processing systems. For example, they foresee the development of knowledge based transaction systems where users can be aided in on-line decision making. However, such ideas are future oriented and not available today. The responses concerning AI were too few to permit statistical comparative analysis between leading edge and norm responses.

FIGURE 5-11
INSTALLED INFORMATION TECHNOLOGIES
BY BUSINESS TYPE AND CAI GROUP

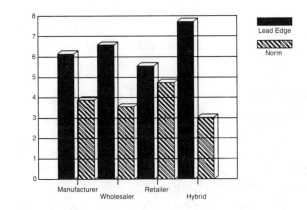

Leading edge firms are closer to the cutting edge of technology. They view the use of information and technology as a way to gain competitive superiority. Leading edge respondents are early adopters of technology that offers cost reduction potential. They are also concerned with implementing technology to enhance revenue generation. Leading edge firms have learned to use information as a strategic resource.

CONCLUSION -
INFORMATION TECHNOLOGY

As a general rule, logistics organizations are not on the frontier when it comes to adopting new technology. However, the adoption rate for EDI is increasing. Manufacturers appear to be taking the lead in planning EDI linkages. AI seems to be a technology of the future. Compared to other hardware technologies, the overall incidence of adoption for AI and EDI is consistent across business types, but the adoption process is slow.

Leading edge firms are ahead of the pack in all areas of technology adoption. It is safe to conclude that the leading edge firms are leaders in testing and adopting new technology.

SUMMARY

Management behavior is the key to understanding what makes a logistics organization successful. In this chapter, practice has been examined in terms of planning, performance measurement, computer applications and information technology adoption. In all categories, leading edge firms were distinctly superior to more typical firms.

Leading edge organizations place a high premium upon planning and the formalization of planning behavior. Leading edge firms are much more likely than norm firms to have formal mission statements and logistics plans to guide their business operations. Logistics executives in leading edge firms indicate high levels of involvement in overall business unit strategic planning. These behavioral patterns are generally consistent across business types.

Leading edge firms are compulsive performance measurers. They reported usage of a greater number of performance measures than did their norm counterparts. Leading edge firms also reported greater utilization of competitive benchmarking than norm firms.

Leading edge firms in all channel categories have superior information systems in comparison to norm firms both in terms of quality of information and application range. Leading edge firms currently have and plan to install more computer applications than norm firms.

In terms of adopting hardware and software technology, leading edge firms lead their norm counterparts. They are more deeply involved in and are planning more EDI and AI applications. Leading edge firms are ahead of norm firms in the adoption of new hardware technologies.

The study of behavior provides considerable insight into how the best of the best practice logistics. In terms of benchmarking leading edge firms to the norm, data analysis supplemented by interview responses support the following generalizations. Leading edge firms:

* Expend more effort on logistics planning.

* Are more apt to publish their performance commitments and standards by issuing specific mission statements.

* Have chief logistics officers who are more apt to be involved in business-unit strategic planning.

* Respond effectively to non-planned events.

* Regularly use a wider range of performance measures, including asset management, cost, customer service, productivity and quality.

* Are more significant users of data processing technology and enjoy a higher quality of information system (IS) support.

* Typically have more state-of-the-art computer applications and are planning more updates and expansions.

* Are more involved in new technologies such as electronic data interchange (EDI) and artificial intelligence (AI).

Chapter Six

EXECUTIVE CAREER PATHING

The level and mobility of logistics executives within a firm is indicative of the general visibility and recognition of their area of responsibility by senior management. Logistics executives in many firms have attained high level visibility and commensurate responsibilities. This chapter presents information concerning logistics executives': (1) current position; (2) tenure in current position; (3) previous position; and (4) reporting relationship.

OFFICER LEVEL STATUS

Logistics executives have achieved high level positions within their organization. The majority of the senior logistics executive of respondent firms have attained the position of Vice President or higher. Table 6-1 presents the distribution of top level logistics executives by business type.

TABLE 6-1
LEVEL OF SENIOR LOGISTICS EXECUTIVES
BY BUSINESS TYPE

	Percent			
Level	Manufacturer	Wholesaler	Retailer	Hybrid
Vice President or Higher	43.9	70.8	80.7	69.3
Director or Higher	78.6	80.3	94.3	82.7

When compared to wholesalers, retailers, and hybrids, manufacturers have a lower representation of logistics executives at the upper levels. Whereas 70-80 percent of senior logistics executives in the wholesaler, retailer and hybrid business types are Vice Presidents or higher, less than one half of the senior manufacturing logistics executives have officer titles. Retailers have the highest level logistics executives. More than 80 percent of retail senior logistics executives are Vice President or higher. Director level and above accounts for 94 percent of senior retail logistics executives.

LEADING EDGE BENCHMARKING - OFFICER LEVEL

Although most respondent firms reported highly positioned logistics executives, leading edge firms have proportionately more executives in the very top positions. Table 6-2 provides a distribution of logistics executives by job title. Once again, manufacturers, both leading edge and norm, have more senior logistics executives at lower levels within the organization than do the other business types. However, senior logistics executives at leading edge manufacturing firms are organizationally higher within the corporate structure than executives of norm manufacturers.

POSITION TENURE

From information obtained during interviews, it appears that the current high visibility and top position of senior logistics executives are relatively recent phenomena. Survey data also indicates the average tenure or length of time in the position is relatively short. The average tenure for the senior logistics executive is 5.06 years for manufacturers, 6.13 years for wholesalers, 6.32 years for retailers and 5.99 years for hybrids. To put these averages in perspective, it is interesting to look at the executives' tenure in their current position somewhat differently. Of every three respondents, two have been in their current position for five years or less. This relationship holds regardless of business type.

TABLE 6-2
LEVEL OF SENIOR LOGISTICS EXECUTIVES
BY BUSINESS TYPE AND CAI GROUP

	Percent			
Title	Manufacturer L.E./Norm	Wholesaler L.E./Norm	Retailer L.E./Norm	Hybrid L.E./Norm
President	0.0/ 2.0	9.1/18.4	6.3/ 5.3	6.7/12.2
Executive Vice President	6.3/ 3.6	13.6/ 6.1	6.3/ 3.5	13.3/ 4.1
Senior Vice President	0.0/ 0.0	18.2/ 7.1	25.0/19.3	20.0/ 6.1
Vice President	64.1/34.4	45.5/41.8	56.3/52.6	53.3/42.9
Director	26.6/37.9	4.6/12.2	6.3/14.0	0.0/16.3
Manager	3.1/21.3	9.1/ 6.1	0.0/ 3.5	6.7/18.4
Other	0.0/ 0.8	0.0/ 8.2	0.0/ 1.8	0.0/ 0.0

LEADING EDGE BENCHMARKING - TENURE

The comparison of leading edge to norm tenure does not offer a conclusive pattern. The data are illustrated in Figure 6-1. The most dramatic difference is between leading edge and norm hybrids. The senior logistics executives at leading edge hybrid firms have been in their current position significantly longer than have the norm executives.

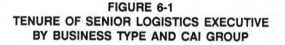

FIGURE 6-1
TENURE OF SENIOR LOGISTICS EXECUTIVE
BY BUSINESS TYPE AND CAI GROUP

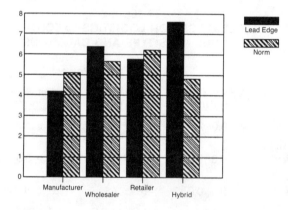

The senior logistics executives at leading edge manufacturers and retailers have actually been in position for a shorter period of time than their norm counterparts. This appears to reflect the especially dynamic nature and changing business practices among firms in recent years. Mergers, reorganizations, and increased awareness of the importance of logistics have impacted job tenure across all business types independent of CAI group.

PREVIOUS POSITION

Information was obtained regarding the senior logistics executive's previous position. Information concerned both the previous title and previous functional area of responsibility. Senior logistics executives are most likely to be promoted or assigned from the level of Vice President. The next most common previous title was director.

Personnel from the functional areas of distribution and operations are more frequently promoted to senior logistical positions than personnel from other areas of business. In contrast, senior logistical executives are much less likely to emerge from merchandising or purchasing. Areas more closely related to logistics such as traffic/transportation and warehousing infrequently provide career paths to the top level logistics positions. The analysis suggests integrated management experience will help an executive reach the top logistics position. Narrow areas of functional specialization offer inadequate preparation for assuming overall responsibility for logistical operations.

LEADING EDGE BENCHMARKING - PREVIOUS POSITION

Differences between leading edge and norm firms are presented in Table 6-3. As a general rule, the senior logistics executives at leading edge firms previously held higher level executive positions within their organizations than did the senior logistics executives at norm firms. This is true independent of business type.

TABLE 6-3
PREVIOUS TITLE OF SENIOR LOGISTICS
EXECUTIVES BY BUSINESS TYPE AND CAI GROUP

Percent

Title	Manufacturer L.E./Norm	Wholesaler L.E./Norm	Retailer L.E./Norm	Hybrid L.E./Norm
President	1.6/ 0.4	0.0/ 5.4	0.0/ 0.0	6.7/ 6.3
Executive Vice President	1.6/ 1.3	0.0/ 8.6	6.3/ 3.7	0.0/ 4.2
Senior Vice President	37.7/17.2	9.1/ 2.2	0.0/ 1.9	0.0/ 0.0
Vice President	32.8/25.0	45.5/29.0	43.8/25.9	40.0/22.9
Director	26.2/49.1	13.6/ 8.6	25.0/50.0	33.3/18.8
Manager	0.0/ 4.7	22.7/29.0	25.0/13.0	13.3/40.0
Supervisor	0.0/ 0.0	0.0/ 5.4	0.0/ 1.9	0.0/ 2.1
Other	0.0/ 2.2	9.1/11.8	0.0/ 3.7	6.7/ 6.3

The previous functional areas of the senior logistics executives were also compared. Table 6-4 provides comparisons of previous assignments for leading edge and norm respondents. As indicated earlier, leading edge wholesalers often select logistics executives who have previously served in distribution/logistics, operations, or sales/marketing. Drawing from such a wide variety of functional areas does not indicate a single or best career path that will give an would-be logistics executive advantage. Rather, career pathing seems to be individualized. However, it is clear that reaching a high level position such as director or manager within a logistics department offers no assurance that one will ultimately get the logistics officer position.

Leading edge manufacturers and retailers report a pattern of choosing senior logistics executives from distribution and operations backgrounds. Senior logistics executives at leading edge wholesalers are most often selected from the areas of distribution, operations and sales/marketing. The most common

TABLE 6-4
PREVIOUS ASSIGNMENT OF SENIOR LOGISTICS
EXECUTIVES BY BUSINESS TYPE AND CAI GROUP

Percent

Area	Manufacturer L.E./Norm	Wholesaler L.E./Norm	Retailer L.E./Norm	Hybrid L.E./Norm
Administration	0.0/ 0.0	4.6/ 9.9	0.0/ 9.3	13.3/10.4
CEO/COO	1.7/ 1.7	0.0/ 3.3	0.0/ 0.0	0.0/ 2.1
Data Processing	0.0/ 0.0	0.0/ 0.0	6.3/ 1.9	0.0/ 6.3
Distribution	41.7/40.8	18.2/14.3	25.0/35.2	26.7/14.6
Merchandising	0.0/ 0.0	4.6/ 2.2	6.3/ 0.0	6.7/ 2.1
Operations	11.7/12.9	18.2/24.2	37.5/13.0	6.7/18.8
Purchasing/ Materials Management	11.7/ 5.6	9.1/ 5.5	0.0/ 0.0	0.0/16.7
Sales/Marketing	0.0/ 0.0	18.2/13.2	6.3/ 5.6	20.0/ 4.2
Traffic/ Transportation	5.0/ 6.4	4.6/ 5.5	0.0/ 9.3	0.0/ 2.1
Warehousing	0.0/ 0.9	4.6/ 9.9	0.0/ 7.4	6.7 /2.1
Other	28.3/31.8	18.2/12.1	18.8/18.5	20.0/20.8

career path for leading edge hybrid executives is via distribution and sales/marketing positions. For all categories, few leading edge senior logistics executives were promoted directly from traffic/transportation, warehousing, data processing, merchandising and purchasing/materials management. This reinforces the hypothesis that integrated management experience is desirable in preparation for top-level positions.

REPORTING RELATIONSHIPS

The level of direct reporting relationships provides an indication of the voice logistics has in overall firm decisions. Direct access to higher level or inner circle firm officials gives the logistics executive an opportunity to offer input and be involved in corporate level decisions. As expected, based upon the earlier presentation concerning senior logistics executive levels, many have direct linkages with top decision makers. Direct access to top level officials is especially prevalent among wholesaler, retailer and hybrid senior logistics executives. As illustrated in Figure 6-2 more than one-half of these executives report directly to the Chief Executive Officer or President. This compares to approximately one-quarter of the senior logistics executives in manufacturing firms. The higher accessibility to

FIGURE 6-2
SENIOR LOGISTICS EXECUTIVE REPORTS
BY BUSINESS TYPE

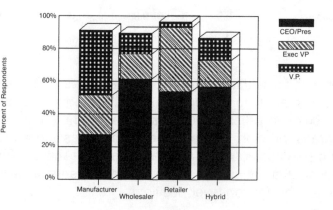

top level corporate executives enjoyed by wholesaler, retailer and hybrid logistics executives provides an opportunity to coordinate logistics with business unit strategy. It also serves to secure increased resource commitment and support for logistical operations.

LEADING EDGE BENCHMARKING - REPORTING RELATIONSHIPS

Senior logistics executives at leading edge firms are more likely to report to higher level executives of the organization than are their norm counterparts. Table 6-5 provides direct comparison leading edge and norm reporting relationships by business type.

For leading edge wholesalers and retailers, approximately 90 percent of the senior logistics executives report either directly to the President or to an Executive Vice President. In manufacturing and hybrid firms, 75 percent of the senior logistics executives report to the President or Executive Vice President.

TABLE 6-5
LEVEL OF THE EXECUTIVE TO WHOM SENIOR
LOGISTICS EXECUTIVE REPORTS BY
BUSINESS TYPE AND CAI GROUP

	Percent			
Reports to:	Manufacturer L.E./Norm	Wholesaler L.E./Norm	Retailer L.E./Norm	Hybrid L.E./Norm
Chairman	0.0/ 0.0	4.8/13.5	0.0/ 7.1	20.0/12.2
President	39.7/24.5	61.9/51.0	50.0/51.8	60.0/40.8
Executive Vice President	27.0/24.5	23.8/12.5	43.8/25.0	13.3/ 8.2
Senior Vice President	0.0/ 0.0	0.0/ 3.1	0.0/14.3	6.7/10.2
Vice President	31.8/41.9	9.5/10.4	0.0/ 1.8	0.0/12.2
Director	1.6/ 4.7	0.0/ 2.1	0.0/ 0.0	0.0/ 4.1
Manager	0.0/ 3.2	0.0/ 1.0	0.0/ 0.0	0.0/ 2.0
Supervisor	0.0/ 0.0	0.0/ 0.0	0.0/ 0.0	0.0/ 2.0
Other	0.0/ 1.2	0.0/ 6.3	6.3/ 0.0	0.0/ 8.2

SUMMARY

A key factor related to the achievement of high performance logistics is the organizational positioning of the senior logistics executives. In leading edge firms, logistical executives are typically placed within the organization at sufficiently high levels to directly interface with very top management. Thus, they are afforded the opportunity to participate in strategic decisions.

Senior logistics executives of wholesaler, retailer and hybrid firms generally hold higher organizational positions than do manufacturing logistics executives. Over 90 percent of leading edge wholesalers, retailers and hybrids' senior logistics executive report directly to the Chairman, President or Executive Vice President.

The senior logistics executives at all types of firms have, on average, been in their current positions a relatively short time. These executives are seasoned managers who typically have previously held high-level positions. Approximately one half of the leading edge senior logistics executives had previously been Vice Presidents or higher. Although distribution/logistics is a common career path for senior logistics executives, a majority of such executives have had senior level experience in some other broad based area.

The career pathing data fully supports the conclusion that logistics executives are typically senior managers. Looking at logistics from the career perspective provides insights to more fully understand the generalizations concerning structure, strategy and behavior presented earlier.

PART III

Service Providers
The Connecting Link

STATEMENT ON SERVICE PROVIDERS

An important part of the overall research was a series of thirty-eight interviews conducted with executives for firms who provide logistics services to manufacturers, wholesalers, retailers and hybrids. The providers of logistical services function in a unique market in that many of their customers have traditionally performed all or the lion's share of their own service requirements using internal or private transportation and warehousing. A major trend during the past decade has been the outsourcing of requirements to be performed by specialized service providers. The traditional providers of logistics services have been transportation and warehouse firms. In today's logistics environment, these traditional services are being augmented with a wide variety of tailored value-added services. Just as found with shippers, selected service companies appear to be way ahead of competition in terms of the quality and range of services provided.

Part III is somewhat different in content from the proceeding chapters. In this part, interview data is weaved into a profile of where the logistics service industry is and where it appears to be headed. Chapter Seven provides an overview of basic logistics services. Emphasis is placed on the new breed service provider and a statistical analysis of the way users select and evaluate their suppliers. Chapter Eight takes a careful look at the near phenomenal growth of strategic alliances between users and providers of logistical services. This chapter offers a classification of various types of logistical alliances and examines the essential characteristics that make them work. The last chapter of Part III is devoted to a closer look at tailored services. While all services provided by a service firm are value-added, they are grouped into two categories. The traditional services, such as timely transportation and safe warehousing, are referred to as basic services. The new services, such as the warehouse packaging or the construction of point of sale displays, are referred to as tailored services. Because value-added tailored services appear to be growing at an exponential rate, it is important to examine the perceptions of industry participants regarding this trend.

Part III brings a change of pace in that tables and charts of the statistical research are supplemented with examples, experiences and opinions expressed by industry leaders. From the overall content, two generalizations emerge:

* Many service providers are providing essential basic and tailored services that users would have great difficulty duplicating in-house. As such, providers of value-added services are becoming increasingly integrated and essential to the North American logistics process.

* *Significant differences exist in the quality and level of performance among the service providers. Just as leading edge firms exist in the shipper community, excellent suppliers also exist. Some service firms are head and shoulders above the competition. Ample evidence exists to conclude that leading edge shipping firms and superior service suppliers find each other and forge strategic alliances. These high performers are joining forces in the channel of distribution.*

192

Restructuring of North American Logistics Service
Outsourcing Expectations
Leading Edge Analysis - Outsourcing Expectations
Factors Influencing the Outsourcing Decision
Leading Edge Analysis - Outsourcing Influence
Factors Used to Evaluate Suppliers
Leading Edge Analysis - Evaluation Factors
New Breed Service Providers
Relational
Responsive
Reliable
Summary

Chapter Seven

BASIC LOGISTICS SERVICES

The logistics service provider industry has changed dramatically over the past decade. New, broader-based service firms have emerged as a result of regulatory policy and information/communication technology. Potential users have become more receptive to outsourcing logistical requirements. The old highly regulated, traditional and predictable group of service providers has been overshadowed by a new breed who are characterized by an innovative customer orientation. These new breed service providers are not constrained by old approaches or conventional business practices. They actively search for new and better solutions to logistical requirements and work closely with customers to provide tailored services. This chapter reviews the way users select and evaluate basic service providers. The procurement of external services is viewed from the perspective of outsourcing expectations, factors influencing outsourcing decisions and evaluation criteria. Consistent with Parts I and II, comparative findings are presented for leading edge and norm respondents. The chapter concludes with a summary profile of the new breed service provider.

RESTRUCTURING OF
NORTH AMERICAN LOGISTICS SERVICE

During the 1980's, the pendulum began to rapidly swing toward less regulation. The 1980 passage of the Motor Carrier Regulatory Reform and Modernization Act and the Staggers Rail Act initiated broad reduction in the federal regulation process. While selected states remain highly regulated, the majority have undergone significant reform.

Deregulation has created significant change in transportation. The name of the game in trucking has been survival of the fittest. Only 10 out of the top 50 United States common motor carriers in 1979 are still significant factors in the industry ten years later. The structure of trucking changed radically. For example, common carriers, who used to command a significant share of truckload traffic, are for all practical purposes out of the market. They have been replaced by a new breed of long haul trucker so effective and efficient that private truck expansion has virtually stopped. The turmoil in the trucking industry is further illustrated by widespread discounting. In selected markets, LTL carriers are discounting 50 to 60 percent off published prices. Despite the degree of competitive interplay, the key performers in the trucking industry are profitable and exhibit impressive growth.

Since the mid-1970's, the rail services of the United States have become increasingly focused. Because of aggressive truck competition, boxcar traffic has virtually disappeared. In most categories of traffic, except coal and automobiles, rail tonnage has declined. While intermodal rail continues to have significant tonnage, equipment is becoming increasingly obsolete. The bright stars on the rail horizon are the long range potential of double stacked containers and the legality of multimodal ownership. Interstate Commerce Commission Rulings and affirmative court review have broken down the traditional single owner-single mode restriction. Today multimodal ownership is permissible. For all practical purposes, that means that railroads can own other modes. While it is legal for a truck firm to start or purchase a railroad, significant rail acquisitions by motor carriers remain remote.

The balance of the transportation infrastructure -- air, water and pipeline -- has experienced significant change. Of particular interest has been the rapid growth and expansion of package services and specialized distribution carriers. The change of the 1980's has extended to service organizations such as brokers, forwarders and agents. While starting later than in the United States, similar deregulatory change is now spreading across Canada.

The nature of public warehousing has also changed during the past decade. The industry structure is shifting from small owner operated to large scale professionally managed firms. The nature of services is shifting toward highly specialized contract arrangements offered on a tailored basis.

Perhaps the most significant dimension of change during the past decade has been growth in the variety of new logistics services. Some service firms literally are willing to provide any legal service desired by a potential buyer. This willingness to expand value-added services fits hand in glove with the desire among business firms to outsource more of their requirements. Most firms are reducing the number of suppliers in all areas of business in an effort to establish closer working arrangements with preferred vendors. The result is an increasing trend toward strategic alliances between shippers and service providers.

OUTSOURCING EXPECTATIONS

North American firms have increased their usage of outside logistical services during the l980's. Survey respondents were asked their perceptions concerning anticipated use of external services during the next five years. Their responses as well as a discussion of the factors influencing outsourcing decisions are presented in this section.

Data were collected concerning the anticipated usage of eight logistical services: (1) transportation; (2) warehousing; (3) order entry and processing; (4) inventory management; (5) freight audit and payment; (6) consolidators; (7) freight forwarders; and (8) fulfillment. Results are presented in Table 7-1.

All categories of respondents indicated the greatest anticipated future use of transportation services. They expect use of warehousing and freight audit/payment services to remain constant or to slightly decrease. More dramatic changes were reported concerning order entry/processing and inventory management services. Overall, respondents anticipate that future use of these two services will decrease.

Transportation and warehousing both involve considerable capital commitment. Many firms have well-established management practices which place emphasis upon taking advantage of available external services especially for peak or overflow demand situations. Outsourcing of these services results in maximum flexibility. Using a service provider a firm can gain almost immediate entry into new markets and offer tailored customer service. Transportation and warehousing present ideal outsourcing candidates because it is relatively easy to separate or partition specific requirements. For example, a portion of a firm's transportation requirements can be obtained externally while the balance is handled by internal private operations.

The use of external consolidators is anticipated to remain constant or to slightly decrease. This is somewhat in contradiction of the trend toward shorter order cycles and smaller shipments.

Respondents anticipate that firms will outsource fewer information-related services in the future. The anticipated use of order entry/processing and inventory management is down across all business types. The responses suggest that firms desire to increase control over information to maintain security of sensitive and proprietary data. Order cycle and inventory information are the lifeblood of logistics management. During interviews, logistical software vendors and systems users indicated they are increasingly purchasing application software to operate in-house hardware in an effort to manage information needs internally.

TABLE 7-1
ANTICIPATED USE OF OUTSIDE LOGISTICAL SERVICES
BY BUSINESS TYPE

Mean Response Ratings*

Outside Service	Manufacturer	Wholesaler	Retail	Hybrid
Transportation	3.27	3.02	3.36	3.13
Warehousing	2.87	2.39	2.70	2.58
Order Entry/Processing	1.77	1.52	1.95	1.90
Inventory Management	1.71	1.59	1.95	1.94
Freight Audit/Payment	2.76	2.31	2.85	2.51
Consolidators	2.71	2.43	3.07	2.42
International Freight Forwarders	3.07	2.54	3.07	2.86
Domestic Freight Forwarders	2.35	2.31	2.60	2.26
Order Fulfillment & Support	2.10	1.70	2.03	2.08

* Scale: 1 = will not use outside logistical services
2 = will use less than current levels
3 = usage will remain constant
4 = will use more outside logistical services
5 = will use many more outside logistical services

Manufacturer's responses were from Phase II.

Freight audit and payment are different from the two operational information-related services in that they represent after the fact processing. In contrast, order entry/processing and inventory management information are integral to day-to-day operations. Respondents anticipate a higher level of future purchasing of freight audit/payment services than order entry/ processing and inventory management information.

Respondents indicated likely increases in future use of international freight forwarders and decreased use of domestic freight forwarders. This is reflective of a general trend toward globalization of business operations and expansion of international trade. International freight forwarders facilitate access to foreign markets.

Survey respondents anticipate a decrease in the use of order fulfillment and support services. In contrast, during interviews, users of fulfillment services expressed strong opinions that they would increase future use of such specialized firms. This contradiction is indicative of industry specific usage patterns. Certain industries have been leaders in the development and heavy use of tailored fulfillment services. For example, fulfillment firms are deeply involved in industries which handle relatively high-cost items, such as pharmaceuticals and beauty aids, where typical shipments involve split cases.

In summary, transportation and warehousing requirements will be outsourced more in the future than information related services. Security concerns and a need for close control, as well as the general availability of lower cost computing, have encouraged firms to plan in-house services. Expanded service options which offer increased flexibility and capability have resulted in a favorable attitude toward the external purchase of transportation and warehousing services. Outsourcing of these basic services and a variety of tailored services are anticipated to keep pace with the overall expansion in the economy. Therefore, the provision of transportation, warehousing and tailored services is perceived by users to represent a growth opportunity.

LEADING EDGE ANALYSIS - OUTSOURCING EXPECTATIONS

Comparison of leading edge to norm firms revealed consistent anticipated use patterns. Overall, leading edge firms plan to utilize outsourced logistical services to a somewhat greater extent than norm firms. Comparisons are presented in Table 7-2.

Leading edge firms anticipate greater use of external transportation and warehousing services and reduced use of order entry/processing, inventory management and freight audit and payment services. The anticipated use of outside transportation services is similar among leading edge and norm firms across business types. Leading edge manufacturing firms are significantly more likely to use outside warehousing services than norm firms. Anticipated use of outside warehousing by the other three channel members is similar for leading edge and norm firms.

For all business types, leading edge firms indicated they would use fewer outside order entry/processing services than norm firms. The intensity of this trend is highlighted by leading edge manufacturers who are considerably less likely to use outside order entry/processing services than norm manufacturers.

Use of outside vendors for inventory management services is anticipated to decrease for all business types. Overall freight audit and payment services is expected to slightly decline. The strongest anticipated use of freight audit and payment services was indicated by manufacturers and retailers. Leading edge retailers anticipated increased use of these services.

Leading edge firms anticipate greater use of external consolidators than norm firms. Leading edge retailers anticipate significantly greater use of consolidators to increase efficiencies and service benefits.

TABLE 7-2
AVERAGE ANTICIPATED USE OF
OUTSIDE LOGISTICAL SERVICES
BY BUSINESS TYPE AND CAI GROUP

Mean Response Ratings*

Outside Service	Manufacturer L.E./Norm	Wholesaler L.E./Norm	Retail L.E./Norm	Hybrid L.E./Norm
Transportation	3.36/3.24	3.18/2.98	3.25/3.43	3.07/3.10
Warehousing	3.20^B/2.73	2.40/2.42	2.69/2.62	2.73/2.52
Order Entry/Processing	1.53/1.91	1.37/1.51	1.86/1.98	1.43^C/2.09
Inventory Management	1.79/1.76	1.65/1.58	1.93/1.92	1.71/2.07
Freight Audit/Payment	2.80/2.83	2.24/2.34	3.06/2.72	2.61/2.58
Consolidators	3.00/2.71	2.73/2.36	3.67^A/2.84	2.64/2.36
International Freight Forwarders	3.13/3.06	2.17/2.59	3.27/2.98	3.55^B/2.71
Domestic Freight Forwarders	2.25/2.42	2.19/2.23	2.75/2.46	2.00/2.29
Order Fulfillment & Support	2.05/2.44	1.85/1.65	2.00/2.11	1.71/2.29

* Scale: 1 = will not use outside logistical services
2 = will use less than current levels
3 = usage will remain constant
4 = will use more outside logistical services
5 = will use many more outside logistical services

A, B, C - Significantly different from the norm at 0.01, 0.05, and 0.10 respectively.

Leading edge hybrids are significantly more likely to use international freight forwarders than norm hybrids. Leading edge manufacturers and retailers indicated greater use of the international freight forwarding services than their norm counterparts. Generally, leading edge firms anticipate greater use of international freight forwarders. One exception was noted. Leading edge wholesalers reported they will utilize international freight forwarders to a lesser extent than norm wholesalers. Use of domestic freight forwarders is expected to decrease for both leading edge and norm firms across all business types.

Order fulfillment and support services are also characterized by low levels of anticipated future use across business types and CAI groups. As noted earlier, this may be a reflection of the relative newness and specialized nature of fulfillment services. Many firms provide such service, but do not refer to it as fulfillment. Another possible explanation for the low levels of anticipated use may be the concentration of fulfillment services within relatively few industries. While the overall anticipated average is low, use may increase in selected industry segments.

In summary, with few exceptions, anticipated use of outsourced services is not remarkably different between leading edge firms and their norm counterparts. It appears that the growth in future use of basic transportation and warehouse services will keep pace or slightly exceed overall industrial expansion. The outlook for other services is less optimistic. It appears the greatest losers among service providers will in the area of operational information and communication services.

FACTORS INFLUENCING
THE OUTSOURCING DECISION

In addition to information regarding anticipated use levels, respondents were asked to identify the relative importance of external factors influencing their logistics service purchase decision. The results are presented in this section.

In the Phase I manufacturing survey, respondents were provided with a choice of six influential factors: (1) deregulation; (2) services available; (3) quality of service; (4) availability of data processing/communication services; (5) vendor management quality; and (6) customer orientation. They were asked to indicate the influence of each factor in outsourcing decisions. The Phase II questionnaire sent to retailers/wholesalers/hybrids contained a modified list of six factors. Deregulation was dropped because of its lack of reported importance in Phase I and vendor reputation was added. Results are presented in Table 7-3.

TABLE 7-3
FACTORS INFLUENCING OUTSOURCING DECISIONS
BY BUSINESS TYPE

Factor	Manufacturer	Wholesaler	Retail	Hybrid
	Mean Response Rating*			
Deregulation	2.64	--	--	--
Services Available	3.23	3.94	4.06	3.87
Service Quality	3.57	4.33	4.45	4.19
Data Processing/ Communications	2.87	3.06	3.12	3.12
Management Quality	3.14	3.75	3.76	3.57
Customer Orientation	3.13	3.83	3.89	3.85
Vendor Reputation	--	4.08	3.99	4.10

* Manufacturer ratings on a 4-point scale:
 1 = not important and 4 = very important

Wholesaler/Retailer/Hybrid ratings on a 5-point scale:
1 = never and 5 = always influences outsourcing decisions

Respondents across all business types rated quality of service as the most important factor influencing outsourcing decisions. Range of services available, vendor reputation, vendor management quality and customer orientation all were ranked as important. Evaluation of vendors involves more than evaluating the basic service. The service package, the services offered and the interaction between buyer and seller are extremely important. These factors reflect the trend toward increased involvement in logistics strategic alliances. Mutual trust and commitment to the business relationship are important features of an alliance. Availability of data processing/communication services was rated least important in the outsourcing decision. This should not be interpreted as meaning that it is not important, but rather that the other factors are more important. Deregulation, which was included only on the manufacturing survey, was rated least important. This is almost certainly a function of the time elapsed since the major transportation deregulatory activity of 1980.

The overall response makes it clear that the quality of the relationship is a prime consideration in the selection of outside service providers. The quality package starts with the basic service and extends to all aspects of the service relationship. In particular, service provider management quality is a significant factor when seeking long-term arrangements.

LEADING EDGE ANALYSIS - OUTSOURCING INFLUENCE

Table 7-4 presents an analysis of responses by business type and CAI group. In most situations, leading edge firms rated the importance higher than norm firms. However, in only one instance -- wholesalers with respect to data processing/communications -- was there a statistically significant difference in mean scores. While leading edge firms place more emphasis on quality, it is not significantly higher or remarkably different than other firms.

FACTORS USED TO EVALUATE SUPPLIERS

Respondents were asked to indicate what criteria they used to evaluate service vendors. After the initial decision is made to outsource a specific logistics service, individual vendors must be selected. Respondents were asked to rate the relative importance of six vendor selection factors: (1) customer support; (2) being easy to work with; (3) good communication; (4) early notification of disruptions; (5) flexibility; and (6) willingness to customize services. Overall mean responses for whole-salers, retailers and hybrids are presented in Table 7-5. These data were only collected in the Phase II survey and, therefore, comparative data are not available for manufacturers.

TABLE 7-4
FACTORS INFLUENCING OUTSOURCING DECISIONS
BY BUSINESS TYPE AND CAI GROUP

Mean Response Rating*

Factor	Manufacturer L.E./Norm	Wholesaler L.E./Norm	Retailer L.E./Norm	Hybrid L.E./Norm
Deregulation	2.70/2.62	--/--	--/--	--/--
Services Available	3.39/3.22	4.05/3.87	4.27/4.04	3.62/3.87
Quality of Service	3.72/3.56	4.33/4.32	4.67/4.41	4.13/4.19
Data Processing/ Communications	3.12/2.87	3.52^B/2.97	3.33/3.02	3.07/3.29
Management Quality	3.38/3.14	3.81/3.73	3.80/3.65	3.67/3.58
Customer Attitudes	3.17/3.16	3.75/3.90	4.20/3.76	3.67/3.88
Vendor Reputation	--/--	4.05/4.07	4.27/3.89	3.93/4.16

* Manufacturer (Phase I) ratings on a 4-point scale:
  1 = not important and 4 = very important

Wholesaler/Retailer/Hybrid ratings on a 5-point scale:
1 = never and 5 = always influences outsourcing decision

B - Significantly different from the norm at 0.05.

Good communication was identified as the factor most often used to evaluate suppliers. This reflects the need for close buyer-seller information interchange in a successful, long-term relationship. Informative interchange is associated with ease of working with as two important factors in selecting a vendor. These two factors are reflective of a general responsiveness on the part of vendors. Responsive vendors focus their customer service in an effort to be easy to do business with and provide flexibility.

TABLE 7-5
FACTORS USED TO EVALUATE SUPPLIERS
BY BUSINESS TYPE

Mean Response Rating*

Factor	Wholesaler	Retailer	Hybrid
Customer Support	3.72	3.63	3.65
Easy to Work with	3.90	3.81	4.00
Good Communication	4.17	3.89	4.22
Early Notification of Disruptions	3.52	3.42	3.54
Flexibility	3.83	3.69	3.95
Willing to Customize Service	3.59	3.68	3.56

* Scale: 1 = never used
          5 = always used to evaluate.

LEADING EDGE ANALYSIS - EVALUATION FACTORS

Results of the data analysis according to business type and CAI group are presented in Table 7-6. Quality of communication remains a very critical factor when leading edge firms evaluate suppliers. Across business type and CAI group, good communications ranks very high. Across almost all factors, leading edge firms place greater emphasis on evaluative criteria than their norm counterparts. This is consistent with other findings that suggest leading edge firms take a more formalized approach to evaluating all aspects of logistical performance.

One result merits further discussion. Leading edge retailers were significantly more likely to use all of the factors than were norm firms. This was an unexpected finding which clearly indicates the importance that leading edge firms place on evaluation. This attention to detail is one of the factors that sets leading edge firms apart from the norm and provides the potential for overall improved performance.

In summary, leading edge firms are especially aware of the advantages inherent in outsourcing arrangements and are more likely to use outside services than norm firms. Participants in the interviews indicated that they believe the range and overall quality of logistics service offerings will continue to increase in the future. The following section presents a discussion of the range of services currently available.

TABLE 7-6
FACTORS USED TO EVALUATE SUPPLIERS
BY BUSINESS TYPE AND CAI GROUP

	Mean Response Rating*		
Factor	Wholesaler L.E./Norm	Retailer L.E./Norm	Hybrid L.E./Norm
Customer Support	4.10^C/3.68	4.28^A/3.47	3.79/3.63
Easy to Work with	4.00/3.88	4.33^A/3.66	4.07/3.90
Good Communication	4.23/4.28	4.27^B/3.74	4.33/4.15
Early Notification of Disruptions	3.59/3.57	3.93^B/3.20	3.50/3.58
Flexibility	3.82/3.89	4.33^B/3.56	4.07/3.88
Willing to Customize Service	3.86/3.59	4.06^B/3.48	3.58/3.54

* Scale: 1 = never used
5 = always used

A, B, C - Significantly different from the norm at 0.01, 0.05, and 0.10 respectively.

NEW BREED SERVICE PROVIDERS

The new breed service provider is critical to the performance of logistics in North America. The phenomenal growth in the number of these service providers reflects the ever increasing awareness of their importance in logistics. As illustrated throughout Parts I and II, reliable high quality handling and product delivery offer a way to gain competitive advantage. In a business environment where products can be duplicated within a matter of days and selling prices can be matched or undercut immediately, value-added logistics service can be used strategically to gain competitive advantage and achieve preferred supplier status.

During interviews with thirty-eight key service provider executives, a profile emerged which describes today's aggressive logistics service providers. The key characteristics of these new breed leaders can be summarized in three words: relational, responsive and reliable.

RELATIONAL

New breed service providers are interested in building and maintaining long-term interactive relations. A wide variety of different types of strategic alliances between users and providers of services is becoming commonplace. The nature of services and the difficulty in specifying exact customer need creates an environment conducive to close working arrangements. Historically, the purchase process has been adversarial in that each party attempted to maximize leverage. The newer alliance type buyer-seller relationship is structured on a win/win incentive basis. By modifying operations, each party seeks to improve service and profitability for all organizations involved. These synergistic relationships are characterized by mutual trust, open communication and senior management commitment.

The trend toward the establishment of alliances has resulted in closer relationships and a reduction in the number of service providers used by a typical shipper. For example, rather than using 10 or 15 different carriers, the trend is to develop close working relations with 3 or 4 carriers. These chosen carriers achieve preferred vendor status contingent upon providing responsive and reliable service delivery.

The one thing that really characterizes this new breed of service provider is their willingness to work with customers.

They develop individualized, flexible services and tend to be very innovative. Information from the interviews suggests firms are likely to outsource to a greater extent in the future in order to take advance of these innovative specialists.

RESPONSIVE

During interviews with users and providers of services, the word responsive was used repeatedly. When shipper executives were asked what sets the best vendors apart from the field, the most common answer was responsiveness. Responsive vendors identify the service requirements of potential customers and create solutions. The key to leading edge service is as simple as that. Or, it may be a more accurate assessment to say as difficult as that.

Leading edge logistics service providers have both the capability and the willingness to satisfy customer requirements. They focus capabilities on specific needs. A great deal of their success can be attributed to outstanding communication. They work closely with customers to gain insight into how to modify basic offerings. Numerous examples of how basic services are being modified to meet customer requirements were cited by users and providers of services. One leading public warehouse firm worked with a major off-shore manufacturer during the introduction of a product line into the United States. The warehouse firm was so successful in providing logistical support that the manufacturer decided to cancel plans to establish private distribution. In other situations, for hire warehouse operations expanded into services to satisfy new customer requirements. A feature of today's logistical practice is that customers are typically ordering more frequently and in smaller quantities per shipment. Pick and repack as well as split case shipments have become more commonplace and currently account for significant public warehouse volume.

Public warehouses today are offering non-traditional or tailored value-added services. Some of the non-traditional services offered by firms interviewed include: order entry and processing, traffic, forward buy services, importing, customized palletizing, display development, bottling, real estate leasing, packaging, customized labeling and software development and maintenance. Such services are discussed and illustrated in Chapter Nine.

An important distribution function that is often overlooked, but vital to logistical effectiveness, is reverse logistics. Handling returns and recalled merchandise is typically difficult for manufacturers whose logistics systems are designed to efficiently move merchandise forward in the channel of distribution. Public warehouses have discovered that reverse logistics can represent a profitable service. One major manufacturer of small appliances has all of its returns consolidated by a public warehouse. The returned goods are reworked or disposed of at the warehouse with only selected high value items being sent back to the manufacturer.

RELIABLE

The new breed of logistics service provider goes far beyond the notion that they need only be *fit, willing and able* to perform their basic duties. These service firms realize that customers place a premium upon reliable service. They explicitly state the services they intend to provide and are committed to their performance. In the case of carriers, delivery standards are spelled out and failure to perform typically results in some form of penalty. A key characteristic of logistical alliances is that service providers typically accept risk and share in the benefits of success. It is not necessary to say a great deal more about need for absolute reliability. Reliability in a service business equates to quality. It is fundamental to the service provision process.

SUMMARY

This chapter has concentrated on logistics service providers. While basic logistics services such as transportation and warehousing have not changed, the manner in which they are performed has changed significantly in recent years and will continue to change.

Outsourcing, or the external purchase of logistics services, has become more commonplace and this trend is expected to remain strong. Certain services, namely transportation and warehousing, will be used to a greater extent than other types of logistics services. This is due in large part to the capital commitment involved in providing such services internally and also because these services can be easily partitioned. For example, a portion of a firm's warehousing can be purchased externally while still performing the balance in-house. Outsourced information-related services are likely to experience less growth by comparison. Security concerns as well as the need for integrated information management are influential in the decision to reduce the degree to which such services are outsourced.

Buyers and sellers of logistics services will continue to enter into long-term partnership-type relationships in the future. Emphasis will continue to be placed upon quality of service and closer working relationships to ensure performance. These trends are discussed in greater detail in Chapter Eight. Vendors who are responsive to customer needs and reliable will continue to emerge as leading edge service providers.

212

Chapter Eight

STRATEGIC ALLIANCES

As awareness of the potential of integrated logistics spread throughout North American business, the incidence of outsourcing logistical service requirements similarly grew. Many of the basic reasons that outsourcing has increased were discussed in Chapter One. This increased incidence of outsourcing has led to the emergence of strategic logistics alliances. A strategic alliance is *a business relationship in which two or more independent organizations decide to work closely together to achieve specific objectives*.

During the course of conducting 100 interviews for this research, numerous strategic alliances were discussed by both shippers and service providers. Most such alliances involved the expansion of traditional or basic for-hire services to encompass a broader array of tailored activities. This chapter directs attention to the nature of strategic logistics alliances and elaborates on what they are and why they are becoming more popular.

Chapter Nine provides a more detailed examination of tailored value-added services provided in strategic arrangements.

THE NATURE OF STRATEGIC ALLIANCES

The essence of a strategic alliance is that it constitutes a cooperative relationship. Such alliances may be directly contrasted to the typical transaction wherein parties are cast in an adversarial setting. When parties are buying and selling a service or product, each seeks to leverage its power at the direct expense of the other. Because alliances are cooperative relationships, they are characterized by participating organizations seeking to establish jointly rewarding relationships. The atmosphere of an alliance should be one of mutual trust. The commitment of the parties involved in an alliance ideally involves the sharing of risk and reward in a joint effort to create synergy.

The following are examples of strategic alliances that were discussed during interviews:

- A manufacturer and a motor carrier created a unique working relationship in an effort to increase joint productivity. The manufacturer agreed to perform several activities that had traditionally been the motor carrier's responsibility. Once the carrier delivered trailers to the manufacturer's holding lot, the manufacturer agreed to position the trailers at docks and load them by geographical area. Freight was sorted and segregated by destination sequence during trailer loading. To complete the dispatch process, the manufacturer electronically produced all shipment related paperwork. This absorption by the manufacturer of traditional carrier responsibility offered unprecedented flexibility for the carrier. Power units could be dispatched to initiate over-the-road movement direct from origin to in-route break bulk terminals. Shipments were scheduled to depart at off peak traffic periods, thereby eliminating traffic congestion and dramatically improving over-the-road driver productivity. The result was a significant reduction in carrier cost, which was shared with the manufacturer in the form of dedicated equipment and lower rates.

- A motor carrier established a dedicated over-the-road service that brought production coordinated component parts into an assembly plant on a just-in-time basis. The purchase of special over-the-road equipment was justified on the basis of a long term commitment by the manufacturer to guarantee backhaul traffic for the carrier.

- A public warehouse and a food manufacturer developed a unique agreement to build, staff and operate a dedicated distribution warehouse. For the manufacturer, the agreement provided state-of-the-art materials handling technology and experience. The long-term relationship incorporated a novel way for both firms to share benefit and risk. Based on a negotiated formula, the manufacturer agreed to help cover fixed facility cost if and when warehouse utilization dropped below a specified threshold. In return, the public warehouse agreed to share productivity cost benefits when utilization achieved capacity-related economies of scale.

These examples illustrate typical logistics alliances. Virtually unheard of a decade ago, such agreements may represent the most fashionable as well as the most direct way to lower logistics operating cost. Even more important is the potential such alliances offer to dramatically improve the quality of customer service.

The typical logistical alliance is between a provider of customized service and one or more firms who are principally engaged in product marketing and manufacturing. In essence, the product marketer arranges for the logistics service company to provide selected services necessary to deliver product assortments to the right location in a timely manner.

At first glance, the practice of outsourcing transportation or warehousing requirements to a service specialist may not appear new or different from the provisions of basic services discussed in Chapter Seven. The unique feature of a logistics alliance is the innovative manner in which the provider and user of logistical services co-mingle their business structures and behaviors for their joint benefit. The typical logistics alliance is a long term arrangement in which involved parties perform their specialized roles in a highly integrated manner. When this orchestration results in competitive advantage for the product marketer, the logistics alliance becomes strategic.

The strategic alliance forms what, in effect, becomes a logistics superorganization. By common consent, the participants establish rules of conduct and specify risk and reward. Roles may be as limited as providing a single logistics function or as extensive as replacing an entire department or division. Within the superorganization, leaders exist. Leadership is typically provided by the party who has the greatest risk. This acknowledgement of disproportionate risk results in a well-defined alliance wherein members pursue common goals in a non-competitive manner.

In some situations, the arrangement is formalized by written contracts. In an impressive number of alliances, the agreement is informal. Many partners work out complex logistics relationships without the benefit of formal contracts. A distinguishing feature of a logistics alliance is that the range of services performed often exceeds traditional or normal practice. Often the arrangements incorporate agreements for the service provider to perform tailored value-added services.

During interviews, a wide range of working relationships were discussed. For purposes of presentation, strategic alliances are classified as partnership agreements, third party arrangements and integrated service agreements. These three categories of strategic alliances are differentiated by the degree of formalization and commitment. Each can be observed in today's logistical environment. Prior to reviewing differences, it is stressed that all three types of alliances are similar in that they are relational as opposed to transactional. They represent different types and degrees of relationship that firms can structure in the pursuit of synergy.

Figure 8-1 illustrates different relationships when a firm seeks to purchase all or part of its logistical services. The buyer/seller service relationship is positioned along a continuum.

FIGURE 8-1
BUYER/SELLER SERVICE RELATIONSHIP

To the extreme left, transactional service purchase arrangements are positioned as having low formalization and commitment. Movement to the right toward strategic alliances reflects increased formalization and commitment. Respondent and interview firms agreed that the procurement of logistical services is becoming increasingly relational and the trend is expected to intensify in the future. In this research, leading edge firms in particular anticipate that service arrangements will become more relational in the future.

PARTNERSHIP AGREEMENTS

The partnership agreement is the most informal type of a strategic alliance. In a partnership, firms acknowledge dependence but typically do not deal in formal or exclusive arrangements. For example, one manufacturer interviewed has cut down the number of outbound carriers to six from an original group of over fifty. The six carriers and the manufacturer are working together to develop a more productive product-customer delivery system. The arrangement includes several innovative features such as the use of a master manifest combining all products transported on a single document as a replacement for individual bills of lading. The tender of freight on a regular basis allows the surviving carriers to plan equipment and routes and to make standing appointments at customer delivery warehouses.

While the parties to a partnership clearly acknowledge dependence, they do not extensively modify their business structure or procedure to facilitate the partnership. Stated differently, the parties to a partnership agreement do whatever is necessary to facilitate the ease and synergy of providing basic services. They stop short of modifying or integrating their basic business systems to the point where separation would be difficult or costly. The fact that partnerships are relational but not fully integrated offers the attraction of joint benefit while retaining independence. For these reasons, the vast majority of logistical alliances are properly viewed as partnerships.

THIRD PARTY ARRANGEMENTS

A third party arrangement is more formalized and expected to last longer than the typical partnership agreement. Because of financial commitment on the part of both the user and the service provider, third party arrangements typically are specified in formal agreements. Two of the most prominent types of third party arrangements are between contract carriers or contract warehouse firms and shippers. These two basic services were discussed in Chapter Seven. When the basic services and related equipment or facilities are modified to meet a specific shipper's logistical requirements, they are classified as third party arrangements. Among many of the firms interviewed, such third party arrangements represent the fastest growing type of logistical service outsourcing.

One distribution service company described its typical comprehensive third party arrangement. The agreement covered statewide distribution of products from a public warehouse to the firm's retail stores. The service company contracted to deliver all required freight to each store on a daily basis for a single flat charge. For example, the charge per-store, per-day was a flat dollar amount, independent of products, weight or pieces delivered. The carrier was permitted to structure efficient LTL routes and combine other for-hire traffic as long as each store was serviced daily. The result was a revenue guarantee for the carrier. For the shipper, the benefit was a simple, reliable store door delivery program that involved no uncertainty regarding cost.

In another situation, a contract carrier worked out a unique arrangement combining two non-competing manufacturers to provide each state-of-technology in over-the-road equipment. Both shippers desired to maintain some private trucking but needed to obtain equipment capacity on short notice to handle business surges and special transportation requirements. The development of a third party arrangement provided the necessary flexibility and synergy to satisfy both shippers' requirements. The shippers enjoyed reliable service while the carrier was guaranteed equipment utilization. A special provision of the contract provided the carrier the right to recover a percentage of the cost of idle equipment from the two manufacturers.

The main benefit of a third party arrangement is that it offers the framework for a service provider and one or more shippers to formally modify their basic logistics practices in order to jointly achieve added benefits. Third party arrangements are typically exclusive. Interviewed shippers and service providers strongly feel that third party arrangements will grow in the future.

INTEGRATED SERVICE AGREEMENTS

The most formalized strategic alliance is a comprehensive or integrated service arrangement. A term often used to describe the provider of fully integrated services is a *logistics utility*. These special service organizations are willing to perform all or any part of logistical requirements, including transportation and warehousing, order fulfillment and even information management. In special situations, they have agreed to take ownership of selected inventory.

Where have these integrated service logistics providers come from? Several emerged from pre-existing service providers. Many truck, rail and warehousing companies have expanded their range of services as a way to expand their business. Others have come into existence as spinoffs from shipper organizations. These spinoffs are created when a shipper organization decides to market its logistical competency. A few firms with long standing reputations for distribution excellence have established internal logistics departments as profit centers with a mission to offer their expertise outside the company.

The integrated service provider seeks to offer part or all of a turnkey distribution system. Functions offered typically include transportation, warehousing, break bulk distribution, consolidation, packaging, light assembly for postponed manufacturing, price marking, sorting, inventory management, returned goods handling, order fulfillment, building point of sale displays and strategic distribution consultation.

The steel service center that functions in the distribution channel between steel mills and users is a prime example of an integrated service company. The centers receive sheet and roll steel which they cut, bend and shape to specific customer requirements. The typical center provides all logistical and customization activities necessary to satisfy customer requirements.

Most integrated service firms operate in a consultative style in the sense that they are problem solvers whose operations are customized to fit their clients' requirements. They offer a management perspective that positions logistical services as an integrated whole. They have staff and facilities geared exclusively to provide a lowest total cost system.

Several integrated service providers have developed services along specific product lines or for individual customers. One well known firm began operations as a packaging company following World War II. The firm now specializes in the distribution and installation of high-tech, high value products such as computers, telecommunications, measurement instrumentation and medical equipment. They offer a warehousing environment customized for these specific products and provide distribution for several firms worldwide. This service provider also offers tailored services such as product testing and modification to accommodate varied world standards.

Another firm that was spun out of a corporate logistics department specializes in serving retail businesses. Their expertise is in full service distribution of small packages to retail stores. This service provider functions as the entire distribution department for one southwestern retailer. When just starting up, the retailer desired to focus available resources on establishing stores in several highly competitive markets. Rather than attempt to develop both retail and physical distribution operations, they chose to outsource their logistical requirements. Orders created by the retail stores are transmitted via electronic data interchange directly to the integrated service firm which warehouses, provides consolidated delivery and supports emergency retail store replenishment on an overnight basis. The arrangement between these two firms specifies no volume commitment. The special service provider is paid according to items distributed and limited warehouse utilization. The service firm supports over 70 percent of the retailer's total inventory requirement under the integrated arrangement.

The overall participation of integrated service providers has thus far been relatively small in terms of the total quantity of goods moved in North America. There are only a handful of such firms operating on anything approaching a large scale. While the future appears to offer potential, service firms have not been willing to confront the risks associated with offering broad-based integrated services. The essential feature of integrated logistics is that it represents a comprehensive commitment to replace internal capability with external expertise. As such, it is the most extensive form of outsourcing. The concept of a logistics utility is not new. It has been discussed for several decades. Emerging technology makes such comprehensive relationships increasingly more feasible. However, for many logistics situations such arrangements remain impractical. Firms interviewed did not report extensive involvement in comprehensive logistics contracts, but they did feel that such arrangements will continue to develop in selected situations. Leading edge firms expressed a stronger belief in the eventual development of such comprehensive arrangements than did norm or emerging firms.

THE ESSENCE OF A STRATEGIC ALLIANCE

The different categories of strategic alliances reflect varied degrees of formalization and commitment. However, as noted earlier, the common feature across partnership agreements, third party arrangements and integrated service agreements is their relational nature. The essence of a logistical alliance is the service provider's agreement to assume risk in the logistics value-added process. They do not normally take risk with respect to inventory ownership. However, when involved in an alliance, service providers may become risk stakeholders at any point in the overall logistics value-added process. The stake occurs in the form of agreements to perform customized services in return for specified rewards. The rewards are often contingent upon performance. They may be supplemented by incentives based on the overall success of the product marketing effort. Likewise, failure to perform may result in reduced revenue and even consequential damages. For example, incentives may be paid for superior performance such as a higher than expected percentage on-time delivery. In contrast, penalties may be automatic when the service is not performed as agreed.

This feature of agreeing to reward and contingent penalty in advance of actual performance of a sequence of services is rare, but becoming more common. Becoming more common is the willingness of the involved parties to modify the range and scope of their basic business in order to jointly perform the value added process more effectively and efficiently.

CREATING A SUCCESSFUL
STRATEGIC LOGISTICS ALLIANCE

Assuming the potential benefit is judged worthwhile, what specific actions are necessary to establish and maintain a successful logistics alliance between a service provider and a product marketer? Based upon interviews with users and service providers, the following guidelines are offered.

CHANNEL PERSPECTIVE

To perform effectively in a logistics alliance, the parties must view their participation from the perspective of the overall purpose of the relationship rather than focusing on specific tasks or roles. This is not to suggest that a service provider need not pay careful attention to the basics or details of the assignment. Rather, the importance of seeing specific tasks or functions in terms of their contribution to the overall value-added process is essential. Retaining a big picture vision protects against the danger of becoming role myopic. Significant changes in practice leading to productivity improvements are best initiated from a global perspective. Understanding the total process offers a safeguard against "continuing to do something well that shouldn't be done at all."

The design of building trailers with soft fabric sides capable of being unloaded from several different locations, rather than only the back door, came from a carrier who understood how timely delivery could favorably impact overall manufacturing efficiency. The introduction of dedicated soft side trailer service allowed just-in-time delivery to stimulate material handling benefits. The soft side trailer could be unloaded from rail docks in close proximity to the point of product assembly, thereby implementing one-time, direct to application material handling. The capability to unload an assortment of products to support assembly from the same trailer introduced unexpected manufacturing economies. The end result was a *win*/*win* situation. The service provider was able to realize greater revenue and long term business guarantees to justify the procurement of specialized equipment. The manufacturer gained through productivity improvements over and above inventory reduction. Material handling cost and time were significantly reduced.

SELECTIVE MATCHING

Not all situations justify or are able to support the extensive commitments necessary to make a logistics alliance work. From a user's perspective, ideal situations are directly related to leverage. Thus, alliances should be concentrated on operating situations that are important to business results.

Because the core business of an enterprise is the typical focus of an alliance, all parties involved must be economically and managerially strong. An alliance is a long-term arrangement that will confront the ups and downs characteristic of most business activity. To maintain a strong alliance, the service provider must have staying power. Thus, equally important to the high side volume that causes a service alliance to flourish is the capability of the service provider to cope with down side business pressure. Several well established partnership arrangements incorporate mechanisms to jointly share the benefit and risk inherent in extraordinarily cyclical business variations.

INFORMATION SHARING

Information sharing is the glue that holds alliances together. This information ranges from strategic planning to operating detail. Joint performance toward shared goals requires open disclosure. Complete information exchange is essential to assure that operations of the user and service provider are synchronized.

Some service providers are establishing full disclosure information systems. Systems are available that provide real time tracking of shipments at case level or stock-keeping unit detail throughout the logistical process. In selected situations, the shippers can access service provider information systems to view in-transit shipment status in terms of projected and desired arrival time. Estimated time of arrival projections provide the basis for evaluating the cost/benefit of expediting shipment delivery. This type of positive shipment control allows a shipment to be upgraded to priority status while in-transit.

The information technology exists to create and control unique and far reaching service packages. Direct computer linkage of user and service providers is essential to fully exploit the power inherent in such technology. To make a logistics alliance work, all parties involved need to trust their operating partners. Such trust does not come easy to generations of managers who were schooled in the belief that information is power and should only be shared on a *need-to-know* basis. Overcoming information hoarding is a key step toward eliminating adversarial relationships.

ROLE SPECIFICATION

Similar to all team efforts, players in a logistics alliance have specified roles. These roles are typically identified and detailed during negotiations that establish the alliance. Performance to expectation requires that each participant have clear operating objectives. The involvement of multiple parties in any process creates the opportunity for details to be overlooked and for functions to be duplicated. The value-added logistics process occurs across a vast geographical playing field in what amounts to a twenty-four hour, seven day a week, fifty-two week a year engagement. No room exists for ambiguity regarding who is responsible for doing what during the value-added process.

One distinguishing feature of logistics service is its event orientation. Each event is unique and important. Average performance means little if anything. As a service provider involved in just-in-time support of manufacturing and assembly operations, the carrier may make all but one delivery during a year as agreed. One failure to deliver on time resulting in the abandonment of planned production or the forced shutdown of a major assembly facility will be significant. In the service business, the service provider is only as good as the most recent engagement.

GROUND RULES

To function effectively day in and day out, a logistics alliance requires clear and comprehensive ground rules. It is essential that a service provider fully understand and internalize or absorb the culture of the user's organization. This translates into the service provider understanding the culture that drives the product marketer's decision process. Cultural absorption becomes tricky when the service provider is simultaneously engaged in more than one strategic alliance. Most observers agree that it is next to impossible for the same people or organizational units to be simultaneously involved in strategic alliances with direct competitors. Even when service users are not direct competitors, providers must learn and acknowledge unique cultural differences between their individual clients.

The prevailing state in any logistical alliance is cooperation. Nevertheless, problems will develop and they need to be promptly resolved. Well established ground rules facilitate conflict resolution. A prime objective is to adjudicate inevitable conflict before it becomes dysfunctional to the goals of the logistics alliance. Pre-negotiated and comprehensive ground rules serve to insure the longevity of an alliance.

FREEDOM TO EXIT

The voluntary and cooperative nature of a typical logistical alliance makes it essential that all parties fully understand that even good relationships sometimes end. While one objective underlying formation of an alliance is to establish a long term and stable arrangement, from time to time one of the participants may desire change.

Because the power balance of the typical logistics alliance favors the user, termination can be a sensitive issue. Traditionally, carriers and other service providers have been at the mercy of service users. Generally, carrier services can be purchased on a trip-to-trip basis in the spot market and many warehouse agreements only involve a minimum 30 day commitment. Logistics alliances introduce longer term stability into such service relationships. This stability must be balanced against each party's freedom to exit if and when it is in the party's long term interest. Success will encourage continuation of the alliance. However, no exit barriers should prohibit termination of the arrangement.

Many logistic alliances discussed during interviews contain dissolution agreements. In situations where special purpose equipment or facilities are involved, there is often a pre-negotiated buy/sell agreement covering termination. This issue is delicate, but cannot be ignored. On the one hand, the relationship needs to be stabilized in order to meet expectations. On the other hand, the parties cannot negate their right of self determination.

TWO DEVELOPMENT STRATEGIES

Given the above general guidelines, the specifics of how to operationalize a strategic alliance still must be addressed. During the research interviews, two significantly different growth and development strategies were expressed. The first is called total conversion. The second is labeled bit-by-bit.

In the total conversion, the service provider and a prospective user negotiate a package plan that will either create or replace specific logistical requirements on a turnkey basis. One logistics provider that follows this comprehensive contract strategy uses a team of several professionals to study a prospective client's requirements. Based upon the analysis, a customized logistics solution is designed. The team negotiates performance standards that become part of the ultimate service contract. The general manager of one service company describes the logic of the team approach as: "the opportunity for those of us who perform value-added services to offer a total system representing maximum value to the customer." He also stated a preference for a total-service orientation for competitive reasons. It is simply extremely difficult for providers of single services to compete for a client's business.

The main difficulties of the total conversion approach are the political circumstances involved in replacing all or most of an entire department. A tactic used to overcome up-front resistance is to initially approach senior executives to gain their support on the basis of improved cost or service performance.

Another obstacle is to convince a potential customer that the services being offered cannot be performed better in-house. The specialized expertise and critical mass of the special service provider are difficult to duplicate. "Most firms can't match us for information systems," says one executive. This service provider uses a sophisticated, highly integrated software package to tie distribution services together. "It took us years and millions of dollars to create this software. We have it available and ready to install today. In-house groups can't start from scratch and duplicate this system without substantial expense and considerable time." In addition, specialized service providers often enjoy benefits of scale economies in operations that clients cannot realize. This gives an inherent cost advantage to a well-managed service provider.

A second major strategy used by service providers is the bit-by-bit approach. A major user of this strategy says simply: "It's easier to get your foot in the door one service at a time." Firms using the step at a time approach have created a modular service offering that can be disaggregated or unbundled. This allows the service provider to fit individual services into the existing conditions found at a client's business. When using the disaggregated product to open the door, the comprehensive service provider typically deals initially with only one distribution area. Decisions for a single area are typically made lower in the organization than those relating to a total system.

The problems in this evolutionary approach lie with the large number of competitors and the multiple competitive arenas in which the third party service provider must operate. Successful firms using the bit-by-bit strategy must have superior products and be extremely flexible.

SUMMARY

This chapter has presented a broad overview of relationships that are developing between users and providers of logistical services. The composite of interviews has resulted in a classification of service providers based upon the degree of formality and time duration of an arrangement. Beyond spot market purchases of services, a wide variety of strategic alliances were presented and illustrated. The most common arrangement is a logistics partnership. Most firms that are seeking to improve logistics performance participate in one or more partnerships. Third party arrangements represent a more formal relationship that typically involves co-mingling of the user and service provider's operations. Such third party arrangements are growing in popularity. The integrated service agreement is a comprehensive offering that seeks to establish client turnkey arrangements. While such integrated service agreements have intrinsic appeal, they are not widespread in today's practice of logistics.

The success of a strategic alliance, regardless of how formal or of its planned duration, will depend upon the vision of the executives involved in its establishment. Success, to some undetermined degree, will depend upon gaining a channel perspective, selecting the right participants, being willing to share information, assigning clearly specified roles, establishing ground rules and freedom to exit. The discussion concluded by presenting alternative development strategies for a service provider who seeks to move from a transactional toward a relational client arrangement.

Chapters Seven and Eight have from time to time referred to tailored value-added services. Chapter Nine is devoted to further discussion of the importance of the expanding number of tailored services being offered by logistical service providers.

232

Chapter Nine

TAILORED SERVICES

At various times the phrase *tailored value-added service* has been used to describe the extraordinary or special activities of logistics service providers. Service providers have always been an integral part of logistics. A characteristic of today's more progressive service providers is the willingness to expand the number and type of activities they perform for their clients. As one president of a progressive service company explained: "Our firm will perform any legal service for our clients providing we can make a profit doing it." While such a statement may be excessively accommodating, it conveys the spirit behind tailored services. Such value-added services are playing an increasingly important role in the logistical strategies of leading edge firms.

In this final chapter of Part III, tailored service practices are highlighted. First, attention is directed to defining the meaning of *tailored* as it is used in today's business world. Second, the basic economic principles that justify outsourcing of selected services are reviewed. The final part of this chapter contains numerous examples of tailored service arrangements being performed as an integral part of strategic logistic alliances. For purpose of this review, examples are grouped according to their motivating business objective.

TAILORED SERVICE - WHAT IS IT?

All services performed by a service provider are expected to be value-added. For example, when a common carrier transports a product from a manufacturer to a retailer when promised, an important value-added service has been performed. The carrier has transported the product to the correct location at the desired time. Thus, the product has been given both time and place value-added utilities.

All of the basic or traditional services provided by logistics service companies are essential -- so essential that their timely and economical accomplishment is expected and demanded. Unless basic services are properly performed, the opportunity does not exist to get involved in tailored situations. A carrier executive put the fundamental necessity of performing traditional services in the following perspective:

> "When our firm is selected as a primary carrier, the shipper assumes that we will provide timely, cost competitive service. They will measure our performance to assure we operate as promised. From that point forward, we begin to get involved in the really exciting and profitable extra services. These extra services are the cream of our operating ratios."

When the logistics professionals talk about tailored value-added services, they are referring to extra activities over and beyond the essential basics.

One example will illustrate the extensiveness of some tailored services. One warehouse operator agreed to repackage bubble gum and soccerballs into a combined promotional package. On the surface, the task sounds simple. However, consider the steps involved: (1) weigh and package three pounds of bubble gum from a bulk carton into a heat sealed tamper proof package; (2) inflate a soccerball; (3) place bubble gum bag into the soccerball box; (4) place soccerball on top of box; (5) shrink wrap ball and box; and (6) place six completed units into a master carton, label and seal. The end result was a customized point of sale promotional package that in reality represented a unique stock or inventory unit. From the vendor's perspective, the activity could be accomplished at lower cost by the warehouse firm. For the warehouse firm, doing the promotional packaging represented a source of significant revenue that was relatively risk free. Performing the tailored service helped the warehouse operator develop a closer working relationship with an important customer.

The tailored value-added services of concern in this chapter are extra and above basic service offerings. These extras have become a significant part of contemporary logistics practice. For service providers, such activities represent significant sources of revenue and profitability. For the user, having such services performed by an outside specialist offers flexibility and in many situations significantly lower cost. As a result of these joint benefits, the performance of tailored services is mushrooming throughout the logistics service industry. The customized performance of such services for users is one of the essential forces behind the rapid growth of strategic logistics alliances.

THE BASIC JUSTIFICATION
FOR OUTSOURCING TAILORED SERVICES

Numerous interviews confirm that strategic alliances are being solidified because of the performance of tailored value-added services. As the service provider and user develop complex working relationships, they are in fact integrating logistical operations. This integration serves to reinforce the basic business relationship. To a significant degree, arrangements to perform tailored services have been facilitated by rapid developments in information technology. Individuals interviewed expressed the opinion that the increased ability to maintain control was the primary reason for expanded outsourcing of key value-added processes.

The basic justifications for external procurement of tailored services are: (1) specialization; (2) risk reduction; and (3) creativity. Each is discussed and illustrated.

SPECIALIZATION

The basic economic justification for using a service provider is that it can perform a specific activity at a lower cost. Such cost advantage results from two sources: (1) lower overall cost structure; and (2) economy of scale.

Many service providers can perform tailored tasks at a lower cost because they are ideally positioned to utilize unskilled labor. For example, the performance of specialized packaging at a manufacturing plant typically involves labor that is highly qualified or even over-trained with respect to the required tasks. When the same service is provided by a service supplier, it is often possible to use part-time or casual labor. One warehouse firm interviewed has developed a division to perform special tailored services for clients. This division is located close to a high school which permits students to work part time as part of a trade skill program. The result is steady employment for the students and a dependable work force for the facilitating division of the warehouse company. This potential to use casual labor at entry level wages is one reason that a large number of tailored services are performed by service providers.

Specialization and economy of scale are the basic economic justifications for using outside service providers. Specialized service companies are able to generate high levels of expertise and low cost performance as a result of their critical mass and dedicated resources. One warehouse firm has several repack lines dedicated to building customized point of sale displays. They are knowledgeable regarding the most effective repack procedures and the use of specialized repackaging equipment. Their personnel have developed a wide variety of do's and don'ts when building special promotional displays. Other services offered by this warehouse include store delivery and in-store promotion detail. The executive interviewed made it very clear that not only do they retain their basic business as a result of this specialized competency, they in fact have expanded the tailored business because client firms wanted to be in a position to utilize the warehouse's extra value-added service support capabilities.

The experience and critical mass associated with the provision of tailored services result in expertise that is hard for the conventional firm to duplicate. Many executives simply do not want to bother with the necessary degree of detail and extreme flexibility required to perform tailored services. Thus, the opportunity exists for a basic service provider to build a specialized competency that generates revenue and profit.

RISK REDUCTION

The performance of tailored value added services can reduce risk in two ways. First, it permits many tailored activities to be ideally postponed with respect to when and where they are performed in the overall business process. Second, many tailored providers are willing to assume a share of the risk associated with providing special services.

The principle of postponement has been widely discussed for years. The essence of the principle is to delay selected activities, such as movement or final product modification, as long as possible in the transaction cycle. For example, if a firm can avoid painting a product until a customer's order is received, then it stands to reason that the probability of painting it the correct color is significantly increased. Service providers are making a substantial business out of performing all types of product modifications based upon unique customer requests.

An example will illustrate. A manufacturer in conjunction with a warehouse service provider is offering to place customized stock numbers and identification symbols on cartons and to arrange such cartons in pallet configuration as requested by customers. In fact, all of this specialized sorting, segregation and identification is performed at the warehouse after customer orders are received. As a consequence, the same basic inventory is being used to satisfy the specialized requirements of a number of different customers. Such customization is being provided as a tailored value-added service by the warehouse firm. Numerous other examples of time and form postponement are presented in the final section of the chapter. The key point is that the practice of customizing to order by service providers in the distribution channel reduces the risk of anticipatory commitment during manufacturing.

A second form of risk reduction results from the close working relationships that develop between product marketers and service providers. As two organizations begin to coordinate and mesh operations, the synergy amounts to risk insurance. As a result of specialized organizations each doing what they do best in a coordinated and focused manner, the chance of error is dramatically reduced. When the relationship involves performance guarantees, failure becomes a shared financial burden. While the typical relationship most often stops short of full consequential damages, firms involved in strategic alliances are committed to quality tailored services. It is often difficult to identify tailored logistical service providers because they operate at a near transparent level in the distribution chain. However, the service provider's employees are very often their client firm's sole contact with the operational side of the client customer's business. One interviewee described a situation in which the service provider's personnel perform in-store inventory and write replenishment orders. In this situation, risk is reduced by having the service provider managing order cycle performance from order entry to delivery. The idea is that two concerned parties working together to maintain customer relations are fundamentally better than each operating independently.

CREATIVITY

A final benefit of tailored service arrangements is the synergy resulting from joint concern regarding how to best perform a series of activities. No firm has a monopoly on creativity. When two or more firms jointly seek creative applications and innovations in a basic process, the chance for a significant productivity or market breakthrough is greatly increased. The unique advantage of relationships among a product manufacturer, a logistics service provider and a retail or wholesaler marketer is that each views the logistics value-added process from a radically different vantage point.

A key concern in negotiating any tailored value-added service is to determine where in the logistical system is the most beneficial place to perform it. While it is normally desirable to perform a tailored service close to the market, it is also necessary to retain economy of scale and maximum flexibility. Joint consideration by all interested parties can be expected to identify the full range of performance location options. Viewing the value-added process from the perspective of the overall distribution chain, including service providers, introduces the widest possible array of potential performance locations.

TYPICAL TAILORED VALUE-ADDED SERVICES

To conclude the discussion of tailored value-added services, a series of examples obtained during interviews is now presented. For ease of presentation, the examples are grouped according to the prime force motivating their development.

CUSTOMER BASED

In a general sense, all tailored services are customer motivated. However, some are specifically aimed at providing a service that directly facilitates or achieves end customer satisfaction.

For example, one public warehouse organization has set up an order entry service and arranges for consumer home delivery of disposable diapers for premature babies. Because of the comparatively low sales volume of such small diapers, they do not represent a profitable product for retailers to stock. However, since premature babies typically grow into normal size diaper users this market segment is significant to manufacturers. The home delivery system provides a unique value-added solution that meets the objectives of all parties.

Several warehouse managers interviewed discussed various forms of special pick-price-repack operations. In the typical situation, the manufacturer services a retail customer who desires to purchase in less than manufacturer's standard carton quantities. Providing this form of tailored service usually requires expanded warehouse layout and the addition of merchandise bins and conveyors to accommodate customized order selection. In performing tailored processing, several warehouses price and/or place retail point of sale identification on individual products during the repack operation. In one facility visited, merchandise was being selected, priced and packed in tote boxes, in store shelving sequence. Using public/contract warehouse operations allows such unique services to be performed locally to the specification of individual retailers.

Customer satisfaction is also the prime motivation behind warehouse or club store repacks. The concept of a club store is that consumers buy larger product quantities at a lower per unit price. While the end customer benefits from lower prices, they are required to purchase a larger quantity of each product. To facilitate distribution, the service provider opens manufacturer cases and shrink wraps individual products into three, six or whatever pack the warehouse club store desires to sell. Since the desired package quantity varies extensively by individual club stores, customized packaging can be most effectively performed in facilities that service specific retailers.

A final example of a customer driven tailored service is the retail store delivery and shelf management service provided by several fulfillment companies. A fulfillment company is a firm that processes customer orders for manufacturers. Some facilitators perform direct store delivery and provide detail personnel to keep retail store shelves fully stocked. These specialized value-added services are extensively used to logistically support new product introduction and high traffic seasonal sales support.

Customer based tailored services evolve because service companies are ideally positioned to accommodate local market requirements. They illustrate how a local flexible service provider can perform customized distribution at a cost difficult to duplicate by firms engaged in national distribution.

PROMOTION BASED

The customer-based special services illustrated above relate in part to unique or local promotional requirements. Other tailored services directly motivated by promotional considerations were identified during the interviews.

The most common promotional tailored service is the building of point-of-sale product display modules. These modules often contain as many as six different products mixed in a multiple tier display unit. The building of such units requires that product master cartons be unpacked and restocked in the desired promotional display pattern. The entire unit is typically shrink wrapped and is often delivered direct to retail stores. Development of such promotional modules facilitates retailer acceptance of special manufacturer deals by reducing the required store level labor.

A similar promotional service is the cutting of master cartons to form shelf ready tray packs for retail display. In some situations, the tailored service provider combines multiple tray packs to facilitate point of sale display. These units are typically configured to meet unique retailer specifications.

Another very common use of special service providers is to arrange for delivery of advertising and in store promotional material. This form of value-added service reduces the burden placed on a manufacturer's sales force to arrange for or to deliver promotional material.

Finally, a common form of a tailored service is the handling and shipment of premium and gift merchandise. A manufacturer offering gifts in return for proof of sale needs to arrange for merchandise redemption and distribution. A common practice is to use a service provider to fulfill these requirements.

The above examples illustrate tailored services designed to support promotional requirements in the distribution channel. Service providers can often provide the required support on a more flexible and lower cost basis than manufacturing, wholesale or retail organizations.

MANUFACTURING BASED

Another highly popular type of special tailored value-added services is those aimed at directly improving manufacturing efficiency. In general, this category is aimed at reducing the risk related to providing unique products while retaining the efficiency of long, high speed manufacturing runs.

One type of manufacturing based special service is finished product custom pack. While somewhat similar to club store bundling, custom product packaging postpones final grouping of individual products into master cartons until customer orders are received. One warehouse firm places a single size of a popular consumer dishwashing soap into as many as six different carton configurations, depending upon class of trade and promotional requirements. Postponement of master carton packing until time of customer order processing allows the manufacturer to produce a custom pack for each customer based upon order receipt. The result is a substantial reduction in forecasting and production scheduling complexity. Such postponement reduces error in packaging to a minimum while retaining maximum marketing flexibility. Another example of product packing is the custom assembly of surgical kits to the specifications of individual physicians. In both examples, manufacturing economy of scale is being retained while the unique requirements of individual market niches are being supported by tailored distribution services.

A similar manufacturing justified value-added service is the assembly of final product configurations at public warehouses. For example, one warehouse cuts and installs various lengths and sizes of hose to pumps. Another firm assembles imported sleds. Still another warehouse bottles water and drink mixes. These and numerous other types of assembly reflect a special category of tailored services wherein the warehouse is involved in final manufacturing.

One of the oldest forms of manufacturing postponement is the remote labeling of packages at warehouses. The **bright can** service is based on a manufacturing practice of packing standardized products without final consumer labeling. This strategy is particularly popular among manufacturers of private label products. Postponement of labeling permits a common inventory to be used to support several different customers.

A final series of manufacturing postponement examples involves the actual packaging of products into consumer retail sale units at warehouses. A number of executives interviewed provided warehouse repackaging illustrations. For example, one warehouse was packing bulk peat-moss into a variety of different consumer retail packages. Another facility was repacking cigarette packages into cartons and master packs. One warehouse reported a value-added service which repackages and relabels bulk chemicals. Another example was a public warehouse that assembled, labeled and packed molded plastic containers into cartons for delivery to a manufacturer's bottling facility.

All of the above examples of initial packaging, repacking, assembly or labeling represent value-added services aimed at risk reduction. While postponement practices are typically more expensive than if they were incorporated as part of a high speed manufacturing process, they reduce anticipatory risk. In other words, products are customized to fill specific customer orders rather than being manufactured in differentiated forms to general inventory.

JUST-IN-TIME BASED

A final form of tailored value-added services includes a wide variety of activities aimed at reducing the cost of manufacturing by assuring the routine flow of zero defect parts and materials. The objectives of these inbound control services are to increase manufacturing specialization and to reduce excessive material and work-in-process inventories.

One of the most popular forms of JIT special service is the feeder warehouse. The purpose of this special warehouse is to receive vendor shipments and then to sort and segregate components to match manufacturing requirements. For example, vendors may make daily deliveries to the feeder warehouse based upon planned production schedules. Located adjacent to the assembly plant, the feeder warehouse sorts multiple vendor components into exacting quantities for delivery to the assembly line when and as needed. The objective is to reduce to an absolute minimum all in plant material handling and inspection.

A similar JIT service combines automotive parts produced in one geographical area and arranges for sorted and segregated delivery to 30 assembly plants. This particular service works to balance parts manufacturing against assembly requirements, allowing each to operate at full economy of scale. The service is provided by a third party warehouse and trucking operation.

Countless examples of inbound consolidation of freight destined to a specific location were discussed during the research interviews. One of the strengths of North American logistics capability is the availability of local distribution carriers who are positioned to receive over-the-road shipments for combination and redistribution within municipalities. Many of these carriers maintain standing delivery appointments at key consignees to facilitate rapid delivery. An impressive and growing array of information services is available with respect to purchase order number, bill of lading, shipment content, special handling requirements and so forth.

A final service being provided by a public warehouse illustrates the degree to which in-house and outsourced services can work in combination. At one warehouse facility, the service provider manages inventory, selects merchandise and loads privately operated driver route trucks. While the trucks are staffed by company drivers during customer delivery, the full maintenance of the fleet is contracted to the warehouse company.

What has been classified as JIT special services works to lubricate the flow of materials, parts and finished goods into manufacturing and throughout the distribution channel. The primary purpose of such tailored services is to permit the manufacturing facilities to focus available resources on the basic challenges of conversion.

SUMMARY

This chapter dealing with tailored services has presented a relatively small sample from a wide assortment of illustrations of how service providers are making significant contributions to the logistics of North America. The intent was not to downplay the importance of basic or traditional services. Timely, economical delivery and strategic storage are essential services that manufacturers, wholesalers and retailers need and will continue to purchase from service providers. The willingness of users and providers of tailored services to join together in unique arrangements is a growing reality. The scope and variety of tailored services illustrates the growing popularity of partnership agreements, third party arrangements and integrated service agreements.

To a significant degree, the popularity of outsourcing tailored service arrangements is directly stimulated by managerial emphasis in shipper firms on downsizing and flattening organization structures. While not supported by statistical evidence, interviews highlighted the commitment that senior managers of leading edge firms have to providers of quality services. They clearly expressed a desire to achieve the benefits of a vertically integrated organization without the burden of ownership. The use of external relationships to gain strategic leverage is analogous to de-verticalization of industry. To conclude, the following edited excerpts from an interview with a senior manufacturing executive summarize the thrust of external arrangements between users and providers of both traditional and tailored value-added services.

"...what it (external networking) amounts to is an attempt to rebuild the Henry Ford dream. During the early Ford Motor company heyday, the firm boasted that iron ore mined in Minnesota could be in an automobile on a dealer's floor in ten days. From ore and coal mines, via private ships, trucks and railroads to company smelters, into manufacturing and assembly and via private transportation to dealers, Ford strived to control the entire value-added process via ownership. The degree of vertical integration extended to internal manufacturing of components such as safety glass and tires.

With time, Ford found he did not have sufficient volume or financial resources to make complete vertical integration a reality. He was forced to outsource to gain economy of scale, reduce risk and achieve technical assistance. However, the dream is alive and well. Somewhat similar levels of control and the related benefits can be achieved from the formation of strategic alliances. The creation of long-term agreements can create monolithic channels that effectively become a superorganization of cooperative vertical asset management."

PART IV

The 1990's and Beyond

STATEMENT ON THE FUTURE

The preceding sections have presented an assortment of statistical and qualitative research results. The discussion has centered on isolating leading edge manufacturers, wholesalers, retailers and hybrids and comparing their practices with more typical or norm firms. These data were augmented with insights collected during interviews with a small, but prestigious, group of shipper, carrier, warehouse and other specialized service providers. Overall, the first nine chapters provided an in-depth look at North American logistics. This final section focuses on the concerns and opportunities for the future.

Part IV contains three concluding chapters. Chapter Ten is devoted to concerns about the future expressed by senior logistics managers. The past decade has been a period of significant turmoil in business life as nearly every public firm has been touched or threatened by merger, acquisition, divestiture or a leveraged buy out. Logistics executives have numerous concerns about the decade ahead. Eight such concerns that were repeatedly mentioned and discussed are reviewed in Chapter Ten.

The impressions, interpretations and concerns of the research team are the subject of Chapter Eleven. While the researchers' interpretations are essentially found throughout any diagnostic report, a deliberate effort was made in the first ten chapters to let both the quantitative and qualitative findings speak for themselves. In Chapter Eleven, the viewpoints and selected concerns of the researchers' are presented. Several of the concerns and opportunities discussed move beyond the scope of the research to speculate on the impact that current events and practice might have on future logistics behavior. The industry's and researcher's concerns and interpretations are presented in two separate chapters to make it clear who is expressing what opinions. Chapter Twelve is devoted to a brief summary and concluding statement regarding the overall research. The balance of the text consists of supporting appendices.

252

Chapter Ten

CHALLENGES -- A RESPONDENT PERSPECTIVE

A major research objective was to identify concerns and future challenges as perceived by senior logistics officers. Data were obtained in two ways. First, in the survey, respondents were asked to indicate the effect that they perceived selected events would have on their logistical operations. The purpose was to identify and isolate events that were viewed as difficult for a logistics organization to accommodate. The second source of data was generated by focusing interviews on challenges that users and providers of logistical services perceive will be important in the future. Concentration on the ability to handle specific events and identification of senior management concerns provided significant insight regarding where resources will be allocated in the future and the areas requiring continued research and development.

The initial section of this chapter presents a statistical overview of how respondents rate the effect of specific events on their logistical operations. These results are presented by business type and CAI grouping. The final section summarizes the eight areas of concern cited most often during interviews.

OPERATIONAL EFFECTS

Respondents were provided with a list of selected events, as detailed in Table 10-1, and asked to indicate the effect each event would have on their logistical operations. The list used in the Phase I manufacturing survey was modified slightly for the Phase II wholesaler/retailer/hybrid questionnaire. To accommodate the second type of respondent, three items were dropped: production planning/scheduling, interface with manufacturing and communication with dealers/distributors. Four items were added: inventory reduction programs, cost reduction programs, load leveling and workforce leveling. Results are presented in Table 10-1.

Respondents across business types reported that computer support has significant effect on their logistical operations. Manufacturers, wholesalers and retailers rated it as the event having the greatest effect. Hybrids rated computer support second, with supplier communication having the highest impact. Computer support is integral to all phases of business operations. The high impact rating came as no surprise. Timely information was reported as having the second highest effect by manufacturers, wholesalers and retailers. Timely information was third highest among hybrids. Communication abilities are vital and allow firms to remain responsive to customer needs.

Manufacturers reported production planning/scheduling and sales forecast accuracy as having significant impact on logistical operations. Manufacturers typically must produce product in anticipation of demand. Accurate projections of sales are crucial to planning for all phases of their operation. This concern is further discussed in the latter part of the chapter dealing with forecasting.

TABLE 10-1
EFFECT OF SELECTED EVENTS ON LOGISTICAL
OPERATIONS BY BUSINESS TYPE

	Mean Response Rating			
Event	Manufacturer[*]	Wholesaler[**]	Retailer[**]	Hybrid[**]
Sales Forecast Accuracy	3.06	3.54	3.73	3.62
Computer Support	3.27	4.24	4.38	4.06
Excessive end-of-month or end-of-quarter Surges	2.76	3.19	3.85	3.37
Communications with Customer	2.76	3.57	3.28	3.68
Production Planning and Scheduling	3.07	---	---	---
Interface with Manufacturing	2.99	---	---	---
Availability of Trained Logistics Personnel	2.58	3.47	3.38	3.33
Vehicle Routing and Scheduling	2.71	3.44	3.35	3.29
Computer Applications Backlog	2.58	3.35	3.54	3.68
Transportation Cost	3.05	3.75	3.74	3.72
Communication with Suppliers	2.60	3.60	3.23	4.46
Communication with Dealers, Distributors, or Brokers	2.53	---	---	---
Warehouse Productivity	2.78	3.94	3.98	3.70
Measurement Tools and Methods	2.54	3.37	3.50	3.25
Communication with Internal Non-Logistics Organizational Units	2.79	3.32	3.73	3.58
Timely Information	3.25	4.02	4.07	3.99
Supplier Performance	2.96	3.50	3.48	3.50
Communication with External Logistical Service Suppliers	2.50	3.03	3.06	3.01
Incompatibility of Computer Equipment and/or Software	2.23	2.79	2.88	2.89
Inventory Reduction Programs	---	3.31	3.39	3.40
Cost Reduction Programs	---	3.40	3.63	3.55
Load Leveling	---	2.96	3.35	3.03
Workforce Leveling	---	3.13	3.41	3.21

[*]   Manufacturer 4-point scale:
    1 = no impact; 4 = very high impact.

[**] Wholesaler/Retailer/Hybrid 5-point scale:
    1 = no impact; 5 = very high impact.

256

Warehouse productivity was rated as having a high effect by wholesalers, retailers and hybrids. A manufacturer's primary concern is producing finished products. In contrast, other channel members must concentrate on moving products as efficiently and effectively as possible. They are concerned with getting products to the point of sale while maximizing utilization of their logistics facilities.

Transportation costs were important to all business types. On average, transportation expenditure is a large percentage of a firm's total logistics costs. Anything that can be done to reduce transportation costs will have a favorable impact on the firm's profit and help insure competitiveness.

By comparison, the events rated as having limited effect on logistics operations include incompatibility of computer equipment and/or software, communication with external service suppliers and load leveling. Many firms today operate with integrated information systems which accounts for the lack of concern with incompatible computer equipment. The low rating concerning load leveling suggests that adequate systems are in place to manage outbound shipments. The low rating in the third area, communication with external service suppliers, is more difficult to understand. It is unlikely that the buyers of external services believe communication with those external vendors is unimportant. The more likely interpretation of the lower rating is that these firms believe they are receiving sufficient information and communications from vendors.

LEADING EDGE ANALYSIS - OPERATIONAL EFFECT

Data were analyzed in order to determine variations in ratings according to business type and CAI group. Results are presented in Table 10-2.

Leading edge manufacturers report three events as having the greatest effect on logistical operations: timely information, computer support and sales forecast accuracy. Leading edge

TABLE 10-2
EFFECT OF SELECTED EVENTS ON LOGISTICAL
OPERATIONS BY BUSINESS TYPE AND CAI GROUP

Event	Manufacturer* L.E./Norm	Wholesaler** L.E./Norm	Retailer** L.E./Norm	Hybrid** L.E./Norm
	Mean Response Rating			
Sales Forecast Accuracy	3.33^B/3.08	4.14^A/3.46	3.88/3.80	3.67/3.71
Computer Support	3.50^C/3.31	4.55/4.27	4.69/4.44	4.40/3.96
Excessive end-of-month or end-of-quarter Surges	2.81/2.74	2.90^C/3.56	4.06/3.81	2.86^B/3.58
Communications with Customer	2.91/2.75	3.91^C/3.53	3.47/3.22	4.07/3.65
Production Planning and Scheduling	3.17/3.09	---	---	---
Interface with Manufacturing	3.11/2.98	---	---	---
Availability of Trained Logistics Personnel	2.91^A/2.56	3.86^A/3.41	3.94^B/3.26	3.64/3.35
Vehicle Routing and Scheduling	2.69/2.74	3.81/3.41	3.40/3.35	3.53/3.23
Computer Applications Backlog	2.87^B/2.58	3.77^C/3.56	4.07^B/3.45	3.33/3.41
Transportation Cost	2.98/3.08	4.05^C/3.64	3.88/3.72	3.93/3.69
Communication with Suppliers	2.60/2.65	3.59/3.54	3.56/3.21	3.47/3.51
Communication with Dealers, Distributors, or Brokers	2.56/2.60	---	---	---
Warehouse Productivity	2.92/2.79	4.45^B/4.01	4.19/4.07	4.13^B/3.62
Measurement Tools and Methods	2.89^A/2.55	3.95^A/3.40	3.81/3.49	3.53/3.23
Communication with Internal Non-Logistic Organizational Units	3.13^A/2.80	3.59/3.31	4.00/3.65	3.73/3.60
Timely Information	3.52^A/3.23	4.27^C/3.95	4.31/4.16	4.27/3.90
Supplier Performance	3.13/3.02	3.86^B/3.36	3.93^C/3.45	3.67/3.51
Communication with External Logistical Service Suppliers	2.60/2.54	3.62^A/2.85	3.50^B/2.93	3.07/3.11
Incompatibility of Computer Equipment and/or Software	2.40/2.21	3.05/2.74	3.38/2.86	3.25/2.83
Inventory Reduction Programs	---	3.73^B/3.22	3.50/3.44	3.40/3.47
Cost Reduction Programs	---	3.64/3.39	3.63/3.67	3.66/3.57
Load Leveling	---	3.62^A/2.95	3.47/3.46	3.71^A/2.83
Workforce Leveling	---	3.86^A/3.11	3.44/3.58	3.67^B/3.09

* Manufacturer 4-point scale:
1 = no impact; 4 = very high impact

** Wholesaler/Retailer/Hybrid 5-point scale:
1 = no impact; 5 = very high impact.

A, B, C - Significantly different from the norm at 0.01, 0.05, and 0.10 respectively.

manufacturers were significantly more likely to rate these three items important than were norm manufacturers. All three of the information-related items are crucial to the logistics planning process. Significant differences were noted between leading edge and norm manufacturers in three additional areas: availability of trained logistics personnel, computer application backlog and measurement tools and methods. Leading edge firms reported that these events have greater effect on their logistics operations than norm respondents. This underlines the importance leading edge firms place upon formal planning and monitoring. Leading edge firms are concerned about future operations, as exemplified by the importance of securing adequately trained personnel and sufficient computer applications. Leading edge firms regularly use more performance measures to guide their operations and planning than do norm firms.

Leading edge wholesalers indicated three events have the greatest effect on their logistics operations: computer support, warehouse productivity and timely information. While the difference between leading edge firms' ratings of computer support and norm firms' ratings are not statistically significant, leading edge firms did rate computer support as having a greater impact than did norm firms. For the other two items, warehouse productivity and timely information, leading edge firms were significantly more likely to rate the items as having greater effect on logistical operations than norm firms.

Leading edge wholesalers reported the following events as having significantly greater effect than norm firms: communications with customers; availability of trained logistics personnel; computer backlog applications; transportation cost; measurement tools; supplier performance; communication with external logistics service supplies; inventory reduction programs; load leveling; and workforce leveling. Leading edge wholesalers found one item, excessive end-of-month or end-of-quarter surges, as having less impact on logistics operations than did norm wholesalers. This could be an indication that leading edge firms either are better at planning, thus reducing the magnitude of end-of-period surges, or that the leading edge firms are more adept at dealing with the surges as they occur.

The three items reported as having the greatest operational effect by leading edge retailers were: computer support, timely information and warehouse productivity. There was no statistically significant difference between the ratings of leading edge and norm firms for these items. Significant differences were found between leading edge and norm firms for four events: availability of trained logistics personnel; computer backlog applications; supplier performance; and communications with external logistical service suppliers. Leading edge retail firms place greater priority on communications/information and longer term planning than do norm retailers.

Computer support, timely information and warehouse productivity were also rated as having the greatest effect by leading edge hybrids. The leading edge hybrid firms' ratings were higher than norm hybrid firms' ratings for all three items. Only the leading edge rating for warehouse productivity was significantly different than the norm rating. Significant differences were found between leading edge and norm firms for: excessive end-of-month or end-of-quarter surges, load leveling and workforce leveling. Leading edge hybrid firms rated excessive end-of-period surges as having significantly lower impact than did norm hybrids. The leading edge firms rated load leveling and workforce leveling as having a significantly greater effect than did norm hybrids. Use of demand management can result in more stable production and shipments of products. To some degree, such stabilization reduces heavy surges which place a burden on their distribution systems.

AREAS OF PRIMARY CONCERN

A focal part of the senior executive interviews was obtaining opinions regarding current events or future trends that they considered significant. The typical procedure was to ask for expressions of concern in a non-structured manner. In situations where it was necessary to prompt discussion, the person being interviewed was asked to consider and comment on a list of events and trends. The responses identified eight areas of widespread concern. In this section, each area is presented with a brief discussion.

FORECAST ACCURACY

A major concern of executives interviewed during the research is their continued inability to accurately forecast detailed business requirements. This deficiency was highlighted in earlier chapters and in Tables 10-1 and 10-2. During interviews, firms reported that no significant improvement in forecast accuracy has been achieved despite substantial advancements in computer and information technology. Typical forecast errors exceeding 20 percent were reported by interview firms. In general, firms reported acceptable or adequate capability with respect to forecasting overall financial results, but indicated extreme inaccuracy when forecasting at the stockkeeping unit (SKU) level. Logistical operations are directly impacted by SKU forecasts, which are used to drive production scheduling and inventory allocation.

While the performance of some firms was hampered by the inability to develop accurate operational forecasts, other firms reported failure of internal organization units to use common forecasts. One part of a firm's operation may use one set of projections, while another part uses a different set of numbers. In many situations, forecasts are not really predictive. The numbers represent target goals of the sales force. One senior logistics manager interviewed said his organization was forced to generate its own operational forecast. He said, "We make no effort to tie to corporate sales objectives or planned incentives because they are a jumble of numbers that have no relevancy for logistics." When his organization receives the official forecast, they make their own projection of how much they think will be shipped and plan operations accordingly. While this situation is somewhat extreme, it illustrates the overall lack of well developed forecast procedures among firms interviewed.

As reported in Table 10-1, overall forecast accuracy ranked above average in its effect upon logistical operations. At the manufacturing level of distribution, inaccurate forecasts lead to producing the wrong items followed by anticipatory distribution to forward stocking warehouses. For the manufacturer, the entire process often results in maldistribution. For the typical wholesaler, the impact of forecast deficiency is somewhat less significant because inventories are managed on a replenishment basis. Retail forecast errors, in contrast, have a critical impact on performance of the overall distribution chain.

One retailer interviewed reflected upon the channel-wide impact of poor forecasting. He stated that his organization is financially unable to assume full responsibility for the conse-quences of inaccurate manufacturer forecasts. He expressed the opinion that a great deal of forecast error was the direct result of poorly planned or ineffective promotions. In such situations, his firm takes the position that it is the fundamental responsibility of the manufacturer to arrange to take the goods back or to issue credits to support mark-downs. He said this policy leads to a constant war with most manufacturers.

A food wholesaler interviewed regards the increasing frequency of returns as an alarming trend. He said that his retail customers were becoming more particular about product quality while at the same time much sloppier in their ordering practices. To protect their vulnerability to such poor ordering practices, his firm instituted strict return authorization policies. In spite of these strict policies, they are currently experiencing an increased level of returned goods. A logistics manager at a drug whole-sale firm also viewed the high level of returns as primarily the result of poor retail management. Regardless of who is in fact responsible, it is clear that channel relations are consistently strained and made more adversarial as a result of maldistribution based on faulty forecasts.

To help mitigate the impact of forecast error, logistical managers reported increased attention to the control of operational variance. If variances can be managed through supply and distribution leadtime, improved forecast procedures can concentrate on estimating demand.

Several executives reported a concentrated effort to formalize coordination between their firms and customers or suppliers. Their belief is that the need to forecast can be substantially reduced by the exchange of information. In other words, the best way to reduce forecast error is to eliminate the need to forecast. Many times the events being forecasted are known facts at a different level in the distribution chain. The objective to reduce anticipatory commitment and associated forecast dependency is the prime motivator behind the widespread attention being directed to all forms of electronic linkage. The potential and implications of electronic linkage are more fully examined in Chapter Eleven.

Because forecasting deals with future events, it is unlikely that error-free procedures will be developed. However, better forecasts are needed to help improve logistical efficiency. Logistical managers are also examining ways to reduce operational dependency upon forecasts.

HUMAN RESOURCES

The process of logistics is highly dependent upon human resources. Executives interviewed expressed widespread concern regarding the continued availability of both entry level management and basic lower skill, manual labor employees.

The demographics of North American continue to rapidly change. The United States Census Bureau projects that the United States population will grow from approximately 241 million in 1986 to over 282 million by the year 2010. Despite an overall expected growth rate of 16.9 percent, the current and projected shortage of personnel is critical. This shortage results from recent full employment, the aging of the population and geographical migration patterns.

Since 1985, employment in the United States has been at record high levels. The impact of full employment is directly felt in the logistics sector. Logistics is a consumer of large quantities of unskilled and manual labor. The employment problem results from the fact that many logistics jobs are not highly attractive. They involve physical labor which often must be performed in less than ideal working environments.

Executives interviewed described a number of programs being used to overcome this human resources shortage. The most popular program is to use part-time or casual labor to fill jobs. In one situation, a service provider interviewed described a flexible work program wherein part-time employees could work from 2 to 8 hours per shift. Others described programs which allow people to work extended hours on a limited number of days. Still others described incentive programs to attract workers, such as housewives, back into the labor pool. The extent of the labor shortage is illustrated in almost every community by the aggressive employment advertising of fast food restaurants.

Interviewed firms are also feeling human resource pressure at the managerial level. Logistics organizations can attract quality people, but express a high degree of difficulty in retaining them. Executives report that many candidates qualified to become senior managers are lost to other areas within the organization. Logistics experience is proving to be a fertile training ground, allowing a young person to gain valuable experience. The perception among the interviewees is that some younger workers are changing jobs with increasing frequency. High visibility management training programs in logistics often serve to benefit competitors. Some firms openly admit the practice of letting other firms bear the cost of training then offering successful individuals a higher salary than they are making at their original firm.

Pertinent dimensions of the human resources dilemma are the aging and migration of the North American population. One statistic especially revealing with respect to the graying of America is that over 200 people turn 100 years of age every day. The median age of the United States population is projected to approach 40 by the year 2000. Despite the popularity of retirement relocation to warm climates, the average age for the industrial Northeast and Midwest is projected to be older than the average age of the South or West.

Migration patterns also result in labor problems for logistics. Population shifts to the West and the South will continue. The projected area of greatest decline in population is the industrial midwest. Some people relocate to find work, relocating from the Appalachian region for example. However, the bulk of migrants consists of young people who are seeking more ideal living climates. These are the type of people most critical to the logistics workforce requirements.

Overall, logistics organizations are becoming leaner and flatter. Thus far, the reduction in headcount has come from early retirement and attrition. The jobs eliminated have been upper middle management positions, some of which became expendable as a result of mergers. However, as the general population ages, some firms are beginning to realize that executive level personnel will need to be retained to staff critical positions. One transportation firm senior executive interviewed described a situation wherein 25 percent of this organization's key executives will become eligible for early retirement during one eighteen-month period. Because of early retirement programs instituted a few years back to trim corporate organization, these executives will be able to take full retirement at the peak of their careers. Unfortunately the firm does not have experienced replacements.

The impact of the above human resource trends is not unique to logistical management. Logistics is significantly affected because of the nature of the manual labor required for distribution-related jobs in comparison to other employment alternatives. People are crucial to the success of any organization. One senior logistics executive who works for a large wholesaler said that state-of-the-art in his firm is people. He noted that no technology will solve the problems created by unproductive and unhappy people. Even with great increases in the level of automation, his organization views its personnel as the "vital link in the system."

SHRINKING SERVICE WINDOW

The overall emphasis that leading edge firms place on achieving customer satisfaction is stimulating rethinking of what constitutes ideal customer service performance. The traditional notion of an expected delivery date plus or minus one day is being replaced by a "point in time" commitment. One executive interviewed explained the growing practice of assigning delivery appointments at the time of purchase order issue. This practice results in the only acceptable delivery performance being "on time."

The emphasis on quality is extending to order fill rate. The importance of high fill rates was noted in numerous interviews and is substantiated by the high attention to measurement expressed by all business types (Table 5-7). During the interviews, the concept of zero defects in fill rate was discussed. One executive explained his company's commitment to shipping complete orders to important customers. His firm instituted a procedure to screen availability of merchandise during order processing. If items are not available, they are located at a secondary stockpoint and shipped to the customer, often arriving before the regular order delivery. While this practice creates split delivery, the firm is attaining zero defect concerning orders shipped complete. Their standard practice is to notify the customer in advance of the split delivery, while highlighting the fact that the order will be 100 percent serviced. As a result of this practice, this firm is turning potential deficiencies into a positive factor as far as customers are concerned. The practice assures key customers that the selling firm cares about them. It goes without saying that a firm has to be really good at the logistics basics to implement the described program.

Interviews confirmed that customer expectations concerning exact delivery time and high fill rate are increasing. Executives report pressure for faster delivery. Order cycles that traditionally have been seven to nine days are currently being reduced to five to seven days, with expectations of further reductions to three to five days. Executives also report that average order sizes are getting smaller and customers are placing increased emphasis on achieving maximum inventory velocity. The general attitude is that tighter schedules, shorter cycles and smaller average orders mean more control. This trend is forcing companies to maintain flexibility while executing near perfectly.

To some degree, the pressure on order cycle management is being reduced by a growing desire among customers to purchase FOB manufacturer's ship point. The pressure for FOB pricing has resulted from a trend to debundle transportation cost from product purchase price. Manufacturer and wholesale executives interviewed are resisting FOB purchase because they lose control and flexibility enjoyed under delivered pricing. Executives from all types of businesses expressed plans to increase control over inbound transportation. When a consignee purchases FOB origin, they assume responsibility for maintaining order cycle consistency. The negotiation of FOB ownership transfer and related responsibility is on the minds of most executives. This situation is in part stimulated by the fact that many wholesale and retail organizations have 48 state common carrier transportation operating authority. Their need for backhaul traffic goes far beyond the typical pick-up allowance.

The nature of what constitutes desired customer service performance is changing rapidly. The overall results of this research clearly illustrate that leading edge organizations are becoming increasingly sensitive to the expectations of key customers.

PROMOTIONAL DYNAMICS

A very popular topic discussed during the interviews was the changing nature of promotions. Handling the dynamics of promotions has always been a major concern for logistics personnel. Survey respondents identified end of period/month/quarter volume surges as having high impact on logistics systems (Table 10-1). Executives interviewed indicated surges were intensifying as a result of forward buy practice, predictable price increases and changing power relationships in the distribution channel. These factors are combining to create large volume surges that are difficult for logistics systems to handle.

Forward buy is a practice that retailers and wholesalers follow to take advantage of special promotion prices. Some firms have adopted deal hopping, or bridging, from trade promotion to trade promotion as a primary purchasing strategy. These firms buy from one trade promotion to the next, procuring large amounts of deal price inventory.

Forward buying creates large demand spikes which tend to cause the manufacturer difficulty in scheduling production and distribution. This practice increases inventory investment for the distributors while at the same time elevating storage and handling costs. According to Dr. Walter Salmon of Harvard University, forward buying is increasing inventories at the distributor level by 40 to 50 percent and distributors' carrying costs for this inventory are approximately $870 million to $1.2 billion annually.[1]

Forward buying has totally changed the purpose of the traffic department at one major food retailer. This retailer is now forced to manage large outside inventories and shuttle trucks back and forth between distribution centers. With the industry buying from "deal to deal," the typical forward buy for this firm is six to eight weeks.

The practice of extensive forward buying has stimulated the growth of diverters. A diverter is a firm that buys and sells inventory involved in forward buy situations. One food cooperative interviewed said that on any given day they could purchase most national branded products from six different sources -- the original supplier and five diverters -- and usually at six different prices. While perhaps an exaggeration, the executive said that on most days the manufacturer's list price could be beat by a diverter, and in some situations product delivery would be faster. It is clear that the practice of regional promotions coupled with extended and repetitive promotions is increasing logistical dynamics.

Pricing practices have also created some special logistics problems. Some firms have become very predictable regarding when they can be expected to increase price. One executive referred to his firm's pricing practice as a "day light savings strategy." Two times a year on precisely the same dates they announce price increases. The result is that customers anticipate increases and advance purchase to avoid higher prices. The fact that such routine price increases occur at quarter endings is just "coincidental."

Within some industries, such as the food industry, the balance of power has shifted from manufacturers to retailers. As a result, retailers are able to negotiate tailored deals. One wholesaler of general merchandise said that the reason retailers in his industry were the most powerful members of the distribution channel was because they were the distribution link that had customer loyalty. Where customers at one time had limited choice, they now have many retail options. This wider choice means that rapidly growing retailers are satisfying a market segment with the right assortment of goods and services at acceptable prices. The power of consumer loyalty strengthens the retailer's capability to request and receive special service consideration from wholesalers and manufacturers. In this context, the interviews provided insight into the origins of tailored distribution arrangements. These arrangements appear to be more driven by retailers who desire special services than by other channel members seeking to differentiate their offerings.

The concern for promotional dynamics and its impact upon logistical performance varies considerably from industry to industry. The surges created by these marketing practices are most extensive in consumer products channels such as food, health and beauty aids, household goods and selected general merchandise. The high incidence of volume surging suggests that many firms do not have a good handle on the true cost/benefit of such activities. Executives continue to report that people who initiate such marketing practices are for the most part not held responsible for the full consequences of their decisions. One retail logistics executive stressed that forward buying looks good in terms of positive purchase cost variance for buyers, but associated logistics costs are charged to different operating accounts and not reconciled to the total cost of such practice. Many executives feel the long-term result of such practice will be a reduction in customer good will. Heavy dealing is risky because reaction time is eliminated. Substantial product deletions, increased damage and general distrust are common.

A limited number of progressive firms have begun to isolate the total cost and assign full accountability for promotion dynamics. The drive of these firms toward negotiating every day low net prices is aimed at leveling the flow of merchandise in the distribution channel. Across the board, logistics executives feel such rationalization is essential to improving logistical performance.

CONVERTING DATA INTO INFORMATION

The importance of data processing to logistical operations was clearly documented in Chapter Five. One of the clearest differentials between leading edge and norm logistical operations was the broader range of logistics data processing applications among leading edge firms (Figure 5-11). Leading edge firms also reported overall higher quality data and better computer support of their logistical operations. It naturally follows that firms seeking to improve overall logistical performance should be highly concerned with data processing development. The interviews confirmed this concern.

There is an abundance of data available to most logistical managers. As one executive explained: "My problem is not data. It's getting data configured into useful information." During the interviews, other logistics managers expressed dissatisfaction with their overall information system support for several reasons.

Logistics organizations report losing ground regarding MIS development. Even though MIS departments are expending great effort, they cannot keep pace with the expanding application requirements of the typical logistics organization. One logistics manager from a large manufacturer expressed no dissatisfaction with the quality of his MIS department. However, he expressed concern over required development time. The systems planned for logistics operations will not be completed for five years. By the time those systems are fully developed, business requirements will have changed dramatically.

Unfortunately for many logistics managers, their MIS requirements are often given lower priority than the needs of other areas of the business. For many logistics professionals, this problem is terribly frustrating. One logistics manager said that "if our group could program as fast as we discover opportunities, we could really move this organization forward." He went on to say that his firm's systems are becoming so complex that each time they are modified, the changes have tremendous impact on related programs. Changing a few lines of code often creates a major problem because other programs or systems are impacted. This manager also states that ninety percent of the deficiency in his firm's logistical performance was directly related to lack of MIS support.

In terms of application development, logistics executives have learned that they must be proactive in assuring that MIS personnel fully understand their user needs and operating environment. Just providing MIS a wish list of general specifications will not get the job done because of the complexity of logistical applications. Many logistics executives indicated that their departments were assuming system ownership from the outset, providing leadership in application design and program validation. In fact, the most frequently noted extended or beyond functional responsibility of leading edge firms is distribution data processing. This expansion in functional responsibility is consistent with reports from the majority of executives interviewed, who said that their logistics departments were the major users of data processing services in the firm.

A complicating factor is that a surprising number of MIS departments are, in the opinion of executives interviewed, not at the leading edge of technology with respect to hardware, data base design and application development aids. Because of the high investment required for computer systems and program development, many firms continue to utilize old technologies and obsolete systems designed more than a decade ago. Some managers report a reluctance to invest in upgraded capability because of the rapid rate of technical advancement. While system reinvestment remains on hold, these firms continue to patch and update their applications on a piecemeal basis, which only serves to increase the MIS backlog and aggravate the problems of achieving interconnected systems and programs.

The managers interviewed fully understand the pressing need to resolve this dilemma. New capabilities for configuring information are available today, given the abundance of microcomputers, mainframe data bases and report writers. Consistent with the survey data, most managers interviewed believed that the desired solution is to increase internal development as contrasted to seeking outside turnkey applications. The internal solution to critical users' needs will not materialize overnight. However, some executives feel it is the only long-term solution.

During the interviews, attention was directed to the degree to which participating executives felt their information systems were fully integrated. The fully integrated system, often referred to as a *seamless transaction system*, ideally would coordinate all information requirements along the value-added chain, from procurement to final end use sale. Naturally, this ideal system is envisioned as being fully integrated with respect to relational data base structure, incorporating knowledge-based user support technology and having extensive report generation capability. No firm interviewed believed its current or planned systems matched these ideals. Most felt that the reality of the seamless system would not materialize until well into the 1990's.

Integrated logistics is dependent upon information management. Leading edge users and service providers place a high premium on developing high quality information to support logistics operations. A significant gap exists between desired and existing level of MIS logistics support. For many firms, closing this gap is a prerequisite to advancing logistical competency.

HAZARDOUS MATERIALS

Logistics executives are very concerned about compliance with increased restrictions concerning hazardous materials. One executive related an experience wherein his firm was fined for an activity that they did not realize was in non-conformance with a shipment regulation. The problem, as expressed by people interviewed, is one of staying current on a rapidly changing situation for which they have had little training or preparation. Usually, special high-cost facilities and equipment are required to accommodate restricted merchandise. For example, firms interviewed discussed special fire provisions they have been forced to follow in distribution centers as a result of such events as aerosol fires.

The problem is compounded by the fact that many individual products can become dangerous as a result of movement through the distribution process. One logistics executive relayed an example wherein a product was adequately protected while in the original master carton. However, when handled in individual split case lots, the individual cans represented a health hazard. The situation is of particular concern in the handling of returned goods.

Carriers and warehouse executives interviewed are concerned with the growing frequency of local restrictions concerning the transport and storage of hazardous materials. A firm responsible for moving hazardous goods through different states and municipalities may confront the existence of local walls or barriers. Local walls are city ordinances that restrict the type and movement of transportation through a geographic area. Some municipalities will not allow hazardous materials to move on streets or highways through their city. Others impose time restrictions. For the firm that must transport or store hazardous materials, these laws create operating headaches.

The impact of hazardous material regulations is greater for some industries than for others. However, few industries are exempt from some consideration, and concern is growing. Executives interviewed are concerned about their ability to remain fully informed and about the capability of their logistics system to accommodate all requirements while maintaining essential efficiency.

MEASUREMENT

One of the most decisive findings of the research was the attention and importance that logistics executives give to all types of performance measurement (Tables 5-7 through 10). In fact, leading edge firms were identified as being near compulsive in their use of a wide variety of different categories of measures and of numerous individual measures within each category. Executives interviewed expressed considerable dissatisfaction with the effectiveness of their current performance measurement capabilities. The scope and relevancy of measures are key problems expressed by logistics managers.

Executives expressed the opinion that measurement gaps have developed. They feel the value of key performance measurements has been negatively affected by the compounding of data errors that leave these measurements either useless or irrelevant. Most logistics managers are quite familiar with large computer printouts of meaningless measurement information.

With the new emphasis in American business on quality, it has become increasingly important to identify and use good performance measurements. Many firms are attempting to force quality control into all areas of their business. One firm interviewed has instituted a unique reward for employees who help reduce error. These employees are given one day to wander around the workplace to think, meet with management and experience the total environment as contrasted to being restricted to an isolated area. These employees are encouraged to critique current procedures and policies and make suggestions to management. Management has committed to review and respond to employees' suggestions. This new attentiveness to employee suggestions has had a significant impact.

The overall improvement of performance measurement is of major concern to logistics executives independent of business type. Executives interviewed expect substantial advancement in overall measurement capabilities in the near future.

MANUFACTURING COORDINATION

A traditional concern of logistics managers has been the coordination of manufacturing and distribution. The increased incidence of using outside services to support aspects of manufacturing and distribution has complicated the coordination process.

Logistics executives interviewed in manufacturing firms reported a great deal of time being devoted to resolving production scheduling conflicts. A major issue in manufacturing is the need to level overall capacity utilization to accommodate work restrictions. Interfacing and supporting new and more complex manufacturing technology have created demand for exacting logistical performance.

One problem discussed during interviews was a temptation among logistics executives to overstep their responsibility and begin to get involved in the how of manufacturing. Logistics managers should be concerned with the what, when and where of manufacturing, but not become involved in the internal aspects of how to produce a product. It is essential that the logistics executive develop a channel-wide vision of the overall value-added process. With exacting customer service require-ments and low allowable margin of error, logistics managers must understand the overall value-added process from inflow to processing to outflow, even if only a portion of the total process is their direct responsibility.

SUMMARY

Logistics executives confront a wide range of strategic and operational problems and have a variety of concerns. The mission of the typical logistics organization has expanded during recent years. Logistics solutions have increased in complexity. Customer expectations regarding level of service and associated quality are higher than ever. The day-to-day problems of logistics managers have increased due to these accelerated forces. In today's operational world, there is limited margin for error. This chapter has highlighted those areas that progressive logistics managers feel offer potential for significant improvement.

276

FOOTNOTE

(1) Dr. Walter Salmon, Food Marketing Institute Executive Conference, January 1988.

278

Chapter Eleven

OPPORTUNITIES -
A RESEARCH TEAM PERSPECTIVE

During the course of conducting this research, ideas were generated that may justify further investigation. These potential
research areas were prompted by survey responses and executive interviews. The topics discussed in this chapter should be
viewed as research team interpretations. The topics are positioned as research opportunities.

The topics are presented in four self-contained sections:
(1) linkage; (2) inventory positioning; (3) transparent organizations; and (4) infrastructure adequacy. No effort is made to
discuss interdependence of the topics.

LINKAGE

One of the most widely discussed areas of logistics is the
potential for electronic data interchange (EDI) between channel

members and between channel members and service providers. This research identified the low current use of EDI (Table 5-19) and an overall perception among leading edge firms that EDI will become more significant in future logistical operations.

The slow acceptance of EDI has been due in part to the fact that different groups are proposing a plethora of technical standards to coordinate industry data interchange. Also, to some as yet undetermined degree, potential participants have exhibited a reluctance to give up the paper-in-hand security and convert to paperless transactions. Finally, during interviews it became clear that some logistics executives simply do not understand EDI or how it can be strategically exploited. Far too many people feel if they electronically transmit a document (FAX), they have participated in EDI. EDI to many logistics executives is roughly translated as "an electronic speed-up of normal orders and invoices." Utilizing technology in this manner will limit EDI benefits to those of an electronic mail service.

To convey the full potential of EDI, the term linkage is indispensable. Linkage consists of tieing two or more firms together electronically so they can conduct full business operations in a paperless environment. Several progressive firms interviewed are exploring ways they can *link* with key customers and providers of materials and services. To implement linkage and exploit the full potential of EDI, it is essential that a firm be willing to modify basic business procedures. In other words, the benefits of this new technology will not be fully realized if it is retrofitted into a traditional business operation.

To illustrate, one firm interviewed is taking the leadership in linking its operations directly to authorized contractors. The ultimate objective is to fully support all contractor inventory requirements by direct job site delivery on a just-in-time basis. The plans call for the total order cycle to be executed without paper exchange.

As an example of an extended application, a major retailer is offering a comprehensive linkage arrangement to select high volume suppliers. The features of this arrangement require a complete change in the way business has been traditionally conducted. The features are:

(1) Operational interfaces such as pallet size and tiers, shrink wrap requirements and bar code display specification are standardized.

(2) The participants agree to a contract period during which a single net price per unit is applicable for all purchases.

(3) At start up time, the retailer agrees to provide the supplier a complete physical count of their warehouse stock by stock-keeping unit (SKU). The retailer also provides a forecast of expected sales by SKU during the contract period.

(4) Once operations are initialized, the retailer agrees to summarize and transmit daily cash register sales at a SKU level for all stores serviced from the warehouse. The retailer also agrees to transmit warehouse receipts and store ship-outs on a daily basis.

(5) The supplier assumes full responsibility for management of the retailer's warehouse inventory. In effect, the supplier creates the order and ships whatever products desired to the warehouse. All associated documents are   electronically transmitted to the retailer. The retailer in turn arranges for electronic bank transfer of funds to pay the invoice.

(6) At the end of the contract period, supplier performance is measured by warehouse fill rate and warehouse inventory turnover.

Examples such as those presented above were not commonly found among research participants. They reflect the efforts of a small group of aggressive firms to fully exploit linkage.

The primary benefit of electronic linkage is the potential to remove variance from the order cycle and reduce the overall complexity of doing business. Through comprehensive two-way information exchange, error rates in orders, invoices and related documents can be virtually eliminated. With satellite tracking of transport vehicles, inventory in the pipeline can be linked to requirements planning even though it is in the possession of a service provider. As operational variance and demand uncertainty are decreased, safety stock becomes less important. In a very real sense, inventory is replaced by quality information.

The perceived barrier to widespread linkage arrangements is the lack of adequate standards. In reality, progressive firms are moving ahead in a proprietary manner with their own unique EDI arrangements. To implement linkage arrangements, it is essential that participating firms be willing to modify the basic ways they conduct business.

A reasonable interpretation of the research findings is that electronic linkage will rapidly expand during the 1990's. As one executive put it: "Linkage is a revolution waiting to happen." Linkage can profoundly change the way a firm engineers, sources, manufactures and distributes products. Most of all, **being linked** changes the ways customers are serviced and service providers are coordinated. Full implementation of linkage will impact all aspects of the involved organizations. Despite the fact that adequate technology currently exists to support comprehensive linkage arrangements, only a relatively few firms have begun to exploit this here-today opportunity. The development and full implementation of electronic linkage arrangements require entrepreneurial leadership and basic research support.

INVENTORY POSITIONING

During the 1980's, a great deal of management attention has been directed to reducing overall inventory and improving quality in the logistics value-added process. The data provided by the United States Bureau of Economic Analysis shows a decline in aggregate inventory from 16.29 percent of Gross National Product in 1981 to 15.17 percent in 1987. These data are presented in greater detail in Appendix F.

To a significant degree, this overall reduction has resulted from the use of improved techniques to control and allocate inventory. Techniques such as MRP and the implementation of just-in-time have substantially reduced raw material and component inventory. A careful examination of trends in the composition of aggregate manufacturing inventory reveal that work-in-process inventory levels have remained relatively constant, raw materials have significantly declined and finished inventory has slightly increased. In other words, while total manufacturing inventory has declined, the ratio of finished inventory appears to be increasing.

In 1987, finished goods inventories were approximately one percent greater than the average of the previous eight years. While one percent may not appear to be a dramatic shift, it represents an increase of nearly $3.4 billion. For the five years inclusive from 1983-87, manufacturing inventory averaged 49 percent of aggregate inventory. In comparison, during the five years from 1978-82, manufacturing inventory averaged 52 percent of total inventory. This shift of three percent in aggregate inventory represented $19.1 billion. While analysis of these data reveals a pattern of forward shift for almost a decade, an abrupt reversal toward manufacturing was reported in 1987. In this one year alone, inventories equivalent to 4.3 percent of the aggregate shifted back to manufacturing. This move represented $27.4 billion of increased inventory reportedly being held by manufacturers. In 1987, new Internal Revenue procedures for the valuation of inventory were implemented, causing a possible one-time adjustment. The availability of 1988 figures will help clarify whether 1987 represents an anomaly or a trend reversal.

It is only possible to speculate why a forward shift in inventory holding might be occurring and why it appears that overall reductions in aggregate inventory have been to some degree accompanied by an increase in the ratio of finished goods. A great deal of managerial attention has been directed to smoothing out the flow of materials and components into manufacturing. The adoption of a JIT philosophy of procurement coupled with the application of planning techniques, such as MRP, has increased attention to improved quality and reduced waste in manufacturing. To maximize JIT benefits, it is necessary to stabilize the manufacturing process by formalizing and adhering to production schedules. The result may be an increase in the frequency of manufacturing to forecasted requirements. Seldom does a statement of dependent demand used in a MRP application represent actual customer orders. It appears that the increase in the volume of finished goods inventory may be necessary to enjoy the full benefits available for new manufacturing and procurement strategies.

It also appears reasonable to surmise that firms have not realized the full potential of JIT in their finished product physical distribution. While some attention has been directed to JIT applications in wholesaling and retailing, it appears safe to generalize that by and large the focal point of these new approaches has been manufacturing. It follows that significant opportunities may exist to gain competitive advantage by integrating inventory planning techniques and strategies throughout the distribution chain.

Some critical research questions stem from the verification of inventory trends and, if determined appropriate, the identification of reasons for the increased forward positioning of inventories. Examples of potential research are the cost/benefit analysis of the associated risk of anticipatory inventory build-up and the examination of ways to extend JIT benefits throughout the overall distribution channel. It is reasonable to theorize that the increased incidence of forward buying discussed in Chapter Ten is directly related to shifts in inventory positioning.

TRANSPARENT ORGANIZATION

Dr. Peter Drucker recently predicted the forthcoming of a major change in organization structures. In his Harvard Business Review article entitled "The Coming of the New Organization," Drucker predicted that major corporations were on the threshold of shifting from a command and control structure that has persisted for over fifty years to an information based organization consisting of knowledge specialists.[1] To Drucker, the organization of the future will "be composed largely of specialists who direct and discipline their own performance through organized feedback from colleagues, customers and headquarters."

During this research, some surprising events have been observed with respect to the reorganization of logistics. The high frequency of reorganization among leading edge logistics organizations were highlighted in Figure 3-6. It is clear that logistics executives continue to search for superior organizational solutions. It is also reasonable to speculate that a great deal of the change in logistics organization is being motivated by forces similar to those discussed by Drucker.

In particular, the practices of six firms interviewed stimulated considerable thought on the part of the research team concerning what might represent the ultimate logistics organization. The six firms at one point in time had highly integrated logistics organizations. They represented ideal command and control structures in that logistics was organized on a centralized basis with comprehensive line and staff responsibility. However, during the research period, these state-of-the-art logistics organizations were essentially dismantled. It is difficult to isolate all of the reasons behind such reorganizations because each situation involved a unique set of circumstances. However, a common perspective of senior management reorganization motivation has emerged in four of the recent reorganizations.

In the four reorganizations of interest, advanced information technology was available. These organizations have repositioned logistical functional responsibility from a centralized department to traditional line organizations. For example, plant related logistics functions have been re-assigned to manufacturing, and sales related functions such as order processing and customer service are now performed by the sales organization. While a formal logistics group remains, it is a staff organization concerned with the coordination of logistical performance across a wide variety of line units. The key to the performance of integrated logistics in an organization characterized by diffused functional responsibility is *information networking*. Senior executives of these four firms expressed the belief that they can retain the benefits of integrated logistics while at the same time making day-to-day functional responsibility an integral part of the prime user's basic effort. As one executive explained: "Under our new approach, logistical performance becomes transparent as an integral part of our operational units. We coordinate activities and generate synergy through information sharing."

These somewhat unorthodox organizational arrangements illustrate that how you manage logistics is more important than how many functions are managed. Commitment to integrated performance is positioned as being more important than formal organization structure.

The idea of logistics being coordinated through information networking at the sacrifice of formal organization raises many interesting research questions. In essence, such information based logistical organizations are forcing authority and responsibility down the formal structure, sharply cutting traditional management layers. A few of the potential long-range implications of these changes are: (1) questions related to the maintenance of critical mass; (2) the retention of pin-pointed or focused accountability; (3) technical training and expertise; and (4) the development of top level executives.

The idea of an invisible logistics organization is intriguing. For the past several decades, logistics organizations have been moving toward increased centralization and formalization. The notion of highly integrated performance being achieved through networking and without formal structure is revolutionary.

INFRASTRUCTURE ADEQUACY

The ultimate success of logistics hinges on the maintenance of an adequate supporting infrastructure. The vision of integrated logistics cannot materialize without the proper combination of roads, rail service corridor, airport and port facilities. Even a brief examination of the adequacy of the North American infrastructure should point out that problems are not limited to **Gorby Gridlock**.

For example, hardly a week goes by without a train derailment due to a deteriorated roadbed. The nation's airways and airports are now experiencing the gridlock that has been developing for years in major populated areas. Forty-five percent of the nation's 557,516 bridges are classified as structurally deficient. Over 8,000 miles of the interstate highway system in the United States are in deteriorated condition and need rebuilding. Rivers need dredging and port facilities are in desperate need of repair. The cost of rebuilding the logistical infrastructure is estimated to exceed one trillion dollars over the next decade.

What can be done to contain and repair the damage and to ensure logistics productivity into the next century? Certainly, the first step is acknowledging that the problem exists and that the deterioration must be stopped. Public support for the maintenance of the national infrastructure must be generated. Practitioners must begin to treat the use of the infrastructure as a scarce national resource. To this end, alternative modes, schedules and agreements must be cordinated in an atmosphere of **voluntary discipline**. For example, voluntary restraints such as those recently agreed to by some commercial airlines and the FAA to reduce peak loads at congested airports, are superior to restrictive laws being considered to reduce freeway gridlock during heavy commuter times in Los Angeles.

Creative, innovative solutions will be required to better utilize the available infrastructure, as well as to reduce operating demand. For example, electronic linkages discussed earlier offer ways to reduce peak loading. Several of the strategic alliances discussed in Chapter Eight serve to reduce excessive duplication and redundancy in the logistical process.

Both specific issues and the rehabilitation needs for the highway system were outlined in a report entitled "Beyond Gridlock," prepared by the staff of the Highway Users Federation.[2] The appealing feature of this report is that it represents views expressed in 65 public forums conducted across the nation by key users of surface transportation. While not a doomsday report, "Beyond Gridlock" makes it very clear that current efforts toward improved use and rebuilding of the infrastructure are simply inadequate.

No easy solution or quick fix exists to resolve the infrastructure dilemma. The main concern of the research team is the general lack of sensitivity to these critical issues among the logistics user community. An action agenda needs to be developed.

SUMMARY

The number of topics discussed in this chapter could have been expanded to include issues related to productivity, standardization, automation and globalization to name but a few. The four areas selected for discussion were most directly related to the objectives of the research.

Linkage involves stimulating logistics executives to seek innovative new ways to fully exploit technology. The trend in inventory positioning raises questions concerning the impact of partial deployment of new techniques and management practices. The long-term impact that information technology will have on organization structure is fundamental. Some recent reorganizations of well managed firms suggest that the impact of information networking upon logistics organization structure could be dramatic and may occur in the near future. Finally, astute senior logistics executives must come to grips with the deterioration of the national logistics infrastructure. Each of these four topics contains a host of research opportunities. Tomorrow's solutions will need to be forged out of the many contradictions contained in today's logistics practice.

290

FOOTNOTES

(1) Peter F. Drucker, "The Coming of the New Organization,"
     <u>Harvard Business Review</u>, 66:1 (January-February), 1988,
     pp. 45-53.

(2) <u>Beyond Gridlock: The Future of Mobility as the Public Sees
     It</u>, Advisory Committee on Highway Policy, 2020 Transpor-
     tation, Public Affairs Highway Users Federation, Washing-
     ton, D.C., 1988.

Proposition One:
The Focal Point of Leading Edge Logistics is An Overriding
Commitment to Customers

Proposition Two:
A Firm Seeking to Exploit Logistics Competency Needs to Perfect
Basic Performance

Proposition Three:
Logistics Solutions Are Becoming Increasingly Sophisticated

Proposition Four:
Leading Edge Firms Emphasize Planning

Proposition Five:
Leading Edge Firms' Logistical Organizations Encompass a Significant
Span of Functional Control

Proposition Six:
Leading Edge Firms Have a Highly Formalized Logistical Process

Proposition Seven:
Leading Edge Firms Place a Premium on Flexibility

Proposition Eight:
Leading Edge Firms Are Committed to External Alliances

Proposition Nine:
Leading Edge Firms Use State of the Art Information Technology

Proposition Ten:
Leading Edge Firms Employ Comprehensive Performance Measurement

The Importance of Benchmarking

Concluding Statement

Chapter Twelve

CONCLUSION

The message of the first eleven chapters is clear. The logistics of North America is large, complex and permeates every aspect of the Canadian and United States economies. The rapidly changing nature of business is increasing the demand for high level logistics performance. Leading edge firms - manufacturers, wholesalers, retailers and hybrids - as well as their service providers are jointly formulating unique and proprietary logistical solutions.

When one reflects upon the relatively few firms that stand out as leading edge performers, it is clear that North America, at best, is only on the threshold of logistical excellence. Using the Common Attributes Index, 117 out of 695 respondents or 17 percent were classified as leading edge. The results are qualified by the fact that only firms identified as being logistically sensitive were included in the survey mailing. It also seems safe to assume that most respondents who completed the comprehensive questionnaire or who agreed to be interviewed had reason to believe that their logistical operations were comparatively sophisticated. Therefore, it is concluded that the overall incidence of leading edge firms is significantly less than ten percent throughout North America.

However, the perspective and insight gained from examining how leading edge firms are going about the management of logistics is encouraging. The lessons of excellence make it safe to predict that the best of the benefits attainable from integrated logistics remain in the future. By way of summarizing the research findings, ten general propositions have been formulated regarding leading edge logistics practice.

PROPOSITION ONE:
THE FOCAL POINT OF LEADING EDGE LOGISTICS IS AN OVERRIDING COMMITMENT TO CUSTOMERS

A common denominator among leading edge firms is an obsession with achieving customer satisfaction. This commitment is based on a well researched understanding that not all customers are equally profitable nor do they have identical potential. Leading edge firms organize their logistical operations to assure that significant customers will receive personalized attention. While these firms desire to provide excellent service to all customers, they seldom if ever fail to meet expectations of key customers. A personalized, key customer program is typically achieved by reducing the bureaucracy of logistical administration. Leading edge firms specialize in human interaction. A typical customer interface is for one person to have complete information and operational authority to fully administer a customer's affairs. This simplification of customer interface extends to such features as single shipment, single invoice and immediate resolution of discrepancies. Streamlined one call communication and focused responsibility in a single person for achieving customer satisfaction serve to increase the discretionary effort given to key accounts.

PROPOSITION TWO:
A FIRM SEEKING TO EXPLOIT LOGISTICS COMPETENCY NEEDS TO PERFECT BASIC PERFORMANCE

A common characteristic among leading edge firms is their high degree of unyielding commitment to basic performance. Being good at the basics appears to be a prerequisite to strategically exploiting logistics. While it was not really a surprise that basic performance is critical to success, it was somewhat of a surprise to find out how highly committed leading edge firms are to the fundamentals. This conclusion is true among leading edge firms independent of position within the distribution channel.

The objective of leading edge logistics is lower cost **and** increased customer service. This objective of simultaneously attaining both flies directly in the face of traditional cost-service trade-off analysis. Doing the basics right means taking system efficiency to new high levels while simultaneously reaching unprecedented effectiveness.

PROPOSITION THREE:
LOGISTICS SOLUTIONS ARE BECOMING INCREASINGLY SOPHISTICATED

The research analyses make it clear that the knowledge base fundamental to contemporary logistics is rapidly growing. This knowledge extends to a growing mastery of technology. Information technology is critical to the improvement of logistical performance. It offers an unprecedented opportunity to control the vast detail that constitutes logistical complexity on a near real time basis. Leading edge firms are forging a future that is being built upon enduring alliances with service providers. As such, the boundaries of logistics are expanding in a creative, innovative and increasingly sophisticated manner. It also follows that, to the degree to which logistical competency becomes a strategic initiative, the internal practices, policies and priorities that guide performance will become increasingly proprietary.

PROPOSITION FOUR:
LEADING EDGE FIRMS EMPHASIZE PLANNING

A hallmark of top level logistical competency is the fact that most operational events occur according to plan. The planning of leading edge logistics begins with direct involvement with and commitment to business unit strategic plans. The details are executed through comprehensive logistics operating plans. These plans constitute much more than operating budgets. They are, in fact, blueprints to guide the allocation of human and financial resources dedicated to the logistical process. Among leading edge firms, such logistics plans are typically projected from three to five years forward and are updated on at least an annual basis.

PROPOSITION FIVE:
LEADING EDGE FIRMS'
LOGISTICAL ORGANIZATIONS ENCOMPASS A
SIGNIFICANT SPAN OF FUNCTIONAL CONTROL

The central thesis of this research has been: *how* logistical functions are managed is more significant than *how many* functions are managed. As a general rule, leading edge firms logistical operations are responsible for more overall and line logistical functions than less advanced firms'. Regardless of the absolute number of functions that directly report to the senior logistics officer, it seems essential that span of control be sufficient to generate a critical mass.

A characteristic of leading edge firms is that they have been delegated sufficient authority and responsibility to assure that planned logistical performance is achieved. It is typical for leading edge firms to have responsibility for logistical functions such as order processing, forecasting, customer service and production scheduling that are boundary spanning in nature. In other words, leading edge logistical operations are positioned to make customer satisfaction become a day in and day out reality. Some evidence suggests that information networking and electronic linkage could significantly reduce functional span of control in the future.

PROPOSITION SIX:
LEADING EDGE FIRMS HAVE
A HIGHLY FORMALIZED LOGISTICAL PROCESS

To guarantee logistical performance, it is essential that a highly routinized set of operating procedures be in place to guide day-to-day activities. Formalization of the logistical process means that what is expected and will be accomplished in terms of customer service is understood throughout the organization. In these organizations, customer service promises are total commitments. Leading edge firms typically have written logistics mission statements that communicate their performance commitment. These commitments are normally very specific concerning what customers can expect in terms of logistical service. Such logistical mission statements are available to all involved parties in advance of entering into a business arrangement. As such, mission statements serve as the logistical game plan or contract.

Presenting a logistical game plan for advanced scrutiny means that an organization must have firmly established procedures to guide routine operations. Among leading edge firms, routine and contingency plans are pre-established to guide the bulk of daily logistical operations. These plans focus authority and responsibility for customer service performance. They become the platform upon which the exceptions, which are bound to develop, can be expeditiously handled.

PROPOSITION SEVEN:
LEADING EDGE FIRMS
PLACE A PREMIUM ON FLEXIBILITY

The very fact that top level performers have highly formalized routine logistical operations tends to reduce the frequency of operational breakdowns. When service failures are true exceptions, they can be resolved in a personalized manner that conveys to key customers an extraordinarily high level of concern and commitment.

Leading edge firms specialize in turning operational adversity into service advantages. When an exception occurs, leading edge firms seek to resolve the operational breakdown in a manner transparent to customers. If it becomes necessary to modify customer expectations, leading edge firms strive to provide advance warning so that customers will not be surprised. In most situations, customers are simultaneously notified of the problem and the suggested method of resolution. Leading edge firms fully realize that customers can live with just about any situation except surprise. They have perfected the process of reducing uncertainty to an absolute minimum.

PROPOSITION EIGHT:
LEADING EDGE FIRMS ARE
COMMITTED TO EXTERNAL ALLIANCES

A remarkable trend during the late 1980's has been a general reduction in the number of vendors used to supply essential materials, component parts and services. In particular, firms that rely extensively on outside transportation and warehousing have significantly reduced the number of service providers they utilize. Prior to 1980, multiple carriers were used to assure firms of high service levels at the then regulated rate. Today's economy is characterized by negotiated rates and tailored service.

Leading edge firms have solidified their service provider relationships by developing extremely close working relationships with key vendors. These strategic alliances serve to help leverage the logistical performance of leading edge firms. In essence, the leading edge firm provides leadership in what becomes a highly coordinated logistical delivery system.

PROPOSITION NINE:
LEADING EDGE FIRMS USE
STATE OF THE ART INFORMATION TECHNOLOGY

As noted in Proposition Three, the utilization of advanced information technology is firmly ingrained in leading edge firms. Leading edge firms have more data processing applications than less advanced firms and plan to significantly enhance their capabilities in the future. They are also more deeply committed to the future use of electronic data interchange and to the research and development of knowledge based/artificial intelligence.

A distinctive feature of leading edge adoption of new information technology is the manner in which advancements are implemented. Leading edge firms seek to exploit new technology by undertaking systematic change. This normally means the reconfiguration of policy, procedure and process to take maximum advantage of new technology. This innovative technology application is contrasted to the more typical approach of putting new technology into a pre-established and somewhat restrictive process. To illustrate, whereas a typical firm may adopt some feature of EDI to improve speed or accuracy of a phase of order cycle management, a leading edge firm is far more likely to totally revamp their entire order cycle to exploit linkage technology. While North American firms tend overall to be slow adopters of new technology, leading edge firms are head and shoulders ahead of the pack.

PROPOSITION TEN:
LEADING EDGE FIRMS EMPLOY
COMPREHENSIVE PERFORMANCE MEASUREMENT

Leading edge firms expend substantial effort to maintain continuous performance monitoring. Such measurements typically focus on asset utilization, cost, customer service, quality and productivity. Every aspect of logistical operations is continuously scrutinized. The process of establishing standards, measuring performance and providing feedback is essential for top level logistical operations.

When a firm enjoys a high level of operational excellence, customer loyalty can be gained by exploiting such competency. Leading edge firms follow the practice of regular customer briefings concerning operational achievements. As such, logistical competency is exploited in a proactive manner.

THE IMPORTANCE OF BENCHMARKING

The technique of benchmarking is designed to help a firm appraise where it stands in comparison to the very best. In some situations, the focus is on key competitive behavior and competency. In other situations, such as logistics, a great deal can be learned by a careful study of those firms that represent leading edge performance.

A major finding of this research is that leading edge firms, regardless of position in the distribution channel, tend to place a premium on similar practices of management. While the typi-

cal logistics missions confronted at various levels in the distribution chain are significantly different, the practices of management
leading to excellence are similar. In fact, leading edge manufacturers, wholesalers, retailers and hybrids are more similar to
each other than they are to norm or emerging firms at their
representative channel levels. Common sense dictates that firms
seeking to improve overall level of performance should make a
careful study of the management practices of leading edge
logistical operations.

CONCLUDING STATEMENT

This overall research suggests that the golden age of
logistics -- when the vast majority of firms will exhibit high levels
of operating competency -- remains for the future. It is clear that
many senior executives have not been convinced that a significant investment in logistics capability will in fact provide a
satisfactory return-on-investment. The question remains: "If we
make a specific investment, will we sell more products and services at margins that will increase bottom line results?"
The answer regarding the probability and amount of payoff
or return on logistical investment is unique to each individual firm
and must be evaluated in terms of each competitive and marketing situation. Two points are emphasized for chief executives
considering the upgrading of logistics competency.
First, convincing evidence is available that a small percentage of existing firms, independent of size, industry or level
in the distribution channel, are strategically positioning to exploit
logistical competency. While formal data collection was limited
to North America, experience gained from foreign travel and presentation of preliminary research results supports the hypothesis
that leading edge logistical firms exist throughout the free world.
The inescapable conclusion is that firms who do not choose to
strategically exploit logistical competency will, either now or in
the future, confront a major competitor who does. In terms of

choosing strategic variables for competitive advantage, logistics is relatively new and unexplored. In contrast to product, promotion and price, logistics competency offers the potential to gain a unique differential advance. Because of the high degree of coordination of human expertise, operating procedure, system design and external alliances required to create logistical competency, it is not likely that excellence can be rapidly duplicated.

Second, if firms wish to exploit logistical competency, it is essential that they fully understand that little or no difference exists between customer expectations and actual performance that will result in customer satisfaction. Logistics deals in specifics of time, place and inventory. As such, it is a very tangible and quantitative field where measurement is precise. Since logistics is event-oriented, it either happens as promised or it does not. While the benefits to be gained are substantial, there is low tolerance for poor performance or failure. The situation is complicated by the fact that leading edge firms tend to seek each other out when building channel alliances. In other words, leading edge retailers tend to concentrate their business with leading edge wholesalers and manufacturers. As such, customer service performance cannot be erratic or used as a one time loss leader. Once a firm chooses to exploit logistics, it is committed to providing continued high level performance or suffer significant erosion of competitive position.

As this book goes to press, the nature of world competition is undergoing radical change. The Single Internal Market Confederation of European Countries will become a business reality by 1992. The trade walls of a unified block of European nations will necessitate increased competency on the part of North American firms.

The plight of the Soviet Union economy is becoming increasingly obvious as we approach the 1990's. Evidence continues to accumulate that the planned approach to economic growth cannot keep pace with the dynamics of a free market system. Among the most deficient of Soviet competencies is the lack of high performance domestic logistics. The horizons of the next decade and beyond suggest an all out effort throughout the world to close the logistical competency gap. The balance of world economic leadership may rest with those nations, East or West, that master logistics.

Selected
Bibliography

BIBLIOGRAPHY

Anderson, David L. and Robert Calabro (1987), "Logistics Productivity Through Strategic Alliances," Proceedings of the Annual Conference of the Council of Logistics Management, Vol. I, pp. 61-74.

Bowersox, Donald J. (1988), "Logistical Partnerships," in Partnerships: A Natural Evolution in Logistics, Joseph E. McKeon, ed., (The Logistics Resource Forum Series: Logistics Resource, Inc.), pp. 1-13.

Bowersox, Donald J. (1986), "A Third Party Partner -- A Timely Concept," Warehousing Forum, 1:11 (October), pp. 1-3.

Bowersox, Donald J. and Patricia J. Daugherty (1987), "Emerging Patterns of Logistics Organizations," Journal of Business Logistics, 8:1, pp. 46-60.

Bowersox, Donald J., Patricia J. Daugherty, Dale S. Rogers, and Daniel L. Wardlow (1987), "Integrated Logistics: A Competitive Weapon/A Study of Organization and Strategy Practices," Proceedings of the Annual Conference of the Council of Logistics Management, Vol. 1, pp. 1-14.

Bowersox, Donald J. and Leland A.W. Buddress (1987), "Logistics Challenges of the Last Decade of the 20th Century," Transportation & Distribution-Presidential Issue 1987/88, 28:10 (September), pp. 18-24.

Bowersox, Donald J., M. Bixby Cooper, Douglas M. Lambert, and Donald A. Taylor (1980), Management in Marketing Channels, (New York: McGraw-Hill Book Company).

Cooke, James Aaron (1988), "Outsourcing: Who'll Do Your Job?" Traffic Management, 27:5 (May), pp. 38-43.

Davisson, John F. (1986), "Third-Party Distribution -- The Growing Alternative," Handling and Shipping Management, 27:11 (October), pp. 69-71.

Delaney, Robert V. (1988), "Freight Transportation Deregulation," Seminar T9 on Road Transport Deregulation: Experience, Evaluation and Research, (Cambridge, MA: Arthur D. Little, Inc.).

DeRose, Louis J. (1988), "What the Buyer-Seller Partnership Requires," Purchasing World, 32:5 (May), pp. 74-75.

Drucker, Peter F. (1988), "The Coming of the New Organization," Harvard Business Review, 88:1 (January-February), pp. 45-53.

Ernst & Whinney (1986), "Corporate Profitability & Logistics-Innovative Guidelines for Executives - Preliminary Findings," Prepared for the Council of Logistics Management, Oak Brook, Illinois.

Ford, D., H. Hakansson, and J. Johanson (1986), "How Do Companies Interact?," Industrial Marketing and Purchasing, 15:1, p. 1.

Fredrickson, James W. (1986), "The Strategic Decision Process and Organizational Structure," Academy of Management Review, 11:2, pp. 280-297.

Gattorna, John and Abby Day (1986), "Strategic Issues in Logistics," International Journal of Physical Distribution and Materials Management (Special Issue), 16:2.

Gustin, Craig M. (1984), "A Re-examination of the Integrated Distribution Concept," Journal of Business Logistics, 5:1, pp. 1-15.

Jackson, Barbara Bund (1985), "Build Customer Relationships That Last," Harvard Business Review, 63:6 (November-December) pp. 120-128.

Kearney, A.T. (1981), "Organizing Physical Distribution to Improve Bottom Line Results," Proceedings of the Annual Conference of the National Council of Physical Distribution Management, pp. 1-14.

Kearney, A.T. (1985), Emerging Top Management Focus for the 1980's, (Chicago, Illinois: Kearney Management Consultants).

Kelsch, John E. (1982), "Benchmarking: Shrewd Way to Keep your Company Ahead of Its Competition," Boardroom Reports, (December 15).

Leifer, Richard P. and Andre Delbecq (1978), "Organization/ Environment Interchange: A Model of Boundary Spanning Activity," Academy of Management Review, 3:1 (January), pp. 40-50.

Lounsbury, Charles B. (1987), "Profit Through Transportation Partnerships," Proceedings of the Annual Conference of the Council of Logistics Management, Vol. II, pp. 105-116.

Martin, Christopher (1986), "Implementing Logistics Strategy," International Journal of Physical Distribution & Materials Management, 16:1, pp. 52-62.

McKeon, Joseph E., Ed. (1988), Partnerships: A Natural Evolution in Logistics, Proceedings of the 1988 Logistics Resource Forum (Columbus, Ohio: Leaseway Transportation Corporation).

Pföhl, Hans-Christian and Werner Zöller (1987), "Organization for Logistics: The Contingency Approach," International Journal of Physical Distribution & Materials Management, 17:1, pp. 3-16.

Plowman, E. Grosvenor (1964), Elements of Business Logistics, (Stanford, CA: Stanford University, Graduate School of Business).

Robeson, James F. (1988), "The Future of Business Logistics: A Delphi Study Predicting Future Trends in Business Logistics," Journal of Business Logistics, 9:2, pp. 1-14.

Ryan, Paul T. (1988), "The Relationship of Logistics to Marketing," Asia Pacific International Journal of Business Logistics, 1:1, pp. 33-36.

Salmon, Walter (1988), Speech given at Food Marketing Institute Executive Conference, (January II).

Staude, Gavin E. (1987), "The Physical Distribution Concept as a Philosophy of Business," International Journal of Physical Distribution & Materials Management, 17:6, pp. 32-37.

Taylor, Charles I., Warren H. Cohen, Kenneth R. Ernst, and Larry M. Koester (1987), "Developing and Managing Distribution Partnerships," Proceedings of the Annual Conference of the Council of Logistics Management, Vol. II, pp. 93-104.

Telem, Moshe (1985), "The Process Organizational Structure," Journal of Management Studies, 22:1, pp. 38-52.

Tucker, Frances G., Seymour M. Zivan, and Robert C. Camp (1987), "How to Measure Yourself Against the Best," Harvard Business Review, 87:1, (January-February), pp. 8-10.

Yanacek, Frank (1987), "The Logic Behind Logistics," Handling and Shipping Management, 28:7 (August), pp. 30-34.

Appendices

APPENDICES

Appendix A: Research Methodology and Data Tabulation

In Appendix A, the development of two questionnaires is described. The first (Phase I) was targeted for manufacturers and the second (Phase II) was targeted for retailers and wholesalers. In addition, a Phase II questionnaire containing certain questions developed during the course of the research, was sent to those manufacturers who responded in Phase I. Appendix A contains the tabulations of the following data:
- (1) U.S. manufacturers: Phase I;
- (2) Canadian manufacturers: Phase I;
- (3) U.S. manufacturers: Phase II;
- (4) Retailers: Phase II;
- (5) Wholesalers: Phase II;

and (6) Hybrids: Phase II.

Hybrids are firms that operate at two or more positions in the channel of distribution. For example, a hybrid firm may be a combination of retailer and wholesaler. Hybrid firms were analyzed as a separate group.

Appendix B: Statistical Comparison by CAI Group

In Appendix B, the "emerging," "norm" and "leading edge" groups are defined on the basis of CAI score classifications. Both the emerging and the leading edge groups are compared to the norm group. Appendix B contains the tabulations by CAI group of the following data:
- (1) U.S. manufacturers: Phase I;
- (2) U.S. manufacturers: Phase II;
- (3) Retailers: Phase II;
- (4) Wholesalers: Phase II;

and (5) Hybrids: Phase II.

Statistical tests are presented of the overall research hypothesis that distinct differences exist among firms due to their classification as emerging, norm or leading edge.

Appendix C: Statistical Comparison of Leading Edge Firms by Business Type

Leading Edge manufacturers, retailers, wholesalers and hybrids are compared to one another in Appendix C. Statistical tests are presented of the overall research hypothesis that leading edge firms exhibit a communality of charac-teristics and behaviors that transcends differences due to position in the distribution chain.

Appendix D: Related Logistics Organization Research

A comparative analysis of the functional span of control over several A.T. Kearney studies versus this research is presented in Appendix D.

Appendix E: The Common Attributes Index (CAI)

The components of the CAI are described in Appendix E. Research on the internal and external validity of the CAI is presented.

Appendix F: Aggregate Logistical Trends

Aggregate logistical trends in the areas of cost, inventory and productivity are analyzed in Appendix F.

APPENDIX A

Research Methodology and Data Tabulation

APPENDIX A: RESEARCH METHODOLOGY AND DATA TABULATION

Two questionnaires were developed, one targeted for manufacturers and one for retailers/wholesalers.   Each of the questionnaires had a section which collected respondent information (name, address), determined professional affiliation (Council of Logistics Management, Canadian Association of Physical Distribution Management), and asked if the respondent would be willing to participate in a short follow-up interview by telephone. The following sections describe the questionnaires, sampling procedures and statistical techniques used.

MANUFACTURER'S QUESTIONNAIRE: PHASE I

The questionnaire targeted for manufacturers was developed in the Fall of 1986.   Michigan State University researchers worked in conjunction with A.T. Kearney Management Consultants, _Traffic Management_ magazine, Gateway Systems Corporation, and the Council of Logistics Management.   The questionnaire was designed to provide continuity and allow direct comparisons to earlier studies conducted by A.T. Kearney and _Traffic Management_.

Michigan State University's 1986 pilot study provided a base for developing this questionnaire.   Personal interviews with sixteen leading United States logistics organizations during the pilot study revealed logistical trends and major concerns within those firms.   In 1987, additional interviews were conducted in order to determine the appropriate focus for a broader based questionnaire.   The survey instrument was subjected to review by two groups: (1) selected practitioners were asked to pre-test the questionnaire;   and (2) members of a special Advisory Board reviewed and commented on the questionnaire. The Advisory Board consisted of two executives from the computer industry, two consultants, two academicians, and a magazine editor.

Input from the pre-test and the advisory board resulted in the following major modifications: (1) more thorough definitions of key terms were added; and (2) the questionnaire was shortened to avoid negatively affecting response rate. Twenty-six questions were retained and/or modified for the final manufacturer's questionnaire. Rationale for question selection follows.

*   Questions 1 through 4 are firm descriptors.

*   Questions 5 and 6 describe executive logistics personnel and typical career paths. Employment history, reporting relationships, and job level give an indication of the visibility of logistics within the organization.

*   Inferences about the firms' commitment to proactive and formalized long term planning were made based upon Questions 7, 8, and 9. The involvement of logistics executives in defining their firms' missions and strategy setting is an indirect measure of their authority and relative position in the organization hierarchy.

*   Questions 10 and 11 provide insight into the dynamic tenure of formal logistics organizations. Respondents were asked how often reorganization of logistics had occurred and what specific areas had been reorganized.

*   In keeping with previous research on logistical organizations, Question 13 asked whether logistics had line or staff responsibility for each of

fifteen functional activities. The results from Question 13 were compared with earlier studies to determine whether the scope of logistics had increased or decreased. In Question 12, direct responsibilities outside of these fifteen traditional functions were elicited in order to determine if the boundaries of logistics had expanded to include new areas.

* Logistics management practices are directly influenced by the organization's structure and strategy orientation (Questions 14 and 15 respectively). Respondents were asked to identify the organization chart that most closely resembled their own structure. The charts illustrated functional versus divisionalized organization, and consolidated versus dispersed logistics responsibilities. Respondents were also asked to choose from a list of strategy options or to describe their primary strategy if it differed from the strategy definitions provided.

* Question 16 asked respondents to indicate how well their logistics system could accommodate events such as product recall, customization requests, and other non-standard business operations. The intent was to determine the degree of flexibility within today's logistical organizations.

* Question 17 gave a list of items - - for example, forecast accuracy and interface with manufacturing. Respondents were asked to specify the impact each item had on logistical operations.

* Question 18 utilized an open-ended format to determine the primary performance measurements used by senior logistics management in four specific performance areas - - cost, customer service, productivity, and quality. The goal was to identify the range of different measures commonly used.

* Data on computer applications and other information related areas was collected using Questions 19 through 22. The purpose was to determine the current level of information availability or data sophistication as well as to get an indication of plans for adding or modifying existing systems.

* Question 23 gauged the characteristics (availability, timeliness, etc.) of the information used to manage logistics. Responses reflect the ability of installed information systems to meet the organization's needs.

* Outsourcing of logistical services has become much more commonplace in recent years. Responses to Questions 24, 25, and 26 reveal future usage trends as well as factors influencing the buying decision. Logistics executives' perceptions of integrated logistical service companies will be crucial in determining their degree of success.

RETAIL/WHOLESALE QUESTIONNAIRE: PHASE II

A retail/wholesale questionnaire was developed in late 1987/early 1988 to extend the study of manufacturers. The Advisory Board was instrumental in the development process, as was a select group of logistics executives who pretested the survey. Following the pre-test, the Advisory Board reviewed the questionnaire, and the following modifications were made: (1) greater use of check-off options (rather than open-ended questions) was made; (2) title options and check-off boxes were added to Question 19; (3) questions concerning competitive benchmarking were added; and (4) various measurement scales and phrasing for some questions were changed.

One important criteria in the questionnaire development process was the degree of consistency between this questionnaire and the manufacturers' questionnaire. Many questions were repeated to allow direct comparisons. Major differences between the questionnaires are discussed below.

* Question 6 was added in order to assess trends in centralization or decentralization of logistics activities.

* Responses to Question 7 were used to gauge power or dominance within the marketing channel.

* Question 19 helped to illustrate organizational structure and reporting relationships.

* Competitive benchmarking is used extensively to measure company performance against competitors. Question 23 was used to define the areas most commonly monitored for competitive benchmarking.

* Question 24 obtained ratings on factors the respondents used to evaluate their suppliers. Responses reveal the factors they use most often.

* The retail/wholesale questionnaire also collected data on information and computer applications (Questions 25 through 30). Present levels of computer applications and planned revisions/installations were determined as well as availability of Electronic Data Interchange (EDI). Questions 27 through 30 gave an indication of the respondents' attitudes regarding point-of-sale scanning and their logistics management information systems.

* Finally, Question 36 was used to determine the current and planned usage of specified technologies (for example, bar coding and robotics) among retailers and wholesalers.

MANUFACTURER'S QUESTIONNAIRE: PHASE II

A second questionnaire was addressed to those manufacturers who had responded to Phase I. The main purpose of this second questionnaire was to allow direct comparisons between manufacturers, retailers and wholesalers on the following key questions:

        * Competitive benchmarking.
        * Performance measurement.
        * Opinions on UPC scanning.
        * Computer applications and EDI.
        * Logistics related technologies.

The manufacturer's Phase I and II (MI and MII) and the retailer's-wholesaler's questionnaire (R/W) correspond as shown in the following table:

R/W Questionnaire	Topic	M-Phase I or II Questionnaire
#4...............	Logistics mission statement	MI - #7
#5 A, B, C.......	Logistics strategic plan, its time..... horizon and its frequency of update.	MI - #8 A, B, C
#6 A, B..........	Centralization versus decentra- .... lization of logistics activities; trend over last three years.	MII - #2 A, B

#8, 9, 10........ Title level and functional area of..... MI - #5 A, B
the most senior logistics executive;
number of years in this position.

#13, 14.......... Title level and functional area .... MI - #6
of the person the senior logistics
executive reports to.

#16.............. Years logistics has been a formal ..... MI - #11
organization.

#17.............. Number of times reorganized in the .... MI - #10
last 5 years.

#18.............. Participation in overall strategic .... MII - #5
planning.   (see also MI - #9)

#20.............. Activities that are currently the ..... MI - #13
formal responsibility of logistics.

#21.............. Responsibility for non-typical .... MI - #12
activities.

#22.............. Analysis of performance measure-....... MII - #7
ments: their use; whether the
information is available; and the
importance of each measure.

#23.............. Use of competitive benchmarking .... MII - #6

#25.............. Use of electronic data interchange .... MII - #14
(EDI).   (see also MI - #20)

#26.............. Logistics computer applications- ...... MII - #13
currently installed and planned.   (see also MI - #19)

#27, 28, 29...... Opinions on point of sale .... MII - #8, 9, 10
scanning (U.P.C.).

#30.............. Comparison of logistics MIS to .... MII - #11
MIS in other functional areas.

#31.............. Characteristics of information used ... MI - #23
to manage logistics.

#32.............. Logistics organization's ability to ... MI - #16
accommodate various events.

#33.............. Factors impacting logistical .... MI - #17
operations.

#34.............. Usage of outside service vendors ...... MII - #12
in the next three years.   (see also MI - #24)

#35.............. Factors influencing the use of .... MI - #25
outside service vendors.

#36.............. Logistics related technologies- .... MII - #16
                 currently used and planned.

SAMPLING PROCEDURES

There were two mailings of the manufacturers' questionnaire (Phase I). The first mailing in April of 1987 was to United States firms. The sample was drawn from a Council of Logistics Management mailing list and a second list provided by A.T. Kearney Management Consultants. Letters were sent to 3,002 firms requesting their participation and giving a mail-back card. A total of 668 cards were received and questionnaires were mailed to these firms. Three hundred eighty usable questionnaires were returned and analyzed.

The second mailing of the manufacturer questionnaire (Phase I) was made in February, 1988. This sample of Canadian manufacturers was drawn from a commercial mailing list and a separate list of members of the Canadian Association of Physical Distribution Management.

The retail/wholesale questionnaire (Phase II) was mailed to 6678 United States and Canadian firms in February, 1988. Two mailing lists were purchased-- one for the United States and one for Canada. The lists specified the senior executive for each firm, and the questionnaire was addressed to this executive. During this time period, the Phase II questionnaire developed for manufacturers was mailed to the 380 respondents in Phase I.

STATISTICAL ANALYSIS

(1)   Testing for an association between two categorical variables in a cross-tabulation table was done using the Pearson chi-square statistic. The cell chi-square statistic (with one degree of freedom) was used to evaluate each cell's contribution to the total chi-square statistic.

(2)   The usual t statistic to test the equality of means was used. Use of this t statistic assumes that the population variances of the two samples are equal. This assumption was tested using an F test for the null hypothesis of equality. If unequal, then the approximate t was computed, and Satterthwaite's (1946) approximation for the degrees of freedom was used (see F.W. Satterthwaite, "An Approximate Distribution of Estimate of Variance Components," Biometrics Bulletin, 2 (1946), 110 - 114).

(3)   When more than two means were being compared, an ANOVA model was used and the significance of the overall ANOVA F test is reported. If significant, pairwise t tests, equivalent to Fisher's least significant difference test (LSD) in the case of equal cell sizes, were performed. The preliminary F test of the overall ANOVA controls for the experimentwise error rate under the complete null hypothesis (i.e., all population means are equal), but not under the partial null hypothesis (i.e., some means are equal, but others differ).

COMPARISON OF MANUFACTURERS: PHASE I VERSUS II

One hundred and eighty seven of the 380 manufacturers who responded in Phase I also responded to the Phase II questionnaire. Thus, 193 did not respond again in Phase II.

To determine whether those that did respond are significantly different from those that didn't, the groups were compared as to CAI groupings:

CAI Grouping	Total manu- facturers	Responded Phase I only	Responded Phase I and II
Emerging	62 (16.3%)	38 (19.7%)	24 (12.8%)
Norm	254 (66.8%)	131 (67.9%)	123 (65.8%)
Leading Edge	64 (16.8%)	24 (12.4%)	40 (21.4%)
Total	380	193	187

Those that responded to Phase I and II have, in general, higher CAI scores than those who did not respond in Phase II. The key questions in this research are: (1) are the 40 leading edge firms in Phase I and I different from the 24 leading edge firms in Phase I only; and (2) are the 123 norm firms in Phase I and II different from the 131 norm firms in Phase I only? To answer these two questions, the "Phase I and II" versus "Phase I only" firms were compared within each of the norm and leading edge groups. The following questions were analyzed: 1, 4 through 17, 19 through 24, SIC grouping and CAI score. Overall, within the leading edge firms, those that answered both Phase I and II had significantly ($p = 0.067$) higher CAI scores than those who responded to Phase I only (means of 73.95 versus 72.25). The same is true of the norm firms: the means were 54.74 versus 51.96 and are significantly different at $p = 0.005$. This confirms that the 187 are generally rated higher in CAI score than the 193. This higher rating reflects in differences found on some questions. For example, Phase I and II leading edge firms have a greater number of total line functions than Phase I only firms ($p = 0.049$) and they are better able to accommodate product recall ($p = 0.061$) and the customization of service levels to specific markets ($p = 0.086$). Overall, however, those that responded to both Phase I and Phase II are a fairly good representation of the 380, keeping in mind that they are somewhat upscale as far as CAI scores are concerned.

TABLES IN APPENDIX A

The following tables may be found in the rest of Appendix A:

(1)   tabulation of the questionnaire sent to U.S. manufacturers in Phase I;
(2)   tabulation of the questionnaire sent to Canadian manufacturers;
(3)   tabulation of the Phase II questionnaire sent to U.S. manufacturers who responded in Phase I;
(4)   tabulation of the questionnaire sent to retailers in Phase II;
(5)   tabulation of the questionnaire sent to wholesalers in Phase II; and
(6)   tabulation of the questionnaire sent to hybrids in Phase II.

QUESTION 1: ANNUAL SALES

(A) Annual dollar sales of the business unit (division or subsidiary) or
of the corporation (if the corporation is the business unit):

```
              Mean = $ 1,852,050,908.
Standard Deviation = $ 8,756,827,958.
   Quartiles:  25% = $    95,000,000.
            Median = $   260,000,000.
               75% = $   994,000,000.
               n = 361
```

(B) Annual dollar sales of the business unit, or of the corporation,
omitting those with sales over $50 billion and those with sales under
$1 million:

```
              Mean = $ 1,066,580,364.
Standard Deviation = $ 2,701,504,695.
   Quartiles:  25% = $   103,500,000.
            Median = $   300,000,000.
               75% = $ 1,000,000,000.
               n = 341
```

QUESTION 3: USE OF DEALERS AND DISTRIBUTORS

In finished products logistics, do you use:	Yes	No	n =
(A) Dealers	151 (44.2%)	191 (55.8%)	342
(B) Distributors	267 (75.0%)	89 (25.0%)	356

QUESTION 4: PERCENTAGE OF MANUFACTURING TO CUSTOMER ORDER VERSUS SOLD FROM INVENTORY

% of Manufacturing:	n=	Mean	Std. Dev.	Quartiles 25%	Median	75%
(A) To Customer Order	362	33.7%	.369	2%	15%	97%
(B) Sold from Inventory	362	65.7%	.372	3%	85%	98%

QUESTION 5: DESCRIPTION OF THE SENIOR LOGISTIC OFFICER

(A) Title of the Senior Logistics Officer

Position:	Number (%)	Department:	Number (%)
President	7 (1.9%)	CEO/COO	8 (2.2%)
Executive V. P.	14 (3.8%)	Operations/Manufacturing	45 (12.2%)
Vice President	141 (38.2%)	Logistics	59 (16.0%)
Director	128 (34.7%)	Physical Distribution	123 (33.4%)
Manager	77 (20.9%)	Traffic/Transportation	36 (9.8%)
Supervisor	2 (0.5%)	Materials Management	62 (16.8%)
Other	0 (0.0%)	Inventory	1 (0.3%)
Total	369	Warehousing	0 (0.0%)
		Purchasing	4 (1.1%)
		Other	30 (8.2%)
		Total	368

(B) Number of years this executive has been in this position:

Years:	Number (%)
1 or less	69 (18.9%)
2	67 (18.4%)
3	47 (12.9%)
4	24 (6.6%)
5	34 (9.3%)
6	29 (7.9%)
7	13 (3.6%)
8	14 (3.8%)
9	7 (1.9%)
10	22 (6.0%)
more than 10	39 (10.7%)
Total	365

(C) Senior logistics executive's previous assignment:

Position:	Number (%)	Department:	Number (%)
President	2 (0.6%)	CEO/COO	5 (1.5%)
Executive V. P.	5 (1.5%)	Operations/Manufacturing	43 (12.8%)
Vice President	66 (19.6%)	Logistics	104 (31.0%)
Director	90 (26.8%)	Physical Distribution	35 (10.4%)
Manager	154 (45.8%)	Traffic/Transportation	23 (6.8%)
Supervisor	14 (4.2%)	Materials Management	22 (6.5%)
Other	5 (1.5%)	Inventory	3 (0.9%)
Total	336	Warehousing	2 (0.6%)
		Purchasing	0 (0.0%)
		Other	99 (29.5%)
		Total	336

QUESTION 6:   TITLE OF THE PERSON THE SENIOR LOGISTICS EXECUTIVE REPORTS TO

(A)   Title of the person reported to:

Position:	Number (%)	Department:	Number (%)
President	102 (27.7%)	CEO/COO	134 (36.5%)
Executive V. P.	88 (23.9%)	Operations/Manufacturing	121 (33.0%)
Vice President	146 (39.7%)	Logistics	19 (5.2%)
Director	17 (4.6%)	Physical Distribution	14 (3.8%)
Manager	12 (3.3%)	Traffic/Transportation	2 (0.5%)
Supervisor	0 (0.0%)	Materials Management	25 (6.8%)
Other	3 (0.8%)	Inventory	8 (2.2%)
Total	368	Warehousing	2 (0.5%)
		Purchasing	0 (0.0%)
		Other	42 (11.4%)
		Total	367

(B)   Previous assignment of the person the senior logistics officer reports to:

Position:	Number (%)	Department:	Number (%)
President	40 (12.7%)	CEO/COO	65 (20.7%)
Executive V. P.	42 (13.4%)	Operations/Manufacturing	86 (27.4%)
Vice President	131 (41.7%)	Logistics	27 (8.6%)
Director	43 (13.7%)	Physical Distribution	22 (7.0%)
Manager	40 (12.7%)	Traffic/Transportation	0 (0.0%)
Supervisor	0 (0.0%)	Materials Management	41 (13.1%)
Other	18 (5.7%)	Inventory	6 (1.9%)
Total	314	Warehousing	2 (0.6%)
		Purchasing	0 (0.0%)
		Other	65 (20.7%)
		Total	314

QUESTION 7:   DO YOU HAVE A FORMAL LOGISTICS MISSION STATEMENT?

Answer:	Number (%)
Yes	120 (32.2%)
No	253 (67.8%)
Total	373

TABULATION OF THE QUESTIONNAIRE
(Manufacturers: Phase I)

QUESTION 8: FORMAL LOGISTICS STRATEGIC PLANS

(A) Do you have a formal logistics strategic plan?

Answer:	Number (%)
Yes	171 (45.4%)
No	206 (54.6%)
Total	377

(B) If yes, what is the time horizon of the plan?

Time Horizon:	Number (%)
1 year or less	28 (16.5%)
2 years	6 (3.5%)
3 years	45 (26.5%)
4 years	1 (0.6%)
5 years	79 (46.5%)
more than 5 years	11 (6.1%)

* mean = 3.94 years,   standard deviation = 2.02,   n = 170

(C) How often is the plan reviewed or updated?

Reviewed Every:	Number (%)
less than 6 mths	39 (23.0%)
half year	12 (7.1%)
1 year	114 (67.1%)
2 years	4 (2.4%)
4 years	1 (0.6%)

* mean = 0.81 years,   standard deviation = 0.47,   n = 170

QUESTION 9: PARTICIPATION IN OVERALL STRATEGIC PLANNING

Do logistics executives participate in overall strategic planning for your business unit:

Answer:	Number (%)
Yes	279 (74.8%)
No	94 (25.2%)
Total	373

QUESTION 10: NUMBER OF TIMES REORGANIZED

Number of Times Reorganized in the Last 5 Years:	Number (%)
0	63 (18.0%)
1	114 (32.6%)
2	86 (24.6%)
3	53 (15.1%)
4	13 (3.7%)
5	6 (1.7%)
6	5 (1.4%)
7	3 (0.9%)
8	3 (0.9%)
10 or more	4 (1.2%)

* mean = 1.89, standard deviation = 2.15, n = 350
NOTE: mean includes the "0" responses

QUESTION 11: HOW MANY YEARS HAS LOGISTICS BEEN A FORMAL ORGANIZATION?

Years a Formal Organization:	Number (%)
0 or missing	20 (5.3%)
less than 1	4 (1.1%)
1 year	24 (6.3%)
2 or 3 years	50 (13.2%)
4 or 5 years	58 (15.3%)
6 or 7 years	28 (7.4%)
8 or 9 years	26 (6.8%)
10 years	44 (11.6%)
11 - 14 years	22 (5.9%)
15 years	24 (6.3%)
16 - 19 years	15 (4.1%)
20 years	30 (7.9%)
over 20 years	35 (9.2%)

* mean = 10.90 years, n = 380
NOTE: mean excludes the "0" responses

TABULATION OF THE QUESTIONNAIRE
(Manufacturers: Phase I)

QUESTION 12: BEYOND FUNCTIONS

Does your logistics organization have responsibilities for any non-typical activities such as data processing, real estate, dealer services and/or facilities?

Answer:	Number (%)
Yes	155 (41.6%)
No	218 (58.4%)
Total	373

QUESTION 13: ANALYSIS OF FUNCTIONS

Activity or Function:	Number who have it in Logistics n =	Likely to be added Yes	No	Nature of Responsibility Line	Staff	Both
Sales Forecasting	118	28	186	51	114	6
Production Planning	193	32	123	135	90	5
Sourcing/Purchasing	192	41	119	144	71	11
Inbound Transportation	285	46	27	222	57	18
Raw/WIP Inventory	163	23	141	114	73	6
Finished Goods Inventory	266	39	48	213	59	12
Intra-co. Transportation	297	23	29	238	36	15
Fin. Gds. Field Warehousing	280	26	37	233	36	7
Order Processing	207	28	97	169	46	6
Customer Service	213	27	92	165	52	12
Outbound Transportation	333	21	15	280	27	12
Logistics Systems Planning	266	45	21	205	47	15
Logistics Engineering	119	39	107	89	42	4
Logistics Administration	259	38	23	217	27	11
International Logistics	174	51	75	131	51	13

-------- * -------- * --------

Total Line or Staff Functions:	Number (%)
5 or less	59 (15.5%)
6 functions	29 (7.6%)
7 functions	29 (7.6%)
8 functions	45 (11.8%)
9 functions	31 (8.2%)
10 functions	48 (12.6%)
11 functions	42 (11.1%)
12 functions	35 (9.2%)
13 functions	32 (8.4%)
14 functions	14 (3.7%)
15 functions	16 (4.2%)

QUESTION 14: ANALYSIS OF LOGISTICS ORGANIZATION

Description:	Number (%)
(A) Functional Organization: Dispersed Responsibilities for Logistics Activities	108 (28.5%)
(B) Functional Organization: Consolidated Logistics Responsibilities	93 (24.5%)
(C) Divisional Organization: Logistics Functions Consolidated Within Business Units	59 (15.6%)
(D) Divisional Organization: Centrally Consolidated Logistics Responsibility	41 (10.8%)
(E) Divisional Organization: Corporate Staff Logistics Function with Line Logistics Functions in the Business Units	59 (15.6%)
(F) Other	19 (5.0%)
Total =	379

QUESTION 15: ANALYSIS OF STRATEGY

Description:	Number (%)
(A) Process: A process-based strategy is concerned with managing a broad group of logistics activities as a value added chain. Emphasis is on achieving efficiency from managing purchasing, manufacturing, scheduling, and physical distribution as an integrated system.	203 (54.1%)
(B) Market: A market-based strategy is concerned with managing a limited group of logistics activities for a multidivision single business unit or across multiple business units. The logistics organization seeks to make joint product shipments to common customers for different product groups and seeks to facilitate sales and logistical coordination by a single order-invoice. Often the senior sales and logistics executives report to the same manager.	104 (27.7%)
(C) Channel: A channel-based strategy is concerned with managing logistics activities performed jointly with dealers and distributors. The strategic orientation places a great deal of attention on external control. Significant amounts of finished inventories are typically maintained forward or downstream in the distribution channel.	34 (9.1%)
(D) Other	34 (9.1%)
Total =	375

TABULATION OF THE QUESTIONNAIRE
(Manufacturers: Phase I)

QUESTION 16: ABILITY TO ACCOMMODATE VARIOUS EVENTS IMPACTING LOGISTICS ACTIVITIES

Number of Firms Rating Their Ability to Accommodate:	n =	Response Rating *: Mean	Std. Dev.
Special Customer Service Requests	368	3.12	0.66
Sales/Marketing Incentive Programs	280	3.04	0.72
Product Introduction	336	3.01	0.71
Product Phaseout	330	2.91	0.76
Disruption in Supply	359	2.78	0.71
Computer Breakdown	343	2.29	0.84
Unexpected Production Schedule Changes	365	2.82	0.66
Product Recall	298	2.79	0.81
Customization of Service Levels to Specific Markets or Customers	355	2.79	0.88
Product Modification or Customization While in the Logistics System	307	2.61	0.86

--------- * --------- * ---------

* Scale was: N.A. = not applicable
1 = current logistics system cannot handle
2 = current logistics system has difficulty handling
3 = current logistics system handles with few problems
4 = current logistics system handles easily

QUESTION 17: IMPACT ON LOGISTICS ACTIVITIES

Impact of:	n =	Response Rating *: Mean	Std. Dev.
Forecast Accuracy	361	3.06	0.75
Computer Support	373	3.27	0.81
Excessive End-of-Month/Quarter Surges	366	2.76	0.89
Communications with Customers	359	2.76	0.85
Production Planning/Scheduling	364	3.07	0.79
Interface with Manufacturing	359	2.99	0.82
Availability of Trained Logistics Personnel	361	2.58	0.87
Vehicle Routing/Scheduling	340	2.71	0.94
Computer Applications Backlog	349	2.58	0.89
Transportation Costs	373	3.05	0.92
Communication with Material Vendors	333	2.60	0.93
Communication with Dealers/Distributors	316	2.53	0.96
Warehouse Productivity	344	2.78	0.90
Measurement Tools/Methods	345	2.54	0.85
Communication with Internal Non-Logistics Units	360	2.79	0.80
Timely Information	374	3.25	0.68
Supplier Performance	356	2.96	0.91
Communication with External Logistics Service Suppliers	348	2.50	0.90
Incompatibility of Computer Equipment/Software	313	2.23	0.96

--------- * --------- * ---------

* Scale was: N.A. = not applicable
                 1 = no impact
                 2 = slight impact
                 3 = high impact
                 4 = very high impact

TABULATION OF THE QUESTIONNAIRE
(Manufacturers: Phase I)

QUESTION 19: LOGISTICS COMPUTER APPLICATIONS

Computer Application:	Is Currently Installed	Number Answering that the Computer Application:	
		Will be Revised in the Next 3-5 Years	Will be Installed in the Next 3-5 Years
Freight Audit/Payment	239	58	62
Purchasing	239	73	50
Sales Forecasting	223	78	44
MRP	187	59	42
DRP	71	60	72
Raw Material Inventory Control	268	53	34
Finished Goods Inventory Control	312	77	20
Warehousing	242	65	41
Order Processing	330	74	12
Order Entry	325	83	14
Vehicle Routing/Scheduling	98	63	86
Inbound Freight Consolidation	63	66	87
Outbound Freight Consolidation	146	69	73
Supporting Financials	275	62	30
Performance Measures	203	81	75
Distribution Modeling	101	67	97

QUESTION 20: EDI APPLICATIONS

Application:	Number Answering EDI is:	
	Currently Used:	Planned in the Next 3-5 Years
Raw Materials Vendors	57	123
Copackers/Contractors	15	60
Public Warehouses	58	91
Carriers	102	139
Customers/Brokers	116	136

QUESTION 21:   USE OF ARTIFICIAL INTELLIGENCE

Artificial Intelligence:	Response: Yes	Response: No	n =
Currently Using	22 (6.0%)	347 (94.0%)	369
Plan to Install (next 3 years)	53 (15.9%)	280 (84.1%)	333

QUESTION 22:   AVAILABILITY OF INFORMATION ON FREIGHT TRACKING,
RATING SYSTEMS AND DELIVERY TIME

Availability of Information (from all sources) on:	Response: Yes	Response: No	n =
Freight Tracking	259 (71.2%)*	105 (28.8%)	364
Real-Time Freight Rating System	182 (51.3%)	173 (48.7%)	355
Accurate Freight Delivery Time	183 (51.1%)	175 (48.9%)	358

QUESTION 23:   CHARACTERISTICS OF INFORMATION USED TO MANAGE LOGISTICS

Characteristic:	Response Rating *: n =	Mean	Std. Dev.
Timely	371	3.85	0.83
Accurate	370	4.03	0.72
Readily Available	368	3.65	0.87
Formatted on an Exception Basis	365	2.85	0.95
Appropriately Formatted to Facilitate Use	361	3.39	0.91

* Scale was: 1 = never
2 = not usually
3 = sometimes
4 = in most instances
5 = always

TABULATION OF THE QUESTIONNAIRE
(Manufacturers: Phase I)

QUESTION 24: USAGE OF OUTSIDE SERVICE VENDORS

	Response Rating *:		
Outside Service:	n =	Mean	Std. Dev.
Transportation	375	3.05	1.07
Warehousing	373	2.75	1.20
Order Entry/Processing	370	1.92	1.15
Inventory Management	373	1.96	1.17
Freight Audit/Payment	377	2.68	1.14

* Scale used:
1 = will not use outside logistical services
2 = will use less than current levels
3 = usage will remain constant
4 = will use more outside logistical services
5 = will use many more outside logistical services

QUESTION 25: FACTORS AFFECTING THE DECISION TO USE OUTSIDE SERVICE VENDORS

	Response Rating *:		
Factor Affecting the Decision:	n =	Mean	Std. Dev.
Deregulation	296	2.64	0.99
Services Available	357	3.23	0.78
Quality of Services	360	3.57	0.70
Data Processing/Communication Services	340	2.87	0.85
Management Quality	341	3.14	0.79
Customer Attitudes	328	3.13	0.88

* Scale was:
N.A. = not applicable
1 = not important
2 = neutral
3 = somewhat important
4 = very important

QUESTION 26: OPINIONS ON INTEGRATED LOGISTICS SERVICE COMPANIES

Item:	n =	Response Rating *: Mean	Std. Dev.
The advantages of using integrated service companies greatly outweigh the disadvantages.	370	3.14	0.89
There is a significant risk in using integrated service companies.	368	2.91	0.90
Integrated logistics service companies are a good idea.	359	3.65	0.68
Few integrated logistics service companies exist today.	357	3.18	0.94
The range of integrated logistics services will increase in the future.	360	3.99	0.67
The real key to such integrated services is the eventual availability of single ownership multimodal transportation.	354	3.23	0.86
Even if commonly available, shippers will not enter into single source turnkey solutions for their logistic requirements.	356	2.88	0.96
Integrated multimodal logistics service companies will increase competition in surface transportation.	368	3.50	0.83
The availability of multimodal transportation will not radically change the way logistics is managed.	357	2.82	0.91
There is really no significant difference between integrated and traditional logistics service companies.	356	2.38	0.81

* Scale used: 1 = strongly disagree
2 = disagree
3 = neutral
4 = agree
5 = strongly agree

TABULATION OF THE QUESTIONNAIRE
(Manufacturers: Phase I)

CHARACTERISTICS OF THE RESPONDENTS

(A) Number who are CLM members: 184 (48.7%)
    Number who are not CLM members: 194 (51.3%)
                     Total   378

(B) Distribution by CAI grouping:

CAI Grouping	Number (%)
Emerging	62 (16.3%)
Norm	254 (66.8%)
Leading Edge	64 (16.8%)
Total	380

(C) Distribution by SIC Code (Industry):

SIC	Number (%)
Mining	39 (10.5%)
Food	89 (23.9%)
Textiles	21 (5.6%)
Forest Related	55 (14.8%)
Electronics/Computers	50 (13.4%)
Motor & Transportation Equipment	45 (12.1%)
Pharmaceuticals	73 (19.6%)
Total	372

DISTRIBUTION BY CAI GROUPING:

CAI Grouping	Number (%)
Emerging	5 (18.5%)
Norm	17 (63.0%)
Leading Edge	5 (18.5%)
Total	**27**

QUESTION 1: ANNUAL SALES

Annual dollar sales of the business unit (division or subsidiary):

Mean = $ 1,053,495,600.
Standard Deviation = $ 3,739,025,770.
Quartiles: 25% = $ 54,159,000.
Median = $ 97,000,000.
75% = $ 300,000,000.
n = 20

QUESTION 5: DESCRIPTION OF THE SENIOR LOGISTICS OFFICER

(A)   Title of the Senior Logistics Officer

Position:	Number (%)	Department:	Number (%)
President	0 (0.0%)	CEO/COO	0 (0.0%)
Executive V. P.	0 (0.0%)	Operations/Manufacturing	4 (16.0%)
Vice President	8 (32.0%)	Logistics	8 (32.0%)
Director	7 (28.0%)	Physical Distribution	2 (8.0%)
Manager	10 (40.0%)	Traffic/Transportation	2 (8.0%)
Supervisor	0 (0.0%)	Materials Management	4 (16.0%)
Other	0 (0.0%)	Inventory	1 (4.0%)
Total	**25**	Warehousing	0 (0.0%)
		Purchasing	0 (0.0%)
		Other	4 (16.0%)
		Total	**25**

TABULATION OF THE QUESTIONNAIRE
(Canadian Manufacturers: Phase I)

QUESTION 5: (CON'T.)

(B) Number of years this executive has been in this position:

Mean = 3.73 years
Standard Deviation = 2.68 years
n = 26

QUESTION 7: DO YOU HAVE A FORMAL LOGISTICS MISSION STATEMENT?

Answer:	Number (%)
Yes	11 (42.3%)
No	15 (57.7%)
Total	26

QUESTION 8: FORMAL LOGISTICS STRATEGIC PLANS

(A) Do you have a formal logistics strategic plan?

Answer:	Number (%)
Yes	11 (44.0%)
No	14 (56.0%)
Total	25

(B) If yes, what is the time horizon of the plan?

Mean = 4.00 years
Standard Deviation = 2.65 years
n = 11

(C) How often is the plan reviewed or updated?

Mean = 0.94 years
Standard Deviation = 0.19 years
n = 10

QUESTION 9:   PARTICIPATION IN OVERALL STRATEGIC PLANNING

Do logistics executives formally participate in overall strategic planning
for your business unit?

Answer:	Number (%)
Yes	21 (77.8%)
No	6 (22.2%)
Total	**27**

QUESTION 10:   NUMBER OF TIMES REORGANIZED

Mean = 2.32 times
Standard Deviation = 1.45
n = 19

QUESTION 11:   HOW MANY YEARS HAS LOGISTICS BEEN A FORMAL ORGANIZATION?

Mean = 10.05 years
Standard Deviation = 9.68
n = 19

QUESTION 12:   BEYOND FUNCTIONS

Does your logistical organization have responsibilities for any non-typical
activities such as data processing, real estate, dealer services and/or facilities?

Answer:	Number (%)
Yes	11 (44.0%)
No	14 (56.0%)
Total	**25**

TABULATION OF THE QUESTIONNAIRE
(Canadian Manufacturers: Phase I)

QUESTION 13:   ANALYSIS OF FUNCTIONS

Activity or Function:	Number who have it in Logistics n =	Likely to be added Yes	No	Nature of Responsibility Line	Staff	Both
Sales Forecasting	11	2	11	3	12	0
Production Planning	18	2	3	13	8	0
Sourcing/Purchasing	15	4	3	11	6	0
Inbound Transportation	16	4	2	17	3	0
Raw/WIP Inventory	12	3	8	10	3	0
Finished Goods Inventory	20	1	3	16	3	1
Intra-Co. Transportation	20	2	2	19	2	0
Fin. Gds. Field Warehousing	18	3	1	19	1	0
Order Processing	13	4	6	11	3	0
Customer Service	15	2	8	11	5	0
Outbound Transportation	19	2	1	18	2	0
Logistics Systems Planning	15	6	1	11	5	1
Logistics Engineering	8	6	5	4	6	0
Logistics Administration	17	2	1	15	3	0
International Logistics	13	2	4	12	1	0

-------- * -------- * --------

	Total Functions:	Total Line Functions:
Mean	8.52	6.99
Standard Deviation	4.60	4.66
n	27	27
Quartiles: 75%	12	10
Median	9	7
25%	6	0

QUESTION 14: ANALYSIS OF LOGISTICS ORGANIZATION

Description	Number (%)
(A) Functional Organization: Dispersed Responsibilities for Logistics Activities	15 (57.7%)
(B) Functional Organization: Consolidated Logistics Responsibilities	5 (19.2%)
(C) Divisional Organization: Logistics Functions Consolidated Within Business Units	1 (3.8%)
(D) Divisional Organization: Centrally Consolidated Logistics Responsibility	3 (11.5%)
(E) Divisional Organization: Corporate Staff Logistics Function with Line Logistics Functions in the Business Units	2 (7.7%)
(F) Other	0 (0.0%)
Total	26

QUESTION 15: ANALYSIS OF STRATEGY

	Number (%)
(A) Process	20 (83.3%)
(B) Market	2 (8.3%)
(C) Channel	2 (8.3%)
(D) Other	0 (0.0%)
Total	24

TABULATION OF THE QUESTIONNAIRE
(Canadian Manufacturers: Phase I)

QUESTION 16: ABILITY TO ACCOMMODATE VARIOUS EVENTS IMPACTING LOGISTICS ACTIVITIES

Number of Firms Rating Their Ability to Accommodate:	n =	Response Rating *: Mean	Std. Dev.
Special Customer Service Requests	27	2.89	0.69
Sales/Marketing Incentive Programs	20	3.00	0.92
Product Introduction	26	3.19	0.94
Product Phaseout	25	3.32	0.80
Disruption in Supply	27	2.70	0.67
Computer Breakdown	27	2.56	0.97
Unexpected Production Schedule Changes	27	2.81	0.68
Product Recall	23	3.00	0.79
Customization of Service Levels to Specific Markets or Customers	25	2.84	0.89
Product Modification or Customization While in the Logistics System	21	2.62	0.80

* Scale was: N.A. = not applicable
1 = current logistics system cannot handle
2 = current logistics system has difficulty handling
3 = current logistics system handles with few problems
4 = current logistics system handles easily

QUESTION 17: IMPACT ON LOGISTICS ACTIVITIES

Impact of:		Response Rating *:	
	n =	Mean	Std. Dev.
Forecast Accuracy	27	3.04	0.85
Computer Support	26	3.35	0.75
Excessive End-of-Month/Quarter Surges	26	2.69	0.88
Communications with Customers	25	2.80	0.71
Production Planning/Scheduling	26	3.58	0.50
Interface with Manufacturing	26	3.46	0.65
Availability of Trained Logistics Personnel	25	2.88	0.93
Vehicle Routing/Scheduling	25	2.48	0.92
Computer Applications Backlog	25	2.80	0.96
Transportation Costs	26	2.54	1.03
Communication with Material Vendors	25	2.68	0.80
Communication with Dealers/Distributors	20	2.55	0.76
Warehouse Productivity	23	2.83	0.78
Measurement Tools/Methods	21	2.67	0.79
Communication with Internal Non-Logistics Units	25	2.68	0.85
Timely Information	26	3.42	0.76
Supplier Performance	26	3.11	0.82
Communication with External Logistics Suppliers	22	2.45	0.86
Incompatibility of Computer Equipment/Software	20	2.25	1.02

* Scale was: N.A. = not applicable
              1 = no impact
              2 = slight impact
              3 = high impact
              4 = very high impact

TABULATION OF THE QUESTIONNAIRE
(Canadian Manufacturers: Phase I)

QUESTION 20: EDI APPLICATIONS

	Number Answering EDI is:	
Application:	Currently Used:	Planned in the Next 3-5 Years
Raw Materials Vendors	3	15
Copackers/Contractors	1	7
Public Warehouses	3	8
Carriers	5	13
Customers/Brokers	10	11

QUESTION 21: USE OF ARTIFICIAL INTELLIGENCE

	Response Rating:		
Artificial Intelligence:	Yes	No	n =
Currently Using	1 (4.0%)	24 (96.0%)	25
Plan to Install (next 3 years)	5 (21.7%)	18 (78.3%)	23

QUESTION 23: CHARACTERISTICS OF INFORMATION USED TO MANAGE LOGISTICS

	Response Rating *:		
Characteristic:	n =	Mean	Std. Dev.
Timely	24	3.71	0.95
Accurate	24	3.75	1.03
Readily Available	24	3.75	0.89
Formatted on an Exception Basis	24	2.88	1.03
Appropriately Formatted to Facilitate Use	23	3.30	1.02

* Scale was: 1 = never
              2 = not usually
              3 = sometimes
              4 = in most instances
              5 = always

QUESTION 24: USAGE OF OUTSIDE SERVICE VENDORS

| | | Response Rating *: | |
Outside Service:	n =	Mean	Std. Dev.
Transportation	26	2.88	1.21
Warehousing	25	2.64	1.25
Order Entry/Processing	25	1.76	1.23
Inventory Management	26	1.73	1.15
Freight Audit/Payment	26	2.38	1.27

* Scale was: 1 = wil not use outside logistical services
2 = will use less than current levels
3 = usage will remain constant
4 = will use more outside logistical services
5 = will use many more outside logistical services

QUESTION 25: FACTORS AFFECTING THE DECISION TO USE OUTSIDE VENDORS

| | | Response Rating *: | |
Factor Affecting the Decision:	n =	Mean	Std. Dev.
Deregulation	14	2.50	0.94
Services Available	22	2.95	1.05
Quality of Services	21	3.43	0.87
Data Processing/Communication Services	21	2.62	1.02
Management Quality	20	2.80	0.95
Customer Attitudes	19	3.16	0.83

* Scale was: N.A. = not applicable
1 = not important
2 = neutral
3 = somewhat important
4 = very important

TABULATION OF THE QUESTIONNAIRE
(Manufacturers - Updates Phase II)

QUESTION 1: ANNUAL SALES

Annual dollar sales of the business unit (division or subsidiary) or of the corporation (if the corporation is the business unit):

$$
\begin{aligned}
\text{Mean} &= \$ \ 1,889,287,000.00 \\
\text{Standard Deviation} &= \$ \ 8,822,776,000.00 \\
\text{Quartiles: } 25\% &= \$ \ \ \ \ 105,000,000.00 \\
\text{Median} &= \$ \ \ \ \ 350,000,000.00 \\
75\% &= \$ \ 1,150,000,000.00 \\
n &= 173
\end{aligned}
$$

QUESTION 2: ANALYSIS OF LOGISTICS ORGANIZATION

(A) Centralization of logistics activities at present:

Description	Number (%)
Completely Decentralized	9 (4.8%)
Somewhat Decentralized	22 (11.8%)
Combination	46 (24.7%)
Somewhat Centralized	62 (33.3%)
Completely Centralized	47 (25.3%)

  * mean 3.62,   standard deviation 1.13,   n = 186

(B)   Trend over the last three years:

Description	Number (%)
Centralization of logistics activities	92 (50.0%)
Decentralization of logistics activities	35 (19.0%)
No Change	57 (31.0%)
Total	**184**

QUESTION 3: DOMINANT CHANNEL MEMBER

The set of relationships defined by manufacturers, wholesalers, and retailers is referred to as a marketing channel. Who is the most influential member of your channel in terms of coordinating logistical relationships:

	Number (%)
This business unit	113 (62.4%)
Wholesaler	20 (11.0%)
Retailer	12 (6.6%)
Broker	2 (1.1%)
Manufacturer	26 (14.4%)
Other	8 (4.4%)
Total	**181**

QUESTION 4: NUMBER OF TIMES REORGANIZED

Number of Times Reorganized in the Last Year:	Number (%)
0	92 (49.7%)
1	73 (39.5%)
2	15 (8.1%)
3	5 (2.7%)

* mean = 0.64, standard deviation = 0.75, n = 185
NOTE: mean includes the "0" responses

QUESTION 5: PARTICIPATION IN OVERALL STRATEGIC PLANNING

Does your senior logistics executive formally participate in overall strategic planning for your business unit?

Answer	Number (%)
Yes	125 (67.6%)
No, but provides input through other executives	54 (29.2%)
No, provides no input	6 (3.2%)
Total	**185**

TABULATION OF THE QUESTIONNAIRE
(Manufacturers - Updates Phase II)

QUESTION 6: COMPETITIVE BENCHMARKING

Benchmarking is a management process used to monitor and measure performance against competitors. Please indicate whether you use competitive benchmarking in each of the following areas:

Area	Number (%) Yes	Number (%) No	n =
Cost	143 (78.1%)	40 (21.9%)	183
Asset management	63 (36.6%)	109 (63.4%)	172
Customer service	157 (84.9%)	28 (15.1%)	185
Productivity	104 (57.5%)	77 (42.5%)	181
Quality	144 (79.1%)	38 (20.9%)	182
Logistics strategy	96 (53.0%)	85 (47.0%)	181
Technology deployment	84 (47.2%)	94 (52.8%)	178
Transportation operations	102 (56.4%)	79 (43.6%)	181
Warehouse operations	92 (51.1%)	88 (48.9%)	180
Order processing operations	94 (51.9%)	87 (48.1%)	181

QUESTION 7: ANALYSIS OF LOGISTICS RELATED PERFORMANCE MEASUREMENTS

Performance Measurement:	Number (%) who said the measure was used:*	Number (%) who said the information was available:*	Average Importance (1 = Unimportant 5 = Important)*
(A) ASSET MANAGEMENT			
Inventory turns	145 (81.9%)	138 (88.5%)	4.10
Inventory carrying costs	120 (68.6%)	113 (72.9%)	3.67
Inventory levels (number of days supply)	152 (86.9%)	139 (92.1%)	4.13
Obsolete inventory	150 (85.7%)	133 (87.5%)	3.68
Return on net assets	115 (66.9%)	118 (76.7%)	3.88
Return on investment	126 (74.6%)	122 (80.3%)	4.04

(CONTINUED...)

* % and means based on the number of respondents who answered the question.

QUESTION 7:   (CON'T)

Performance Measurement:	Number (%) who said the measure was used:*	Number (%) who said the information was available:*	Average Importance (1 = Unimportant 5 = Important)*
(B) COST (logistics cost only)			
Total cost analysis	155 (87.6%)	138 (87.9%)	4.47
Cost per unit	141 (79.7%)	136 (88.9%)	4.14
Cost as a percentage of sales	150 (83.3%)	144 (91.7%)	3.91
Inbound freight costs	154 (86.0%)	139 (87.4%)	3.82
Outbound freight costs	170 (94.4%)	150 (96.2%)	4.43
Warehouse costs	153 (89.0%)	136 (91.3%)	4.05
Administrative costs	140 (80.0%)	139 (92.1%)	3.61
Order processing costs	89 (52.0%)	91 (62.3%)	3.31
Direct labor costs	136 (78.6%)	128 (85.3%)	3.82
Comparison of actual versus budget	172 (96.6%)	148 (95.5%)	4.19
Cost trend analysis	133 (76.9%)	117 (77.5%)	3.78
Direct product profitability	100 (59.2%)	102 (67.5%)	3.82
(C) CUSTOMER SERVICE (to your customer)			
Fill rate	129 (78.2%)	118 (81.9%)	4.26
Stockouts	133 (80.6%)	115 (82.7%)	4.20
Shipping errors	142 (83.0%)	129 (86.0%)	4.06
On time delivery	143 (82.7%)	121 (80.1%)	4.35
Backorders	128 (77.1%)	120 (83.3%)	3.88
Cycle time	114 (69.9%)	106 (76.3%)	3.75
Customer feedback	159 (90.3%)	136 (86.6%)	4.38
Sales force feedback	152 (87.9%)	131 (85.6%)	4.04
Customer Surveys	119 (68.8%)	104 (68.9%)	3.76

(CONTINUED...)

* % and means based on the number of respondents who answered the question.

TABULATION OF THE QUESTIONNAIRE
(Manufacturers - Updates Phase II)

QUESTION 7: (CON'T)

Performance Measurement:	Number (%) who said the measure was used:*	Number (%) who said the information was available:*	Average Importance (1 = Unimportant 5 = Important)*
(D) PRODUCTIVITY			
Units shipped per employee	91 (54.8%)	104 (73.2%)	3.37
Units per labor dollar	84 (51.9%)	98 (69.5%)	3.38
Orders per sales rep.	58 (38.7%)	78 (60.0%)	2.99
Comparison to historical standards	129 (76.3%)	120 (81.6%)	3.55
Goal programs	128 (76.2%)	108 (75.0%)	3.82
Productivity Index	91 (55.8%)	86 (61.0%)	3.65
(E) QUALITY			
Frequency of damage	118 (67.4%)	101 (66.0%)	3.77
Dollar amount of damage	129 (74.6%)	111 (73.0%)	3.73
Number of credit claims	128 (75.7%)	116 (79.5%)	3.70
Number of customer returns	135 (77.1%)	123 (80.4%)	3.75
Cost of returned goods	115 (68.0%)	103 (71.5%)	3.55

* % and means based on the number of respondents who answered the question.

-------- * -------- * --------

TOTAL NUMBER OF PERFORMANCE MEASUREMENTS

Category	n =	Mean	Std. Dev.
Asset Management	187	4.32	1.93
Cost	187	9.05	2.70
Customer Service	187	6.52	2.61
Productivity	187	3.11	2.02
Quality	187	3.34	1.83

TABULATION OF THE QUESTIONNAIRE
(Manufacturers - Updates Phase II)

QUESTIONS 8, 9, 10:   OPINIONS ABOUT POINT OF SALE SCANNING (UPC)

(A) "UPC has given retailers a unique advantage over other members of the distribution channel"

Answer:	Number (%)
Strongly disagree/Disagree	13 (7.3%)
Neutral	59 (33.3%)
Strongly agree/Agree	105 (59.3%)
Total	177

* mean = 3.66, standard deviation 0.90, n = 177

(B) "Information derived from point of sale scanning has made your business unit competitively stronger in comparison to other members of your distribution channel"

Answer:	Number (%)
Strongly disagree/Disagree	39 (23.8%)
Neutral	80 (48.8%)
Strongly agree/Agree	45 (27.4%)
Total	164

* mean = 3.03, standard deviation 0.99, n = 164

(C) "Point of sale scanning information is more important to retailers than wholesalers"

Answer:	Number (%)
Strongly disagree/Disagree	45 (26.2%)
Neutral	47 (27.3%)
Strongly agree/Agree	80 (46.5%)
Total	172

* mean = 3.22, standard deviation 1.02, n = 172

TABULATION OF THE QUESTIONNAIRE
(Manufacturers - Updates Phase II)

QUESTION 11: COMPARATIVE EVALUATION OF LOGISTICS MANAGEMENT
INFORMATION SYSTEM

How do your company's logistics management information systems compare overall
to the management information systems designed to support other areas of the
business? (i.e. Accounting, Finance, Sales, etc.)

Answer:	Number (%)
Much Worse	10 (5.4%)
Worse	49 (26.5%)
Same	59 (31.9%)
Better	50 (27.0%)
Much better	17 (9.2%)
Total	**185**

* mean = 3.08, standard deviation 1.06, n = 185

QUESTION 12: USAGE OF OUTSIDE SERVICE VENDORS

Outside Service:	Response Rating *:		
	n =	Mean	Std. Dev.
Transportation	183	3.27	0.86
Warehousing	176	2.87	1.18
Order entry/processing	178	1.77	1.10
Inventory management	173	1.71	1.04
Freight audit/payment	177	2.76	1.07
Consolidators	169	2.71	1.11
International freight forwarders	168	3.07	0.96
Domestic freight forwarders	164	2.35	1.12
Order fulfillment and support	131	2.10	1.22

* Scale used: N.A. = not applicable
1 = will not use outside logistical services
2 = will use less than current levels
3 = usage will remain constant
4 = will use more outside logistical services
5 = will use many more outside logistical services

QUESTION 13:   LOGISTICS COMPUTER APPLICATIONS

Logistics Computer Application:	Number who answered:			
	Currently installed and no plans for revision	Currently installed but will be revised in next 3 years	Not currently installed but will be in next 3 years	Not currently installed & no plans to install
Freight Audit and Payment	57	60	31	35
Purchasing	56	77	37	12
Sales Forecasting	40	97	25	14
Raw Materials Inventory Control	56	83	25	11
In Process Inventory Control	55	87	20	15
Finished Gds. Inventory Control	66	100	9	4
Warehouse Order Selection	49	76	24	28
Warehouse On-Line Receiving	43	65	43	27
Warehouse Merchandise Locator	48	58	33	38
Warehouse Workload Balancing	21	35	41	79
Warehouse Short Interval Scheduling	24	30	30	86
Order Processing	61	114	6	1
Order Entry	62	114	7	0
Vehicle Routing and Scheduling	17	42	43	78
Inbound Freight Consolidation	25	29	49	78
Outbound Freight Consolidation	43	55	32	52
Supporting Financials	67	78	18	12
Performance Measurement	45	85	32	21
Distribution Modeling	28	54	42	53
Direct Product Profitability	37	47	33	57
Direct Store Delivery	24	30	16	100
Shelf Management	17	26	18	101
MRP	35	65	26	38
DRP	14	45	41	57

TABULATION OF THE QUESTIONNAIRE
(Manufacturers - Updates Phase II)

QUESTION 14:   EDI USAGE

Number who are currently using, or planning to use Electronic Data Interchange
(EDI) to facilitate order or other communications with the following:

	Number who answered:			
Entity	Currently installed	Plan to install in next 3 years	No Plans to install	Not Applicable
Manufacturers	41	54	43	39
Wholesalers	43	48	44	40
Public Warehouses	37	47	50	42
Carriers	46	75	52	8
Financial Institutions	47	36	45	37
Retailers	28	31	47	57
Customers	49	75	36	18
Copackers/Contractors	10	32	56	69

QUESTION 15:   FINANCIAL AND PERSONNEL RESOURCES AVAILABLE TO IMPLEMENT
LOGISTICS COMPUTER APPLICATIONS?

Answer:	Number (%)
Yes	140 (75.7%)
No	45 (24.3%)
Total	185

TABULATION OF THE QUESTIONNAIRE
(Manufacturers - Updates Phase II)

QUESTION 16:   TECHNOLOGY APPLICATIONS WITHIN THE BUSINESS UNIT

Technology	Number who answered:				
	Currently used in logistics	Currently used in firm but not in logistics	Planned to be installed in logistics next 3 years	Not planned to be installed in logistics	Have not evaluated
Bar codes	50	24	77	22	13
Optical scanning	29	19	45	47	39
Robotics	15	44	11	65	46
Artificial intelligence/ knowledge based systems	7	14	38	58	60
Automated storage and retrieval systems	32	9	14	92	31
Automated material handling equipment	44	20	32	61	22
Local area networks	43	16	36	32	44
Computer-aided warehouse design	31	8	23	59	58
Handheld data entry devices	35	22	60	28	35
Electronic order transmission	100	16	42	11	13
On board computers - delivery vehicles	29	2	28	59	60
On board computers - lift trucks	22	4	30	55	67
Voice data capture	11	9	16	63	74
IBM PC or PC XT compatible	154	9	14	4	5
80286 Microcomputers (IBM AT or compatible)	84	13	16	25	38

(CONTINUED...)

TABULATION OF THE QUESTIONNAIRE
(Manufacturers - Updates Phase II)

QUESTION 16: (CON'T.)

			Number who answered:		
Technology	Currently used in logistics	Currently used in firm but not in logistics	Planned to be installed in logistics next 3 years	Not planned to be installed in logistics	Have not evaluated
80386 Microcomputers	44	20	11	34	60
CD-ROM	12	11	9	37	93
WORM (write once, read many) discs	15	5	5	34	107
68020 - based micro-computers (Macintosh 2 or Sun)	14	7	5	51	89
Fiber Optics	11	5	4	51	94

CHARACTERISTICS OF THE RESPONDENTS

Number who are CLM or CAPDM members:	111 (60.0%)
Number who are not:	74 (40.0%)
Total	**185**

Distribution by CAI grouping:

CAI Grouping	Number (%)
Emerging	24 (12.8%)
Norm	123 (65.8%)
Leading Edge	40 (21.4%)
Total	**187**

QUESTION 1: ANNUAL SALES

Annual dollar sales of the business unit (division or subsidiary) or of the
corporation (if the corporation is the business unit):

$$
\begin{aligned}
\text{Mean} &= \$~2,288,720,735.00 \\
\text{Standard Deviation} &= \$~4,493,455,168.00 \\
\text{Quartiles: } 25\% &= \$~~~~150,000,000.00 \\
\text{Median} &= \$~~~~570,000,000.00 \\
75\% &= \$~2,188,000,000.00 \\
n &= 83
\end{aligned}
$$

QUESTION 4:   DO YOU HAVE A FORMAL LOGISTICS MISSION STATEMENT?

Answer:	Number (%)
Yes	34 (39.1%)
No	53 (60.9%)
Total	87

QUESTION 5: FORMAL LOGISTICS STRATEGIC PLANS

(A) Do you have a formal logistics strategic plan?

Answer:	Number (%)
Yes	50 (57.5%)
No	37 (42.5%)
Total	87

(B) If yes, what is the time horizon of the plan?

Time Horizon:	Number (%)
1 year or less	5 (10.6%)
2 years	5 (10.6%)
3 years	5 (10.6%)
4 years	2 (4.3%)
5 years	28 (59.6%)
more than 5 years	2 (4.3%)

* mean = 4.13 years, standard deviation = 1.69, n = 47

TABULATION OF THE QUESTIONNAIRE
(Retailers: Phase II)

QUESTION 5:   (CON'T.)

(C)   How often is the plan reviewed or updated?

Reviewed Every:	Number (%)
less than 6 mths	7 (14.9%)
half year	4 (8.5%)
1 year	32 (68.1%)
2 years	3 (6.4%)
3 or more	1 (2.1%)

* mean = 11.94 months,   standard deviation = 8.66,   n = 47

QUESTION 6:   ANALYSIS OF LOGISTICS ORGANIZATION

(A)   Centralization of logistics activities at present:

Description	Number (%)
Completely Decentralized	3 (3.4%)
Somewhat Decentralized	6 (6.7%)
Combination	24 (27.0%)
Somewhat Centralized	25 (28.1%)
Completely Centralized	31 (34.8%)

* mean 3.84,   standard deviation 1.09,   n = 89

(B)   Trend over the last three years:

Description	Number (%)
Centralization of logistics activities	49 (56.3%)
Decentralization of logistics activities	11 (12.6%)
No Change	27 (31.0%)
Total	**87**

QUESTION 7: DOMINANT CHANNEL MEMBER

The set of relationships defined by manufacturers, wholesalers, and retailers is referred to as a marketing channel. Who is the most influential member of your channel in terms of coordinating logistical relationships:

	Number (%)
This business unit	62 (72.9%)
Wholesaler	2 (2.4%)
Retailer	12 (14.1%)
Broker	0 (0.0%)
Manufacturer	9 (10.6%)
Other	0 (0.0%)
Total	**85**

QUESTIONS 8 - 12: DESCRIPTION OF THE SENIOR LOGISTICS OFFICER

(A) Title of the Senior Logistics Officer

Position:	Number (%)	Department:	Number (%)
President	5 (5.7%)	Administration	2 (2.3%)
Executive V. P.	4 (4.5%)	CEO/COO	5 (5.7%)
Senior V.P.	19 (21.6%)	Data Processing	1 (1.1%)
Vice President	43 (48.9%)	Distribution	38 (43.2%)
Director	12 (13.6%)	Logistics	4 (4.5%)
Manager	2 (2.3%)	Merchandising	1 (1.1%)
Supervisor	1 (1.1%)	Operations	15 (17.0%)
Other	2 (2.3%)	Purchasing/Materials Mgt.	1 (1.1%)
Total	**88**	Sales/Marketing	2 (2.3%)
		Traffic/Transportation	2 (2.3%)
		Warehousing	1 (1.1%)
		Other	16 (18.2%)
		Total	**88**

TABULATION OF THE QUESTIONNAIRE
(Retailers: Phase II)

QUESTIONS 8 - 12:   (CON'T.)

(B) Number of years this executive has been in this position:

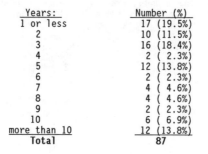

Years:	Number (%)
1 or less	17 (19.5%)
2	10 (11.5%)
3	16 (18.4%)
4	2 (2.3%)
5	12 (13.8%)
6	2 (2.3%)
7	4 (4.6%)
8	4 (4.6%)
9	2 (2.3%)
10	6 (6.9%)
more than 10	12 (13.8%)
Total	87

(C) Senior logistics executive's previous assignment:

Position:	Number (%)
President	1 (1.2%)
Executive V. P.	3 (3.5%)
Senior V.P.	3 (3.5%)
Vice President	26 (30.6%)
Director	34 (40.0%)
Manager	14 (16.5%)
Supervisor	2 (2.4%)
Other	2 (2.4%)
Total	85

Department:	Number (%)
Administration	6 (7.0%)
CEO/COO	1 (1.2%)
Data Processing	2 (2.4%)
Distribution	27 (31.8%)
Logistics	0 (0.0%)
Merchandising	1 (1.2%)
Operations	18 (21.2%)
Purchasing/Materials Mgt.	0 (0.0%)
Sales/Marketing	4 (4.7%)
Traffic/Transportation	6 (7.0%)
Warehousing	4 (4.7%)
Other	16 (18.8%)
Total	85

TABULATION OF THE QUESTIONNAIRE
(Retailers: Phase II)

QUESTIONS 13, 14, 15: DESCRIPTION OF THE PERSON
THE SENIOR LOGISTICS EXECUTIVE REPORTS TO

(A) Title of the person reported to:

Position:	Number (%)	Department:	Number (%)
Chairman	6 (6.9%)	Administration	15 (17.9%)
President	41 (47.1%)	CEO/COO	42 (50.0%)
Executive V.P.	22 (25.3%)	Data Processing	0 (0.0%)
Senior V.P.	12 (13.8%)	Distribution	1 (1.2%)
Vice President	3 (3.4%)	Logistics	0 (0.0%)
Director	0 (0.0%)	Merchandising	4 (4.8%)
Manager	0 (0.0%)	Operations	8 (9.5%)
Supervisor	0 (0.0%)	Purchasing/Materials Mgt.	0 (0.0%)
Other	3 (3.4%)	Sales/Marketing	1 (1.2%)
Total	87	Traffic/Transportation	0 (0.0%)
		Warehousing	0 (0.0%)
		Other	13 (15.5%)
		Total	84

(B) Number of years this executive has been in this position:

Years:	Number (%)
1 or less	17 (19.8%)
2	7 (8.1%)
3	8 (9.3%)
4	6 (7.0%)
5	13 (15.1%)
6	2 (2.3%)
7	0 (0.0%)
8	2 (2.3%)
9	2 (2.3%)
10	8 (9.3%)
more than 10	21 (24.4%)
Total	86

TABULATION OF THE QUESTIONNAIRE
(Retailers: Phase II)

QUESTION 16: HOW MANY YEARS HAS LOGISTICS BEEN A FORMAL ORGANIZATION?

Years a Formal Organization:	Number (%)
zero	1 (1.3%)
1 year or less	5 (6.3%)
2 or 3 years	15 (19.0%)
4 or 5 years	12 (15.2%)
6 or 7 years	2 (2.6%)
8 or 9 years	3 (3.8%)
10 years	12 (15.2%)
11 - 14 years	3 (3.8%)
15 years	8 (10.1%)
16 - 19 years	4 (5.1%)
20 years	9 (11.4%)
over 20 years	5 (6.3%)

* mean = 11.82 years, standard deviation = 14.44, n = 79
NOTE: mean excludes the "0" responses

QUESTION 17: NUMBER OF TIMES REORGANIZED

Number of Times Reorganized in the Last 5 Years:	Number (%)
0	10 (12.7%)
1	17 (21.5%)
2	24 (30.4%)
3	17 (21.5%)
4	5 (6.3%)
5	4 (5.1%)
6	1 (1.3%)
7	0 (0.0%)
8	0 (0.0%)
10 or more	1 (1.3%)

* mean = 2.30, standard deviation = 2.44, n = 79
NOTE: mean includes the "0" responses

QUESTION 18:   PARTICIPATION IN OVERALL STRATEGIC PLANNING

Does your senior logistics executive formally participate in overall strategic
planning for your business unit?

Answer	Number (%)
Yes	76 (86.4%)
No, but provides input through other executives	9 (10.2%)
No, provides no input	3 (3.4%)
Total	88

QUESTION 19:   TITLE LEVELS OF THOSE REPORTING TO THE SENIOR LOGISTICS OFFICER

Respondents were asked to indicate the titles of each person who reports
directly to the senior logistics executive.

Title:	Total number of times this title was reported
Executive Vice President	1
Senior Vice President	2
Vice President	52
Director	116
Manager	170
Supervisor	3
Other	16

TABULATION OF THE QUESTIONNAIRE
(Retailers: Phase II)

QUESTION 20: ANALYSIS OF FUNCTIONS

Activity or Function:	Number who have it in Logistics n =	Likely to be added Yes	No	Nature of Responsibility Line	Staff	Both
Sales Forecasting	17	5	41	9	15	1
Purchasing	34	5	28	18	21	2
Inbound Transportation	70	4	5	43	32	2
Inventory Management	38	11	17	26	19	1
Intra-Co. Transportation	53	5	8	39	16	3
Warehousing	67	4	0	56	18	3
Order Processing	40	7	15	34	15	1
Customer Service	28	6	31	19	12	3
Outbound Transportation	65	2	5	46	20	5
Logistics Systems Planning	55	6	5	22	38	1
Facilities Design	56	3	9	18	45	1
Materials Handling	58	2	6	40	24	3
Logistics Administration	55	5	5	23	39	1
International	30	7	19	13	20	1
Capital Equipment Procurement	53	5	7	25	36	3
Data Processing for Distribution Applications	44	8	15	22	28	3

-------- * -------- * --------

Total Line or Staff Functions:	Number (%)
5 or less	25 (27.8%)
6 functions	4 (4.4%)
7 functions	7 (7.8%)
8 functions	2 (2.2%)
9 functions	3 (3.3%)
10 functions	9 (10.0%)
11 functions	11 (12.2%)
12 functions	11 (12.2%)
13 functions	7 (7.8%)
14 functions	1 (1.1%)
15 functions	7 (7.8%)
16 functions	3 (3.3%)

QUESTION 21: BEYOND FUNCTIONS

In some companies the senior logistics executive manages activities that are not typically part of a logistics organization. For example, some logistics organizations have responsibility for real estate and facilities.

Does your logistical organization have responsibility for any such non-typical activities?

Answer:	Number (%)
Yes	40 (49.4%)
No	41 (50.6%)
Total	81

If yes, the number of such activities was:

# of activities	Number (%)
1 activity	18 (46.2%)
2 activities	18 (46.2%)
3 activities	3 (7.7%)
Total	39

QUESTION 22: ANALYSIS OF LOGISTICS RELATED PERFORMANCE MEASUREMENTS

Performance Measurement:	Number (%) who said the measure was used:*	Number (%) who said the information was available:*	Average Importance (1 = Unimportant 5 = Important)*
(A) ASSET MANAGEMENT			
Inventory turns	71 (82.6%)	68 (89.5%)	4.35
Inventory carrying costs	45 (55.6%)	52 (76.5%)	3.85
Inventory levels (number of days supply)	60 (74.1%)	59 (85.5%)	4.03
Obsolete inventory	57 (73.1%)	53 (81.5%)	3.67
Return on net assets	44 (55.0%)	49 (79.0%)	3.79
Return on investment	55 (67.9%)	55 (85.9%)	4.14

(CONTINUED...)

* % and means based on the number of respondents who answered the question.

TABULATION OF THE QUESTIONNAIRE
(Retailers: Phase II)

QUESTION 22:   (CON'T)

Performance Measurement:	Number (%) who said the measure was used:*	Number (%) who said the information was available:*	Average Importance (1 = Unimportant 5 = Important)*
(B) COST (logistics cost only)			
Total cost analysis	69 (82.1%)	63 (85.1%)	4.30
Cost per unit	66 (78.6%)	62 (84.9%)	3.92
Cost as a percentage of sales	70 (79.5%)	69 (93.2%)	4.10
Inbound freight costs	77 (87.5%)	64 (86.5%)	4.13
Outbound freight costs	77 (90.6%)	66 (94.3%)	4.36
Warehouse costs	79 (89.9%)	71 (93.4%)	4.44
Administrative costs	66 (76.7%)	68 (90.7%)	3.59
Order processing costs	37 (45.7%)	40 (61.5%)	3.34
Direct labor costs	75 (86.2%)	65 (91.5%)	4.26
Comparison of actual versus budget	77 (86.5%)	68 (91.9%)	4.46
Cost trend analysis	51 (61.4%)	53 (77.9%)	3.94
Direct product profitability	22 (27.8%)	26 (41.3%)	3.30
(C) CUSTOMER SERVICE (to your customer)			
Fill rate	51 (66.2%)	45 (77.6%)	4.22
Stockouts	58 (71.6%)	50 (80.6%)	4.32
Shipping errors	68 (81.9%)	52 (83.9%)	4.21
On time delivery	60 (76.9%)	51 (85.0%)	4.32
Backorders	44 (58.7%)	38 (66.7%)	3.80
Cycle time	44 (56.4%)	41 (67.2%)	3.54
Customer feedback	69 (84.1%)	47 (81.0%)	4.27
Sales force feedback	34 (51.5%)	25 (58.1%)	3.78
Customer Surveys	43 (58.9%)	33 (68.8%)	3.87

(CONTINUED...)

* % and means based on the number of respondents who answered the question.

TABULATION OF THE QUESTIONNAIRE
(Retailers: Phase II)

QUESTION 22: (CON'T)

Performance Measurement:	Number (%) who said the measure was used:*	Number (%) who said the information was available:*	Average Importance (1 = Unimportant 5 = Important)*
(D) PRODUCTIVITY			
Units shipped per employee	51 (61.4%)	48 (76.2%)	3.98
Units per labor dollar	53 (63.9%)	49 (77.8%)	4.05
Orders per sales rep.	9 (15.5%)	13 (36.1%)	3.11
Comparison to historical standards	70 (86.4%)	59 (95.2%)	4.04
Goal programs	69 (82.1%)	54 (85.7%)	4.29
Productivity Index	45 (56.3%)	35 (66.0%)	4.00
(E) QUALITY			
Frequency of damage	48 (60.8%)	43 (71.7%)	3.86
Dollar amount of damage	53 (67.1%)	45 (75.0%)	3.97
Number of credit claims	52 (67.5%)	40 (70.2%)	3.78
Number of customer returns	46 (63.9%)	37 (72.5%)	3.62
Cost of returned goods	39 (54.2%)	31 (67.4%)	3.60

* % and means based on the number of respondents who answered the question.

-------- * -------- * --------

TOTAL NUMBER OF PERFORMANCE MEASUREMENTS

Category	n =	Mean	Std. Dev.
Asset Management	90	3.69	1.92
Cost	90	8.51	2.50
Customer Service	90	5.23	2.54
Productivity	90	3.30	1.55
Quality	90	2.64	1.90

TABULATION OF THE QUESTIONNAIRE
(Retailers: Phase II)

QUESTION 23: COMPETITIVE BENCHMARKING

Benchmarking is a management process used to monitor and measure performance against competitors. Please indicate whether you use competitive benchmarking in each of the following areas:

Area	Number (%)		
	Yes	No	n =
Cost	44 (56.4%)	34 (43.6%)	78
Asset management	18 (24.3%)	56 (75.7%)	74
Customer service	31 (40.3%)	46 (59.7%)	77
Productivity	36 (46.8%)	41 (53.2%)	77
Quality	29 (38.2%)	47 (61.8%)	76
Logistics strategy	29 (39.2%)	45 (60.8%)	74
Technology deployment	24 (34.8%)	45 (65.2%)	69
Transportation operations	46 (60.5%)	30 (39.5%)	76
Warehouse operations	44 (57.9%)	32 (42.1%)	76
Order processing operations	21 (28.8%)	52 (71.2%)	73

QUESTION 24: FACTORS USED TO EVALUATE SUPPLIERS

Factor:		Response Rating *:	
	n =	Mean	Std. Dev.
On time delivery	74	4.12	0.91
Percentage of complete orders	69	3.70	1.05
Automatic substitutions rates	55	2.53	1.40
Customer support	65	3.63	1.10
Easy to work with	73	3.81	0.94
Maintains short order cycle	63	3.68	0.93
Good communication	74	3.89	0.88

(CONTINUED...)

---

* Scale was:
  1 = never used
  2 = rarely used
  3 = sometimes used
  4 = often used
  5 = always used

QUESTION 24:   (CON'T.)

Factor:	n =	Response Rating *: Mean	Std. Dev.
Early notification of disruptions	69	3.42	1.08
Flexibility	70	3.69	0.96
Willing to customize service	71	3.68	1.07
Management quality	69	3.36	1.07
Service quality	72	4.00	1.01
Positive attitude	69	3.42	1.09
Master carton packaging quality	64	3.27	1.20
Shelf unit packaging quality	62	3.13	1.25
Price	72	4.46	0.95
Consistency of order cycle	64	3.64	1.09

* Scale was: 1 = never used
                  2 = rarely used
                  3 = sometimes used
                  4 = often used
                  5 = always used

QUESTION 25:   EDI USAGE

Number who are currently using, or planning to use Electronic Data Interchange (EDI) to facilitate order or other communications with the following:

Entity	Currently installed	Plan to install in next 3 years	No Plans to install	Not Applicable
Manufacturers	30	26	18	5
Wholesalers	13	13	25	23
Public Warehouses	8	6	26	34
Carriers	24	27	23	5
Financial Institutions	29	13	22	11
Retailers	19	10	13	40
Customers	16	8	22	27
Copackers/Contractors	3	7	25	39

TABULATION OF THE QUESTIONNAIRE
(Retailers: Phase II)

<u>QUESTION 26:</u> LOGISTICS COMPUTER APPLICATIONS

Logistics Computer Application:	Number who answered:			
	Currently installed and no plans for revision	Currently installed but will be revised in next 3 years	Not currently installed but will be in next 3 years	Not currently installed & no plans to install
Freight Audit and Payment	23	24	14	20
Purchasing	28	40	11	4
Sales Forecasting	21	38	14	9
Inventory Control	31	46	9	2
Warehouse Order Selection	23	43	6	9
Warehouse On-Line Receiving	28	30	16	10
Warehouse Merchandise Locator	31	34	8	12
Warehouse Workload Balancing	11	19	23	26
Warehouse Short Interval Scheduling	10	13	18	37
Order Processing	38	40	8	0
Order Entry	39	41	6	1
Vehicle Routing and Scheduling	8	19	18	34
Inbound Freight Consolidation	12	17	20	33
Outbound Freight Consolidation	16	21	12	32
Supporting Financials	34	32	6	7
Performance Measurement	28	27	15	12
Distribution Modeling	18	16	19	27
Direct Product Profitability	7	12	18	41
Direct Store Delivery	17	20	9	36
Shelf Management	10	10	12	45

QUESTION 27, 28, 29:   OPINIONS ABOUT POINT OF SALE SCANNING (UPC)

(A)   "UPC has given retailers a unique advantage over other members of the distribution channel"

Answer:	Number (%)
Strongly disagree/Disagree	10 (11.8%)
Neutral	14 (16.5%)
Strongly agree/Agree	61 (71.8%)
Total	**85**

* mean = 3.80,   standard deviation 1.08,   n = 85

(B)   "Information derived from point of sale scanning has made your business unit competitively stronger in comparison to other members of your distribution channel"

Answer:	Number (%)
Strongly disagree/Disagree	9 (11.4%)
Neutral	31 (39.2%)
Strongly agree/Agree	39 (49.4%)
Total	**79**

* mean = 3.52,   standard deviation 1.00,   n = 79

(C)   "Point of sale scanning information is more important to retailers than wholesalers"

Answer:	Number (%)
Strongly disagree/Disagree	21 (25.3%)
Neutral	24 (28.9%)
Strongly agree/Agree	38 (45.8%)
Total	**83**

* mean = 3.24,   standard deviation 1.07,   n = 83

TABULATION OF THE QUESTIONNAIRE
(Retailers: Phase II)

QUESTION 30: COMPARATIVE EVALUATION OF LOGISTICS MANAGEMENT INFORMATION SYSTEM

How do your company's logistics management information systems compare overall to
the management information systems designed to support other areas of the business?
(i.e. Accounting, Finance, Sales, etc.)

Answer:	Number (%)
Much Worse	4 (4.5%)
Worse	25 (28.4%)
Same	28 (31.8%)
Better	22 (25.0%)
Much better	9 (10.2%)
Total	**88**

* mean = 3.08,   standard deviation 1.06,   n = 88

QUESTION 31:   CHARACTERISTICS OF INFORMATION USED TO MANAGE LOGISTICS

Characteristic:	n =	Response Rating *: Mean	Std. Dev.
Timely	85	4.11	0.89
Accurate	85	4.25	0.71
Readily Available	84	3.96	0.74
Formatted on an Exception Basis	76	2.97	1.05
Appropriately Formatted to Facilitate Use	78	3.55	0.88

* Scale was: N.A. = not applicable
1 = never
2 = rarely
3 = sometimes
4 = in most instances
5 = always

QUESTION 32: ABILITY TO ACCOMMODATE VARIOUS EVENTS IMPACTING LOGISTICS ACTIVITIES

		Response Rating *:	
Ability to Accommodate:	n =	Mean	Std. Dev.
Special customer service requests	82	3.38	1.00
Sales/Marketing incentive programs	53	3.53	0.97
Product introduction	71	3.85	0.87
Product phase out	70	3.59	0.99
Disruption in supply	75	3.12	1.05
Computer breakdown	82	2.35	1.02
Product recall	72	3.18	1.04
Customization of service levels to specific markets or customers	69	3.30	0.97
Product modification or customization while in the logistics system (e.g. pricing, packaging, mixing)	69	3.00	1.07
Returned goods	82	3.40	1.03

--------- * --------- * ---------

* Scale was: N.A. = not applicable
1 = cannot accommodate
2 = accommodates with difficulty
3 = accommodates with few problems
4 = accommodates easily
5 = accommodates very easily

TABULATION OF THE QUESTIONNAIRE
(Retailers: Phase II)

QUESTION 33: IMPACT ON LOGISTICS ACTIVITIES

Impact of:	Response Rating *:		
	n =	Mean	Std. Dev.
Sales forecast accuracy	86	3.73	0.98
Computer support	89	4.38	0.73
Excessive end-of-month/quarter surges	82	3.85	1.00
Communications with customers	78	3.28	1.18
Availability of trained logistics personnel	87	3.38	1.01
Vehicle routing and scheduling	82	3.35	1.17
Computer applications backlog	83	3.54	1.05
Transportation cost	89	3.74	1.09
Communication with suppliers	83	3.23	1.04
Warehouse productivity	87	3.98	1.02
Measurement tools/methods	84	3.50	0.96
Communication with internal non-logistics organizational units	84	3.73	0.92
Timely information	90	4.07	0.86
Supplier logistical performance	83	3.48	1.02
Communication with external logistics service suppliers	79	3.06	1.02
Incompatibility of computer equipment and/or software	80	2.88	1.30
Inventory reduction programs	85	3.39	1.10
Cost reduction programs	86	3.63	0.88
Load leveling	75	3.35	1.05
Workforce leveling	80	3.41	0.96

--------- * --------- * ---------

* Scale was: N.A. = not applicable
                  1 = no impact
                  2 = slight impact
                  3 = medium impact
                  4 = high impact
                  5 = very high impact

QUESTION 34:   USAGE OF OUTSIDE SERVICE VENDORS

Outside Service:	n =	Response Rating *: Mean	Std. Dev.
Transportation	88	3.36	0.78
Warehousing	81	2.70	1.16
Order entry/processing	74	1.95	1.08
Inventory management	77	1.95	1.10
Freight audit/payment	84	2.85	1.11
Consolidators	76	3.07	1.05
International freight forwarders	76	3.07	1.09
Domestic freight forwarders	77	2.60	1.16
Order fulfillment and support	70	2.03	1.09

* Scale used: N.A. = not applicable
1 = will not use outside logistical services
2 = will use less than current levels
3 = usage will remain constant
4 = will use more outside logistical services
5 = will use many more outside logistical services

QUESTION 35:   FACTORS AFFECTING THE DECISION TO USE OUTSIDE SERVICE VENDORS

Factor Affecting the Decision:	n =	Response Rating *: Mean	Std. Dev.
Services available	86	4.06	0.86
Quality of services	86	4.45	0.76
Data processing/communication services	83	3.12	1.06
Management quality	84	3.76	1.07
Customer orientation	83	3.89	1.07
Vendor reputation	83	3.99	0.89

* Scale was: N.A. = not applicable
1 = never
2 = rarely
3 = sometimes
4 = often
5 = always

TABULATION OF THE QUESTIONNAIRE
(Retailers: Phase II)

QUESTION 36:   TECHNOLOGY APPLICATIONS WITHIN THE BUSINESS UNIT

Technology	Currently used in logistics	Currently used in firm but not in logistics	Planned to be installed in logistics next 3 years	Not planned to be installed in logistics	Have not evaluated
Bar codes	42	8	24	10	5
Optical scanning	36	10	14	19	8
Robotics	3	0	5	49	29
Artificial intelligence/ knowledge based systems	3	4	13	34	32
Automated storage and retrieval systems	16	0	11	44	16
Automated material handling equipment	37	3	17	17	13
Local area networks	19	11	20	19	12
Computer-aided warehouse design	23	2	15	27	19
Handheld data entry devices	28	14	27	9	10
Electronic order transmission	48	14	17	2	7
On board computers - delivery vehicles	4	0	17	44	19
On board computers - lift trucks	2	0	19	42	21
Voice data capture	2	5	6	31	38
IBM PC or PC XT compatible	70	10	3	4	3
80286 Microcomputers (IBM AT or compatible)	44	7	5	13	13

(CONTINUED...)

QUESTION 36:   (CON'T.)

Technology	Currently used in logistics	Currently used in firm but not in logistics	Planned to be installed in logistics next 3 years	Not planned to be installed in logistics	Have not evaluated
80386 Microcomputers	19	11	9	15	25
CD-ROM	5	4	2	21	43
WORM (write once, read many) discs	3	5	1	18	48
68020 - based micro-computers (Macintosh 2 or Sun)	5	4	1	22	45
Fiber Optics	4	5	3	18	46

TABULATION OF THE QUESTIONNAIRE
(Retailers: Phase II)

CHARACTERISTICS OF THE RESPONDENTS

(A) Number who are CLM or CAPDM members: 54 (60.0%)

Number who are not: 36 (40.0%)

                        Total   **90**

(B) Distribution by CAI grouping:

CAI Grouping	Number (%)
Emerging	17 (18.9%)
Norm	57 (63.3%)
Leading Edge	16 (17.8%)
Total	**90**

(C) Distribution by Industry:

Industry	Number (%)
Building Materials, Hardware and Garden Supply	7 (7.9%)
General Merchandise	24 (27.0%)
Food	11 (12.4%)
Automotive	5 (5.6%)
Apparel and Accessory	20 (22.5%)
Furniture, Home Furnishings, and Equipment	10 (11.2%)
Eating and Drinking Establishments	1 (1.1%)
Drugs, Health and Beauty Aids	6 (6.7%)
Fuel	3 (3.4%)
Paper/Office Supplies	1 (1.1%)
Other	1 (1.1%)
Total	**89**

QUESTION 1: ANNUAL SALES

Annual dollar sales of the business unit (division or subsidiary) or of the corporation (if the corporation is the business unit):

$$
\begin{aligned}
\text{Mean} &= \$ \quad 482,806,759.00 \\
\text{Standard Deviation} &= \$ \ 1,104,611,345.00 \\
\text{Quartiles: } 25\% &= \$ \quad 61,000,000.00 \\
\text{Median} &= \$ \quad 122,987,000.00 \\
75\% &= \$ \quad 400,000,000.00 \\
n &= 141
\end{aligned}
$$

QUESTION 4: DO YOU HAVE A FORMAL LOGISTICS MISSION STATEMENT?

Answer:	Number (%)
Yes	26 (17.9%)
No	119 (82.1%)
Total	145

QUESTION 5: FORMAL LOGISTICS STRATEGIC PLANS

(A) Do you have a formal logistics strategic plan?

Answer:	Number (%)
Yes	46 (31.3%)
No	101 (68.7%)
Total	147

(B) If yes, what is the time horizon of the plan?

Time Horizon:	Number (%)
1 year or less	7 (15.9%)
2 years	4 (9.1%)
3 years	10 (22.7%)
4 years	0 (0.0%)
5 years	21 (47.7%)
more than 5 years	2 (4.5%)

* mean = 3.82 years, standard deviation = 1.92, n = 44

TABULATION OF THE QUESTIONNAIRE
(Wholesalers: Phase II)

QUESTION 5: (CON'T.)

(C) How often is the plan reviewed or updated?

Reviewed Every:	Number (%)
less than 6 mths	5 (11.1%)
half year	6 (13.3%)
1 year	32 (71.1%)
2 years	1 (2.2%)
3 or more	1 (2.2%)

* mean = 11.44 months, standard deviation = 8.44, n = 45

QUESTION 6: ANALYSIS OF LOGISTICS ORGANIZATION

(A) Centralization of logistics activities at present:

Description	Number (%)
Completely Decentralized	9 (6.2%)
Somewhat Decentralized	17 (11.7%)
Combination	45 (31.0%)
Somewhat Centralized	36 (24.8%)
Completely Centralized	38 (26.2%)

* mean 3.53, standard deviation 1.18, n = 145

(B) Trend over the last three years:

Description	Number (%)
Centralization of logistics activities	68 (47.9%)
Decentralization of logistics activities	23 (16.2%)
No Change	51 (35.9%)
Total	**142**

QUESTION 7: DOMINANT CHANNEL MEMBER

The set of relationships defined by manufacturers, wholesalers, and retailers is referred to as a marketing channel. Who is the most influential member of your channel in terms of coordinating logistical relationships:

	Number (%)
This business unit	85 (59.9%)
Wholesaler	17 (12.0%)
Retailer	15 (10.6%)
Broker	1 (0.7%)
Manufacturer	21 (14.8%)
Other	3 (2.1%)
Total	**142**

QUESTIONS 8 - 12: DESCRIPTION OF THE SENIOR LOGISTICS OFFICER

(A) Title of the Senior Logistics Officer

Position:	Number (%)	Department:	Number (%)
President	26 (17.7%)	Administration	15 (10.3%)
Executive V. P.	12 (8.2%)	CEO/COO	21 (14.5%)
Senior V.P.	11 (7.5%)	Data Processing	0 (0.0%)
Vice President	55 (37.4%)	Distribution	28 (19.3%)
Director	14 (9.5%)	Logistics	7 (4.8%)
Manager	18 (12.2%)	Merchandising	0 (0.0%)
Supervisor	1 (0.7%)	Operations	33 (22.8%)
Other	10 (6.8%)	Purchasing/Materials Mgt.	6 (4.1%)
Total	**147**	Sales/Marketing	8 (5.5%)
		Traffic/Transportation	10 (6.9%)
		Warehousing	3 (2.1%)
		Other	14 (9.7%)
		Total	**145**

TABULATION OF THE QUESTIONNAIRE
(Wholesalers: Phase II)

QUESTIONS 8 - 12:　(CON'T.)

(B) Number of years this executive has been in this position:

Years:	Number (%)
1 or less	24 (16.8%)
2	28 (19.6%)
3	17 (11.9%)
4	10 (7.0%)
5	14 (9.8%)
6	3 (2.1%)
7	7 (4.9%)
8	5 (3.5%)
9	4 (2.8%)
10	12 (8.4%)
more than 10	19 (13.3%)
Total	143

(C) Senior logistics executive's previous assignment:

Position:	Number (%)
President	7 (5.0%)
Executive V. P.	11 (7.9%)
Senior V.P.	4 (2.9%)
Vice President	40 (28.8%)
Director	12 (8.6%)
Manager	42 (30.2%)
Supervisor	8 (5.8%)
Other	15 (10.8%)
Total	139

Department:	Number (%)
Administration	11 (8.0%)
CEO/COO	4 (2.9%)
Data Processing	0 (0.0%)
Distribution	17 (12.3%)
Logistics	0 (0.0%)
Merchandising	4 (2.9%)
Operations	30 (21.7%)
Purchasing/Materials Mgt.	8 (5.8%)
Sales/Marketing	24 (17.4%)
Traffic/Transportation	11 (8.0%)
Warehousing	12 (8.7%)
Other	17 (12.3%)
Total	138

TABULATION OF THE QUESTIONNAIRE
(Wholesalers: Phase II)

QUESTIONS 13, 14, 15: DESCRIPTION OF THE PERSON
THE SENIOR LOGISTICS EXECUTIVE REPORTS TO

(A) Title of the person reported to:

Position:	Number (%)	Department:	Number (%)
Chairman	17 (11.9%)	Administration	25 (18.8%)
President	71 (49.7%)	CEO/COO	74 (55.6%)
Executive V.P.	18 (12.6%)	Data Processing	0 (0.0%)
Senior V.P.	4 (2.8%)	Distribution	4 (3.0%)
Vice President	18 (12.6%)	Logistics	0 (0.0%)
Director	5 (3.5%)	Merchandising	2 (1.5%)
Manager	2 (1.4%)	Operations	1 (0.8%)
Supervisor	0 (0.0%)	Purchasing/Materials Mgt.	3 (2.3%)
Other	8 (5.6%)	Sales/Marketing	8 (6.0%)
Total	143	Traffic/Transportation	0 (0.0%)
		Warehousing	0 (0.0%)
		Other	16 (12.0%)
		Total	133

(B) Number of years this executive has been in this position:

Years:	Number (%)
1 or less	25 (18.2%)
2	13 (9.5%)
3	14 (10.2%)
4	8 (5.8%)
5	9 (6.6%)
6	1 (0.7%)
7	6 (4.4%)
8	5 (3.6%)
9	2 (1.5%)
10	14 (10.2%)
more than 10	40 (29.2%)
Total	137

TABULATION OF THE QUESTIONNAIRE
(Wholesalers: Phase II)

QUESTION 16:　HOW MANY YEARS HAS LOGISTICS BEEN A FORMAL ORGANIZATION?

Years a Formal Organization:	Number (%)
zero	15 (12.9%)
1 year or less	6 (5.2%)
2 or 3 years	23 (19.8%)
4 or 5 years	16 (13.8%)
6 or 7 years	6 (5.2%)
8 or 9 years	5 (4.3%)
10 years	8 (6.9%)
11 - 14 years	3 (2.6%)
15 years	8 (6.9%)
16 - 19 years	6 (5.2%)
20 years	5 (4.3%)
over 20 years	15 (12.9%)

* mean = 10.14 years, standard deviation = 12.45, n = 116
 NOTE: mean excludes the "0" responses

QUESTION 17:　NUMBER OF TIMES REORGANIZED

Number of Times Reorganized in the Last 5 Years:	Number (%)
0	34 (26.6%)
1	31 (24.2%)
2	36 (28.1%)
3	17 (13.3%)
4	4 (3.1%)
5	5 (3.9%)
6	0 (0.0%)
7	1 (0.8%)
8	0 (0.0%)
10 or more	0 (0.0%)

* mean = 1.58, standard deviation = 1.40, n = 128
NOTE: mean includes the "0" responses

QUESTION 18:   PARTICIPATION IN OVERALL STRATEGIC PLANNING

Does your senior logistics executive formally participate in overall strategic
planning for your business unit?

Answer	Number (%)
Yes	122 (84.1%)
No, but provides input through other executives	18 (12.4%)
No, provides no input	5 (3.4%)
Total	**145**

QUESTION 19:   TITLE LEVELS OF THOSE REPORTING TO THE SENIOR LOGISTICS OFFICER

Respondents were asked to indicate the titles of _each_ person who reports
directly to the senior logistics executive.

Title:	Total number of times this title was reported
Executive Vice President	18
Senior Vice President	14
Vice President	85
Director	74
Manager	222
Supervisor	56
Other	30

TABULATION OF THE QUESTIONNAIRE
(Wholesalers: Phase II)

QUESTION 20: ANALYSIS OF FUNCTIONS

Activity or Function:	Number who have it in Logistics n =	Likely to be added Yes	No	Nature of Responsibility Line	Staff	Both
Sales Forecasting	48	9	59	25	35	1
Purchasing	60	7	42	46	31	2
Inbound Transportation	77	12	18	50	41	5
Inventory Management	86	10	15	54	50	1
Intra-Co. Transportation	78	4	13	55	35	3
Warehousing	97	5	7	72	33	6
Order Processing	63	5	36	37	35	4
Customer Service	63	6	35	40	32	3
Outbound Transportation	98	6	7	67	40	6
Logistics Systems Planning	74	15	12	38	51	1
Facilities Design	76	5	19	36	52	2
Materials Handling	84	7	8	55	37	6
Logistics Administration	74	10	16	38	48	1
International	20	4	51	17	14	0
Capital Equipment Procurement	71	8	21	34	45	3
Data Processing for Distribution Applications	57	14	37	23	41	2

-------- * -------- * --------

Total Line or Staff Functions:	Number (%)
5 or less	43 (29.1%)
6 functions	12 (8.1%)
7 functions	6 (4.1%)
8 functions	12 (8.1%)
9 functions	12 (8.1%)
10 functions	17 (11.5%)
11 functions	11 (7.4%)
12 functions	12 (8.1%)
13 functions	8 (5.4%)
14 functions	7 (4.7%)
15 functions	7 (4.7%)
16 functions	1 (0.7%)

QUESTION 21: BEYOND FUNCTIONS

In some companies the senior logistics executive manages activities that are not typically part of a logistics organization. For example, some logistics organizations have responsibility for real estate and facilities.

Does your logistical organization have responsibility for any such non-typical activities?

Answer:	Number (%)
Yes	76 (54.7%)
No	63 (45.3%)
Total	139

If yes, the number of such activities was:

# of activities	Number (%)
1 activity	30 (41.7%)
2 activities	33 (45.8%)
3 activities	9 (12.5%)
Total	72

QUESTION 22: ANALYSIS OF LOGISTICS RELATED PERFORMANCE MEASUREMENTS

Performance Measurement:	Number (%) who said the measure was used:*	Number (%) who said the information was available:*	Average Importance (1 = Unimportant 5 = Important)*
(A) ASSET MANAGEMENT			
Inventory turns	121 (85.2%)	115 (92.7%)	4.48
Inventory carrying costs	95 (68.3%)	95 (81.9%)	4.00
Inventory levels (number of days supply)	113 (80.7%)	104 (89.7%)	4.04
Obsolete inventory	110 (79.7%)	101 (87.8%)	3.96
Return on net assets	87 (65.9%)	99 (86.8%)	3.91
Return on investment	104 (74.8%)	106 (89.8%)	4.11
(CONTINUED...)			

* % and means based on the number of respondents who answered the question.

TABULATION OF THE QUESTIONNAIRE
(Wholesalers: Phase II)

QUESTION 22: (CON'T)

Performance Measurement:	Number (%) who said the measure was used:*	Number (%) who said the information was available:*	Average Importance (1 = Unimportant 5 = Important)*
(B) COST (logistics cost only)			
Total cost analysis	98 (74.8%)	89 (78.8%)	4.23
Cost per unit	83 (63.8%)	80 (71.4%)	3.74
Cost as a percentage of sales	108 (81.2%)	102 (90.3%)	4.18
Inbound freight costs	108 (80.0%)	99 (87.6%)	3.81
Outbound freight costs	121 (88.3%)	104 (92.0%)	4.12
Warehouse costs	114 (85.7%)	101 (91.8%)	4.24
Administrative costs	106 (79.1%)	101 (91.0%)	3.78
Order processing costs	60 (45.8%)	67 (63.2%)	3.52
Direct labor costs	95 (71.4%)	85 (81.0%)	4.02
Comparison of actual versus budget	118 (86.6%)	102 (88.7%)	4.17
Cost trend analysis	75 (59.1%)	69 (66.3%)	3.74
Direct product profitability	59 (46.8%)	61 (56.0%)	4.04
(C) CUSTOMER SERVICE (to your customer)			
Fill rate	93 (71.0%)	78 (77.2%)	4.56
Stockouts	94 (72.9%)	76 (76.0%)	4.44
Shipping errors	105 (78.9%)	73 (71.6%)	4.29
On time delivery	93 (70.5%)	64 (62.1%)	4.29
Backorders	92 (69.2%)	75 (73.5%)	4.12
Cycle time	43 (34.7%)	39 (39.8%)	3.44
Customer feedback	119 (85.6%)	80 (74.8%)	4.31
Sales force feedback	113 (85.0%)	78 (75.7%)	4.14
Customer Surveys	66 (51.6%)	50 (52.1%)	3.80

(CONTINUED...)

* % and means based on the number of respondents who answered the question.

QUESTION 22:   (CON'T)

Performance Measurement:	Number (%) who said the measure was used:*	Number (%) who said the information was available:*	Average Importance (1 = Unimportant 5 = Important)*
(D) PRODUCTIVITY			
Units shipped per employee	68 (53.1%)	63 (63.0%)	3.88
Units per labor dollar	55 (43.7%)	59 (59.6%)	3.69
Orders per sales rep.	62 (51.7%)	67 (72.8%)	3.62
Comparison to historical standards	97 (74.6%)	82 (79.6%)	3.91
Goal programs	90 (69.2%)	75 (72.1%)	4.08
Productivity Index	57 (44.9%)	53 (53.0%)	3.74
(E) QUALITY			
Frequency of damage	55 (44.7%)	39 (41.5%)	3.74
Dollar amount of damage	70 (55.6%)	53 (54.1%)	3.93
Number of credit claims	91 (68.9%)	74 (74.0%)	3.90
Number of customer returns	89 (69.0%)	75 (78.1%)	3.97
Cost of returned goods	71 (57.7%)	60 (65.2%)	3.88

* % and means based on the number of respondents who answered the question.

-------- * -------- * --------

TOTAL NUMBER OF PERFORMANCE MEASUREMENTS

Category	n =	Mean	Std. Dev.
Asset Management	148	4.26	1.84
Cost	148	7.74	3.14
Customer Service	148	5.53	2.41
Productivity	148	2.90	1.98
Quality	148	2.54	1.89

TABULATION OF THE QUESTIONNAIRE
(Wholesalers: Phase II)

QUESTION 23: COMPETITIVE BENCHMARKING

Benchmarking is a management process used to monitor and measure performance against competitors. Please indicate whether you use competitive benchmarking in each of the following areas:

	Number (%)		
Area	Yes	No	n =
Cost	80 (59.7%)	54 (40.3%)	134
Asset management	40 (30.3%)	92 (69.7%)	132
Customer service	73 (53.7%)	63 (46.3%)	136
Productivity	56 (41.5%)	79 (58.5%)	135
Quality	61 (46.2%)	71 (53.8%)	132
Logistics strategy	37 (27.8%)	96 (72.2%)	133
Technology deployment	48 (36.4%)	84 (63.6%)	132
Transportation operations	60 (44.4%)	75 (55.6%)	135
Warehouse operations	70 (51.5%)	66 (48.5%)	136
Order processing operations	53 (39.6%)	81 (60.4%)	134

QUESTION 24: FACTORS USED TO EVALUATE SUPPLIERS

	Response Rating *:		
Factor:	n =	Mean	Std. Dev.
On time delivery	133	3.96	1.02
Percentage of complete orders	119	3.62	1.31
Automatic substitutions rates	91	2.19	1.29
Customer support	123	3.72	1.09
Easy to work with	130	3.90	0.86
Maintains short order cycle	117	3.50	1.13
Good communication	132	4.17	0.87

(CONTINUED...)

---

* Scale was: 1 = never used
2 = rarely used
3 = sometimes used
4 = often used
5 = always used

QUESTION 24:   (CON'T.)

Factor:		Response Rating *:	
	n =	Mean	Std. Dev.
Early notification of disruptions	124	3.52	1.19
Flexibility	129	3.83	0.93
Willing to customize service	122	3.59	1.10
Management quality	124	3.65	1.04
Service quality	128	4.30	0.85
Positive attitude	125	3.77	1.11
Master carton packaging quality	100	3.08	1.40
Shelf unit packaging quality	99	3.20	1.32
Price	126	4.49	0.79
Consistency of order cycle	111	3.59	1.12

* Scale was:
    1 = never used
    2 = rarely used
    3 = sometimes used
    4 = often used
    5 = always used

QUESTION 25:   EDI USAGE

Number who are currently using, or planning to use Electronic Data Interchange
(EDI) to facilitate order or other communications with the following:

Entity	Number who answered:			
	Currently installed	Plan to install in next 3 years	No Plans to install	Not Applicable
Manufacturers	46	40	43	9
Wholesalers	22	17	42	53
Public Warehouses	2	5	61	59
Carriers	18	22	75	17
Financial Institutions	34	17	61	19
Retailers	29	19	53	30
Customers	55	32	37	15
Copackers/Contractors	5	7	50	63

TABULATION OF THE QUESTIONNAIRE
(Wholesalers: Phase II)

QUESTION 26: LOGISTICS COMPUTER APPLICATIONS

Logistics Computer Application:	Currently installed and no plans for revision	Currently installed but will be revised in next 3 years	Not currently installed but will be in next 3 years	Not currently installed & no plans to install
		Number who answered:		
Freight Audit and Payment	37	29	27	48
Purchasing	57	58	12	14
Sales Forecasting	44	45	19	27
Inventory Control	64	70	4	7
Warehouse Order Selection	53	46	13	27
Warehouse On-Line Receiving	45	40	33	21
Warehouse Merchandise Locator	41	38	26	34
Warehouse Workload Balancing	14	23	31	69
Warehouse Short Interval Scheduling	13	18	20	83
Order Processing	81	50	6	6
Order Entry	87	47	8	4
Vehicle Routing and Scheduling	14	26	39	61
Inbound Freight Consolidation	16	18	27	74
Outbound Freight Consolidation	27	23	26	60
Supporting Financials	65	43	14	19
Performance Measurement	40	42	33	27
Distribution Modeling	12	17	30	74
Direct Product Profitability	36	29	36	30
Direct Store Delivery	20	19	13	76
Shelf Management	20	17	17	76

QUESTION 27, 28, 29:   OPINIONS ABOUT POINT OF SALE SCANNING (UPC)

(A) "UPC has given retailers a unique advantage over other members of the
     distribution channel"

Answer:	Number (%)
Strongly disagree/Disagree	8 (5.8%)
Neutral	30 (21.9%)
Strongly agree/Agree	99 (72.3%)
Total	137

* mean = 3.86, standard deviation 0.88, n = 137

(B) "Information derived from point of sale scanning has made your business
     unit competitively stronger in comparison to other members of your
     distribution channel"

Answer:	Number (%)
Strongly disagree/Disagree	28 (25.7%)
Neutral	50 (45.9%)
Strongly agree/Agree	31 (28.4%)
Total	109

* mean = 3.03, standard deviation 1.08, n = 109

(C) "Point of sale scanning information is more important to retailers
     than wholesalers"

Answer:	Number (%)
Strongly disagree/Disagree	53 (39.8%)
Neutral	22 (16.5%)
Strongly agree/Agree	58 (43.6%)
Total	133

* mean = 3.00, standard deviation 1.09, n = 133

TABULATION OF THE QUESTIONNAIRE
(Wholesalers: Phase II)

QUESTION 30: COMPARATIVE EVALUATION OF LOGISTICS MANAGEMENT INFORMATION SYSTEM

How do your company's logistics management information systems compare overall to the management information systems designed to support other areas of the business? (i.e. Accounting, Finance, Sales, etc.)

Answer:	Number (%)
Much Worse	9 (6.3%)
Worse	38 (26.6%)
Same	51 (35.7%)
Better	40 (28.0%)
Much better	5 (3.5%)
Total	**143**

* mean = 2.96, standard deviation 0.97, n = 143

QUESTION 31: CHARACTERISTICS OF INFORMATION USED TO MANAGE LOGISTICS

Characteristic:	Response Rating *:		
	n =	Mean	Std. Dev.
Timely	141	3.98	0.89
Accurate	141	4.11	0.86
Readily Available	138	3.70	1.01
Formatted on an Exception Basis	124	3.11	1.09
Appropriately Formatted to Facilitate Use	129	3.50	1.02

* Scale was: N.A. = not applicable
1 = never
2 = rarely
3 = sometimes
4 = in most instances
5 = always

QUESTION 32: ABILITY TO ACCOMMODATE VARIOUS EVENTS IMPACTING LOGISTICS ACTIVITIES

Ability to Accommodate:	Response Rating *:		
	n =	Mean	Std. Dev.
Special customer service requests	143	3.56	0.98
Sales/Marketing incentive programs	124	3.58	0.91
Product introduction	128	3.68	0.95
Product phase out	124	3.23	0.96
Disruption in supply	131	2.89	0.93
Computer breakdown	140	2.31	0.99
Product recall	106	3.07	1.02
Customization of service levels to specific markets or customers	134	3.22	1.16
Product modification or customization while in the logistics system (e.g. pricing, packaging, mixing)	121	3.04	1.02
Returned goods	132	3.47	0.87

--------- * --------- * ---------

* Scale was: N.A. = not applicable
1 = cannot accommodate
2 = accommodates with difficulty
3 = accommodates with few problems
4 = accommodates easily
5 = accommodates very easily

TABULATION OF THE QUESTIONNAIRE
(Wholesalers: Phase II)

QUESTION 33: IMPACT ON LOGISTICS ACTIVITIES

Impact of:	n =	Response Rating *: Mean	Std. Dev.
Sales forecast accuracy	138	3.54	1.15
Computer support	144	4.24	0.88
Excessive end-of-month/quarter surges	131	3.19	1.13
Communications with customers	141	3.57	1.02
Availability of trained logistics personnel	135	3.47	0.88
Vehicle routing and scheduling	131	3.44	1.20
Computer applications backlog	128	3.35	1.11
Transportation cost	138	3.75	1.04
Communication with suppliers	138	3.60	1.03
Warehouse productivity	128	3.94	1.03
Measurement tools/methods	128	3.37	1.16
Communication with internal non-logistics organizational units	131	3.32	1.05
Timely information	141	4.02	0.87
Supplier logistical performance	134	3.50	1.03
Communication with external logistics service suppliers	124	3.03	1.10
Incompatibility of computer equipment and/or software	132	2.79	1.31
Inventory reduction programs	132	3.31	1.06
Cost reduction programs	138	3.40	1.03
Load leveling	118	2.96	1.10
Workforce leveling	122	3.13	1.14

--------- * --------- * ---------

* Scale was: N.A. = not applicable
                   1 = no impact
                   2 = slight impact
                   3 = medium impact
                   4 = high impact
                   5 = very high impact

QUESTION 34:   USAGE OF OUTSIDE SERVICE VENDORS

Outside Service:	n =	Response Rating *: Mean	Std. Dev.
Transportation	140	3.02	1.08
Warehousing	127	2.39	1.25
Order entry/processing	124	1.52	0.94
Inventory management	130	1.59	1.04
Freight audit/payment	131	2.31	1.21
Consolidators	112	2.43	1.26
International freight forwarders	102	2.54	1.27
Domestic freight forwarders	109	2.31	1.21
Order fulfillment and support	119	1.70	1.02

* Scale used: N.A. = not applicable
                    1 = will not use outside logistical services
                    2 = will use less than current levels
                    3 = usage will remain constant
                    4 = will use more outside logistical services
                    5 = will use many more outside logistical services

QUESTION 35:   FACTORS AFFECTING THE DECISION TO USE OUTSIDE SERVICE VENDORS

Factor Affecting the Decision:	n =	Response Rating *: Mean	Std. Dev.
Services available	127	3.94	0.91
Quality of services	129	4.33	0.84
Data processing/communication services	112	3.06	1.11
Management quality	123	3.75	1.00
Customer orientation	120	3.83	1.08
Vendor reputation	122	4.08	0.91

* Scale was: N.A. = not applicable
                    1 = never
                    2 = rarely
                    3 = sometimes
                    4 = often
                    5 = always

TABULATION OF THE QUESTIONNAIRE
(Wholesalers: Phase II)

QUESTION 36: TECHNOLOGY APPLICATIONS WITHIN THE BUSINESS UNIT

Technology	Currently used in logistics	Currently used in firm but not in logistics	Planned to be installed in logistics next 3 years	Not planned to be installed in logistics	Have not evaluated
Bar codes	32	8	55	19	28
Optical scanning	25	5	42	33	32
Robotics	4	2	6	77	48
Artificial intelligence/ knowledge based systems	4	5	8	55	63
Automated storage and retrieval systems	15	3	18	64	37
Automated material handling equipment	36	5	21	46	32
Local area networks	19	12	25	33	46
Computer-aided warehouse design	21	3	21	46	46
Handheld data entry devices	40	8	49	19	23
Electronic order transmission	78	16	27	7	11
On board computers - delivery vehicles	20	0	19	49	47
On board computers - lift trucks	6	0	20	59	54
Voice data capture	11	2	7	57	59
IBM PC or PC XT compatible	101	15	14	8	6
80286 Microcomputers (IBM AT or compatible)	60	10	7	29	27

(CONTINUED...)

QUESTION 36:   (CON'T.)

Technology	Number who answered:				
	Currently used in logistics	Currently used in firm but not in logistics	Planned to be installed in logistics next 3 years	Not planned to be installed in logistics	Have not evaluated
80386 Microcomputers	33	7	12	32	39
CD-ROM	11	2	8	32	70
WORM (write once, read many) discs	5	3	5	36	77
68020 - based micro-computers (Macintosh 2 or Sun)	13	5	4	43	60
Fiber Optics	5	2	4	41	67

TABULATION OF THE QUESTIONNAIRE
(Wholesalers: Phase II)

CHARACTERISTICS OF THE RESPONDENTS

(A) Number who are CLM or CAPDM members: 47 (31.8%)

  Number who are not: 101 (68.2%)

                        Total   **148**

(B) Distribution by CAI grouping:

CAI Grouping	Number (%)
Emerging	28 (18.9%)
Norm	98 (66.2%)
Leading Edge	22 (14.9%)
Total	**148**

(C) Distribution by Industry:

Industry	Number (%)
Building Materials, Hardware and Garden Supply	36 (24.3%)
General Merchandise	7 (4.7%)
Food	36 (24.3%)
Automotive	15 (10.1%)
Apparel and Accessory	4 (2.7%)
Furniture, Home Furnishings, and Equipment	20 (13.5%)
Eating and Drinking Establishments	3 (2.0%)
Drugs, Health and Beauty Aids	8 (5.4%)
Fuel	9 (6.1%)
Paper/Office Supplies	8 (5.4%)
Other	2 (1.4%)
Total	**148**

QUESTION 1: ANNUAL SALES

Annual dollar sales of the business unit (division or subsidiary) or of the
corporation (if the corporation is the business unit):

```
                    Mean = $ 1,207,831,395.00
      Standard Deviation = $ 6,493,641,810.00
        Quartiles:  25% = $    69,250,000.00
                 Median = $   124,500,000.00
                    75% = $   461,250,000.00
                      n = 76
```

QUESTION 4: DO YOU HAVE A FORMAL LOGISTICS MISSION STATEMENT?

Answer:	Number (%)
Yes	19 (25.3%)
No	56 (74.7%)
Total	75

QUESTION 5: FORMAL LOGISTICS STRATEGIC PLANS

(A) Do you have a formal logistics strategic plan?

Answer:	Number (%)
Yes	28 (37.8%)
No	46 (62.2%)
Total	74

(B) If yes, what is the time horizon of the plan?

Time Horizon:	Number (%)
1 year or less	4 (14.8%)
2 years	3 (11.1%)
3 years	6 (22.2%)
4 years	1 (3.7%)
5 years	13 (48.1%)
more than 5 years	0 (0.0%)

* mean = 3.59 years, standard deviation = 1.55, n = 27

TABULATION OF THE QUESTIONNAIRE
(Hybrids: Phase II)

QUESTION 5: (CON'T.)

(C) How often is the plan reviewed or updated?

Reviewed Every:	Number (%)
less than 6 mths	1 (3.8%)
half year	3 (11.5%)
1 year	19 (73.1%)
1 1/2 years	1 (3.8%)
2 years	2 (7.7%)
3 or more	0 (0.0%)

* mean = 12.12 months, standard deviation = 4.53, n = 26

QUESTION 6: ANALYSIS OF LOGISTICS ORGANIZATION

(A) Centralization of logistics activities at present:

Description	Number (%)
Completely Decentralized	5 (6.6%)
Somewhat Decentralized	14 (18.4%)
Combination	27 (35.5%)
Somewhat Centralized	18 (23.7%)
Completely Centralized	12 (15.8%)

* mean 3.24, standard deviation 1.13, n = 76

(B) Trend over the last three years:

Description	Number (%)
Centralization of logistics activities	33 (44.6%)
Decentralization of logistics activities	14 (18.9%)
No Change	27 (36.5%)
Total	**74**

QUESTION 7:   DOMINANT CHANNEL MEMBER

The set of relationships defined by manufacturers, wholesalers, and retailers is referred to as a marketing channel. Who is the most influential member of your channel in terms of coordinating logistical relationships:

	Number (%)
This business unit	47 (64.4%)
Wholesaler	9 (12.3%)
Retailer	7 (9.6%)
Broker	3 (4.1%)
Manufacturer	5 (6.8%)
Other	2 (2.7%)
Total	**73**

QUESTIONS 8 - 12:   DESCRIPTION OF THE SENIOR LOGISTICS OFFICER

(A)   Title of the Senior Logistics Officer

Position:	Number (%)	Department:	Number (%)
President	11 (14.7%)	Administration	4 (5.3%)
Executive V. P.	4 (5.3%)	CEO/COO	8 (10.7%)
Senior V.P.	6 (8.0%)	Data Processing	0 (0.0%)
Vice President	31 (41.3%)	Distribution	16 (21.3%)
Director	10 (13.3%)	Logistics	3 (4.0%)
Manager	12 (16.0%)	Merchandising	0 (0.0%)
Supervisor	1 (1.3%)	Operations	17 (22.7%)
Other	0 (0.0%)	Purchasing/Materials Mgt.	8 (10.7%)
Total	**75**	Sales/Marketing	4 (5.3%)
		Traffic/Transportation	4 (5.3%)
		Warehousing	0 (0.0%)
		Other	11 (14.7%)
		Total	**75**

TABULATION OF THE QUESTIONNAIRE
(Hybrids: Phase II)

QUESTIONS 8 - 12:   (CON'T.)

(B) Number of years this executive has been in this position:

Years:	Number (%)
1 or less	13 (18.3%)
2	7 (9.9%)
3	7 (9.9%)
4	9 (12.7%)
5	10 (14.1%)
6	4 (5.6%)
7	3 (4.2%)
8	3 (4.2%)
9	0 (0.0%)
10	5 (7.0%)
more than 10	10 (14.1%)
Total	71

(C) Senior logistics executive's previous assignment:

Position:	Number (%)	Department:	Number (%)
President	6 (8.5%)	Administration	8 (11.3%)
Executive V. P.	3 (4.2%)	CEO/COO	3 (4.2%)
Senior V.P.	0 (0.0%)	Data Processing	3 (4.2%)
Vice President	18 (25.4%)	Distribution	13 (18.3%)
Director	15 (21.1%)	Logistics	2 (2.8%)
Manager	23 (32.4%)	Merchandising	0 (0.0%)
Supervisor	2 (2.8%)	Operations	10 (14.1%)
Other	4 (5.6%)	Purchasing/Materials Mgt.	8 (11.3%)
Total	71	Sales/Marketing	5 (7.0%)
		Traffic/Transportation	2 (2.8%)
		Warehousing	2 (2.8%)
		Other	15 (21.1%)
		Total	71

TABULATION OF THE QUESTIONNAIRE
(Hybrids: Phase II)

QUESTIONS 13, 14, 15:   DESCRIPTION OF THE PERSON
THE SENIOR LOGISTICS EXECUTIVE REPORTS TO

(A) Title of the person reported to:

Position:	Number (%)	Department:	Number (%)
Chairman	11 (14.9%)	Administration	11 (15.1%)
President	31 (41.9%)	CEO/COO	37 (50.7%)
Executive V.P.	6 (8.1%)	Data Processing	0 (0.0%)
Senior V.P.	6 (8.1%)	Distribution	1 (1.4%)
Vice President	10 (13.5%)	Logistics	1 (1.4%)
Director	2 (2.7%)	Merchandising	0 (0.0%)
Manager	1 (1.4%)	Operations	4 (5.5%)
Supervisor	1 (1.4%)	Purchasing/Materials Mgt.	1 (1.4%)
Other	6 (8.1%)	Sales/Marketing	5 (6.8%)
Total	74	Traffic/Transportation	0 (0.0%)
		Warehousing	0 (0.0%)
		Other	13 (17.8%)
		Total	73

(B) Number of years this executive has been in this position:

Years:	Number (%)
1 or less	14 (19.2%)
2	7 (9.6%)
3	9 (12.3%)
4	3 (4.1%)
5	8 (11.0%)
6	2 (2.7%)
7	3 (4.1%)
8	4 (5.5%)
9	2 (2.7%)
10	7 (9.6%)
more than 10	14 (19.2%)
Total	73

TABULATION OF THE QUESTIONNAIRE
(Hybrids: Phase II)

QUESTION 16: HOW MANY YEARS HAS LOGISTICS BEEN A FORMAL ORGANIZATION?

Years a Formal Organization:	Number (%)
zero	3 (5.3%)
1 year or less	6 (10.5%)
2 or 3 years	6 (10.5%)
4 or 5 years	12 (21.0%)
6 or 7 years	2 (3.5%)
8 or 9 years	3 (5.3%)
10 years	9 (15.8%)
11 - 14 years	2 (3.5%)
15 years	6 (10.5%)
16 - 19 years	0 (0.0%)
20 years	2 (3.5%)
over 20 years	6 (10.5%)

* mean = 10.39 years, standard deviation = 12.03, n = 57
NOTE: mean excludes the "0" responses

QUESTION 17: NUMBER OF TIMES REORGANIZED

Number of Times Reorganized in the Last 5 Years:	Number (%)
0	8 (12.7%)
1	16 (25.4%)
2	14 (22.2%)
3	17 (27.0%)
4	3 (4.8%)
5	4 (6.3%)
6	1 (1.6%)
7	0 (0.0%)
8	0 (0.0%)
10 or more	0 (0.0%)

* mean = 2.11, standard deviation = 1.44, n = 63
NOTE: mean includes the "0" responses

QUESTION 18: PARTICIPATION IN OVERALL STRATEGIC PLANNING

Does your senior logistics executive formally participate in overall strategic
planning for your business unit?

Answer	Number (%)
Yes	58 (78.4%)
No, but provides input through other executives	15 (20.3%)
No, provides no input	1 (1.4%)
Total	**74**

QUESTION 19: TITLE LEVELS OF THOSE REPORTING TO THE SENIOR LOGISTICS OFFICER

Respondents were asked to indicate the titles of each person who reports
directly to the senior logistics executive.

Title:	Total number of times this title was reported
Executive Vice President	4
Senior Vice President	0
Vice President	45
Director	66
Manager	99
Supervisor	47
Other	25

TABULATION OF THE QUESTIONNAIRE
(Hybrids: Phase II)

QUESTION 20:   ANALYSIS OF FUNCTIONS

Activity or Function:	Number who have it in Logistics n =	Likely to be added		Nature of Responsibility		
		Yes	No	Line	Staff	Both
Sales Forecasting	32	6	23	17	13	3
Purchasing	40	4	16	23	18	2
Inbound Transportation	48	5	10	34	15	1
Inventory Management	51	4	9	31	19	3
Intra-Co. Transportation	46	5	6	36	9	3
Warehousing	55	2	7	43	13	2
Order Processing	40	4	19	25	15	1
Customer Service	38	4	22	26	12	3
Outbound Transportation	61	3	4	43	17	3
Logistics Systems Planning	46	5	9	23	23	2
Facilities Design	40	4	17	22	16	3
Materials Handling	47	1	13	37	9	4
Logistics Administration	47	2	10	25	19	3
International	20	4	25	16	5	1
Capital Equipment Procurement	46	3	13	26	19	3
Data Processing for Distribution Applications	32	9	16	13	19	3

-------- * -------- * --------

Total Line or Staff Functions:	Number (%)
5 or less	13 (16.9%)
6 functions	5 (6.5%)
7 functions	6 (7.8%)
8 functions	6 (7.8%)
9 functions	10 (13.0%)
10 functions	6 (7.8%)
11 functions	7 (9.1%)
12 functions	7 (9.1%)
13 functions	6 (7.8%)
14 functions	7 (9.1%)
15 functions	3 (3.9%)
16 functions	1 (1.3%)

QUESTION 21: BEYOND FUNCTIONS

In some companies the senior logistics executive manages activities that are not
typically part of a logistics organization. For example, some logistics organizations have responsibility for real estate and facilities.

Does your logistical organization have responsibility for any such non-typical
activities?

Answer:	Number (%)
Yes	38 (53.5%)
No	33 (46.5%)
Total	71

If yes, the number of such activities was:

# of activities	Number (%)
1 activity	11 (30.6%)
2 activities	24 (66.7%)
3 activities	1 (2.8%)
Total	36

QUESTION 22: ANALYSIS OF LOGISTICS RELATED PERFORMANCE MEASUREMENTS

Performance Measurement:	Number (%) who said the measure was used:*	Number (%) who said the information was available:*	Average Importance (1 = Unimportant 5 = Important)*
(A) ASSET MANAGEMENT			
Inventory turns	64 (84.2%)	62 (92.5%)	4.27
Inventory carrying costs	55 (74.3%)	48 (75.0%)	3.72
Inventory levels (number of days supply)	66 (88.0%)	62 (93.9%)	4.18
Obsolete inventory	62 (84.9%)	55 (91.7%)	3.92
Return on net assets	38 (54.3%)	47 (82.5%)	3.81
Return on investment	52 (71.2%)	53 (88.3%)	4.08

(CONTINUED...)

* % and means based on the number of respondents who answered the question.

TABULATION OF THE QUESTIONNAIRE
(Hybrids: Phase II)

QUESTION 22: (CON'T)

Performance Measurement:	Number (%) who said the measure was used:*	Number (%) who said the information was available:*	Average Importance (1 = Unimportant 5 = Important)*
(B) COST (logistics cost only)			
Total cost analysis	58 (82.9%)	53 (86.9%)	4.29
Cost per unit	59 (79.7%)	51 (79.7%)	4.17
Cost as a percentage of sales	61 (83.6%)	55 (88.7%)	3.97
Inbound freight costs	53 (73.6%)	51 (81.0%)	3.61
Outbound freight costs	65 (90.3%)	60 (95.2%)	4.10
Warehouse costs	65 (89.0%)	55 (85.9%)	3.99
Administrative costs	57 (77.0%)	59 (89.4%)	3.52
Order processing costs	22 (33.8%)	34 (58.6%)	3.14
Direct labor costs	60 (85.7%)	56 (90.3%)	4.00
Comparison of actual versus budget	65 (90.3%)	57 (91.9%)	4.18
Cost trend analysis	43 (62.3%)	47 (74.6%)	3.88
Direct product profitability	41 (58.6%)	42 (68.9%)	3.82
(C) CUSTOMER SERVICE (to your customer)			
Fill rate	41 (61.2%)	33 (62.3%)	4.44
Stockouts	45 (67.2%)	37 (69.8%)	4.15
Shipping errors	50 (73.5%)	40 (71.4%)	4.11
On time delivery	45 (67.2%)	34 (61.8%)	4.36
Backorders	41 (63.1%)	36 (70.6%)	4.00
Cycle time	29 (46.8%)	23 (44.2%)	3.65
Customer feedback	63 (88.7%)	45 (78.9%)	4.49
Sales force feedback	53 (80.3%)	42 (80.8%)	4.29
Customer Surveys	32 (47.8%)	26 (47.3%)	3.67

(CONTINUED...)

* % and means based on the number of respondents who answered the question.

QUESTION 22:   (CON'T)

Performance Measurement:	Number (%) who said the measure was used:*	Number (%) who said the information was available:*	Average Importance (1 = Unimportant 5 = Important)*
(D) PRODUCTIVITY			
Units shipped per employee	42 (60.0%)	38 (67.9%)	3.82
Units per labor dollar	44 (61.1%)	41 (70.7%)	3.82
Orders per sales rep.	27 (42.2%)	29 (56.9%)	3.83
Comparison to historical standards	59 (83.1%)	47 (82.5%)	4.11
Goal programs	54 (76.1%)	42 (77.8%)	4.25
Productivity Index	31 (44.9%)	28 (54.9%)	4.05
(E) QUALITY			
Frequency of damage	34 (50.0%)	34 (60.7%)	3.78
Dollar amount of damage	40 (58.8%)	36 (63.2%)	3.69
Number of credit claims	42 (62.7%)	41 (73.2%)	3.68
Number of customer returns	51 (72.9%)	42 (75.0%)	3.96
Cost of returned goods	38 (55.1%)	34 (64.2%)	4.02

* % and means based on the number of respondents who answered the question.

-------- * -------- * --------

TOTAL NUMBER OF PERFORMANCE MEASUREMENTS

Category	n =	Mean	Std. Dev.
Asset Management	77	4.38	1.50
Cost	77	8.43	2.84
Customer Service	77	5.18	2.78
Productivity	77	3.34	1.73
Quality	77	2.66	1.77

TABULATION OF THE QUESTIONNAIRE
(Hybrids: Phase II)

QUESTION 23:   COMPETITIVE BENCHMARKING

Benchmarking is a management process used to monitor and measure performance against competitors. Please indicate whether you use competitive benchmarking in each of the following areas:

	Number (%)		
Area	Yes	No	n =
Cost	44 (61.1%)	28 (38.9%)	72
Asset management	19 (26.4%)	53 (73.6%)	72
Customer service	32 (47.1%)	36 (52.9%)	68
Productivity	28 (38.9%)	44 (61.1%)	72
Quality	38 (52.8%)	34 (47.2%)	72
Logistics strategy	18 (26.5%)	50 (73.5%)	68
Technology deployment	28 (40.6%)	41 (59.4%)	69
Transportation operations	28 (40.0%)	42 (60.0%)	70
Warehouse operations	26 (37.7%)	43 (62.3%)	69
Order processing operations	19 (27.5%)	50 (72.5%)	69

QUESTION 24:   FACTORS USED TO EVALUATE SUPPLIERS

	Response Rating *:		
Factor:	n =	Mean	Std. Dev.
On time delivery	65	4.29	0.86
Percentage of complete orders	60	3.67	1.05
Automatic substitutions rates	44	2.05	0.94
Customer support	62	3.65	0.87
Easy to work with	66	4.00	0.78
Maintains short order cycle	58	3.59	0.94
Good communication	67	4.22	0.76

(CONTINUED...)

---

* Scale was: 1 = never used
                2 = rarely used
                3 = sometimes used
                4 = often used
                5 = always used

QUESTION 24:   (CON'T.)

Factor:		Response Rating *:	
	n =	Mean	Std. Dev.
Early notification of disruptions	63	3.54	0.95
Flexibility	66	3.95	0.81
Willing to customize service	61	3.56	0.87
Management quality	64	3.75	0.82
Service quality	66	4.38	0.67
Positive attitude	66	3.86	0.86
Master carton packaging quality	52	3.06	1.19
Shelf unit packaging quality	47	3.26	1.21
Price	64	4.59	0.61
Consistency of order cycle	58	3.91	0.84

* Scale was: 1 = never used
                 2 = rarely used
                 3 = sometimes used
                 4 = often used
                 5 = always used

QUESTION 25:   EDI USAGE

Number who are currently using, or planning to use Electronic Data Interchange (EDI) to facilitate order or other communications with the following:

Entity	Number who answered:			
	Currently installed	Plan to install in next 3 years	No Plans to install	Not Applicable
Manufacturers	23	19	20	11
Wholesalers	11	12	25	20
Public Warehouses	7	5	25	30
Carriers	15	11	28	14
Financial Institutions	20	7	23	16
Retailers	18	9	17	24
Customers	27	17	12	17
Copackers/Contractors	4	2	20	39

TABULATION OF THE QUESTIONNAIRE
(Hybrids: Phase II)

QUESTION 26: LOGISTICS COMPUTER APPLICATIONS

Logistics Computer Application:	Number who answered:			
	Currently installed and no plans for revision	Currently installed but will be revised in next 3 years	Not currently installed but will be in next 3 years	Not currently installed & no plans to install
Freight Audit and Payment	28	3	15	26
Purchasing	38	23	6	6
Sales Forecasting	22	24	11	14
Inventory Control	36	32	4	4
Warehouse Order Selection	26	24	7	16
Warehouse On-Line Receiving	24	14	17	18
Warehouse Merchandise Locator	21	22	11	18
Warehouse Workload Balancing	5	14	19	34
Warehouse Short Interval Scheduling	7	8	15	40
Order Processing	39	28	5	3
Order Entry	37	29	5	3
Vehicle Routing and Scheduling	11	9	20	31
Inbound Freight Consolidation	9	8	9	45
Outbound Freight Consolidation	16	15	13	28
Supporting Financials	37	27	5	6
Performance Measurement	24	24	12	12
Distribution Modeling	9	12	15	34
Direct Product Profitability	19	9	19	23
Direct Store Delivery	13	10	8	35
Shelf Management	9	5	8	40

QUESTION 27, 28, 29:   OPINIONS ABOUT POINT OF SALE SCANNING (UPC)

(A) "UPC has given retailers a unique advantage over other members of the
distribution channel"

Answer:	Number (%)
Strongly disagree/Disagree	5 (7.0%)
Neutral	18 (25.4%)
Strongly agree/Agree	48 (67.6%)
Total	71

* mean = 3.82,   standard deviation 0.90, n = 71

(B) "Information derived from point of sale scanning has made your business
unit competitively stronger in comparison to other members of your
distribution channel"

Answer:	Number (%)
Strongly disagree/Disagree	13 (22.0%)
Neutral	27 (45.8%)
Strongly agree/Agree	19 (32.2%)
Total	59

* mean = 3.08,   standard deviation 1.06, n = 59

(C) "Point of sale scanning information is more important to retailers
than wholesalers"

Answer:	Number (%)
Strongly disagree/Disagree	21 (29.6%)
Neutral	15 (21.1%)
Strongly agree/Agree	35 (49.3%)
Total	71

* mean = 3.23,   standard deviation 1.04, n = 71

TABULATION OF THE QUESTIONNAIRE
(Hybrids: Phase II)

QUESTION 30:   COMPARATIVE EVALUATION OF LOGISTICS MANAGEMENT INFORMATION SYSTEM

How do your company's logistics management information systems compare overall to the management information systems designed to support other areas of the business? (i.e. Accounting, Finance, Sales, etc.)

Answer:	Number (%)
Much Worse	6 (8.1%)
Worse	23 (31.1%)
Same	23 (31.1%)
Better	18 (24.3%)
Much better	4 (5.4%)
Total	**74**

* mean = 2.88,   standard deviation 1.05,   n = 74

QUESTION 31:   CHARACTERISTICS OF INFORMATION USED TO MANAGE LOGISTICS

	Response Rating *:		
Characteristic:	n =	Mean	Std. Dev.
Timely	74	4.07	0.90
Accurate	74	4.19	0.72
Readily Available	74	3.77	0.90
Formatted on an Exception Basis	67	2.88	1.04
Appropriately Formatted to Facilitate Use	69	3.52	0.87

* Scale was: N.A. = not applicable
1 = never
2 = rarely
3 = sometimes
4 = in most instances
5 = always

QUESTION 32: ABILITY TO ACCOMMODATE VARIOUS EVENTS IMPACTING LOGISTICS ACTIVITIES

Ability to Accommodate:	n =	Response Rating *: Mean	Std. Dev.
Special customer service requests	73	3.52	1.00
Sales/Marketing incentive programs	65	3.51	1.00
Product introduction	71	3.69	0.92
Product phase out	68	3.47	1.00
Disruption in supply	71	2.85	0.90
Computer breakdown	70	2.33	0.94
Product recall	56	2.88	0.92
Customization of service levels to specific markets or customers	68	3.21	0.99
Product modification or customization while in the logistics system (e.g. pricing, packaging, mixing)	67	3.24	1.03
Returned goods	69	3.45	0.83

--------- * --------- * ---------

* Scale was: N.A. = not applicable
1 = cannot accommodate
2 = accommodates with difficulty
3 = accommodates with few problems
4 = accommodates easily
5 = accommodates very easily

TABULATION OF THE QUESTIONNAIRE
(Hybrids: Phase II)

QUESTION 33: IMPACT ON LOGISTICS ACTIVITIES

Impact of:	n =	Response Rating *: Mean	Std. Dev.
Sales forecast accuracy	74	3.62	1.09
Computer support	72	4.06	0.87
Excessive end-of-month/quarter surges	70	3.37	1.05
Communications with customers	74	3.68	1.02
Availability of trained logistics personnel	73	3.33	0.87
Vehicle routing and scheduling	68	3.29	1.13
Computer applications backlog	68	3.37	1.08
Transportation cost	74	3.72	1.04
Communication with suppliers	72	3.46	0.98
Warehouse productivity	69	3.70	0.90
Measurement tools/methods	71	3.25	0.95
Communication with internal non-logistics organizational units	72	3.58	0.93
Timely information	75	3.99	0.78
Supplier logistical performance	72	3.50	0.86
Communication with external logistics service suppliers	67	3.01	0.98
Incompatibility of computer equipment and/or software	64	2.89	1.11
Inventory reduction programs	70	3.40	1.06
Cost reduction programs	75	3.55	0.95
Load leveling	62	3.03	0.99
Workforce leveling	66	3.21	0.94

--------- * --------- * ---------

* Scale was: N.A. = not applicable
1 = no impact
2 = slight impact
3 = medium impact
4 = high impact
5 = very high impact

QUESTION 34:   USAGE OF OUTSIDE SERVICE VENDORS

Outside Service:	Response Rating *:		
	n =	Mean	Std. Dev.
Transportation	75	3.13	0.78
Warehousing	71	2.58	1.18
Order entry/processing	71	1.90	1.12
Inventory management	69	1.94	1.10
Freight audit/payment	69	2.51	1.05
Consolidators	57	2.42	1.13
International freight forwarders	56	2.86	1.03
Domestic freight forwarders	61	2.26	1.08
Order fulfillment and support	64	2.08	1.17

* Scale used: N.A. = not applicable
                 1 = will not use outside logistical services
                 2 = will use less than current levels
                 3 = usage will remain constant
                 4 = will use more outside logistical services
                 5 = will use many more outside logistical services

QUESTION 35:   FACTORS AFFECTING THE DECISION TO USE OUTSIDE SERVICE VENDORS

Factor Affecting the Decision:	Response Rating *:		
	n =	Mean	Std. Dev.
Services available	70	3.87	1.10
Quality of services	72	4.19	0.87
Data processing/communication services	68	3.12	1.11
Management quality	68	3.57	1.01
Customer orientation	68	3.85	0.97
Vendor reputation	69	4.10	0.86

* Scale was: N.A. = not applicable
                1 = never
                2 = rarely
                3 = sometimes
                4 = often
                5 = always

TABULATION OF THE QUESTIONNAIRE
(Hybrids: Phase II)

QUESTION 36: TECHNOLOGY APPLICATIONS WITHIN THE BUSINESS UNIT

Technology	Number who answered:				
	Currently used in logistics	Currently used in firm but not in logistics	Planned to be installed in logistics next 3 years	Not planned to be installed in logistics	Have not evaluated
Bar codes	21	4	26	12	12
Optical scanning	15	3	25	17	13
Robotics	4	3	7	36	24
Artificial intelligence/ knowledge based systems	3	0	8	28	31
Automated storage and retrieval systems	6	3	8	38	18
Automated material handling equipment	14	2	13	28	17
Local area networks	11	5	9	22	24
Computer-aided warehouse design	12	2	10	26	23
Handheld data entry devices	23	7	17	15	11
Electronic order transmission	39	4	17	5	8
On board computers - delivery vehicles	7	1	12	33	21
On board computers - lift trucks	4	1	13	34	22
Voice data capture	4	1	4	31	33
IBM PC or PC XT compatible	52	6	10	2	3
80286 Microcomputers (IBM AT or compatible)	31	8	5	10	15

(CONTINUED...)

QUESTION 36:   (CON'T.)

Technology	Number who answered:				
	Currently used in logistics	Currently used in firm but not in logistics	Planned to be installed in logistics next 3 years	Not planned to be installed in logistics	Have not evaluated
80386 Microcomputers	22	6	7	12	19
CD-ROM	5	2	4	11	34
WORM (write once, read many) discs	4	0	3	13	43
68020 - based micro-computers (Macintosh 2 or Sun)	5	2	0	20	37
Fiber Optics	3	0	1	16	45

TABULATION OF THE QUESTIONNAIRE
(Hybrids: Phase II)

CHARACTERISTICS OF THE RESPONDENTS

(A) Number who are CLM or CAPDM members: 23 (29.9%)

Number who are not: 54 (70.1%)

Total   77

(B) Distribution by CAI grouping:

CAI Grouping	Number (%)
Emerging	13 (16.9%)
Norm	49 (63.6%)
Leading Edge	15 (19.5%)
Total	77

(C) Distribution by Industry:

Industry	Number (%)
Building Materials, Hardware and Garden Supply	7 (9.1%)
General Merchandise	4 (5.2%)
Food	24 (31.2%)
Automotive	10 (13.0%)
Apparel and Accessory	3 (3.9%)
Furniture, Home Furnishings, and Equipment	11 (14.3%)
Eating and Drinking Establishments	0 (0.0%)
Drugs, Health and Beauty Aids	2 (2.6%)
Fuel	12 (15.6%)
Paper/Office Supplies	4 (5.2%)
Other	0 (0.0%)
Total	77

APPENDIX B

Statistical Comparison
by CAI Group

APPENDIX B: STATISTICAL COMPARISON BY CAI GROUP

In Appendix B, selected questions from the Phase I and Phase II question-naires are analyzed by CAI group. Emerging and leading edge respondents are each compared to the norm. Statistical test results are presented which test the overall research hypothesis that differences in responses exist due to CAI group. Usually, significance levels are indicated by: (1) * meaning signifi-cantly different at p = 0.10; (2) ** meaning significantly different at p = 0.05; and (3) *** meaning significantly different at p = 0.01. Sometimes exact significance levels are given in the footnotes of tables. Space limitations precluded giving exact significance levels for every item of every question.

The analyses for the following questions appear in the rest of Appendix B:

(1) Phase I questionnaire sent to manufacturers--Questions 5A, 5B, 6A, 7, 8A, 8B, 8C, 9, 10, 11, 12, 13, 14, 15, 16, 17, 23 and 25;
(2) Phase II questionnaire sent to manufacturers--Questions 2A, 2B, 5, 6, 7, 8, 9, 10, 11, 12, 13 and 14;
(3) Phase II questionnaire sent to retailers--Questions 4, 5A, 5B, 5C, 6A, 6B, 8, 10, 13, 16, 17, 18, 20, 22, 23, 25, 26, 27, 28, 29, 30, 31, 32, 33, 34 and 35;
(4) Phase II questionnaire sent to wholesalers--see list for retailers; and
(5) Phase II questionnaire sent to hybrids--see list for retailers.

COMPARISON OF EMERGING, NORM AND LEADING EDGE
(Manufacturers Phase I Only)

QUESTION 5A: TITLE LEVEL OF THE MOST SENIOR LOGISTICS EXECUTIVE

	Emerging	Norm	Leading Edge
President	2 (3.85%)	5 (1.98%)	0 (0.00%)
Executive V.P.	1 (1.92%)	9 (3.56%)	4 (6.25%)
Vice President	13 (25.00%)	87 (34.39%)	41 (64.06%)
Director	15 (28.85%)	96 (37.94%)	17 (26.56%)
Manager	21 (40.38%)	54 (21.34%)	2 (3.13%)
Supervisor	0 (0.00%)	2 (0.79%)	0 (0.00%)
Total	52*	253	64**

* Chi-square table (versus the NORM) is significant at p = 0.078.
** Chi-square table (versus the NORM) is significant at p = 0.000.

QUESTION 5B: YEARS IN THIS POSITION

Mean	(Standard Deviation)	
Emerging	Norm	Leading Edge
6.11	5.08	4.16
(5.22)*	(4.30)	(4.38)

* Significantly different from the NORM at 0.10.

QUESTION 6A: TITLE OF THE PERSON THE SENIOR LOGISTICS EXECUTIVE REPORTS TO

	Emerging	Norm	Leading Edge
President	15 (28.85%)	62 (24.51%)	25 (39.68%)
Executive V.P.	9 (17.31%)	62 (24.51%)	17 (26.98%)
Vice-President	20 (38.46%)	106 (41.90%)	20 (31.75%)
Director	4 (7.69%)	12 (4.74%)	1 (1.59%)
Manager	4 (7.69%)	8 (3.16%)	0 (0.00%)
Other	0 (0.00%)	3 (1.19%)	0 (0.00%)
Total	52	253	63*

* Chi-square table (versus the NORM) is significant at p = 0.087.

QUESTION 7: DO YOU HAVE A FORMAL LOGISTICS MISSION STATEMENT?

Answer:	Emerging	Norm	Leading Edge
Yes	5 (8.06%)	70 (27.89%)	45 (75.00%)
No	57 (91.94%)	181 (72.11%)	15 (25.00%)
Total	62*	251	60**

* Chi-square table (versus the NORM) is significant at p = 0.001.
** Chi-square table (versus the NORM) is significant at p = 0.000.

QUESTION 8: LOGISTICS STRATEGIC PLAN

(A) Do you have a written logistics strategic plan?

Answer:	Emerging	Norm	Leading Edge
Yes	1 (1.64%)	106 (42.06%)	64 (100.00%)
No	60 (98.36%)	146 (47.94%)	0 (0.00%)
Total	61*	252	64*

(B) If yes, what is the time horizon?

	Mean (Standard Deviation)	
Emerging	Norm	Leading Edge
**	3.67	4.40****
(**)	(2.01)	(1.97)

(C) If yes, how often is the plan reviewed or updated?

	Mean (Standard Deviation)	
Emerging	Norm	Leading Edge
**	0.75 yrs.	0.92 years***
(**)	(0.40)	(0.57)****

* Chi-square table (versus the NORM) is significant at p = 0.000.
** Only one respondent answered this question.
****, *** Significantly different from the NORM at 0.05 and 0.01 respectively.

COMPARISON OF EMERGING, NORM AND LEADING EDGE
(Manufacturers Phase I Only)

QUESTION 9: DO LOGISTICS EXECUTIVES FORMALLY PARTICIPATE IN OVERALL STRATEGIC PLANNING

Answer:	Emerging	Norm	Leading Edge
Yes	24 (40.68%)	192 (76.80%)	63 (98.44%)
No	35 (59.32%)	58 (23.20%)	1 (1.56%)
Total	59*	250	64*

* Chi-square tables (versus the NORM) are significant at p = 0.000.

QUESTIONS 10, 11: FORMAL ORGANIZATION OF LOGISTICS ACTIVITIES

(A) How many years has logistics been a formal organization?

	Mean (Standard Deviation)	
Emerging	Norm	Leading Edge
8.25	10.59	11.31
(10.68)	(10.29)	(8.92)

(B) Within the last five years, how many times has logistics been reorganized?

	Mean (Standard Deviation)	
Emerging	Norm	Leading Edge
1.48	1.87	2.33*
(3.55)***	(1.87)	(1.52)*

***, * Significantly different from the NORM at 0.01 and 0.10 respectively.

QUESTION 12: BEYOND FUNCTIONS?

Answer:	Emerging	Norm	Leading Edge
Yes	15 (26.79%)	109 (43.08%)	31 (48.44%)
No	41 (73.21%)	144 (56.92%)	33 (51.56%)
Total	56*	253	64

* Chi-square table (versus the NORM) is significant at p = 0.024.

QUESTION 13: ANALYSIS OF FUNCTIONS

Total # of Functions:	Overall Mean (Standard Deviation)		
	Emerging	Norm	Leading Edge
Line or staff	4.26*** (3.23)	9.10 (3.15)	12.19*** (1.90)***
Line only	2.89*** (3.01)	6.64 (3.56)	9.89*** (3.26)

*** Significantly different from the NORM at 0.01

Function	Number (%) Who Have It (Line or Staff)		
	Emerging	Norm	Leading Edge
Sales Forecasting	4 (6.45)***	78 (30.71)	36 (56.25)***
Production Planning	12 (19.35)***	130 (51.18)	51 (79.69)***
Sourcing/Purchasing	18 (29.03)***	126 (49.61)	38 (59.38)
Inbound Transportation	37 (59.68)**	191 (75.20)	57 (89.06)**
Raw/WIP Inventory	13 (20.97)***	111 (43.70)	39 (60.94)**
Finished Goods Inventory	19 (30.65)***	187 (73.62)	60 (93.75)***
Intra-co. Transportation	33 (53.23)***	205 (80.71)	59 (92.19)**
Fin. Gds. Field Warehousing	26 (41.94)***	193 (75.98)	61 (95.31)***
Order Processing	10 (16.13)***	142 (55.91)	55 (85.94)***
Customer Service	9 (14.52)***	147 (57.87)	57 (89.06)***
Outbound Transportation	37 (59.68)***	232 (91.34)	64 (100.00)**
Logistics Systems Planning	16 (25.81)***	189 (74.41)	61 (95.31)***
Logistics Engineering	5 (8.06)***	76 (29.92)	38 (59.38)***
Logistics Administration	15 (24.19)***	183 (72.05)	61 (95.31)***
International Logistics	10 (16.13)***	121 (47.64)	43 (67.19)***

***, ** Chi-square tables (versus the NORM) are significant at 0.01 and 0.05 respectively.

COMPARISON OF EMERGING, NORM AND LEADING EDGE
(Manufacturers Phase I Only)

QUESTION 14: ORGANIZATIONAL CONFIGURATION

	Emerging	Norm	Leading Edge
Type A: Functional Organization with Dispersed Logistics Activities	34 (58.62%)	67 (27.69%)	7 (11.67%)
Type B: Functional Organization with Consolidated Activities	5 (8.62%)	63 (26.03%)	25 (41.67%)
Type C: Divisional Organization with Logistics Consolidated Within Business Units	8 (13.79%)	44 (18.18%)	7 (11.67%)
Type D: Divisional Organization with Logistics Consolidated Centrally	4 (6.90%)	23 (9.50%)	14 (23.33%)
Type E: Divisional Organization with Corporate Staff and Line Functions Within Business Units	7 (12.07%)	45 (18.60%)	7 (11.67%)
Total	**58***	**242**	**60****

* Chi-square table (versus the NORM) is significant at $p = 0.000$.
** Chi-square table (versus the NORM) is significant at $p = 0.001$.

QUESTION 15: STRATEGY

	Emerging	Norm	Leading Edge
Type A: Process	32 (65.31%)	129 (55.60%)	42 (70.00%)
Type B: Market	12 (24.49%)	78 (33.62%)	14 (23.33%)
Type C: Channel	5 (10.20%)	25 (10.78%)	4 (6.67%)
Total	**49**	**232**	**60**

QUESTION 16: ABILITY TO ACCOMODATE VARIOUS EVENTS IMPACTING
LOGISTICS ACTIVITIES
(1 = CANNOT ACCOMMODATE, 4 = ACCOMMODATES EASILY)

Event	Mean on a 4-point scale (Standard Deviation)		
	Emerging	Norm	Leading Edge
Special customer service requests	3.05 (0.82)***	3.11 (0.63)	3.22 (0.63)
Sales/Marketing incentive programs	2.79 (0.96)**	3.03 (0.69)	3.18 (0.64)
Product introduction	2.76* (0.83)	2.99 (0.69)	3.27*** (0.62)
Product phase out	2.60** (0.81)	2.92 (0.74)	3.06 (0.77)
Disruptions in supply	2.63 (0.66)	2.77 (0.71)	2.91 (0.71)
Computer breakdown	2.51* (0.89)	2.26 (0.83)	2.25 (0.82)
Unexpected production schedule changes	2.72 (0.70)	2.80 (0.63)	3.02** (0.72)
Product recall	2.54 (1.04)***	2.77 (0.76)	3.02** (0.78)
Customization of service levels	2.90 (0.88)	2.72 (0.89)	2.98** (0.81)
Product modification while in logistics system	2.46 (0.81)	2.59 (0.86)	2.76 (0.88)

***, **, * Significantly different from the NORM at 0.01, 0.05, and 0.10
respectively.

COMPARISON OF EMERGING, NORM AND LEADING EDGE
(Manufacturers Phase I Only)

QUESTION 17: PLEASE RATE EACH OF THE FOLLOWING IN TERMS OF THEIR IMPACT ON YOUR LOGISTICAL OPERATIONS.

Item:	Mean for each of the CAI Groups (1)		
	Emerging	Norm	Leading Edge
Forecast accuracy	2.63***	3.08	3.33**
Computer support	2.86***	3.31	3.50*
Excessive end-of-month or end-of-quarter surges	2.76	2.74	2.81
Communications with customer	2.65	2.75	2.91
Production planning & scheduling	2.91	3.09	3.17
Interface with manufacturing	2.89	2.98	3.11
Availability of trained logistics personnel	2.32*	2.56	2.91***
Vehicle routing and scheduling	2.61	2.74	2.69
Computer applications backlog	2.24**	2.58	2.87**
Transportation cost	2.98	3.08	2.98
Communication with material vendors	2.41*	2.65	2.60
Communication with dealers, distributors, or brokers	2.20**	2.60	2.56
Warehouse productivity	2.58	2.79	2.92
Measurement tools and methods	2.02***	2.55	2.89***
Communication with internal non-logistics organizational units	2.35***	2.80	3.13***
Timely information	3.09	3.23	3.52***
Supplier performance	2.49***	3.02	3.13
Communication with external logistical service suppliers	2.18**	2.54	2.60
Incompatibility of computer equipment and/or software	2.12	2.21	2.40

(1) - Scale was 1 = no impact
                2 = slight impact
                3 = high impact
                4 = very high impact

***, **, * Significantly different from the norm at 0.01, 0.05 and 0.10 respectively.

QUESTION 23: CHARACTERISTICS OF INFORMATION USED TO MANAGE LOGISTICS
(1 = NEVER, 5 = ALWAYS)

	Mean on a 5-point scale (Standard Deviation)		
Characteristic	Emerging	Norm	Leading Edge
Accurate	3.66***	4.09	4.13
	(0.92)***	(0.67)	(0.60)
Timely	3.58**	3.87	4.00
	(1.02)**	(0.82)	(0.67)*
Readily available	3.45	3.61	4.00***
	(1.01)	(0.86)	(0.70)*
Formatted on an exception basis	2.69	2.79	3.23***
	(0.95)	(0.94)	(0.92)
Appropriately formatted to facilitate use	2.83***	3.42	3.76***
	(1.08)***	(0.82)	(0.86)

***, **, * Significantly different from the NORM at 0.01, 0.05, and 0.10
respectively.

QUESTION 25: IN ADDITION TO COST, WHICH FACTORS INFLUENCE THE DECISION TO USE
OUTSIDE SERVICE VENDORS? (1 = not important, 4 = very important)

	Mean for each CAI Group		
Factor	Emerging	Norm	Leading Edge
Deregulation	2.64	2.62	2.70
Services available	3.09	3.22	3.39
Quality of services	3.47	3.56	3.72
Data processing/ communications services	2.60	2.87	3.12
Management quality	2.87	3.14	3.38
Customer attitudes	2.91	3.16	3.17

COMPARISON OF EMERGING, NORM AND LEADING EDGE
(Manufacturers Phase II Only)

<u>QUESTION 2:</u> ANALYSIS OF LOGISTICS ORGANIZATION

(A) Centralization (=5) versus decentralization (=1)

	Mean (Standard Deviation)	
Emerging	Norm	Leading Edge
3.13**	3.70	3.69
(1.23)	(1.06)	(1.21)

** Significantly different from the NORM at 0.05.

(B) Trend over the last three years?

	Emerging	Norm	Leading Edge
Centralization	6 (26.09%)	62 (52.10%)	23 (57.50%)
Decentralization	5 (21 74%)	21 (17.65%)	9 (22.50%)
No Change	12 (52.17%)	36 (30.25%)	8 (20.00%)
Total	23*	119	40

* Chi-square table of NORM versus EMERGING is significant at p = 0.060.

<u>QUESTION 5:</u> PARTICIPATION IN OVERALL STRATEGIC PLANNING

Answer:	Emerging	Norm	Leading Edge
Yes	14 (63.64%)	77 (63.64%)	34 (85.00%)
No, but provides input	7 (31.82%)	41 (33.88%)	5 (12.50%)
No	1 (4.55%)	3 (2.48%)	1 (2.50%)
Total	22	121	40*

* Chi-square table of NORM versus LEADING EDGE is significant at p = 0.033.

QUESTION 6: COMPETITIVE BENCHMARKING

	Number (%) of Those Who Responded, Who Said Benchmarking Was Used		
Area	Emerging	Norm	Leading Edge
Cost	13 (61.90)	94 (77.69)	34 (87.18)
Asset Management	3 (15.00)	38 (33.33)	22 (59.46)***
Customer Service	18 (81.82)	102 (84.30)	35 (87.50)
Productivity	10 (45.45)	66 (55.00)	28 (73.68)**
Quality	18 (85.71)	90 (75.63)	34 (85.00)
Logistics Strategy	7 (33.33)	60 (50.42)	29 (74.36)***
Technology Deployment	11 (52.38)	48 (41.03)	24 (63.16)**
Transportation Operations	10 (47.62)	66 (55.00)	25 (65.79)
Warehouse Operations	9 (40.91)	60 (50.85)	23 (60.53)
Order Processing Operations	6 (28.57)**	64 (53.78)	24 (61.54)

***, **, * Chi-square table (versus the NORM) is significant at 0.01, 0.05 and 0.10 respectively.

QUESTION 7: ANALYSIS OF LOGISTICS RELATED PERFOMANCE MEASUREMENT

	Number (%) of Those Who Responded, Who Said The Measure Was Used		
(A) ASSET MANAGEMENT	Emerging	Norm	Leading Edge
Inventory turns	10 (47.62)***	97 (84.35)	36 (92.31)
Inventory carrying costs	12 (54.55)	73 (65.18)	33 (84.62)**
Inventory levels (# of days supply)	15 (75.00)	98 (85.96)	37 (94.87)
Obsolete inventory	13 (61.90)***	98 (85.73)	37 (94.87)
Return on net assets	11 (50.00)	73 (66.36)	29 (76.32)
Return on investment	12 (60.00)	80 (73.39)	32 (84.21)

***, ** Chi-square table (versus the NORM) is significant at 0.01 and 0.05 respectively.

COMPARISON OF EMERGING, NORM AND LEADING EDGE
(Manufacturers Phase II Only)

QUESTION 7: (CON'T)

	Number (%) of Those Who Responded, Who Said The Measure Was Used		
(B) COST (logistics cost)			
Total cost analysis	16 (80.00)	100 (86.96)	38 (95.00)
Cost per unit	15 (71.43)	93 (80.87)	33 (84.62)
Cost as a percentage of sales	18 (81.82)	96 (82.76)	35 (87.50)
Inbound freight costs	17 (77.27)	98 (85.22)	37 (92.50)
Outbound freight costs	19 (86.36)	110 (94.02)	40 (100.00)
Warehouse costs	14 (66.67)***	100 (91.74)	37 (92.50)
Administrative costs	13 (61.90)**	91 (80.53)	35 (87.50)
Order processing costs	6 (28.57)*	54 (48.65)	28 (73.68)***
Direct labor costs	16 (72.73)	89 (80.18)	30 (78.95)
Comparison of actual versus budget	19 (86.36)**	112 (97.39)	39 (100.00)
Cost trend analysis	12 (57.14)*	85 (76.58)	34 (87.18)
Direct product profitability	10 (47.62)	65 (60.19)	24 (63.16)

(C) CUSTOMER SERVICE	Emerging	Norm	Leading Edge
Fill rate	8 (50.00)**	87 (79.09)	33 (86.84)
Stockouts	5 (33.33)***	92 (83.64)	34 (89.47)
Shipping errors	12 (66.67)*	94 (83.19)	34 (89.47)
On time delivery	18 (90.00)	86 (77.48)	37 (92.50)**
Backorders	13 (65.00)	86 (78.90)	27 (77.14)
Cycle time	6 (40.00)**	76 (69.72)	30 (81.08)
Customer feedback	18 (90.00)	103 (90.35)	36 (90.00)
Sales force feedback	17 (80.95)	97 (88.18)	37 (92.50)
Customer Surveys	10 (47.62)*	77 (69.37)	30 (76.92)

***, **, * Chi-square table (versus the NORM) is significant at 0.01, 0.05 and 0.10 respectively.

QUESTION 7: (CON'T)

Number (%) of Those Who
Responded, Who Said The Measure Was Used

(D) PRODUCTIVITY

	Emerging	Norm	Leading Edge
Units shipped per employee	3 (15.79)***	61 (57.01)	27 (69.23)
Units per labor dollar	6 (30.00)*	54 (52.43)	24 (63.16)
Orders per sales rep.	4 (22.22)*	42 (43.30)	12 (35.29)
Comparison to historical standards	13 (65.00)	85 (77.27)	31 (81.58)
Goal programs	8 (42.11)***	86 (78.90)	34 (87.18)
Productivity Index	7 (36.84)	55 (51.89)	29 (78.38)***

(E) QUALITY

	Emerging	Norm	Leading Edge
Frequency of damage	11 (52.38)	70 (62.50)	35 (87.50)***
Dollar amount of damage	13 (61.90)	79 (71.17)	35 (89.74)**
Number of credit claims	14 (73.68)	79 (71.82)	34 (89.47)**
Number of customer returns	13 (61.90)	86 (76.79)	36 (90.00)*
Cost of returned goods	11 (57.89)	70 (64.22)	34 (85.00)**

***, **, * Chi-square table (versus the NORM) is significant at 0.01, 0.05 and 0.10 respectively.

TOTAL NUMBER OF PERFORMANCE MEASURES

Performance Category	Mean (Standard Deviation)		
	Emerging	Norm	Leading Edge
Asset Management	3.17** (2.19)	4.25 (1.93)	5.10*** (1.43)*
Cost	7.61** (2.82)	8.96 (2.75)	10.25*** (1.95)**
Customer Service	4.65*** (2.77)	6.54 (2.63)	7.45** (1.89)**
Productivity	1.78*** (1.98)	3.14 (1.95)	3.93** (1.79)
Quality	2.69 (1.94)	3.15 (1.87)	4.35*** (1.25)***

***, **, * Significantly different from NORM at 0.01, 0.05 & 0.10 respectively.

COMPARISON OF EMERGING, NORM AND LEADING EDGE
(Manufacturers Phase II Only)

QUESTIONS 8, 9, 10: OPINIONS ABOUT U.P.C. SCANNING
(1 = STRONGLY DISAGREE, 5 = STRONGLY AGREE)

(A) "UPC has given retailers a unique advantage over other members of the distribution channel"

Mean (Standard Deviation)		
Emerging	Norm	Leading Edge
3.50	3.67	3.68
(1.05)	(0.82)	(1.05)*

* Significantly different from the NORM at 0.10.

(B) "Information derived from point of sale scanning has made your business unit competitively stronger in comparison to other members of your distribution channel"

Mean (Standard Deviation)		
Emerging	Norm	Leading Edge
2.94	2.98	3.16
(0.97)	(0.95)	(1.08)

(C) "Point of sale scanning information is more important to retailers than wholesalers"

Mean (Standard Deviation)		
Emerging	Norm	Leading Edge
3.33	3.25	3.15
(1.08)	(1.04)	(0.90)

QUESTION 11: COMPARATIVE EVALUATION OF LOGISTICS MANAGEMENT INFORMATION SYSTEM
(1 = MUCH WORSE,   5 = MUCH BETTER)

How do your company's logistics management information systems compare overall
to the management information systems designed to support other areas of the
business?

Mean (Standard Deviation)		
Emerging	Norm	Leading Edge
2.77	3.01	3.50**
(0.97)	(1.05)	(1.04)

** Significantly different from the NORM at 0.05.

QUESTION 12: USAGE OF OUTSIDE SERVICE VENDORS
(1 = will not use, 5 = will use many more outside services)

	Mean for each of the CAI Groups		
Outside Service Vendor	Emerging	Norm	Leading Edge
Transportation	3.19	3.24	3.36
Warehousing	3.11	2.73	3.20**
Order Entry and Processing	1.48*	1.91	1.53*
Inventory Management	1.32*	1.76	1.79
Freight Audit and Payment	2.35*	2.83	2.80
Consolidators	2.00***	2.71	3.00
International Freight Forwarders	3.25	3.06	3.13
Domestic Freight Forwarders	2.20	2.42	2.25
Order Fulfillment and Support	1.67	2.04	2.44

***, **, * Significantly different from the norm at 0.01, 0.05 and
0.10 respectively

COMPARISON OF EMERGING, NORM AND LEADING EDGE
(Manufacturers Phase II Only)

<u>QUESTION 13:</u> LOGISTICS COMPUTER APPLICATIONS

Number (%) of Those Who Responded, Who Said The Application
Was Currently Installed (With or Without Revision Plans)

Application	Emerging	Norm	Leading Edge
Freight Audit and Payment	8 (36.37)*	77 (63.73)	31 (79.49)
Purchasing	12 (57.15)**	88 (73.34)	31 (79.49)
Sales Forecasting	11 (61.11)	70 (75.63)	34 (91.89)
Inventory Control - Raw Materials	14 (66.67)	93 (80.87)	30 (81.09)
Inventory Control - In Process	16 (76.19)*	95 (81.20)	30 (81.90)
Inventory Control - Finished Goods	16 (76.19)**	111 (93.27)	38 (100.00)
Warehouse Order Selection	10 (47.62)	80 (69.83)	32 (84.21)
Warehouse On-Line Receiving	8 (38.10)*	71 (60.68)	28 (73.69)
Warehouse Merchandise Locator	9 (40.91)	71 (61.21)	25 (65.79)
Warehouse Workload Balancing	3 (15.00)	35 (29.17)	18 (47.37)
Warehouse Short Interval Scheduling	3 (14.28)	34 (30.36)	17 (47.23)
Order Processing	21 (91.30)*	114 (95.80)	39 (100.00)
Order Entry	21 (91.30)**	116 (96.67)	38 (97.44)
Vehicle Routing and Scheduling	5 (22.73)	35 (29.92)	18 (47.50)
Inbound Freight Consolidation	5 (22.73)**	30 (25.42)	18 (45.00)**
Outbound Freight Consolidation	7 (31.82)	60 (50.42)	30 (75.00)**
Supporting Financials	13 (68.42)	95 (81.20)	36 (94.79)
Performance Measurement	13 (59.09)***	81 (67.50)	34 (87.18)
Distribution Modeling	5 (25.00)	49 (41.88)	27 (71.05)**
Direct Product Profitability	9 (50.00)	56 (47.46)	19 (51.35)
Direct Store Delivery	3 (15.79)	34 (30.36)	17 (44.74)
Shelf Management	4 (22.23)	24 (22.23)	15 (52.86)**
MRP	8 (47.06)	64 (59.26)	26 (70.27)
DRP	4 (23.52)	37 (35.58)	18 (52.94)***

***, **, * Chi-square table (versus the NORM) is significant at 0.01, 0.05 and
0.10 respectively.

QUESTION 14: ELECTRONIC DATA INTERCHANGE

	Number (%) of Those Who Responded, Who Said EDI Was Currently Installed		
Application	Emerging	Norm	Leading Edge
Manufacturers	3 (13.64)*	23 (20.18)	14 (35.90)**
Wholesalers	2 (9.52)***	27 (23.68)	14 (35.90)*
Public Warehouses	2 (9.09)*	21 (18.42)	13 (33.33)*
Carriers	2 (9.09)	29 (24.79)	15 (37.50)***
Financial Institutions	7 (33.33)	28 (26.67)	12 (31.58)
Retailers	1 (4.76)	17 (16.19)	10 (27.78)*
Customers	2 (8.70)**	26 (22.81)	20 (51.28)***
Copackers/Contracters	0 (0.00)*	6 (5.50)	4 (10.81)

***, **, * Overall chi-square table (versus the NORM) is significant at 0.01, 0.05, and 0.10 respectively.

	Number (%) of Those Who Responded, Who Said EDI Was Planned in Next Three Years		
Application	Emerging	Norm	Leading Edge
Manufacturers	2 (9.09)	37 (32.46)	15 (38.46)
Wholesalers	1 (4.76)	31 (27.19)	15 (38.46)
Public Warehouses	3 (13.64)	30 (26.32)	14 (35.90)
Carriers	6 (27.27)	44 (37.61)	24 (60.00)
Financial Institutions	1 (4.76)	23 (21.90)	12 (31.58)
Retailers	3 (14.29)	18 (17.14)	10 (27.78)
Customers	7 (30.43)	51 (44.74)	16 (41.03)
Copackers/Contracters	1 (5.00)	21 (19.27)	10 (27.03)

COMPARISON OF EMERGING, NORM AND LEADING EDGE
(Retailers Only)

QUESTION 4: DO YOU HAVE A WRITTEN LOGISTICS MISSION STATEMENT?

Answer:	Emerging	Norm	Leading Edge
Yes	0 (0.00%)	21 (38.18%)	13 (81.25%)
No	16 (100.00%)	34 (61.82%)	3 (18.75%)
Total	16*	55	16**

* Chi-square table of NORM versus EMERGING is significant at p = 0.003.
** Chi-square table of NORM versus LEADING EDGE is significant at p = 0.0002.

QUESTION 5: LOGISTICS STRATEGIC PLAN

(A) Do you have a written logistics strategic plan?

Answer:	Emerging	Norm	Leading Edge
Yes	2 (12.50%)	33 (60.00%)	15 (93.75%)
No	14 (87.50%)	22 (40.00%)	1 (6.25%)
Total	16*	55	16**

* Chi-square table of NORM versus EMERGING is significant at p = 0.001.
** Chi-square table of NORM versus LEADING EDGE is significant at p = 0.011.

(B) If yes, what is the time horizon?

	Mean (Standard Deviation)	
Emerging	Norm	Leading Edge
*	4.32	3.67
(*)	(1.74)	(1.59)

* Only one respondent answered this question.

QUESTION 5: (CON'T)

(C) If yes, how often is the plan reviewed or updated?

	Mean (Standard Deviation)	
Emerging	Norm	Leading Edge
*	12.48	10.00
(*)	(10.10)	(3.53)**

* Only one respondent answered this question.
** Significantly different from the NORM at 0.01

QUESTION 6: ANALYSIS OF LOGISTICS ORGANIZATION

(A) Centralization (=5) versus decentralization (=1)

	Mean (Standard Deviation)	
Emerging	Norm	Leading Edge
4.00	3.81	3.81
(1.03)	(1.16)	(0.91)

(B) Trend over the last three years?

	Emerging	Norm	Leading Edge
Centralization	8 (53.33%)	31 (55.36%)	10 (62.50%)
Decentralization	1 (6.67%)	8 (14.29%)	2 (12.50%)
No Change	6 (40.00%)	17 (30.36%)	4 (25.00%)
Total	15	56	16

COMPARISON OF EMERGING, NORM AND LEADING EDGE
(Retailers Only)

QUESTION 8: TITLE LEVEL OF THE MOST SENIOR LOGISTICS EXECUTIVE

	Emerging	Norm	Leading Edge
President	1 (6.67%)	3 (5.26%)	1 (6.25%)
Executive V.P.	1 (6.67%)	2 (3.51%)	1 (6.25%)
Senior V.P.	4 (26.67%)	11 (19.30%)	4 (25.00%)
Vice-President	4 (26.67%)	30 (52.63%)	9 (56.25%)
Director	3 (20.00%)	8 (14.04%)	1 (6.25%)
Manager	0 (0.00%)	2 (3.51%)	0 (0.00%)
Supervisor	1 (6.67%)	0 (0.00%)	0 (0.00%)
Other	1 (6.67%)	1 (1.75%)	0 (0.00%)
Total	**15**	**57**	**16**

QUESTION 10: YEARS IN THIS POSITION

Mean	(Standard Deviation)	
Emerging	Norm	Leading Edge
6.67	6.21	6.38
(8.25)	(6.74)	(6.04)

QUESTION 13: TITLE OF THE PERSON THE SENIOR LOGISTICS EXECUTIVE REPORTS TO

	Emerging	Norm	Leading Edge
Chairman	2 (13.33%)	4 (7.14%)	0 (0.00%)
President	4 (26.67%)	29 (51.79%)	8 (50.00%)
Executive V.P.	1 (6.67%)	14 (25.00%)	7 (43.75%)
Senior V.P.	4 (26.67%)	8 (14.29%)	0 (0.00%)
Vice-President	2 (13.33%)	1 (1.79%)	0 (0.00%)
Director	0 (0.00%)	0 (0.00%)	0 (0.00%)
Manager	0 (0.00%)	0 (0.00%)	0 (0.00%)
Supervisor	0 (0.00%)	0 (0.00%)	0 (0.00%)
Other	2 (13.33%)	0 (0.00%)	1 (6.25%)
Total	**15**	**56**	**16**

QUESTIONS 16, 17: FORMAL ORGANIZATION OF LOGISTICS ACTIVITIES

(A) How many years has logistics been a formal organization?

	Mean (Standard Deviation)	
Emerging	Norm	Leading Edge
9.00	10.09	20.00
(6.42)	(8.74)	(27.55)***

*** Significantly different from the NORM at 0.001

(B) Within the last five years, how many times has logistics been reorganized?

	Mean (Standard Deviation)	
Emerging	Norm	Leading Edge
3.00	2.13	2.40
(5.76)***	(1.35)	(1.45)

*** Significantly different from the NORM at 0.01

QUESTION 18: PARTICIPATION IN OVERALL STRATEGIC PLANNING

Answer:	Emerging	Norm	Leading Edge
Yes	9 (60.00%)	51 (89.47%)	16 (100.00%)
No, but provides input	4 (26.67%)	5 (8.77%)	0 (0.00%)
No	2 (13.33%)	1 (1.75%)	0 (0.00%)
Total	15*	57	16

* Chi-square table of NORM versus EMERGING is significant at p = 0.017.

COMPARISON OF EMERGING, NORM AND LEADING EDGE
(Retailers Only)

QUESTION 20: ANALYSIS OF FUNCTIONS

Total # of Functions:	Overall Mean (Standard Deviation)		
	Emerging	Norm	Leading Edge
Line or staff	3.00***	8.77	13.25***
	(3.10)	(4.30)	(1.87)***
Line only	1.76***	4.95	6.06
	(2.01)***	(3.81)	(3.99)

*** Significantly different from the NORM at 0.01

Function	Number (%) Who Have It (Line or Staff)		
	Emerging	Norm	Leading Edge
Sales Forecasting	1 (5.88)	12 (19.67)	4 (33.33)
Purchasing	3 (17.65)*	24 (39.34)	7 (58.33)
Inbound Transportation	7 (41.18)***	51 (83.61)	12 (100.00)
Inventory Management	0 (0.00)***	29 (47.54)	9 (75.00)*
Intra-Co. Transportation	5 (29.41)**	37 (60.66)	11 (91.67)**
Warehousing	8 (47.06)**	47 (77.05)	12 (100.00)*
Order Processing	2 (11.76)**	27 (44.26)	11 (91.67)***
Customer Service	3 (17.65)	18 (29.51)	7 (58.33)*
Outbound Transportation	7 (41.18)***	46 (75.41)	12 (100.00)*
Logistics Systems Planning	1 (5.88)***	43 (70.49)	11 (91.67)
Facilities Design	2 (11.76)***	43 (70.49)	11 (97.67)
Materials Handling	3 (17.65)***	43 (70.49)	12 (100.00)**
Logistics Administration	2 (11.76)***	41 (67.21)	12 (100.00)**
International	3 (17.65)	23 (37.70)	4 (33.33)
Capital Equipment Procurement	2 (11.76)***	39 (63.93)	12 (100.00)**
Data Processing for Distribution Applications	2 (11.76)***	30 (49.18)	12 (100.00)***

***, **, * Chi-square table (versus the NORM) is significant at 0.01, 0.05, and 0.10 respectively.

QUESTION 21: BEYOND FUNCTIONS?

Answer:	Emerging	Norm	Leading Edge
Yes	4 (33.33%)	25 (47.17%)	11 (68.75%)
No	8 (66.67%)	28 (52.83%)	5 (31.25%)
Total	12	53	16

QUESTION 22: ANALYSIS OF LOGISTICS RELATED PERFOMANCE MEASUREMENT

	Number (%) of Those Who Responded, Who Said The Measure Was Used		
(A) ASSET MANAGEMENT	Emerging	Norm	Leading Edge
Inventory turns	9 (52.94)***	47 (87.04)	15 (100.00)
Inventory carrying costs	3 (21.43)**	30 (57.69)	12 (80.00)
Inventory levels (# of days supply)	7 (43.75)***	39 (78.00)	14 (93.33)
Obsolete inventory	5 (38.46)***	39 (78.00)	13 (86.67)
Return on net assets	8 (47.06)	23 (47.92)	13 (86.67)***
Return on investment	10 (58.82)	31 (63.27)	14 (93.33)**
(B) COST (logistics cost)			
Total cost analysis	10 (62.50)*	44 (84.62)	15 (93.75)
Cost per unit	10 (62.50)*	44 (83.02)	12 (80.00)
Cost as a percentage of sales	11 (64.71)	44 (80.00)	15 (93.75)
Inbound freight costs	11 (64.71)***	51 (92.73)	15 (93.75)
Outbound freight costs	11 (68.75)***	52 (96.30)	14 (93.33)
Warehouse costs	13 (76.47)*	51 (92.73)	15 (93.75)
Administrative costs	7 (43.75)***	46 (83.64)	13 (86.67)
Order processing costs	4 (25.00)	20 (40.82)	13 (81.25)***
Direct labor costs	11 (68.75)**	49 (89.09)	15 (93.75)
Comparison of actual versus budget	11 (64.71)***	51 (91.07)	15 (93.75)
Cost trend analysis	8 (47.06)	30 (60.00)	13 (81.25)
Direct product profitability	2 (12.50)	13 (27.08)	7 (46.67)

COMPARISON OF EMERGING, NORM AND LEADING EDGE
(Retailers Only)

QUESTION 22: (CON'T)

	Number (%) of Those Who Responded, Who Said The Measure Was Used		
(C) CUSTOMER SERVICE	Emerging	Norm	Leading Edge
Fill rate	4 (28.57)***	32 (68.09)	15 (93.75)**
Stockouts	6 (40.00)***	38 (76.00)	14 (87.50)
Shipping errors	7 (50.00)***	47 (88.68)	14 (87.50)
On time delivery	7 (50.00)**	38 (79.17)	15 (93.75)
Backorders	2 (14.29)***	30 (66.67)	12 (75.00)
Cycle time	3 (21.43)**	28 (58.33)	13 (81.25)*
Customer feedback	11 (73.33)	42 (82.35)	16 (100.00)*
Sales force feedback	4 (28.57)**	24 (58.54)	6 (54.55)
Customer Surveys	5 (33.33)*	26 (61.90)	12 (75.00)

(D) PRODUCTIVITY			
Units shipped per employee	7 (46.67)	33 (63.46)	11 (68.75)
Units per labor dollar	4 (26.67)***	35 (67.31)	14 (87.50)
Orders per sales rep.	0 (0.00)**	7 (21.88)	2 (18.18)
Comparison to historical standards	10 (62.50)**	44 (89.80)	16 (100.00)
Goal programs	8 (50.00)***	47 (88.68)	14 (93.33)
Productivity Index	5 (31.25)**	31 (63.27)	9 (60.00)

(E) QUALITY			
Frequency of damage	3 (21.43)***	33 (67.35)	12 (75.00)
Dollar amount of damage	5 (33.33)**	32 (66.67)	16 (100.00)***
Number of credit claims	6 (40.00)**	32 (69.57)	14 (87.50)
Number of customer returns	3 (20.00)***	28 (66.67)	15 (100.00)***
Cost of returned goods	1 (7.14)***	23 (53.49)	15 (100.00)***

***, **, * Chi-square table (versus the NORM) is significant at 0.01, 0.05 and 0.10 respectively.

QUESTION 22:   (CON'T)

TOTAL NUMBER OF PERFORMANCE MEASURES

Performance Category	Mean (Standard Deviation)		
	Emerging	Norm	Leading Edge
Asset Management	2.47** (1.81)	3.67 (1.88)	5.06*** (1.24)*
Cost	6.41*** (2.79)	8.68 (2.16)	10.13** (1.86)
Customer Service	2.88*** (1.83)	5.35 (2.40)	7.31*** (1.49)*
Productivity	2.00*** (1.58)	3.46 (1.40)	4.13* (1.20)
Quality	1.06*** (1.52)	2.60 (1.79)	4.50*** (0.73)***

***, **, * Significantly different from the NORM at 0.01, 0.05 and
0.10 respectively.

QUESTION 23:   COMPETITIVE BENCHMARKING

Area	Number (%) of Those Who Responded, Who Said Benchmarking Was Used		
	Emerging	Norm	Leading Edge
Cost	6 (37.50)	27 (58.70)	11 (68.75)
Asset Management	2 (13.33)	11 (25.58)	5 (31.25)
Customer Service	5 (31.25)	21 (46.67)	5 (31.25)
Productivity	5 (31.25)*	25 (55.56)	6 (37.50)
Quality	3 (21.43)	18 (39.13)	8 (50.00)
Logistics Strategy	1 (7.69)**	20 (44.44)	8 (50.00)
Technology Deployment	3 (25.00)	13 (31.71)	8 (50.00)
Transportation Operations	5 (35.71)**	31 (67.39)	10 (62.50)
Warehouse Operations	5 (35.71)*	28 (60.87)	11 (68.75)
Order Processing Operations	1 (8.33)	13 (28.89)	7 (43.75)

**, * Chi-square table (versus the NORM) is significant at 0.05 and 0.10
respectively

COMPARISON OF EMERGING, NORM AND LEADING EDGE
(Retailers Only)

QUESTION 25: ELECTRONIC DATA INTERCHANGE

	Number (%) of Those Who Responded, Who Said EDI Was Currently Installed		
Application	Emerging	Norm	Leading Edge
Manufacturers	4 (30.77)	20 (39.22)	6 (40.00)
Wholesalers	2 (15.38)	7 (15.22)	4 (26.67)
Public Warehouses	0 (0.00)	6 (12.50)	2 (14.29)
Carriers	2 (16.67)	16 (31.37)	6 (37.50)
Financial Institutions	2 (16.67)	19 (40.43)	8 (50.00)
Retailers	4 (26.67)	12 (22.64)	3 (21.43)
Customers	2 (18.18)	8 (16.67)	6 (42.86)***
Copackers/Contracters	0 (0.00)	2 (4.26)	1 (6.67)

*** Overall chi-square table (versus the NORM) is significant at 0.01.

	Number (%) of Those Who Responded, Who Said EDI Was Planned in Next Three Years		
Application	Emerging	Norm	Leading Edge
Manufacturers	5 (38.46)	14 (27.45)	7 (46.67)
Wholesalers	3 (23.08)	6 (13.04)	4 (26.67)
Public Warehouses	2 (16.67)	3 (6.25)	1 (7.14)
Carriers	7 (58.33)	13 (25.49)	7 (43.75)
Financial Institutions	3 (25.00)	7 (14.89)	3 (18.75)
Retailers	2 (13.33)	6 (11.32)	2 (14.29)
Customers	1 (9.09)	3 (6.25)	4 (28.57)
Copackers/Contracters	1 (8.33)	4 (8.51)	2 (13.33)

QUESTION 26: LOGISTICS COMPUTER APPLICATIONS

	Number (%) of Those Who Responded, Who Said The Application Was Currently Installed (With or Without Revision Plans)		
Application	Emerging	Norm	Leading Edge
Freight Audit and Payment	8 (57.14)	27 (51.92)	12 (80.00)*
Purchasing	11 (73.33)	41 (78.84)	16 (100.00)**
Sales Forecasting	7 (46.67)	36 (70.59)	16 (100.00)
Inventory Control	11 (73.33)*	50 (87.72)	16 (100.00)
Warehouse Order Selection	9 (69.23)	43 (81.14)	14 (93.33)
Warehouse On-Line Receiving	4 (30.76)*	39 (70.91)	15 (93.75)
Warehouse Merchandise Locator	8 (61.53)	42 (75.00)	15 (93.75)
Warehouse Workload Balancing	3 (25.00)*	18 (34.62)	9 (60.00)
Warehouse Short Interval Scheduling	2 (16.67)*	15 (30.00)	6 (37.50)
Order Processing	12 (80.00)	50 (91.01)	16 (100.00)
Order Entry	11 (78.57)	53 (92.98)	16 (100.00)
Vehicle Routing and Scheduling	4 (33.33)	16 (31.37)	7 (43.75)
Inbound Freight Consolidation	5 (41.67)	18 (33.33)	6 (37.50)
Outbound Freight Consolidation	4 (36.36)	23 (41.82)	10 (66.67)
Supporting Financials	5 (41.67)***	46 (90.20)	15 (93.75)
Performance Measurement	6 (46.16)	35 (66.04)	14 (87.50)
Distribution Modeling	4 (30.76)	23 (44.23)	7 (46.67)
Direct Product Profitability	2 (14.28)	11 (22.45)	6 (40.00)
Direct Store Delivery	3 (21.43)	25 (47.17)	9 (60.00)
Shelf Management	5 (35.72)	11 (23.41)	4 (25.00)

***, **, * Chi-square table (versus the NORM) is significant at 0.01, 0.05, and 0.10 respectively.

COMPARISON OF EMERGING, NORM AND LEADING EDGE
(Retailers Only)

QUESTIONS 27, 28, 29: OPINIONS ABOUT U.P.C. SCANNING
(1 = STRONGLY DISAGREE, 5 = STRONGLY AGREE)

(A) "UPC has given retailers a unique advantage over other members of the distribution channel"

Mean (Standard Deviation)		
Emerging	Norm	Leading Edge
3.63	3.87	3.73
(1.26)	(1.06)	(0.96)

(B) "Information derived from point of sale scanning has made your business unit competitively stronger in comparison to other members of your distribution channel"

Mean (Standard Deviation)		
Emerging	Norm	Leading Edge
3.29	3.70	3.13
(0.99)	(0.95)	(1.06)**

(C) "Point of sale scanning information is more important to retailers than wholesalers"

Mean (Standard Deviation)		
Emerging	Norm	Leading Edge
3.13	3.43	2.67**
(0.99)	(1.07)	(0.98)

** Significantly different from the NORM at 0.05.

QUESTION 30: COMPARATIVE EVALUATION OF LOGISTICS MANAGEMENT INFORMATION SYSTEM
(1 = MUCH WORSE, 5 = MUCH BETTER)

How do your company's logistics management information systems compare overall
to the management information systems designed to support other areas of the
business?

Mean	(Standard Deviation)	
Emerging	Norm	Leading Edge
2.35***	3.16	3.56
(0.86)	(1.07)	(0.89)

*** Significantly different from the NORM at 0.01.

QUESTION 31: CHARACTERISTICS OF INFORMATION USED TO MANAGE LOGISTICS
(1 = NEVER, 5 = ALWAYS)

Characteristic	Mean on a 5-point scale	(Standard Deviation)	
	Emerging	Norm	Leading Edge
Timely	3.57*	4.20	4.25
	(1.16)*	(0.80)	(0.77)
Accurate	3.79**	4.31	4.44
	(0.89)	(0.66)	(0.51)
Readily available	3.54	4.00	4.19
	(1.05)**	(0.64)	(0.66)
Formatted on an exception basis	2.50	2.92	3.50**
	(1.31)	(0.96)	(0.89)
Appropriately formatted to facilitate use	2.83***	3.64	3.81
	(1.03)	(0.80)	(0.75)

***, **, * Significantly different from the NORM at 0.01, 0.05, and
0.10 respectively.

COMPARISON OF EMERGING, NORM AND LEADING EDGE
(Retailers Only)

QUESTION 32: ABILITY TO ACCOMODATE VARIOUS EVENTS IMPACTING
LOGISTICS ACTIVITIES
(1 = CANNOT ACCOMMODATE, 5 = ACCOMMODATES VERY EASILY)

Event	Mean on a 5-point scale (Standard Deviation)		
	Emerging	Norm	Leading Edge
Special customer service requests	2.92 (1.44)***	3.38 (0.87)	3.75 (0.86)
Sales/Marketing incentive programs	2.75** (1.28)	3.50 (0.84)	4.08** (0.76)
Product introduction	3.70 (1.25)**	3.80 (0.79)	4.06 (0.85)
Product phase out	3.55 (1.13)	3.57 (0.95)	3.67 (1.05)
Disruption in supply	2.80 (1.23)	3.10 (0.95)	3.40 (1.24)
Computer breakdown	2.17 (1.19)	2.35 (1.01)	2.50 (0.97)
Product recall	3.00 (1.05)	3.15 (1.06)	3.40 (0.99)
Customization of service levels to specific markets or customers	3.44 (1.13)	3.15 (0.93)	3.77** (0.93)
Product modification or customization while in the logistics system (e.g. pricing, packaging, mixing)	3.00 (1.22)	2.92 (1.03)	3.29 (1.20)
Returned goods	3.62 (1.19)	3.28 (0.99)	3.63 (1.02)

***, ** Significantly different from the NORM at 0.01 and 0.05 respectively.

QUESTION 33: ON A SCALE OF 1 TO 5, RATE THE LEVEL OF IMPACT EACH OF
THE FOLLOWING HAS ON YOUR LOGISTICAL OPERATIONS

Item:	Mean for each of the CAI Groups (1)		
	Emerging	Norm	Leading Edge
Sales forecast accuracy	3.29	3.80	3.88
Computer support	3.88**	4.44	4.69
Excessive end-of-month or end-of-quarter surges	3.79	3.81	4.06
Communications with customer	3.33	3.22	3.47
Availability of trained logistics personnel	3.21	3.26	3.94**
Vehicle routing and scheduling	3.31	3.35	3.40
Computer applications backlog	3.33	3.45	4.07**
Transportation cost	3.69	3.72	3.88
Communication with suppliers	2.93	3.21	3.56
Warehouse productivity	3.40**	4.07	4.19
Measurement tools and methods	3.15	3.49	3.81
Communication with internal non-logistics organizational units	3.69	3.65	4.00
Timely information	3.53***	4.16	4.31
Supplier logistical performance	3.13	3.45	3.93*
Communication with external logistical services suppliers	3.00	2.93	3.50**
Incompatibility of computer equipment and/or software	2.31	2.86	3.38
Inventory reduction programs	3.07	3.44	3.50
Cost reduction programs	3.47	3.67	3.63
Load leveling	2.60	3.46	3.47
Workforce leveling	2.66**	3.58	3.44

(1) - Scale was 1 = no impact
                 2 = slight impact
                 3 = medium impact
                 4 = high impact
                 5 = very high impact

***, **, * Significantly different from the norm at 0.01, 0.05 and 0.10
respectively.

COMPARISON OF EMERGING, NORM AND LEADING EDGE
                              (Retailers Only)

QUESTION 34: USAGE OF OUTSIDE SERVICE VENDORS
                 (1 = will not use, 5 = will use many more outside services)

	Mean for each of the CAI Groups		
Outside Service Vendor	Emerging	Norm	Leading Edge
Transportation	3.25	3.43	3.25
Warehousing	3.00	2.62	2.69
Order Entry and Processing	1.92	1.98	1.86
Inventory Management	2.08	1.92	1.93
Freight Audit and Payment	3.07	2.72	3.06
Consolidators	3.38	2.84	3.67***
International Freight Forwarders	3.23	2.98	3.27
Domestic Freight Forwarders	3.00	2.46	2.75
Order Fulfillment and Support	1.75	2.11	2.00

*** Significantly different from the norm at 0.01

QUESTION 35: FACTORS INFLUENCING THE DECISION TO USE OUTSIDE SERVICE VENDORS
                 (1 = never, 5 = always)

	Mean for each of the CAI Groups		
Factor	Emerging	Norm	Leading Edge
Services available	3.93	4.04	4.27
Quality of services	4.40	4.41	4.67
Data processing/ communications services	3.29	3.02	3.33
Management quality	4.13	3.65	3.80
Customer orientation	4.07	3.76	4.20
Vendor reputation	4.07	3.89	4.27

QUESTION 4: DO YOU HAVE A WRITTEN LOGISTICS MISSION STATEMENT?

Answer:	Emerging	Norm	Leading Edge
Yes	0 (0.00%)	10 (10.42%)	16 (76.19%)
No	28 (100.00%)	86 (89.58%)	5 (23.81%)
Total	28*	96	21**

* Chi-square table of NORM versus EMERGING is significant at p = 0.075.
** Chi-square table of NORM versus LEADING EDGE is significant at p = 0.000.

QUESTION 5: LOGISTICS STRATEGIC PLAN

(A) Do you have a written logistics strategic plan?

Answer:	Emerging	Norm	Leading Edge
Yes	1 (3.57%)	25 (25.77%)	20 (90.91%)
No	27 (96.43%)	72 (74.23%)	2 (9.09%)
Total	28*	97	22**

* Chi-square table of NORM versus EMERGING is significant at p = 0.011.
** Chi-square table of NORM versus LEADING EDGE is significant at p = 0.000.

(B) If yes, what is the time horizon?

	Mean (Standard Deviation)	
Emerging	Norm	Leading Edge
*	3.65	3.95
(*)	(1.97)	(1.93)

* Only one respondent answered this question.

QUESTION 5: (CON'T)

(C) If yes, how often is the plan reviewed or updated?

Mean	(Standard Deviation)	
Emerging	Norm	Leading Edge
*	11.46	11.40
(*)	(11.55)	(1.85)**

* Only one respondent answered this question.
** Significantly different from the NORM at 0.01

QUESTION 6: ANALYSIS OF LOGISTICS ORGANIZATION

(A) Centralization (=5) versus decentralization (=1)

Mean	(Standard Deviation)	
Emerging	Norm	Leading Edge
3.63	3.53	3.41
(1.08)	(1.19)	(1.30)

(B) Trend over the last three years?

	Emerging	Norm	Leading Edge
Centralization	14 (53.85%)	47 (50.00%)	7 (31.82%)
Decentralization	2 (7.69%)	16 (17.02%)	5 (22.73%)
No Change	10 (38.46%)	31 (32.98%)	10 (45.45%)
Total	26	94	22

QUESTION 8: TITLE LEVEL OF THE MOST SENIOR LOGISTICS EXECUTIVE

	Emerging	Norm	Leading Edge
President	6 (22.22%)	18 (18.37%)	2 (9.09%)
Executive V.P.	3 (11.11%)	6 (6.12%)	3 (13.64%)
Senior V.P.	0 (0.00%)	7 (7.14%)	4 (18.18%)
Vice-President	4 (14.81%)	41 (41.84%)	10 (45.45%)
Director	1 (3.70%)	12 (12.24%)	1 (4.55%)
Manager	10 (37.04%)	6 (6.12%)	2 (9.09%)
Supervisor	1 (3.70%)	0 (0.00%)	0 (0.00%)
Other	2 (7.41%)	8 (8.16%)	0 (0.00%)
Total	27	98	22

QUESTION 10: YEARS IN THIS POSITION

	Mean (Standard Deviation)	
Emerging	Norm	Leading Edge
8.07	5.66	5.77
(9.41)*	(5.66)	(5.42)

* Significantly different from the NORM at 0.004.

QUESTION 13: TITLE OF THE PERSON THE SENIOR LOGISTICS EXECUTIVE REPORTS TO

	Emerging	Norm	Leading Edge
Chairman	3 (11.54%)	13 (13.54%)	1 (4.76%)
President	9 (34.62%)	49 (51.04%)	13 (61.90%)
Executive V.P.	1 (3.85%)	12 (12.50%)	5 (23.81%)
Senior V.P.	1 (3.85%)	3 (3.13%)	0 (0.00%)
Vice-President	6 (23.08%)	10 (10.42%)	2 (9.52%)
Director	3 (11.54%)	2 (2.08%)	0 (0.00%)
Manager	1 (3.85%)	1 (1.04%)	0 (0.00%)
Supervisor	0 (0.00%)	0 (0.00%)	0 (0.00%)
Other	2 (7.69%)	6 (6.25%)	0 (0.00%)
Total	26	96	21

QUESTIONS 16, 17: FORMAL ORGANIZATION OF LOGISTICS ACTIVITIES

(A) How many years has logistics been a formal organization?

	Mean (Standard Deviation)	
Emerging	Norm	Leading Edge
2.00***	8.84	22.20***
(3.71)***	(9.33)	(18.68)***

*** Significantly different from the NORM at 0.01.

(B) Within the last five years, how many times has logistics been reorganized?

	Mean (Standard Deviation)	
Emerging	Norm	Leading Edge
0.74***	1.71	1.77
(1.10)	(1.47)	(1.07)*

***, * Significantly different from the NORM at 0.01 and 0.10 respectively.

QUESTION 18: PARTICIPATION IN OVERALL STRATEGIC PLANNING

Answer:	Emerging	Norm	Leading Edge
Yes	14 (51.85%)	86 (89.58%)	22 (100.00%)
No, but provides input	10 (37.04%)	8 (8.33%)	0 (0.00%)
No	3 (11.11%)	2 (2.08%)	0 (0.00%)
Total	27*	96	22

* Chi-square table of NORM versus EMERGING is significant at p = 0.000.

QUESTION 20: ANALYSIS OF FUNCTIONS

Total # of Functions:	Overall Mean (Standard Deviation)		
	Emerging	Norm	Leading Edge
Line or staff	3.29***	8.11	10.86***
	(3.85)	(4.36)	(4.33)
Line only	1.21***	4.32	5.77
	(2.51)***	(3.91)	(5.44)*

***, * Significantly different from the NORM at 0.01 and 0.10 respectively.

Function	Number (%) Who Have It (Line or Staff)		
	Emerging	Norm	Leading Edge
Sales Forecasting	7 (25.00)	31 (31.63)	10 (45.45)
Purchasing	7 (25.00)	41 (41.84)	12 (54.55)
Inbound Transportation	6 (21.43)***	53 (54.08)	18 (81.82)**
Inventory Management	11 (39.29)**	61 (62.24)	14 (63.64)
Intra-Co. Transportation	6 (21.43)***	57 (58.16)	15 (68.18)
Warehousing	8 (28.57)***	70 (71.43)	19 (86.36)
Order Processing	7 (25.00)**	47 (47.96)	9 (40.91)
Customer Service	7 (25.00)*	44 (44.90)	12 (54.55)
Outbound Transportation	10 (35.71)***	68 (69.39)	20 (90.91)**
Logistics Systems Planning	5 (17.86)***	50 (51.02)	19 (86.36)***
Facilities Design	3 (10.71)***	54 (55.10)	19 (86.36)***
Materials Handling	3 (10.71)***	62 (63.27)	19 (86.36)**
Logistics Administration	5 (17.86)***	52 (53.06)	17 (77.27)**
International	1 (3.57)*	16 (16.33)	3 (13.64)
Capital Equipment Procurement	3 (10.71)***	50 (51.02)	18 (81.82)***
Data Processing for Distribution Applications	3 (10.71)***	39 (39.80)	15 (68.18)**

***, **, * Chi-square table (versus the NORM) is significant at 0.01, 0.05, and 0.10 respectively.

COMPARISON OF EMERGING, NORM AND LEADING EDGE
(Wholesalers Only)

QUESTION 21: BEYOND FUNCTIONS?

Answer:	Emerging	Norm	Leading Edge
Yes	8 (32.00%)	54 (58.06%)	14 (66.67%)
No	17 (68.00%)	39 (41.94%)	7 (33.33%)
Total	25*	93	21

* Chi-square table of NORM versus EMERGING is significant at p = 0.021.

QUESTION 22: ANALYSIS OF LOGISTICS RELATED PERFOMANCE MEASUREMENT

	Emerging	Norm	Leading Edge
(A) ASSET MANAGEMENT			
Inventory turns	16 (64.00)***	84 (88.42)	21 (95.45)
Inventory carrying costs	14 (56.00)	64 (69.57)	17 (77.27)
Inventory levels (# of days supply)	17 (70.83)	75 (79.79)	21 (95.45)*
Obsolete inventory	15 (62.50)**	75 (81.52)	20 (90.91)
Return on net assets	11 (47.83)	55 (63.22)	21 (95.45)***
Return on investment	17 (65.38)	67 (73.63)	20 (90.91)*
(B) COST (logistics cost)			
Total cost analysis	12 (52.17)**	65 (74.71)	21 (100.00)***
Cost per unit	12 (57.14)	54 (61.36)	17 (80.95)*
Cost as a percentage of sales	9 (40.91)***	77 (86.52)	22 (100.00)*
Inbound freight costs	17 (73.91)	73 (81.11)	18 (81.92)
Outbound freight costs	18 (81.82)	82 (88.17)	21 (95.45)
Warehouse costs	13 (61.90)***	79 (87.78)	22 (100.00)*
Administrative costs	14 (60.87)*	71 (79.98)	21 (95.45)*
Order processing costs	6 (27.27)	41 (46.07)	13 (65.00)
Direct labor costs	9 (45.00)**	65 (71.43)	21 (95.45)**
Comparison of actual versus budget	17 (73.91)	79 (86.81)	22 (100.00)*
Cost trend analysis	8 (40.00)	47 (54.65)	20 (95.24)***
Direct product profitability	6 (30.00)*	45 (52.33)	8 (40.00)

Number (%) of Those Who Responded, Who Said The Measure Was Used

QUESTION 22: (CON'T)

	Number (%) of Those Who Responded, Who Said The Measure Was Used		
(C) CUSTOMER SERVICE	Emerging	Norm	Leading Edge
Fill rate	6 (27.27)***	65 (74.71)	22 (100.00)***
Stockouts	7 (35.00)***	66 (75.86)	21 (95.45)**
Shipping errors	9 (39.13)***	76 (85.39)	20 (95.24)
On time delivery	9 (39.13)***	64 (72.73)	20 (95.24)**
Backorders	12 (50.00)**	66 (77.86)	14 (63.64)**
Cycle time	0 (0.00)***	30 (35.71)	13 (65.00)
Customer feedback	16 (66.67)***	85 (90.43)	18 (85.71)
Sales force feedback	11 (50.00)***	83 (91.21)	19 (95.00)
Customer Surveys	7 (33.33)	42 (48.28)	17 (85.00)***
(D) PRODUCTIVITY			
Units shipped per employee	3 (17.67)**	44 (49.44)	21 (95.45)***
Units per labor dollar	2 (11.76)**	35 (40.23)	18 (81.82)***
Orders per sales rep.	6 (35.29)	45 (52.33)	11 (64.71)
Comparison to historical standards	6 (35.29)***	70 (76.92)	21 (95.45)**
Goal programs	9 (50.00)	62 (68.89)	19 (86.36)
Productivity Index	5 (27.78)	37 (42.53)	15 (68.18)**
(E) QUALITY			
Frequency of damage	3 (17.65)**	37 (43.02)	15 (75.00)***
Dollar amount of damage	4 (22.22)**	47 (54.02)	19 (90.48)***
Number of credit claims	8 (42.11)**	66 (71.74)	17 (80.95)
Number of customer returns	7 (35.00)***	64 (72.73)	18 (85.71)
Cost of returned goods	3 (17.65)***	50 (58.82)	18 (85.71)**

***, **, * Chi-square table (versus the NORM) is significant at 0.01, 0.05, and 0.10 respectively.

COMPARISON OF EMERGING, NORM AND LEADING EDGE
(Wholesalers Only)

QUESTION 22: (CON'T)

TOTAL NUMBER OF PERFORMANCE MEASURES

Performance Category	Mean (Standard Deviation)		
	Emerging	Norm	Leading Edge
Asset Management	3.21*** (2.06)	4.29 (1.71)	5.45*** (1.34)
Cost	5.04*** (3.56)*	7.94 (2.68)	10.27*** (1.67)**
Customer Service	2.75*** (2.01)	5.89 (1.99)	7.45*** (1.44)*
Productivity	1.11*** (1.47)	2.99 (1.81)	4.77*** (1.23)*
Quality	0.89*** (1.31)*	2.69 (1.75)	3.95*** (1.68)

***, **, * Significantly different from the NORM at 0.01, 0.05, and 0.10 respectively.

QUESTION 23: COMPETITIVE BENCHMARKING

Area	Number (%) of Those Who Responded, Who Said Benchmarking Was Used		
	Emerging	Norm	Leading Edge
Cost	11 (47.83)	51 (57.30)	18 (81.82)**
Asset Management	6 (26.09)	21 (23.86)	13 (61.90)***
Customer Service	9 (37.50)	44 (48.89)	20 (90.91)***
Productivity	6 (26.09)	34 (37.36)	16 (76.19)***
Quality	5 (20.83)**	39 (44.83)	17 (80.95)***
Logistics Strategy	6 (25.00)	19 (21.35)	12 (60.00)***
Technology Deployment	3 (13.04)*	29 (32.95)	16 (76.19)***
Transportation Operations	8 (33.33)	36 (40.00)	16 (76.19)***
Warehouse Operations	5 (20.83)***	47 (51.65)	18 (85.71)***
Order Processing Operations	4 (16.67)**	37 (41.11)	12 (60.00)

***, **, * Chi-square table (versus the NORM) is significant at 0.01, 0.05, and 0.10 respectively.

QUESTION 25: ELECTRONIC DATA INTERCHANGE

	Number (%) of Those Who Responded, Who Said EDI Was Currently Installed		
Application	Emerging	Norm	Leading Edge
Manufacturers	9 (36.00)	27 (29.35)	10 (47.62)
Wholesalers	2 (8.33)***	16 (17.78)	4 (20.00)
Public Warehouses	0 (0.00)	2 (2.35)	0 (0.00)
Carriers	2 (8.33)*	14 (15.73)	2 (10.53)
Financial Institutions	1 (4.35)*	22 (25.29)	11 (52.38)*
Retailers	1 (4.17)**	19 (21.84)	9 (45.00)
Customers	5 (20.00)***	37 (39.78)	13 (61.90)
Copackers/Contracters	0 (0.00)	2 (2.35)	3 (17.65)*

***, **, * Overall chi-square table (versus the NORM) is significant at 0.01, 0.05, and 0.10 respectively.

	Number (%) of Those Who Responded, Who Said EDI Was Planned in Next Three Years		
Application	Emerging	Norm	Leading Edge
Manufacturers	4 (16.00)	30 (32.61)	6 (28.57)
Wholesalers	3 (12.50)	11 (12.22)	3 (15.00)
Public Warehouses	1 (4.35)	3 (3.53)	1 (5.26)
Carriers	2 (8.33)	15 (16.85)	5 (26.32)
Financial Institutions	2 (8.70)	12 (13.79)	3 (14.29)
Retailers	1 (4.17)	15 (17.24)	3 (15.00)
Customers	2 (8.00)	26 (27.96)	4 (19.05)
Copackers/Contracters	0 (0.00)	6 (7.06)	1 (5.88)

COMPARISON OF EMERGING, NORM AND LEADING EDGE
(Wholesalers Only)

QUESTION 26: LOGISTICS COMPUTER APPLICATIONS

Number (%) of Those Who Responded,
Who Said The Application Was Currently
Installed (With or Without Revision Plans)

Application	Emerging	Norm	Leading Edge
Freight Audit and Payment	7 (26.94)	44 (47.31)	15 (68.18)**
Purchasing	13 (52.00)***	81 (86.17)	21 (95.45)
Sales Forecasting	6 (28.57)***	64 (68.83)	19 (90.48)
Inventory Control	17 (65.38)***	55 (97.93)	22 (100.00)
Warehouse Order Selection	5 (21.74)***	73 (77.66)	21 (95.45)
Warehouse On-Line Receiving	6 (26.09)***	60 (63.16)	20 (90.48)*
Warehouse Merchandise Locator	6 (26.09)***	53 (56.48)	20 (90.91)**
Warehouse Workload Balancing	0 (0.00)***	22 (23.40)	15 (75.00)***
Warehouse Short Interval Scheduling	0 (0.00)*	20 (21.51)	11 (57.89)**
Order Processing	17 (68.00)***	92 (95.84)	22 (100.00)
Order Entry	18 (69.23)***	94 (95.91)	22 (100.00)
Vehicle Routing and Scheduling	1 (4.17)**	29 (30.53)	10 (47.61)**
Inbound Freight Consolidation	0 (0.00)*	24 (25.81)	10 (52.64)**
Outbound Freight Consolidation	1 (4.35)**	37 (39.78)	12 (60.00)
Supporting Financials	14 (66.00)**	75 (78.95)	19 (90.47)
Performance Measurement	8 (32.00)***	57 (58.76)	17 (85.00)**
Distribution Modeling	1 (4.55)	15 (16.30)	13 (68.43)***
Direct Product Profitability	7 (33.33)**	50 (53.19)	8 (50.00)
Direct Store Delivery	1 (5.00)	26 (28.57)	12 (70.59)***
Shelf Management	2 (9.09)	23 (25.27)	12 (70.59)***

***, **, * Chi-square table (versus the NORM) is significant at 0.01, 0.05, and 0.10 respectively.

QUESTIONS 27, 28, 29: OPINIONS ABOUT U.P.C. SCANNING
(1 = STRONGLY DISAGREE, 5 = STRONGLY AGREE)

(A) "UPC has given retailers a unique advantage over other
members of the distribution channel"

Mean (Standard Deviation)		
Emerging	Norm	Leading Edge
3.78	3.92	3.68
(0.80)	(0.84)	(1.08)

(B) "Information derived from point of sale scanning has made your
business unit competitively stronger in comparison to other
members of your distribution channel"

Mean (Standard Deviation)		
Emerging	Norm	Leading Edge
3.00	3.00	3.14
(1.08)	(1.12)	(0.96)

(C) "Point of sale scanning information is more important to
retailers than wholesalers"

Mean (Standard Deviation)		
Emerging	Norm	Leading Edge
3.04	3.00	2.95
(0.98)	(1.12)	(1.12)

COMPARISON OF EMERGING, NORM AND LEADING EDGE
(Wholesalers Only)

QUESTION 30: COMPARATIVE EVALUATION OF LOGISTICS MANAGEMENT INFORMATION SYSTEM
(1 = MUCH WORSE, 5 = MUCH BETTER)

How do your company's logistics management information systems compare overall
to the management information systems designed to support other areas of the
business?

Mean (Standard Deviation)		
Emerging	Norm	Leading Edge
2.46**	2.92	3.68***
(0.98)	(0.92)	(0.78)

***, ** Significantly different from the NORM at 0.01 and 0.05 respectively.

QUESTION 31: CHARACTERISTICS OF INFORMATION USED TO MANAGE LOGISTICS
(1 = NEVER, 5 = ALWAYS)

Characteristic	Mean on a 5-point scale (Standard Deviation)		
	Emerging	Norm	Leading Edge
Timely	3.65	3.99	4.27
	(1.11)*	(0.86)	(0.63)
Accurate	3.65*	4.11	4.54**
	(1.11)**	(0.79)	(0.59)
Readily available	3.23**	3.76	3.95
	(1.23)	(0.96)	(0.90)
Formatted on an exception basis	2.71	3.07	3.62**
	(1.10)	(1.08)	(0.97)
Appropriately formatted to facilitate use	2.89*	3.51	3.95**
	(1.32)**	(0.93)	(0.84)

**, * Significantly different from the NORM at 0.05 and 0.10 respectively.

QUESTION 32: ABILITY TO ACCOMODATE VARIOUS EVENTS IMPACTING
LOGISTICS ACTIVITIES
(1 = CANNOT ACCOMMODATE, 5 = ACCOMMODATES VERY EASILY)

Event	Mean on a 5-point scale (Standard Deviation)		
	Emerging	Norm	Leading Edge
Special customer service requests	3.52 (1.00)	3.60 (1.00)	3.41 (0.91)
Sales/Marketing incentive programs	3.65 (0.88)	3.54 (0.93)	3.68 (0.89)
Product introduction	3.13** (0.91)	3.70 (0.90)	3.95 (1.05)
Product phase out	3.00 (0.85)	3.20 (0.91)	3.45 (1.18)*
Disruption in supply	2.56 (0.78)	2.92 (1.00)	3.05 (0.65)**
Computer breakdown	2.62 (1.02)	2.30 (1.03)	2.09 (0.68)**
Product recall	2.82 (1.08)	3.04 (1.03)	3.27 (0.94)
Customization of service levels to specific markets or customers	3.05 (1.24)	3.30 (1.16)	3.09 (1.11)
Product modification or customization while in the logistics system (e.g. pricing, packaging, mixing)	2.63** (1.02)	3.19 (1.02)	2.76* (0.89)
Returned goods	3.16 (1.07)*	3.51 (0.81)	3.59 (0.91)

**, * Significantly different from the NORM at 0.05 and 0.10 respectively.

COMPARISON OF EMERGING, NORM AND LEADING EDGE
(Wholesalers Only)

QUESTION 33: ON A SCALE OF 1 TO 5, RATE THE LEVEL OF IMPACT EACH OF
THE FOLLOWING HAS ON YOUR LOGISTICAL OPERATIONS

Item:	Mean for each of the CAI Groups (1)		
	Emerging	Norm	Leading Edge
Sales forecast accuracy	3.33	3.46	4.14***
Computer support	3.84*	4.27	4.55
Excessive end-of-month or end-of-quarter surges	2.75**	3.56	2.90*
Communications with customer	3.43	3.53	3.91*
Availability of trained logistics personnel	3.30	3.41	3.86***
Vehicle routing and scheduling	3.23	3.41	3.81
Computer applications backlog	2.84	3.56	3.77*
Transportation cost	3.88	3.64	4.05*
Communication with suppliers	3.86	3.54	3.59
Warehouse productivity	2.88***	4.01	4.45**
Measurement tools and methods	2.58***	3.40	3.95***
Communication with internal non-logistics organizational units	3.05	3.31	3.59
Timely information	4.08	3.95	4.27*
Supplier logistical performance	3.71	3.36	3.86**
Communication with external logistical services suppliers	3.24	2.85	3.62***
Incompatibility of computer equipment and/or software	2.71	2.74	3.05
Inventory reduction programs	3.24	3.22	3.73**
Cost reduction programs	3.23	3.39	3.64
Load leveling	2.18***	2.95	3.62***
Workforce leveling	2.35***	3.11	3.86***

(1) - Scale was 1 = no impact
                 2 = slight impact
                 3 = medium impact
                 4 = high impact
                 5 = very high impact

***, **, * Significantly different from the norm at 0.01, 0.05 and 0.10
respectively.

QUESTION 34: USAGE OF OUTSIDE SERVICE VENDORS
(1 = will not use, 5 = will use many more outside services)

Outside Service Vendor	Mean for each of the CAI Groups		
	Emerging	Norm	Leading Edge
Transportation	3.04	2.98	3.18
Warehousing	2.28	2.41	2.40
Order Entry and Processing	1.70	1.51	1.37
Inventory Management	1.57	1.58	1.65
Freight Audit and Payment	2.24	2.34	2.24
Consolidators	2.36	2.36	2.73
International Freight Forwarders	2.71	2.59	2.17
Domestic Freight Forwarders	2.82*	2.23	2.19
Order Fulfillment and Support	1.72	1.65	1.85

* Significantly different from the norm at 0.10

QUESTION 35: FACTORS INFLUENCING THE DECISION TO USE OUTSIDE SERVICE VENDORS
(1 = never, 5 = always)

Factor	Mean for each of the CAI Groups		
	Emerging	Norm	Leading Edge
Services available	4.10	3.87	4.05
Quality of services	4.35	4.32	4.33
Data processing/ communications services	2.87	2.97	3.52**
Management quality	3.78	3.73	3.81
Customer orientation	3.59	3.90	3.75
Vendor reputation	4.18	4.07	4.05

** Significantly different from the norm at 0.05.

COMPARISON OF EMERGING, NORM AND LEADING EDGE
(Hybrids Only)

QUESTION 4: DO YOU HAVE A WRITTEN LOGISTICS MISSION STATEMENT?

Answer:	Emerging	Norm	Leading Edge
Yes	1 (8.33%)	9 (18.37%)	9 (64.29%)
No	11 (91.67%)	40 (81.63%)	5 (35.71%)
Total	12	49	14*

* Chi-square table of NORM versus LEADING EDGE is significant at $p = 0.001$.

QUESTION 5: LOGISTICS STRATEGIC PLAN

(A) Do you have a written logistics strategic plan?

Answer:	Emerging	Norm	Leading Edge
Yes	0 (0.00%)	15 (31.25%)	13 (92.86%)
No	12 (100.00%)	33 (68.75%)	1 (7.14%)
Total	12*	48	14**

* Chi-square table of NORM versus EMERGING is significant at $p = 0.025$.
** Chi-square table of NORM versus LEADING EDGE is significant at $p = 0.000$.

(B) If yes, what is the time horizon?

Mean	(Standard Deviation)	
Emerging	Norm	Leading Edge
*	3.79	3.38
(*)	(1.42)	(1.71)

* No respondents answered this question.

QUESTION 5: (CON'T)

(C) If yes, how often is the plan reviewed or updated?

	Mean (Standard Deviation)	
Emerging	Norm	Leading Edge
*	12.21	12.00
(*)	(5.82)	(2.55)***

* No respondents answered this question.
*** Significantly different from the NORM at 0.01.

QUESTION 6: ANALYSIS OF LOGISTICS ORGANIZATION

(A) Centralization (=5) versus decentralization (=1)

	Mean (Standard Deviation)	
Emerging	Norm	Leading Edge
3.00	3.18	3.60
(1.41)	(1.07)	(1.06)

(B) Trend over the last three years?

	Emerging	Norm	Leading Edge
Centralization	3 (25.00%)	21 (43.75%)	9 (64.29%)
Decentralization	1 (8.33%)	10 (20.83%)	3 (21.43%)
No Change	8 (66.67%)	17 (35.42%)	2 (14.29%)
Total	12	48	14

COMPARISON OF EMERGING, NORM AND LEADING EDGE
(Hybrids Only)

QUESTION 8: TITLE LEVEL OF THE MOST SENIOR LOGISTICS EXECUTIVE

	Emerging	Norm	Leading Edge
President	4 (36.36%)	6 (12.24%)	1 (6.67%)
Executive V.P.	0 (0.00%)	2 (4.08%)	2 (13.33%)
Senior V.P.	0 (0.00%)	3 (6.12%)	3 (20.00%)
Vice-President	2 (18.18%)	21 (42.86%)	8 (53.33%)
Director	2 (18.18%)	8 (16.33%)	0 (0.00%)
Manager	2 (18.18%)	9 (18.37%)	1 (6.67%)
Supervisor	1 (9.09%)	0 (0.00%)	0 (0.00%)
Other	0 (0.00%)	0 (0.00%)	0 (0.00%)
Total	**11**	**49**	**15**

QUESTION 10: YEARS IN THIS POSITION

	Mean (Standard Deviation)	
Emerging	Norm	Leading Edge
9.00	4.80	7.60*
(10.01)***	(3.84)	(5.75)**

***, **, * Significantly different from the NORM at 0.01, 0.05, and 0.10 respectively.

QUESTION 13: TITLE OF THE PERSON THE SENIOR LOGISTICS EXECUTIVE REPORTS TO

	Emerging	Norm	Leading Edge
Chairman	2 (20.00%)	6 (12.24%)	3 (20.00%)
President	2 (20.00%)	20 (40.82%)	9 (60.00%)
Executive V.P.	0 (0.00%)	4 (8.16%)	2 (13.33%)
Senior V.P.	0 (0.00%)	5 (10.20%)	1 (6.67%)
Vice-President	4 (40.00%)	6 (12.24%)	0 (0.00%)
Director	0 (0.00%)	2 (4.08%)	0 (0.00%)
Manager	0 (0.00%)	1 (2.04%)	0 (0.00%)
Supervisor	0 (0.00%)	1 (2.04%)	0 (0.00%)
Other	2 (20.00%)	4 (8.16%)	0 (0.00%)
Total	**10**	**49**	**15**

QUESTIONS 16, 17: FORMAL ORGANIZATION OF LOGISTICS ACTIVITIES

(A) How many years has logistics been a formal organization?

Mean	(Standard Deviation)	
Emerging	Norm	Leading Edge
6.50	11.74	7.71
(4.65)*	(13.86)	(6.28)***

***, * Significantly different from the NORM at 0.01 and 0.10 respectively.

(B) Within the last five years, how many times has logistics been reorganized?

Mean	(Standard Deviation)	
Emerging	Norm	Leading Edge
1.50	2.12	2.43
(1.69)	(1.44)	(1.28)

QUESTION 18: PARTICIPATION IN OVERALL STRATEGIC PLANNING

Answer:	Emerging	Norm	Leading Edge
Yes	4 (40.00%)	40 (81.63%)	14 (93.33%)
No, but provides input	6 (60.00%)	8 (16.33%)	1 (6.67%)
No	0 (0.00%)	1 (2.04%)	0 (0.00%)
Total	10*	49	15

* Chi-square table of NORM versus EMERGING is significant at p = 0.012.

COMPARISON OF EMERGING, NORM AND LEADING EDGE
(Hybrids Only)

QUESTION 20: ANALYSIS OF FUNCTIONS

Total # of Functions:	Overall Mean (Standard Deviation)		
	Emerging	Norm	Leading Edge
Line or staff	3.38*** (3.64)	9.51 (3.45)	11.93*** (2.49)
Line only	1.69*** (2.72)	6.37 (4.00)	6.80 (3.99)

*** Significantly different from the NORM at 0.01.

Function	Number (%) Who Have It (Line or Staff)		
	Emerging	Norm	Leading Edge
Sales Forecasting	2 (15.38)**	23 (46.00)	7 (50.00)
Purchasing	3 (23.08)**	29 (58.00)	8 (57.14)
Inbound Transportation	3 (23.08)***	34 (68.00)	11 (78.57)
Inventory Management	4 (30.77)***	38 (76.00)	9 (64.29)
Intra-Co. Transportation	1 (7.69)***	37 (74.00)	8 (57.14)
Warehousing	3 (23.08)***	38 (76.00)	14 (100.00)**
Order Processing	5 (38.46)	26 (52.00)	9 (64.29)
Customer Service	5 (38.46)	23 (46.00)	10 (71.43)*
Outbound Transportation	6 (46.15)***	42 (84.00)	13 (92.86)
Logistics Systems Planning	3 (23.08)**	31 (62.00)	12 (85.71)*
Facilities Design	1 (7.69)***	27 (54.00)	12 (85.71)**
Materials Handling	2 (15.38)***	33 (66.00)	12 (85.71)
Logistics Administration	1 (7.69)***	35 (70.00)	11 (78.57)
International	2 (15.38)	12 (24.00)	6 (42.86)
Capital Equipment Procurement	2 (15.38)***	31 (62.00)	13 (92.86)**
Data Processing for Distribution Applications	1 (7.69)**	21 (42.00)	10 (71.43)**

***, **, * Chi-square table (versus the NORM) is significant at 0.01, 0.05, and 0.10 respectively.

QUESTION 21: BEYOND FUNCTIONS?

Answer:	Emerging	Norm	Leading Edge
Yes	4 (40.00%)	25 (53.19%)	9 (64.29%)
No	6 (60.00%)	22 (46.81%)	5 (35.71%)
Total	10	47	14

QUESTION 22: ANALYSIS OF LOGISTICS RELATED PERFOMANCE MEASUREMENT

	Number (%) of Those Who Responded, Who Said The Measure Was Used		
(A) ASSET MANAGEMENT	Emerging	Norm	Leading Edge
Inventory turns	10 (76.92)	40 (83.33)	14 (93.33)
Inventory carrying costs	7 (58.33)	34 (72.34)	14 (93.33)*
Inventory levels (# of days supply)	10 (76.92)	43 (91.49)	13 (86.67)
Obsolete inventory	11 (84.62)	38 (84.44)	13 (86.67)
Return on net assets	7 (53.85)	21 (50.00)	10 (66.67)
Return on investment	9 (69.23)	30 (66.67)	13 (86.67)
(B) COST (logistics cost)			
Total cost analysis	7 (63.64)*	38 (86.36)	13 (86.67)
Cost per unit	8 (66.67)	39 (82.98)	12 (80.00)
Cost as a percentage of sales	9 (75.00)	38 (82.61)	14 (93.33)
Inbound freight costs	7 (63.64)	35 (76.09)	11 (73.33)
Outbound freight costs	9 (81.82)	41 (89.13)	15 (100.00)
Warehouse costs	8 (66.67)**	42 (91.30)	15 (100.00)
Administrative costs	8 (66.67)	36 (76.60)	13 (86.67)
Order processing costs	2 (20.00)	11 (27.50)	9 (60.00)**
Direct labor costs	7 (70.00)	38 (84.44)	15 (100.00)
Comparison of actual versus budget	7 (63.64)***	43 (93.48)	15 (100.00)
Cost trend analysis	4 (40.00)	27 (61.36)	12 (80.00)
Direct product profitability	3 (30.00)**	29 (64.44)	9 (60.00)

COMPARISON OF EMERGING, NORM AND LEADING EDGE
(Hybrids Only)

QUESTION 22: (CON'T)

	Number (%) of Those Who Responded, Who Said The Measure Was Used		
(C) CUSTOMER SERVICE	Emerging	Norm	Leading Edge
Fill rate	5 (45.45)	24 (58.54)	12 (80.00)
Stockouts	7 (58.33)	26 (65.00)	12 (80.00)
Shipping errors	6 (54.55)	31 (73.81)	13 (86.67)
On time delivery	4 (36.36)**	29 (70.73)	12 (80.00)
Backorders	4 (36.36)*	26 (66.67)	11 (73.33)
Cycle time	4 (36.36)	14 (38.89)	11 (73.33)**
Customer feedback	10 (83.33)	38 (86.36)	15 (100.00)
Sales force feedback	10 (90.91)	32 (78.05)	11 (78.57)
Customer Surveys	6 (50.00)	12 (30.00)	14 (93.38)***
(D) PRODUCTIVITY			
Units shipped per employee	3 (27.27)**	27 (61.36)	12 (80.00)
Units per labor dollar	5 (41.67)	27 (60.00)	12 (80.00)
Orders per sales rep.	4 (36.36)	15 (38.46)	8 (57.14)
Comparison to historical standards	7 (63.64)*	39 (86.67)	13 (86.67)
Goal programs	5 (45.45)**	36 (80.00)	13 (86.67)
Productivity Index	3 (25.00)	19 (45.24)	9 (60.00)
(E) QUALITY			
Frequency of damage	4 (33.33)	18 (43.90)	12 (80.00)**
Dollar amount of damage	4 (33.33)	22 (53.38)	14 (100.00)***
Number of credit claims	5 (45.45)	23 (56.10)	14 (93.33)***
Number of customer returns	6 (50.00)	32 (74.42)	13 (86.67)
Cost of returned goods	4 (36.36)	23 (52.27)	11 (78.57)*

***, **, * Chi-square table (versus the NORM) is significant at 0.01, 0.05, and 0.10 respectively.

QUESTION 22: (CON'T)

TOTAL NUMBER OF PERFORMANCE MEASURES

Performance Category	Mean (Standard Deviation)		
	Emerging	Norm	Leading Edge
Asset Management	4.15 (1.77)	4.20 (1.47)	5.13** (1.19)
Cost	6.08** (3.66)*	8.51 (2.55)	10.21*** (1.26)***
Customer Service	4.31 (3.01)	4.73 (2.68)	7.40*** (1.72)*
Productivity	2.08** (1.98)	3.33 (1.52)	4.47*** (1.46)
Quality	1.77 (1.92)	2.41 (1.66)	4.27*** (0.80)***

***, **, * Significantly different from the NORM at 0.01, 0.05 and 0.10 respectively.

QUESTION 23: COMPETITIVE BENCHMARKING

Area	Number (%) of Those Who Responded, Who Said Benchmarking Was Used		
	Emerging	Norm	Leading Edge
Cost	4 (36.36)*	30 (65.22)	10 (66.67)
Asset Management	3 (27.27)	11 (23.91)	5 (33.33)
Customer Service	4 (36.36)	18 (41.86)	10 (71.43)**
Productivity	4 (36.36)	15 (32.61)	9 (60.00)*
Quality	5 (45.45)	22 (47.83)	11 (73.33)*
Logistics Strategy	0 (0.00)	9 (20.93)	9 (60.00)***
Technology Deployment	4 (40.00)	16 (36.36)	8 (53.33)
Transportation Operations	3 (27.27)	18 (40.91)	7 (46.67)
Warehouse Operations	3 (27.27)	15 (34.88)	8 (53.33)
Order Processing Operations	3 (27.27)	11 (25.58)	5 (33.33)

***, **, * Significantly different from the NORM at 0.01, 0.05, and 0.10 respectively.

COMPARISON OF EMERGING, NORM AND LEADING EDGE
(Hybrids Only)

QUESTION 25: ELECTRONIC DATA INTERCHANGE

	Number (%) of Those Who Responded, Who Said EDI Was Currently Installed		
Application	Emerging	Norm	Leading Edge
Manufacturers	2 (16.67)	12 (26.09)	9 (60.00)**
Wholesalers	2 (16.67)	5 (11.96)	4 (33.33)
Public Warehouses	1 (9.09)	4 (9.30)	2 (15.38)
Carriers	3 (25.00)	8 (19.05)	4 (28.57)
Financial Institutions	1 (8.33)	12 (29.27)	7 (53.85)
Retailers	3 (25.00)	9 (20.93)	6 (46.15)
Customers	3 (25.00)	16 (34.78)	8 (53.33)***
Copackers/Contracters	0 (0.00)	4 (9.52)	0 (0.00)

***, ** Overall chi-square table (versus the NORM) is significant at 0.01 and 0.05 respectively.

	Number (%) of Those Who Responded, Who Said EDI Was Planned in Next Three Years		
Application	Emerging	Norm	Leading Edge
Manufacturers	3 (25.00)	12 (26.09)	4 (26.67)
Wholesalers	2 (16.67)	9 (20.45)	1 (8.33)
Public Warehouses	0 (0.00)	4 (9.30)	1 (7.69)
Carriers	0 (0.00)	7 (16.67)	4 (28.57)
Financial Institutions	1 (8.33)	4 (9.76)	2 (15.38)
Retailers	0 (0.00)	7 (16.28)	2 (15.38)
Customers	1 (8.33)	9 (19.57)	7 (46.67)
Copackers/Contracters	0 (0.00)	1 (2.38)	1 (8.33)

QUESTION 26: LOGISTICS COMPUTER APPLICATIONS

Application	Number (%) of Those Who Responded, Who Said The Application Was Currently Installed (With or Without Revision Plans)		
	Emerging	Norm	Leading Edge
Freight Audit and Payment	3 (27.27)	20 (43.48)	8 (53.33)
Purchasing	8 (72.72)	40 (83.34)	13 (92.86)
Sales Forecasting	4 (36.36)	29 (64.45)	13 (86.67)
Inventory Control	8 (66.67)	45 (91.84)	15 (100.00)
Warehouse Order Selection	5 (45.45)	32 (68.08)	13 (86.67)
Warehouse On-Line Receiving	4 (36.36)	23 (49.94)	12 (73.33)
Warehouse Merchandise Locator	3 (30.00)**	28 (59.57)	12 (80.00)*
Warehouse Workload Balancing	1 (10.00)	11 (23.41)	7 (46.67)
Warehouse Short Interval Scheduling	2 (20.00)	6 (13.05)	7 (50.00)***
Order Processing	10 (83.33)	42 (87.50)	15 (100.00)
Order Entry	10 (83.33)	42 (87.50)	14 (100.00)
Vehicle Routing and Scheduling	4 (36.36)	12 (26.08)	4 (28.57)
Inbound Freight Consolidation	1 (10.00)	11 (23.41)	5 (35.71)*
Outbound Freight Consolidation	2 (20.00)	20 (42.56)	9 (60.00)
Supporting Financials	9 (91.92)	42 (85.71)	13 (86.67)
Performance Measurement	4 (40.00)	33 (68.08)	12 (80.00)
Distribution Modeling	1 (11.11)	14 (30.44)	6 (40.00)
Direct Product Profitability	3 (30.00)**	20 (43.48)	5 (35.71)
Direct Store Delivery	2 (20.00)	14 (32.55)	7 (53.85)
Shelf Management	0 (0.00)	9 (23.07)	5 (35.72)

***, **, * Chi-square table (versus the NORM) is significant at 0.01, 0.05, and 0.01 respectively.

COMPARISON OF EMERGING, NORM AND LEADING EDGE
(Hybrids Only)

QUESTIONS 27, 28, 29: OPINIONS ABOUT U.P.C. SCANNING
(1 = STRONGLY DISAGREE, 5 = STRONGLY AGREE)

(A) "UPC has given retailers a unique advantage over other members of the distribution channel"

Mean	(Standard Deviation)	
Emerging	Norm	Leading Edge
3.82	3.83	3.79
(0.60)	(0.85)	(1.25)*

(B) "Information derived from point of sale scanning has made your business unit competitively stronger in comparison to other members of your distribution channel"

Mean	(Standard Deviation)	
Emerging	Norm	Leading Edge
2.56	3.05	3.58
(1.13)	(0.96)	(1.16)

(C) "Point of sale scanning information is more important to retailers than wholesalers"

Mean	(Standard Deviation)	
Emerging	Norm	Leading Edge
3.18	3.32	2.93
(1.08)	(0.94)	(1.33)*

* Significantly different from the NORM at 0.10.

QUESTION 30: COMPARATIVE EVALUATION OF LOGISTICS MANAGEMENT INFORMATION SYSTEM
(1 = MUCH WORSE, 5 = MUCH BETTER)

How do your company's logistics management information systems compare overall
to the management information systems designed to support other areas of the
business?

Mean	(Standard Deviation)	
Emerging	Norm	Leading Edge
2.55	2.73	3.60***
(1.21)	(0.98)	(0.83)

*** Significantly different from the NORM at 0.01.

QUESTION 31: CHARACTERISTICS OF INFORMATION USED TO MANAGE LOGISTICS
(1 = NEVER, 5 = ALWAYS)

	Mean on a 5-point scale	(Standard Deviation)	
Characteristic	Emerging	Norm	Leading Edge
Timely	4.00	4.00	4.33
	(0.77)	(0.95)	(0.82)
Accurate	4.36	4.06	4.47**
	(0.50)	(0.78)	(0.52)*
Readily available	3.91	3.58	4.27***
	(0.83)	(0.92)	(0.70)
Formatted on an exception basis	2.38	2.70	3.67***
	(1.06)	(0.98)	(0.82)
Appropriately formatted to facilitate use	3.44	3.38	4.00***
	(1.13)	(0.78)	(0.85)

***, **, * Significantly different from the NORM at 0.01, 0.05, and
0.10 respectively.

COMPARISON OF EMERGING, NORM AND LEADING EDGE
(Hybrids Only)

QUESTION 32: ABILITY TO ACCOMODATE VARIOUS EVENTS IMPACTING
LOGISTICS ACTIVITIES
(1 = CANNOT ACCOMMODATE, 5 = ACCOMMODATES VERY EASILY)

Event	Mean on a 5-point scale (Standard Deviation)		
	Emerging	Norm	Leading Edge
Special customer service requests	3.55 (1.13)	3.40 (1.01)	3.87 (0.83)
Sales/Marketing incentive programs	4.00** (0.76)	3.21 (0.99)	4.14*** (0.77)
Product introduction	3.80 (0.92)	3.57 (0.86)	4.00 (1.07)
Product phase out	3.33 (1.00)	3.34 (0.96)	3.93** (1.03)
Disruption in supply	2.90 (1.20)	2.78 (0.84)	3.00 (0.93)
Computer breakdown	2.40 (1.07)	2.26 (0.88)	2.50 (1.09)
Product recall	2.20 (1.10)	2.84 (0.87)	3.21 (0.89)
Customization of service levels to specific markets or customers	3.56* (1.01)	3.00 (0.86)	3.60** (1.18)
Product modification or customization while in the logistics system (e.g. pricing, packaging, mixing)	3.25 (1.16)	3.16 (0.99)	3.47 (1.13)
Returned goods	3.50 (0.93)	3.37 (0.80)	3.67 (0.90)

***, **, * Significantly different from the NORM at 0.01, 0.05, and
0.10 respectively.

QUESTION 33: ON A SCALE OF 1 TO 5, RATE THE LEVEL OF IMPACT EACH OF
THE FOLLOWING HAS ON YOUR LOGISTICAL OPERATIONS

Item:	Mean for each of the CAI Groups (1)		
	Emerging	Norm	Leading Edge
Sales forecast accuracy	3.18	3.71	3.67
Computer support	4.00	3.96	4.40
Excessive end-of-month or end-of-quarter surges	3.00	3.58	2.86**
Communications with customer	3.27	3.65	4.07
Availability of trained logistics personnel	2.80*	3.35	3.64
Vehicle routing and scheduling	3.22	3.23	3.53
Computer applications backlog	3.14	3.41	3.33
Transportation cost	3.50	3.69	3.93
Communication with suppliers	3.20	3.51	3.47
Warehouse productivity	3.33	3.62	4.13**
Measurement tools and methods	2.89	3.23	3.53
Communication with internal non-logistics organizational units	3.30	3.60	3.73
Timely information	4.00	3.90	4.27
Supplier logistical performance	3.20	3.51	3.67
Communication with external logistical services suppliers	2.38**	3.11	3.07
Incompatibility of computer equipment and/or software	2.67	2.83	3.25
Inventory reduction programs	3.00	3.47	3.40
Cost reduction programs	3.27	3.57	3.66
Load leveling	2.86	2.83	3.71***
Workforce leveling	3.00	3.09	3.67**

(1) - Scale was 1 = no impact
                 2 = slight impact
                 3 = medium impact
                 4 = high impact
                 5 = very high impact

***, **, * Significantly different from the norm at 0.01, 0.05 and 0.10 respectively.

COMPARISON OF EMERGING, NORM AND LEADING EDGE
(Hybrids Only)

QUESTION 34: USAGE OF OUTSIDE SERVICE VENDORS
(1 = will not use, 5 = will use many more outside services)

Outside Service Vendor	Mean for each of the CAI Groups		
	Emerging	Norm	Leading Edge
Transportation	3.36	3.10	3.07
Warehousing	2.60	2.52	2.73
Order Entry and Processing	1.73	2.09	1.43*
Inventory Management	1.73	2.07	1.71
Freight Audit and Payment	2.09	2.58	2.61
Consolidators	2.30	2.36	2.64
International Freight Forwarders	2.60	2.71	3.55**
Domestic Freight Forwarders	2.50	2.29	2.00
Order Fulfillment and Support	1.67	2.29	1.71

**, * Significantly different from the norm at 0.05 and 0.10 respectively.

QUESTION 35: FACTORS INFLUENCING THE DECISION TO USE OUTSIDE SERVICE VENDORS
(1 = never, 5 = always)

Factor	Mean for each of the CAI Groups		
	Emerging	Norm	Leading Edge
Services available	4.18	3.87	3.62
Quality of services	4.27	4.19	4.13
Data processing/ communications services	2.55**	3.29	3.07
Management quality	3.40	3.58	3.67
Customer orientation	4.00	3.88	3.67
Vendor reputation	4.09	4.16	3.93

** Significantly different from the norm at 0.05.

Statistical Comparison of Leading Edge Firms by Business Type

**APPENDIX C: STATISTICAL COMPARISON OF
LEADING EDGE FIRMS BY BUSINESS TYPE**

In Appendix C, leading edge manufacturers, retailers, wholesalers and hybrids were compared with one another. The overall research hypothesis was that leading edge firms exhibit communalities in spite of the different missions inherent in their respective positions in the distribution chain. Specifically, it was tested whether leading edge firms across the four types of businesses were:

(1) equally likely to have formal mission statements and plans (questions 4 and 5A);

(2) similar with respect to the time horizon and frequency of update of their logistics plans (questions 5B and 5C);

(3) centralized to the same degree (question 6);

(4) similar with respect to the position in the organization of the senior logistics officer and this officer's immediate superior (questions 8, 10 and 13);

(5) similar in terms of years organized and number of times reorganized in the past 5 years (questions 16 and 17);

(6) equally likely to participate in overall strategic planning (question 18);

(7) equally likely to control each of 13 typical activities or functions (question 20) and to have control over non-typical activities (question 21);

(8) equally likely to use each of 6 asset management performance measurements, 12 cost measurements, 9 measurements of customer service, 6 of productivity and 5 of quality (question 22);

(9) equally likely to engage in competitive benchmarking in each of 10 areas (question 23);

(10) similar in their opinions about UPC (questions 27, 28 and 29);

(11) similar in their evaluation of logistics management information system as compared to the systems designed to support other areas (question 30);

(12) similar in their descriptions of the characteristics of information used to manage logistics (question 31);

and   (13) similar in their ability to accommodate various events (question 32).

COMPARISON OF MANUFACTURERS, HYBRIDS, RETAILERS AND WHOLESALERS (M, H, R and W):
(Leading Edge Only)

QUESTION 4: DO YOU HAVE A FORMAL LOGISTICS MISSION STATEMENT

	M	H	R	W
YES	45 (75.00%)	9 (64.29%)	13 (81.25%)	16 (76.19%)
NO	15 (25.00%)	5 (35.71%)	3 (18.75%)	5 (23.81%)
TOTAL	60	14	16	21

Chi-square (3 df) = 1.20, p = 0.754

QUESTION 5: FORMAL LOGISTICS STRATEGIC PLAN

(A) Do you have a formal logistics strategic plan?

	M	H	R	W
YES	64 (100.00%)	13 (92.86%)	15 (93.75%)	20 (90.91%)
NO	0 (0.00%)	1 (7.14%)	1 (6.25%)	2 (9.09%)
TOTAL	64	14	16	22

Chi-square (3 df) = 5.34, p = 0.148

(B) What is the time horizon of the plan?

In years:

M = 4.398   W = 3.950   R = 3.667   H = 3.385

These means are not significantly different (p = 0.231)

(C) How often is the plan reviewed or updated?

In months:

H = 12.000   W = 11.400   M = 11.048   R = 10.000

These means are not significantly different (p = 0.805)

COMPARISON OF MANUFACTURERS,
HYBRIDS, RETAILERS AND WHOLESALERS (M, H, R and W):
(Leading Edge Only)

QUESTION 6: ANALYSIS OF LOGISTICS ORGANIZATIONS

(A) Centralization of logistics activities at present:
(1 = Decentralized, 5 = Centralized)

R = 3.813   M = 3.692   H = 3.600   W = 3.409

These means are not significantly different (p = 0.729)

(B) Trend over the last three years:

	M	H	R	W
Centralization	23 (57.50%)	9 (64.29%)	10 (62.50%)	7 (31.82%)
Decentralization	9 (22.50%)	3 (21.43%)	2 (12.50%)	5 (22.73%)
No Change	8 (20.00%)	2 (14.29%)	4 (25.00%)	10 (45.45%)
TOTAL	40	14	16	22

Chi-square (6 df) = 7.73, p = 0.259

QUESTIONS 8, 10: DESCRIPTION OF SENIOR LOGISTICS OFFICER

(A) Title	M	H	R	W
V.P. and above	45 (70.31%)	14 (93.33%)	15 (93.75%)	19 (86.36%)
Below V.P.	19 (29.69%)*	1 (6.67%)	1 (6.25%)**	3 (13.64%)
TOTAL	64	15	16	22

Chi-square (6 df) = 7.702, p = 0.053
* More than expected under the null hypothesis
** Less than expected under the null hypothesis

(B) Number of years in this position

H = 7.600   R = 6.375   W = 5.773   M = 4.166

Underlined means are not significantly different (p = 0.068)

**COMPARISON OF MANUFACTURERS,
HYBRIDS, RETAILERS AND WHOLESALERS (M, H, R and W):**
(Leading Edge Only)

QUESTION 13: TITLE OF THE PERSON THE SENIOR LOGISTICS OFFICER REPORTS TO

	M	H	R	W
Senior V.P. and above	43 (67.19%)	15 (100.00%)	15 (93.75%)	20 (90.91%)
V.P., director	21 (32.81%)*	0 (0.00%)	0 (0.00%)	2 (9.09%)
Mgr., Supervisor, Other	0 (0.00%)	0 (0.00%)	1 (6.25%)	0 (0.00%)
TOTAL	64	15	16	22

Chi-square (6 df) = 22.072, p = 0.001
* More than expected under the null hypothesis

QUESTIONS 16, 17: YEARS A FORMAL ORGANIZATION AND NUMBER OF TIMES
REORGANIZED IN THE LAST 5 YEARS

Years a formal organization:

W = 22.200   R = 20.000   M = 11.313   H = 7.714

Underlined means are not significantly different (p = 0.004)

Number of times reorganized:

H = 2.429   R = 2.400   M = 2.328   W = 1.773

These means are not significantly different (p = 0.381)

QUESTION 18: PARTICIPATION IN OVERALL STRATEGIC PLANNING

	M	H	R	W
YES	34 (85.00%)	14 (93.33%)	16 (100.00%)	22 (100.00%)
NO	1 (2.50%)	1 (6.67%)	0 (0.00%)	0 (0.00%)
SOME	5 (12.50%)	0 (0.00%)	0 (0.00%)	0 (0.00%)
TOTAL	40	15	16	22

COMPARISON OF MANUFACTURERS,
HYBRIDS, RETAILERS AND WHOLESALERS (M, H, R and W):
(Leading Edge Only)

QUESTION 20: NUMBER (%) OF THE SAMPLES OF M, H, R, AND W WHO HAVE
EACH ACTIVITY (LEADING EDGE ONLY)

	P-value from X^2 Table	M	H	R	W
Sales Forecasting	0.537	36 (56.25)	8 (53.33)	6 (37.50)	10 (45.55)
Purchasing	0.965	38 (59.38)	9 (60.00)	10 (62.50)	12 (54.55)
Inbound Transportation	0.265	57 (89.06)	12 (80.00)	16 (100.00)	18 (81.82)
Inventory Management *	0.003	60 (93.75)[4]	10 (66.67)	12 (75.00)	14 (63.64)[2]
Intra-Company Trans.	0.002	59 (92.19)[4]	9 (60.00)[2]	15 (93.75)	15 (68.18)[2]
Warehousing	0.174	61 (95.31)	15 (100.00)	16 (100.00)	19 (86.36)
Order Processing	0.000	55 (85.94)[4]	10 (66.67)	15 (93.75)	9 (40.90)[2,3]
Customer Service	0.004	57 (89.06)[4]	11 (73.33)	10 (62.50)	12 (54.55)[2]
Outbound Transportation	0.153	64 (100.00)	14 (93.33)	15 (93.75)	20 (90.91)
Logistics Systems Planning	0.453	61 (95.31)	13 (86.67)	15 (93.75)	19 (86.36)
Facilities Design **	0.005	38 (59.38)[2]	13 (86.67)	15 (93.75)	19 (86.36)
Logistics Administration	0.053	61 (95.31)	12 (80.00)	15 (93.75)	17 (77.27)
International	0.000	43 (67.19)[1,4]	6 (40.00)	6 (37.50)	3 (13.64)[2,3]

* Finished goods inventory management on M's questionnaire
** Logistics engineering on M's questionnaire
1,2,3,4: Superscripts mean more than expected said yes (=1), said no (=2);
less than expected said yes (=3), said no (=4).

Total functions (line or staff), means:

R = 13.250   M = 12.188   H = 11.933   W = 10.864

Underlined means are not significantly different (p = 0.047)

Total line functions, means:

M = 9.891   H = 6.800   R = 6.063   W = 5.773

Underlined means are not significantly different (p = 0.0001)

COMPARISON OF MANUFACTURERS,
HYBRIDS, RETAILERS AND WHOLESALERS (M, H, R and W):
(Leading Edge Only)

QUESTION 21: NUMBER (%) HAVING NON-TYPICAL ACTIVITIES (LEADING EDGE ONLY)

	M	H	R	W
YES	31 (48.44%)	9 (64.29%)	11 (68.75%)	14 (66.67%)
NO	33 (51.56%)	5 (35.71%)	5 (31.25%)	7 (33.33%)
TOTAL	64	14	16	21

Chi-square = 3.898, p = 0.273

QUESTION 22: NUMBER (%) OF THOSE WHO RESPONDED OF M, H, R, AND W WHO USE THE FOLLOWING PERFORMANCE MEASUREMENT

Performance Measurement	P-value from X^2 Table	M	H	R	W
(A) ASSET MANAGEMENT					
Inventory turns	0.726	36 (92.31)	14 (93.33)	15 (100.00)	21 (95.45)
Inventory carrying costs	0.606	33 (84.62)	14 (93.33)	12 (80.00)	17 (77.27)
Inventory levels (number of days supply)	0.707	37 (94.87)	13 (86.67)	14 (93.33)	21 (95.45)
Obsolete inventory	0.699	37 (94.87)	13 (86.67)	13 (86.67)	20 (90.91)
Return on net assets	0.118	29 (76.37)	10 (66.67)	13 (86.67)	21 (95.45)
Return on investment	0.777	32 (84.21)	13 (86.67)	14 (93.33)	20 (90.91)
(B) COST (logistics cost only)					
Total cost analysis	0.382	38 (95.00)	13 (86.67)	15 (93.75)	21 (100.00)
Cost per unit	0.964	33 (84.62)	12 (80.00)	12 (80.00)	17 (80.95)
Cost as a percentage of sales	0.352	35 (87.50)	14 (93.33)	15 (93.75)	22 (100.00)
Inbound freight costs	0.192	37 (92.50)	11 (73.33)	15 (93.75)	18 (81.82)
Outbound freight costs	0.358	40 (100.00)	15 (100.00)	14 (93.33)	21 (91.45)
Warehouse costs	0.423	37 (92.50)	15 (100.00)	15 (93.75)	22 (100.00)
Administrative costs	0.752	35 (87.50)	13 (86.67)	13 (86.67)	21 (95.45)
Order processing costs	0.538	28 (73.68)	9 (60.00)	13 (81.25)	13 (65.00)

(CONTINUED...)

QUESTION 22: CON'T.

Performance Measurement	P-value from X^2 Table	M	H	R	W
(B) COST (logistics cost only) CON'T.					
Direct labor costs	0.069	30 (78.95)[2]	15 (100.00)	15 (93.75)	21 (95.45)
Comparison of actual versus budget	0.187	39 (100.00)	15 (100.00)	15 (93.75)	22 (100.00)
Cost trend analysis	0.504	34 (87.18)	12 (80.00)	13 (81.25)	20 (95.24)
Direct product profitability	0.334	24 (53.33)	9 (60.00)	7 (46.67)	8 (40.00)
(C) CUSTOMER SERVICE (to your customer)					
Fill rate	0.185	33 (86.84)	12 (80.00)	15 (93.75)	22 (100.00)
Stockouts	0.527	34 (89.47)	12 (80.00)	14 (87.50)	21 (95.45)
Shipping error	0.814	34 (89.47)	13 (86.67)	14 (87.50)	20 (95.74)
On time delivery	0.389	37 (92.50)	12 (80.00)	15 (93.74)	20 (95.24)
Backorders	0.728	27 (77.14)	11 (73.33)	12 (75.00)	14 (63.64)
Cycle time	0.540	30 (81.08)	11 (73.33)	13 (81.25)	13 (65.00)
Customer feedback	0.240	36 (90.00)	15 (100.00)	16 (100.00)	18 (85.71)
Sales force feedback	0.006	37 (92.50)	11 (78.57)	6 (54.55)	19 (95.00)
Customer Surveys	0.476	30 (76.92)	14 (93.33)	12 (75.00)	17 (85.00)
(D) PRODUCTIVITY					
Units shipped per employee	0.099	27 (69.23)[2]	12 (80.00)	11 (68.75)	21 (95.45)[4]
Units per labor dollar	0.181	24 (63.16)	12 (80.00)	14 (87.50)	18 (81.82)
Orders per sales rep.	0.047	12 (35.29)	8 (57.14)	2 (18.18)	11 (64.71)[1]
Comparison to historical standards	0.162	31 (81.58)	13 (86.67)	16 (100.00)	21 (95.45)
Goal programs	0.918	34 (87.18)	13 (86.77)	14 (93.33)	19 (86.36)
Productivity Index	0.444	29 (78.38)	9 (60.00)	9 (60.00)	15 (68.18)

(CONTINUED...)

**COMPARISON OF MANUFACTURERS,
HYBRIDS, RETAILERS AND WHOLESALERS (M, H, R and W):**
(Leading Edge Only)

QUESTION 22: CON'T.

Performance Measurement	P-value from X^2 Table	M	H	R	W
(E) QUALITY					
Frequency of damage	0.579	35 (87.50)	12 (80.00)	12 (75.00)	15 (75.00)
Dollar amount of damage	0.358	35 (89.74)	14 (100.00)	16 (100.00)	19 (90.48)
Number of credit claims	0.695	34 (89.47)	14 (93.33)	14 (87.50)	17 (80.95)
Number of customer returns	0.512	36 (90.00)	13 (86.67)	15 (100.00)	18 (85.71)
Cost of returned goods	0.360	34 (85.00)	11 (78.57)	15 (100.00)	18 (85.71)

1,2,3,4: Superscripts mean more than expected said yes (=1), said no (=2);
less than expected said yes (=3), said no (=4).

-------- * -------- * --------

TOTAL NUMBER OF PERFORMANCE MEASUREMENTS

Underlined means are not significantly different:

p =	Measure:	Means:			
0.752	Asset Management	W = 5.455	H = 5.133	M = 5.100	R = 5.063
0.994	Cost	W = 10.273	M = 10.250	H = 10.200	R = 10.125
0.993	Customer Service	W = 7.455	M = 7.450	H = 7.400	R = 7.313
0.196	Productivity	W = 4.773	H = 4.667	R = 4.125	M = 3.925
0.547	Quality	R = 4.500	M = 4.350	H = 4.267	W = 3.955

QUESTION 23: NUMBER (%) OF M, H, R, AND W WHO USED COMPETITIVE BENCHMARKING

Area	P-value from X^2 Table	M	H	R	W
Cost	0.250	34 (87.18)	10 (66.67)	11 (68.75)	18 (81.82)
Asset management	0.093	22 (59.46)	5 (33.33)	5 (31.25)	13 (61.90)
Customer service	0.000	35 (87.50)	10 (66.67)	5 (31.25)*	20 (90.91)
Productivity	0.047	28 (73.68)	9 (60.00)	6 (37.50)*	16 (76.19)
Quality	0.045	34 (85.00)	11 (73.33)	8 (50.00)*	17 (80.95)
Logistics strategy	0.330	29 (74.36)	9 (60.00)	8 (50.00)	12 (60.00)
Technology deployment	0.351	24 (63.16)	8 (53.33)	8 (50.00)	16 (76.19)
Transportation operations	0.335	25 (65.79)	7 (46.67)	10 (62.50)	16 (76.19)
Warehouse operations	0.151	23 (60.53)	8 (53.33)	11 (68.75)	18 (85.71)
Order processing operations	0.220	24 (61.54)	5 (33.33)	7 (43.75)	12 (60.00)

* In each of the significant tables, retailers are more likely to say no
  and less likely to say yes.

QUESTIONS 27, 28, 29: OPINIONS ABOUT POINT OF SALE SCANNING (UPC):
                       MEANS ACROSS M, H, R, AND W*.

(A) "UPC has given retailers a unique advantage over other members of the
    distribution channel" (1 = strongly disagree, 5 = strongly agree)

    H = 3.786   R = 3.733   W = 3.682   M = 3.675

(B) "Information derived from point of sale scanning has made your business
    unit competitively stronger in comparison to other members of your
    distribution channel" (1 = strongly disagree, 5 = strongly agree)

    H = 3.583   M = 3.157   W = 3.143   R = 3.133

(C) "Point of sale scanning information is more important to retailers
    than wholesalers" (1 = stronly disagree, 5 = strongly agree

    M = 3.154   W = 2.952   H = 2.929   R = 2.667

    * Underlined means are not significantly different (#27: p = 0.989;
    #28: p = 0.629; #29: p =0.482)

**COMPARISON OF MANUFACTURERS,
HYBRIDS, RETAILERS AND WHOLESALERS (M, H, R and W):**
(Leading Edge Only)

QUESTION 30: COMPARATIVE EVALUATION OF LOGISTICS MANAGEMENT
INFORMATION SYSTEM

How do your company's logistics management information systems compare overall
to the management information systems designed to support other areas of the
business? (i.e. Accounting, Finance, Sales, etc.)
(1 = much worse, 5 = much better)

Means were:

W = 3.682	H = 3.600	R = 3.563	M = 3.500

Underlined means are not significantly different (p = 0.904)

QUESTION 31: CHARACTERISTICS OF INFORMATION USED TO MANAGE LOGISTICS:
DIFFERENCES BETWEEN M, H, R, AND W.

p =	Descriptor:	Means:			
0.184	Timely	H = 4.33	W = 4.27	R = 4.25	M = 4.00
0.010	Accurate	W = 4.55	H = 4.47	R = 4.44	M = 4.13
0.477	Readily Available	H = 4.26	R = 4.19	M = 4.00	W = 3.95
0.196	Formatted on an Exception Basis	H = 3.67	W = 3.62	R = 3.50	M = 3.23
0.672	Appropriately Formatted to Facilitate Use	H = 4.00	W = 3.95	R = 3.81	M = 3.76

NOTE: Scale was 1 = never to 5 = always.
Underlined means are not significantly different.

QUESTION 32:   ABILITY TO ACCOMMODATE VARIOUS EVENTS IMPACTING
LOGISTICS ACTIVITIES

p =	Event	Means (on 4-point scales)*:			
0.080	Special customer service requests	M = 3.22	H = 3.15	R = 3.06	W = 2.81
0.402	Sales/Marketing incentive programs	H = 3.35	R = 3.31	M = 3.18	W = 3.01
0.986	Product introduction	R = 3.30	M = 3.27	H = 3.25	W = 3.22
0.566	Product phase out	H = 3.20	M = 3.06	R = 3.00	W = 2.84
0.074	Disruption in supply	M = 2.91	R = 2.80	W = 2.53	H = 2.50
0.153	Computer breakdown	M = 2.25	H = 2.13	R = 2.13	W = 1.82
0.216	Product recall	M = 3.02	R = 2.80	W = 2.70	H = 2.67
0.180	Customization of service levels to specific markets or customers	R = 3.08	M = 2.98	H = 2.95	W = 2.57
0.177	Product modification or customization while in the logistics system	H = 2.85	M = 2.76	R = 2.71	W = 2.32

* Underlined means are not significantly different.
NOTE: These questions had 4-point scales on the M questionnaire and 5-point scales on the R/W/H questionnaire. The latter were recoded with 1 left at 1, 2 set to 1.75, 3 set to 2.5, 4 set to 3.25, and 5 set to 4.

APPENDIX D

Related Logistics
Organization Research

APPENDIX D: RELATED LOGISTICS ORGANIZATION RESEARCH

The research presented in this book represents an extension of the organization surveys completed by A.T. Kearney Consultants and Traffic Management Magazine in 1973, 1980 and 1985. Relevant data and results of the earlier research were made available to the Michigan State University Research Team.

The earlier research focused on the span of control of logistics organization. A three stage typology was developed to classify firms. The basic Kearney/Traffic Management hypothesis was that organizations evolve over time through three stages. In their classification scheme, line control over selected functions was used to determine stage. To qualify as Stage I, a company would have to have outbound and intracompany transportation, finished goods field warehousing, logistics systems planning, logistics control and logistics management under direct line control of the logistics organization. Using their typology, the typical Stage II logistics organization would have direct line control over all of the Stage I functions mentioned above plus customer service, order processing, finished goods inventory management, finished goods plant warehousing and inbound transportation. The typical Stage III firm would have direct line control over all of the Stage I and II functions plus sales forecasting, production planning, purchasing, raw materials and work in process inventories, logistics engineering and international logistics.

The results of the 1980 study were:

1. Increasing numbers of companies were bringing an expanding group of logistics activities under centralized planning control.
2. The senior logistics executive was being elevated to corporate officer status on par with senior marketing, sales, finance and manufacturing executives.
3. The common pattern of organizational change involves three distinct stages of management development and reorientation- the Stage I, II and III companies.
4. Successful companies produce superior financial results by managing that process of change (Farrell, 1980).

In the 1980 study, the researchers concluded that firms classified as Phase III respondents become more productive as they move closer toward fully integrated logistics management. Logistics performance in terms of operations, finance and administration was seen as improving as the organization became more integrated.

Another conclusion of the 1980 study was that, as the logistics organizations gained responsibilities, their logistics costs/sales ratios improved. For warehousing, inventory, order processing and administrative costs, there was a noticeable difference between Stage I, II and III companies. Among firms studied, Phase II and III companies had on average lower cost/sales ratios than did Phase I firms.

The 1985 Logistics Organization study resulted in conclusions similar to the 1980 research. The major findings were as follows:

1. Logistics groups of all types have steadily widened the scope of their responsibilities.

2. Broader responsibilities have resulted in enhanced performance.

3. A centralized approach to logistics management materially improves the bottom line.
4. Increased logistics purchasing power is a reflection of greater corporate and management interest.
5. Most logistics departments expect to expand their scope of responsibilities even more in the near future (Farrell, 1985).

The 1985 research found that the number of Stage I companies had decreased, while Stage II and III increased. Stage I companies went from 60 to 42.2 percent of all firms surveyed, whereas Stage II firms moved from 30 in 1980 to 37.5 percent in 1985. Stage III firms more than doubled from 10 in 1980 to 20.1 percent in 1985.

Another conclusion of the 1985 study was that Canadian firms had greatly increased the number of functions they managed. On average, Canadian firms managed 10.6 overall functions compared to 9.4 overall functions for all companies included in the research.

The 1987-1988 MSU research found that while many firms may evolve from a Stage I firm through Stage II and eventually to Stage III, many firms do not. Some firms organize logistics in a manner that qualifies for an advanced stage firm at the outset. The MSU research was based on its belief that the management of functions is more important than how many functions are managed. Thus, attention was directed to a combination of structure, strategy and behavior in the performance of logistics. However, research results point out that leading edge logistics organizations are more integrated than norm or emerging organizations.

In terms of functional expansion, the pattern is consistent. The first study in 1973 found that firms averaged 2.24 overall functions. In 1981, the survey found that the average number of functions had increased to 3.62 functions per firm. By 1985, the number of overall functions had grown to 6.99. The 1987 MSU research found that manufacturers averaged overall 8.82 functions. The 1988 retail/wholesale research project respondents were similar to the 1987 respondents. Wholesalers averaged 7.61 functions, retailers averaged 8.84, and hybrid firms averaged 8.94 functions.

Based on the upwardly moving trend of both average number of line and overall functions, it is clear that the typical firm's functional critical mass is expanding. Although it is necessary to have sufficient span of control to create a positive impact, the key to understanding strategic logistics is an appreciation of how logistical functions are managed.

REFERENCES

Farrell, Jack. (1985). New Clout for Logistics. Traffic Management, September.

Farrell, Jack. (1980). Distribution Departments Gain Ground. Traffic Management, September.

APPENDIX E

The Common Attributes Index (CAI)

APPENDIX E: THE COMMON ATTRIBUTES INDEX (CAI)

The logistical organization of a firm has traditionally been rated on the basis of the breadth of its span of control over logistical functions or activities. This rating system was based on the assumptions that: (1) a greater number of controlled activities is reflective of a greater degree of logistics integration; and (2) greater logistics integration is related to enhanced logistical performance. Hence, the number of controlled activities was hypothesized to be directly related to logistical performance.

There are several problems with this traditional rating system. First, merely having control over an activity does not necessarily mean that the activity is well managed. Second, having control over a number of activities does not necessarily imply a commitment to the integrated logistics concept. To illustrate, consider the following example. Which firm has the "better" logistical organization: one that controls 10 activities which are non-integrated, or one that controls 7 activities which are fully integrated? A third problem with the traditional rating system is that it does not necessarily reflect the power and influence of logistics within the firm's organization. For example, the logistical organization may control many logistics activities and yet the senior logistics executive may have little or no say in the overall strategic planning of the business unit. Thus the logistics executive may have considerable authority and responsibility within the logistics hierarchy, but little power within the organization as a whole. This situation would make full implementation of the integrated logistics concept difficult.

The Common Attributes Index (CAI) was developed by a panel of experts attempting to address some of the above concerns. The panel consisted of academicians and logistics professionals. Using a Delphi method, the panel determined both the components of the CAI and the weighing of each component so that the sum would be 100. The aim was to create an index that measured logistical excellence as well as the importance of the logistics organization within the firm.

CAI COMPONENTS

The components chosen by the panel are listed below:

* The title level of the senior logistics executive officer and the title level of the executive to whom this officer reports;

* The existence and comprehensiveness of the logistics mission statement;

* The existence and comprehensiveness of the logistics strategic plan;

* The time horizon of the logistics plan and its frequency of update;

* The inclusion of the senior logistics executive officer in overall corporate strategic planning;

* The length of time logistics has been a formal organization and the number of times logistics has been reorganized in the last five years;

* The number of traditional logistics activities that are the responsibility of the logistics organization;

* The number of non-typical activities (or "beyond" functions) that are the responsibility of logistics;

* The ability to accommodate selected events;

* The number and type of performance measurements used in logistics;

* The number and type of computer applications currently installed and used in logistics;

* The extent to which electronic data interchange (EDI) is used (if planned, partial points were assigned);

* The extent to which artificial intelligence (AI) or expert systems software is used in logistics (if planned, partial points were assigned); and

* The quality and relevance of information used to manage logistics.

Every company that returned a questionnaire was assigned points for each of the above components. It was possible to receive a zero for any particular component. The maximum points for any one of the components listed above was 15. The component points were added, and each respondent received a CAI score. The means and standard deviations were calculated for manufacturers, retailers, wholesalers and hybrids separately. Within each of these four channel categories, the leading edge firms were defined as those whose CAI score was more than the mean CAI plus one standard deviation, and the emerging firms were defined as those whose CAI score was less than the mean CAI minus one standard deviation. Norm firms had CAI scores within one standard deviation of the mean CAI of their respective category.

VALIDITY OF THE CAI

CAI was calculated as the weighted sum of scores the respondents were assigned on a variety of items from the questionnaires. When total CAI is regressed against these items one at a time, each regression is significant at $p = 0.001$. The R-squares for these regressions are listed in the first column of Table E-1. In rank order, the best predictors of total CAI score are: (1) the number of traditional functions; (2) the existence and comprehensiveness of the logistics strategic plan; (3) the time horizon of the plan; (4) the inclusion of the senior logistics officer in corporate strategic planning; (5) the frequency of plan updates; and (6) performance measurements. For each of these six items, the R-square is over 0.30. The least related items to total CAI score are the use of artificial intelligence and the number of non-typical (non-traditional) functions. The R-squares for these were both well under 0.10.

Since each of the items is a component of CAI, it is not surprising that each is statistically related to CAI. However, when a particular item's score is subtracted from the total CAI and then the partial CAI score is regressed against that item, the regression is still significant at 0.001 for every item. In each of these models, the partial CAI score, or the total CAI score minus the score on item "i", is the dependent variable and the score on item "i" is the independent variable. The R-squares for these regressions are listed in the second column of Table E-1. In rank order, the items whose R-squares are over 0.30 are: (1) the time horizon of the strategic plan; (2) the existence and comprehensiveness of the strategic plan; (3) the frequency of plan updates; and (4) the inclusion of the senior logistics officer in corporate strategic planning. These four items are the best predictors of partial CAI score, and all four were among the top six predictors of total CAI score. The number of traditional functions, which was the best predictor of total CAI (with an R-square of 0.483), did not achieve an R-square of over 0.30 in predicting partial CAI. However, the R-square for the total number of functions as independent

---

Table E-1

R-SQUARE FROM SIMPLE REGRESSIONS*

Item	Total CAI (1)	Partial CAI (2)
Senior Logistics Executive's Title	0.240	0.186
Title of Immediate Superior	0.110	0.063
Mission Statement	0.203	0.109
Strategic Plan	0.444	0.334
Time Horizon of Strategic Plan	0.424	0.356
Frequency of Plan Updates	0.379	0.320
Inclusion in Corporate Planning	0.389	0.308
Years Logistics Has Been Organized	0.120	0.065
Number of Times Reorganized	0.100	0.054
Number of Traditional Functions	0.483	0.266
Number of Nontypical Functions	0.037	0.014
Ability to Accommodate Events	0.226	0.150
Performance Measurements	0.374	0.171
Computer Applications	0.294	0.207
Use of EDI	0.160	0.111
Use of Artificial Intelligence	0.055	0.040
Information Characteristics	0.135	0.061

*   All regressions are significant at p = 0.001.
(1) Each firm's actual CAI score was used.
(2) Each firm's total CAI score minus its score on the particular item was used.
    Thus the R-square value for item "i" comes from the regression of (total CAI)-(score on item "i") as the dependent variable and item "i" as independent variable.

---

variable and partial CAI as dependent variable was 0.266, which is highly significant. In conclusion, the best predictors of both total CAI and partial CAI are fairly consistent. The items most related to both total CAI and partial CAI are a variety of items focusing on planning. The items least related to partial CAI were the use of artificial intelligence and the number of nontypical functions. This also represents the same pattern as found for the total CAI regressions.

The analyses of CAI and partial CAI suggest that a higher level planning construct may exist that is comprised of: (1) the existence and comprehensiveness of the strategic plan; (2) its time horizon; (3) the frequency of update; and (4) the inclusion of the senior logistics officer in corporate strategic planning. An exploratory factor analysis of all items in the CAI confirms that this is the case. The principle components analysis yielded five factors with eigenvalues greater than 1.0. These explain about 58% of the variance. The factor loading pattern following varimax rotation was not representative of a simple factor structure. For example, the number of traditional functions did not load over 0.5 on any factor. However, the four planning items did load together on the first factor. The loadings were quite high and ranged from 0.66 to 0.94.

Finally, the relationships of CAI to sales volume (as reported by the respondents) and to the percent of products made-to-stock were analyzed. For the latter, only the manufacturer's data is relevant. Sales volume was analyzed because it may be a prime determinant of a firm's logistical organization and competencies. If a firm is large, its very size may be reflective of competitive success due, at least in part, to strong logistics performance. On the other hand, small firms may not have the resources to install, manage and maintain complex logistical systems. The results of the regression analyses with CAI as independent variable and sales volume as dependent variable are presented in Table E-2.

Table E-2

RELATIONSHIP OF SALES VOLUME TO CAI BY BUSINESS TYPE

Business Type	R-square	p-Value
Manufacturers	0.033	0.001
Wholesalers	0.026	0.060
Retailers	0.012	0.330
Hybrids	0.053	0.051

The relationship of sales to CAI is highly significant (p = 0.001) in the case of manufacturers, significant in the case of hybrids, somewhat significant for wholesalers and not significant in the case of retailers. All R-squares are between 0.05 and 0.01, indicating that less than 5% of the variance is explained and that the correlations are between 0.23 and 0.11. Thus there is a small, but statistically significant relationship between sales and CAI when the reported sales volume is used as dependent variable.

For manufacturers, the relationship between CAI score and percentage of made-to-stock was analyzed because a high made-to-stock percentage may imply the necessity of a more sophisticated logistics system to manage the continuous flow of goods through the system. Conversely, firms with low made-to-stock percentages may succeed with less complex logistics organizations due to job-shop orientations that result in an interval or unit flow of goods. The R-square for this regression analysis was 0.028, which was statistically significant at p = 0.002. Again the relationship was statistically significant but small, explaining about 3% of the variance.

ANCHORING THE CAI

Two data sets were obtained in order to determine whether CAI score was related to such key indicators of performance as operating cost, inventory turns and inventory to assets ratio. The first data set consisted of publicly available data that was collected for 135 of the manufacturers who responded in Phase I. Sales, assets, cost of goods sold, operating profit, operating cost, raw materials inventory, WIP inventory, finished goods inventory and inventory turns are some of the key indicators in this data set. The second data set was collected from logistics executives in 24 manufacturers. When contacted by the research team, these executives provided data on cost as a percentage of sales for indicators such as inbound transportation, plant warehousing and logistics administration. These two data sets were analyzed separately.

The Relationship of CAI to Key Publicly Available Indicators

Table E-3 contains the correlations of several key indicators with CAI score for: (1) all manufacturers for whom some or all of this data was available; and (2) a subset of these manufacturers whose organizational structure was given as A or B on the questionnaire. Those manufacturers who described the organizational structure of logistics activities as either dispersed across functional areas (structure A) or consolidated within a logistics functional area (as in

Table E-3
CORRELATIONS OF CAI SCORE WITH SELECTED INDICATORS
(PUBLICLY AVAILABLE DATA)

Correlation of CAI score with: (p-value in brackets)	Manufacturers (n=135), all organizational structures (Structures A, B, C, D, E)	Manufacturers (n=46), only functional organizations (Structures A and B)
Sales	-0.141 (0.112)	0.033 (0.828)
Cost of Goods Sold	-0.120 (0.173)	-0.038 (0.800)
Operating Profit	-0.111 (0.207)	-0.014 (0.928)
Operating Cost (1)	-0.120 (0.178)	0.141 (0.357)
Operating Cost/Sales	0.061 (0.497)	0.167 (0.272)
Return on Assets (2)	0.088 (0.320)	0.185 (0.219)
Raw Materials Inventory	-0.099 (0.339)	-0.146 (0.419)
WIP Inventory	-0.084 (0.495)	-0.191 (0.360)
Finished Goods Inventory	-0.139 (0.200)	0.183 (0.316)
Total 1986 Inventory	-0.145 (0.092)	-0.038 (0.798)
Total 1987 Inventory	-0.120 (0.172)	-0.081 (0.593)
% Change in Inventory (3)	0.058 (0.512)	-0.110 (0.466)
Inventory Turns (4)	-0.129 (0.143)	0.100 (0.509)
Return on Inventory (5)	0.008 (0.933)	0.075 (0.624)
Inventory/Assets (6)	0.143 (0.106)	-0.118 (0.433)

(1) Operating cost = sales-COGS-profit.
(2) Return on assets = profit/assets.
(3) % Change in inventory = (1987-1986)/1987.
(4) Inventory turns = COGS/(average 1986, 1987 inventory).
(5) Return on inventory = profit/(average 1986, 1987 inventory).
(6) Inventory/assets = (average 1986, 1987 inventory)/assets.

structure B) were analyzed separately because these firms are not organized by business unit at the corporate level. Firms with structures C, D and E are organized by business units and thus the relationship of CAI score with the publicly available corporate data may be confounded by the differential successes of various business units.[*]

Table E-3 also contains the p-values for every correlation. A p-value of less than 0.10 would indicate that the corresponding correlations are significantly different from zero. With the possible exception of Total 1986 Inventory, none of the correlations is statistically different from zero. Total 1986 Inventory is negatively correlated with CAI score, but this correlation is only

---

[*] Although structure D has business units, logistics is organized not within these units but at the corporate level. Here both line and staff logistics responsibilities reside. When structure D was analyzed along with A and B, the substantive results were not significantly different.

somewhat significant at p = 0.092. This negative correlation is probably reflective of the fact that sales in negatively correlated with CAI score in this sample of 135, although the correlation of sales and CAI score does not reach statistical significance.

In order to examine the relationships of CAI score with key indicators more closely, the covariate adjusted means of each of six indicators were compared across emerging, norm and leading edge CAI groups. Two separate series of ANCOVAS (analysis of covariance) were analyzed: one with total assets as covariate and one with sales as covariate. The six indicators chosen were return on assets, operating cost to sales ratio, percentage change in inventory (1986 to 1987), inventory turns, return on inventory and inventory to assets ratio. The covariate adjusted means for each CAI group are presented in Table E-4 (covariate: total assets) and Table E-5 (covariate: sales). The p-values for equality of adjusted means are also presented in these tables. If the p-values are over 0.10, the null hypothesis that the adjusted means are equal cannot be rejected. The results for the entire sample, as well as the results for manufacturers with structures A and B only, are presented in the tables.

Table E-4

COMPARISON OF THE EMERGING, NORM AND LEADING EDGE
MEANS ON SELECTED INDICATORS: MEANS ADJUSTED FOR
THE COVARIATE TOTAL ASSETS (ALL MANUFACTURERS/
MANUFACTURERS WITH STRUCTURES A AND B ONLY)

	Covariate Adjusted Means for CAI Group:		
Indicator	Emerging	Norm	Leading Edge
Return on Assets	0.112/0.102	0.135/0.131	0.133/0.146
Operating Cost/Sales	0.259/0.277	0.279/0.271	0.298/0.354
% Change in Inventory	0.084/0.161	0.077/0.089	0.087/0.090
Inventory Turns	4.906/3.939	4.620/4.938	5.141/5.132
Return on Inventory	0.839/0.703	0.894/0.831	0.881/1.002
Inventory/Assets	0.208/0.249	0.192/0.192	0.172/0.169

	p-values for the Test of Equality of Adjusted Means		
Indicator	Test of Leading Edge vs. Norm	Test of Leading Edge vs. Emerging	Test of Norm vs. Emerging
Return on Assets	0.906/0.528	0.341/0.179	0.254/0.317
Operating Cost/Sales	0.499/0.132	0.351/0.299	0.588/0.924
% Change in Inventory	0.814/0.997	0.971/0.495	0.895/0.443
Inventory Turns	0.315/0.814	0.765/0.296	0.687/0.326
Return on Inventory	0.919/0.365	0.833/0.281	0.759/0.611
Inventory/Assets	0.234/0.439	0.169/0.049	0.507/0.109

An examination of Table E-4 reveals only one significant difference in means adjusted for the covariate total assets. At p = 0.049, one can conclude that the inventory to assets ratio for leading edge firms is significantly different from that of emerging firms in the subsample of manufacturers with structures A and B.

The covariance adjusted means' relationships to CAI group is interesting despite the fact that, with one exception, none of the tests achieve statistical significance. As can be seen from Table E-4, adjusted return on assets is lowest in the emerging group, as are inventory turns, return on inventory and operating cost to sales ratio. The inventory to assets ratio (adjusted) is highest for emerging firms and lowest for leading edge firms. Leading edge firms also have the highest inventory turns.

When the means adjusted for the covariate sales (rather than assets) are examined, the same general pattern described above emerges. As seen in Table E-5, the only difference in adjusted means that achieves statistical significance is the difference between the leading edge and emerging firms on inventory to assets ratio in the case of the subsample containing only structures A and B. An examination of the sales covariate adjusted means across CAI group presents the same overall picture as that described previously for the means adjusted for total assets.

Table E-5

COMPARISON OF THE EMERGING, NORM AND LEADING EDGE
MEANS ON SELECTED INDICATORS: MEANS ADJUSTED FOR
THE COVARIATE TOTAL SALES (ALL MANUFACTURERS/
MANUFACTURERS WITH STRUCTURES A AND B ONLY)

Covariate Adjusted Means for CAI Group

Indicator	Emerging	Norm	Leading Edge
Return on Assets	0.113/0.103	0.134/0.131	0.133/0.151
Operating Cost/Sales	0.256/0.279	0.279/0.271	0.302/0.354
% Change in Inventory	0.106/0.157	0.079/0.089	0.098/0.110
Inventory Turns	4.939/3.948	4.582/4.946	5.030/4.851
Return on Inventory	0.823/0.734	0.892/0.828	0.893/1.033
Inventory/Assets	0.212/0.247	0.192/0.192	0.170/0.172

p-Values for the Test of Equality of Adjusted Means

Indicator	Test of Leading Edge vs. Norm	Test of Leading Edge vs. Emerging	Test of Norm vs. Emerging
Return on Assets	0.937/0.422	0.339/0.152	0.252/0.332
Operating Cost/Sales	0.419/0.129	0.250/0.306	0.501/0.900
% Change in Inventory	0.663/0.795	0.897/0.666	0.626/0.478
Inventory Turns	0.401/0.908	0.906/0.415	0.601/0.306
Return on Inventory	0.994/0.301	0.727/0.294	0.698/0.710
Inventory/Assets	0.235/0.511	0.113/0.076	0.382/0.136

The Relationship of CAI to Indicators Provided by Contacted Manufacturers

Table E-6 contains the correlations of CAI with several key cost indicators, which are expressed as a percentage of sales. Not all of the 24 contacted manufacturers gave estimates of each indicator listed, as shown by the sample size upon which each correlation is based. Since the sample size was so small, division of the data by structure was not practical.

As can be seen from Table E-6, the correlations of CAI score with total transportation costs as a percent of sales, total warehousing costs as a percent of sales, inventory as a percent of sales and total logistics costs as a percent of sales are negative. The correlations with total logistics costs less inventory and with total logistics costs less administration (both expressed as a percentage of sales) are also negative. Logistics administration cost as a percentage of sales is positively correlated with CAI score.

It is important to note that none of these correlations is significantly different from zero. This can be seen from the p-values in the table: all are greater than 0.10 and hence no correlation achieves statistical significance. However, p-values are dependent on sample size and these samples are very small. Thus the consistency of the directions of these correlations may indicate substantive meaning that is not reflected in statistical testing alone.

Table E-6

CORRELATIONS OF CAI SCORE WITH SELECTED
INDICATORS (n = 24 CONTACTED MANUFACTURERS)

Cost as a Percentage of Sales (1) of:	Correlation With CAI	n =	p-Value =
Inbound Transportation	-0.071	18	0.780
Intra-Company Transportation	0.195	19	0.424
Outbound Transportation	-0.205	21	0.372
Total Transportation (2)	-0.182	16	0.500
Plant Warehousing	-0.299	20	0.200
Field Warehousing	-0.025	19	0.918
Total Warehousing (3)	-0.358	16	0.174
Inventory	-0.017	19	0.944
Logistics Administration	0.168	21	0.468
Total Logistics Costs (4)	-0.228	12	0.474
Total Less Inventory	-0.215	13	0.480
Total Less Administration	-0.215	12	0.502

---

(1) Sales is correlated with CAI at 0.269 (n = 24; p = 0.203).
(2) Total transportation = inbound + intra-company + outbound.
(3) Total warehousing = plant + field.
(4) Total logistics costs = transportation + warehousing + inventory + adminis-
    tration.

Table E-7

COMPARISON OF MEANS OF LEADING EDGE VERSUS
EMERGING AND NORM ON SELECTED INDICATORS
(n = 24 CONTACTED MANUFACTURERS)

Cost as a Percentage of Sales of:	Division of Data by CAI Group			
	Leading Edge		Emerging Norm	
	Mean (1)	n =	Mean (1)	n =
Inbound Transportation	1.428	8	1.519	10
Intra-Company Transportation	1.077	10	0.706	9
Outbound Transportation	2.901	10	2.790	11
Total Transportation	5.250	7	5.370	9
Plant Warehousing	1.128	11	1.452	9
Field Warehousing	0.598	9	0.720	10
Total Warehousing	1.536	8	1.184	8
Inventory	1.824	10	1.880	9
Logistics Administration	1.116	10	0.955	11
Total Logistics Costs	9.838	5	9.974	7
Total Less Inventory	8.290	5	7.800	8
Total Less Administration	9.266	5	9.289	7

(1) None of these pairs of means are significantly different from one another (p > 0.10).

In Table E-7, the results of comparing the leading edge firms versus the emerging and norm firms are presented. The emerging and norms firm were grouped together due to sample size limitations. Table E-7 lists the means and the sample sizes for each group. None of the means are significantly different from one another since all p-values are over 0.10. These costs (as a percentage of sales), even when adjusted for sales level as a covariate, appear not to differ across the CAI leading edge group versus the emerging/norm group.

In conclusion, most logistics costs examined, expressed as a percentage of sales, do not appear to be increasing with increasing CAI score. The mean costs across CAI groups appears to be stable. While there is no statistical evidence of any correlation between CAI and these costs, the frequency with which negative correlations were found gives some indication that a statistically significant inverse relationship may be detectable in a larger sample. The major exception may be logistics administration costs, which may be increasing with increasing CAI.

APPENDIX F

Aggregate Logistical Trends

APPENDIX F: AGGREGATE LOGISTICAL TRENDS

The purpose of this appendix is to provide supporting data on (1) aggregate logistics cost, (2) inventory and (3) productivity. These data are to support statements made in the main body of the text.

UNITED STATES AGGREGATE LOGISTICS COST

This section presents an estimate of aggregate United States logistics cost. The calculations are based on work completed by Robert V. Delaney over a number of years. Table F-1 presents aggregate cost by primary components, total cost and total cost as a percent of Gross National Product. Aggregate inventory and cost figures from Tables F-2 and F-3 were used in the construction of Table F-1. To construct Table F-1, the Delaney procedure was modified with respect to the inventory cost calculation. The total inventory size estimates were adopted from the Delaney work. These inventory data are presented in Table F-2. For the inventory cost calculation, the Alford and Bang formulation was modified with respect to cost of inventory as follows: (1) average prime rate was calculated for each year; (2) average cost of borrowing was specified at 1.5 times the average prime rate; and (3) additional cost percentages were accepted as .25 percent for storage, .25 percent for insurance, .5 percent for taxes, and 10 percent for obsolescence. Inventory carrying costs using the above procedure are presented in Table F-3.

Table F-1

UNITED STATES LOGISTICS COST 1977-87
($BILLIONS)

Year	GNP $ Trillion	Inventory Holding/ Carrying Costs	Transpor- tation Costs	Adminis- trative Costs	Total U.S. Logistics Costs	Percent GNP
1977	1.92	71.76	150	10	231.76	12.07
1978	2.16	93.69	175	12	280.69	12.99
1979	2.42	128.12	193	14	335.12	13.85
1980	2.63	156.57	205	15	376.57	14.32
1981	2.94	201.63	236	17	454.63	15.46
1982	3.07	168.45	240	17	425.45	13.86
1983	3.31	139.73	244	15	398.73	12.05
1984	3.66	167.39	250	16	433.39	11.84
1985	3.89	150.97	265	18	433.97	11.16
1986	3.98	138.62	271	18	427.62	10.74
1987	4.50	158.01	285	19	462.01	10.27

Source: Robert V. Delaney "Freight Transportation Deregulation" SEMINAR T9 on Road Transport Deregulation: Experience Evaluation and Research, (Cambridge, MA: Arthur D. Little, Inc.) (Modified) 1988.

INVENTORY ANALYSIS

Matters of concern in the research were the composition of manufacturing inventory and the relative position of overall channel of distribution inventory. To examine the issue of composition, it was necessary to convert durable and nondurable manufacturing inventory into categories of: (1) raw material, (2) work-in-process and (3) finished goods. Business inventory-to-sales ratios were multiplied by sales for each month from 1979 through 1988. The Bureau of Economic Analysis provides monthly ratios of raw material, work-in-process and finished goods for durable and nondurable goods. The products of these monthly calculations were summed for each year and averaged to project an annual dollar distribution for each inventory category. These averages were used to project manufacturing inventory level. These data do not include wholesale or retail inventory.

Table F-4 provides the distribution by category of manufacturers durable goods. Table F-5 provides the distribution for manufacturer nondurable goods. Table F-6 presents overall manufacturer inventory.

Table F-2

RATIO OF INVENTORY TO GROSS NATIONAL PRODUCT: UNITED STATES 1977-87
(Current Dollars)

Year	GNP $ Trillion	Inventory $ Billion	Percent of GNP
1977	1.92	338	17.6
1978	2.16	381	17.64
1979	2.42	427	17.65
1980	2.63	462	17.57
1981	2.94	513	17.45
1982	3.07	506	16.48
1983	3.31	514	15.53
1984	3.66	576	15.49
1985	3.89	583	14.99
1986	3.98	590	14.82
1987	4.50	683	15.17

Source: Robert V. Delaney "Freight Transportation Deregulation" Seminar T9 on Road Transport Deregulation: Experience Evaluation and Research, (Cambridge, MA: Arthur D. Little, Inc.), 1988.

Table F-3

INVENTORY CARRYING CALCULATIONS 1977-87
(Percent)

Year	Prime Rate	Cost of Borrowing	Effective Interest	Additional Costs	Carrying Cost %
1977	6.82 *	1.5 =	10.23 +	11.00 =	21.23
1978	9.06 *	1.5 =	13.59 +	11.00 =	24.59
1979	12.67 *	1.5 =	19.00 +	11.00 =	30.00
1980	15.26 *	1.5 =	22.89 +	11.00 =	33.89
1981	18.87 *	1.5 =	28.30 +	11.00 =	39.30
1982	14.86 *	1.5 =	22.29 +	11.00 =	33.29
1983	10.79 *	1.5 =	16.18 +	11.00 =	27.18
1984	12.04 *	1.5 =	18.06 +	11.00 =	29.06
1985	9.93 *	1.5 =	14.89 +	11.00 =	25.89
1986	8.33 *	1.5 =	12.50 +	11.00 =	23.50
1987	8.09 *	1.5 =	12.13 +	11.00 =	23.13

Table F-4

MANUFACTURE DURABLE INVENTORY: UNITED STATES 1979-88
($Millions)

Year	Total	RM%	WIP%	FG%
1979	142049	32.03	43.25	24.72
1980	158843	31.38	44.82	23.80
1981	180502	31.27	45.65	23.08
1982	183672	30.34	44.03	25.63
1983	170817	29.82	44.82	25.36
1984	182724	29.84	45.78	24.38
1985	191445	28.50	47.19	24.31
1986	186825	27.46	48.42	24.12
1987	210896	28.29	46.16	25.55
1988	221568	28.40	46.26	25.34

Source: Business Conditions Digest, Bureau of Economic Analysis United States
Department of Commerce (Modified)

Table F-5

MANUFACTURER NONDURABLE INVENTORY: UNITED STATES 1979-88
($Million)

Year	Total	RM%	WIP%	FG%
1979	72867	39.24	15.71	45.06
1980	82027	38.97	15.39	45.64
1981	90751	40.24	16.08	43.68
1982	91925	39.87	16.87	43.26
1983	89452	39.70	16.16	44.13
1984	93733	39.67	15.83	44.49
1985	93042	38.65	15.73	45.62
1986	90659	39.02	15.29	45.68
1987	116123	38.54	16.54	44.92
1988	116538	38.90	16.32	44.78

Source: Business Conditions Digest, Bureau of Economic Analysis United States
Department of Commerce (Modified)

TABLE F-6

MANUFACTURERS COMBINED DURABLE AND NONDURABLE INVENTORY:
UNITED STATES 1979-88
($Million)

Year	Total	RM%	WIP%	FG%
1979	214916	34.47	33.91	31.61
1980	240870	33.96	34.80	31.24
1981	271253	34.27	35.76	29.98
1982	275597	33.52	34.97	31.51
1983	260269	33.21	34.98	31.81
1984	276457	33.17	35.63	31.20
1985	284487	31.82	36.90	31.28
1986	277483	31.24	37.60	31.16
1987	327020	31.91	35.67	32.42
1988	338106*	32.01	35.94	32.04

Source: Tables F-4 and F-5 Combined
*   Projected based on first eight months

Using the above methodology to decompose aggregate manufacturing inventory, durable and nondurable combined for 1988 consisted of 32 percent raw materials, 36 percent work-in-process and 32 percent finished goods. The relative shares shift significantly when durables are compared to nondurable manufacturing inventory. In terms of nondurables, finished goods represent the largest category of inventory at 44.8 percent of the 1988 total. For durables, work-in-process is the largest category at 46.3 percent of 1988 total. The relationships mirror historical patterns and represent the relative incidence of build-to-order and build-to-stock characteristic for each type of inventory.

Of particular concern is the subtle forward shift in both categories of manufacturers inventory. In the past two years, a shift forward in total inventory of one percent or $3.4 billion dollars compared to the average of the previous eight years is noted. While a positive shift forward exists in both durable and nondurable inventories, the durable category has experienced the most significant shift forward at approximately $2.2 billion.

The above noted shifts may be cyclical or they could be reflective of a long-term trend. Evidence to support the cyclical assumption is found in the relatively high level of finished goods manufacturers' inventory during 1982-83, when it averaged 31.6 percent of the total. These two years experienced high durable finished goods inventories at an average of 25.5 percent, compared to an average of 25.4 percent for 1987-88.

The support for the assumption of a trend toward forward positioning of manufacturers inventory depends upon continuation of the 1987-88 composition. The data projected for 1988 reflects a slight reversal. These data are based on light months which do not reflect the period of traditional manufacturing inventory build-up to support fourth quarter seasonal retail sales. Therefore, it is reasonable to assume that final 1988 figures will be adjusted downward.

The analysis of this data suggests that continued careful examination of manufacturing inventory composition is in order. The aggregate inventory, as reported in Table F-2, is declining as a percentage of GNP. To benefit from this drop, the composition of manufacturing inventories should remain at least the same. To fully benefit from the aggregate drop, inventory composition should ideally shift backward in the value-added chain not forward. To the degree inventory shifts forward, the ingredient of anticipatory distribution, with all of its related risk, is increased.

When aggregate manufacturing inventories are related to overall inventory, the existence of a forward trend is further confirmed. Table F-7 combines the data from Tables F-2 and F-6. Analyses of these data support the hypothesis that inventory ownership is moving forward in the distribution channel. With the exception of 1987, data from the last five years support a shift in overall manufacturing inventory to combined wholesale/retail inventory. In comparison, during the five years inclusive from 1978-82, manufacturing inventory represented 52 percent of aggregate material inventory. For the five years inclusive from 1983-87, it averaged 49 percent. The drop of 3 percent in aggregate inventory represents a shift forward of 19.1 billion dollars based on 1987 totals. However, when 1987 totals are compared to 1986, a shift back toward manufacturing of 4.3 percent or 27.4 billion is reported. Once again, the evidence is not conclusive. In 1987 new Internal Revenue Service procedures for valuation of inventory were implemented, introducing a possible one time impact in reporting relationships. The availability of 1988 figures should help in determining 1987 represents an anomaly or the start of a reversal in trend.

While the analyses of these data do not support a final conclusion regarding a forward inventory shift, it does offer reasonable support. Once again, 1988 figures will be extremely useful in further examination of the ratio of aggregate manufacturing to natural aggregate inventory.

The fact remains that for a majority of years during the decade from 1978 to 1987, manufacturing inventories have been shifting toward finished goods while inventories in total have been shifting forward in the channel of distribution. These trends, if substantiated, have significant implications for logistical management.

Table F-7

PERCENT OF MANUFACTURING INVENTORY TO AGGREGATE INVENTORY
UNITED STATES 1978-87
(Current Dollars)

Year	Aggregate Inventory ($Billion)	Manufacturers Total ($Billion)	Manufacturers Percent	Wholesale/Retail Total ($Billion)	Wholesale/Retail Percent
1978	381	190	49.86	191	50.14
1979	427	215	50.35	212	49.65
1980	462	240	51.95	222	48.05
1981	513	271	52.83	242	47.17
1982	506	275	54.35	231	45.65
1983	514	260	50.58	254	49.42
1984	576	276	47.91	300	52.09
1985	583	284	48.71	299	51.29
1986	590	277	46.95	313	53.05
1987	638	327	51.25	311	48.75

PRODUCTIVITY

While gains have been made in lowering the overall cost of logistics as a percentage of Gross National Product and in the total inventory levels carried by U.S. firms, the productivity growth of American workers has slowed dramatically. The following table shows important measures illustrating the sluggish growth pattern.

As shown in Table F-8, annual growth in output per hour has averaged less than one percent during the 1970's and 1980's. This represents a significant decline from the growth experienced in the two previous decades.

Manufacturing output, in absolute terms, has increased since 1980. However, the increase can largely be attributed to boosts in the employment level. Workers have not been more productive. Rather, there have been more workers.

Table F-8

UNITED STATES PRODUCTIVITY ANALYSIS

Decade	Annual Increase Real GNP	Real Gross Domestic Product Per Person	Ratio of Employment to Population	Avg. Hourly Earnings in 1977 Dollars	Annual Growth In Output Per Hour
1950's	3.3%	+1.5%	40%	$3.30	+3.00%
1960's	3.8%	+2.5%	39%	$4.25	+1.90%
1970's	2.8%	+1.6	40%	$5.05	+0.75%
1980's	2.4%	+1.6%	44%	$4.87	+1.00%

Source: Bureau of Labor Statistics

There is uncertainty as to what will happen regarding United States manufacturing productivity.   Automation and high-technology innovations offer the potential for productivity breakthroughs.   However, manufacturing firms must be willing to make the required investments to promote growth.   A Business Week June 1988 special report emphasized the importance of capital spending in order to ensure competitiveness and suggested United States manufacturers may be falling short.   "Though capital spending is expected to jump 10 percent or so this year, many fear that it's still not enough and, worse yet, not of the variety to boost productivity" (p. 102).

ST. JOHN FISHER COLLEGE LIBRARY
HD38.5 .L4 1989

010101   000

Leading edge logistics : compe

0 1219 0099749 9